BRACKETED BELONGING

A volume in the series
Police/Worlds: Studies in Security, Crime, and Governance
Edited by Kevin Karpiak, Sameena Mulla, William Garriott, and Ilana Feldman

A list of titles in this series is available at cornellpress.cornell.edu.

BRACKETED BELONGING

Gurkha Migrant Warriors and Transnational Lives

Kelvin E. Y. Low

CORNELL UNIVERSITY PRESS   ITHACA AND LONDON

First published 2025 by Cornell University Press

Library of Congress Cataloging-in-Publication Data

Names: Low, Kelvin E. Y., author.
Title: Bracketed belonging : Gurkha migrant warriors and transnational lives / Kelvin E.Y. Low.
Description: Ithaca : Cornell University Press, 2025. | Series: Police/worlds : studies in security, crime, and governance | Includes bibliographical references and index.
Identifiers: LCCN 2024040234 (print) | LCCN 2024040235 (ebook) | ISBN 9781501781612 (hardcover) | ISBN 9781501781629 (paperback) | ISBN 9781501781636 (epub) | ISBN 9781501781643 (pdf)
Subjects: LCSH: Gurkha soldiers—Employment—Foreign countries. | Private security services—Employees—Relocation. | Private military companies—Employees—Relocation. | Gorkha (South Asian people)—Foreign countries—Ethnic identity. | Gorkha (South Asian people)—Migrations. | Transnationalism—Social aspects. | Belonging (Social psychology) | Nepal—Emigration and immigration—Social aspects.
Classification: LCC DS493.9.G8 L69 2025 (print) | LCC DS493.9.G8 (ebook) | DDC 305.8914—dc23/eng/20250121
LC record available at https://lccn.loc.gov/2024040234
LC ebook record available at https://lccn.loc.gov/2024040235

For the warrior/s in my life

Contents

Acknowledgments

A book several years in the making necessarily incurs many chalked-up debts. I gratefully acknowledge the inestimable kindness, generosity, hospitality, and warmth of numerous individuals who have together nourished me on this protracted journey since I embarked on it more than a decade ago. Needless to say, Gurkhas and their families form the very backbone of this book. They have generously opened up their homes and shared their life histories, dreams, and aspirations with me. Throughout my continual visits to Nepal, Hong Kong, and the United Kingdom over the past several years, they have offered me gracious hospitality, cherished patience, goodwill, and good food as I learned so much from each of them about what it means to leave home, and what it takes to make someplace or somewhere else home in their lives. I cannot summon the right words to convey my deepest gratitude to all of them who have made this book possible.

Friends and colleagues at my home institution, the Department of Sociology and Anthropology, National University of Singapore, have continued to stand with me through time. The magnitude of Vineeta Sinha's stalwart support, friendship, and invaluable insights offered over these past several years is not lost on me. Good-humored corridor conversations, friendship, and moral support come through such individuals as Maribeth Erb, Feng Qiushi, Narayanan Ganapathy, Indira Arumugam, and Anne Raffin. Friends whom I know will always have my back, laugh and cry with me, and journey together through various celebrations and challenges in life manifest munificently in the forms of Sidharthan Maunaguru, Anojaa Karunananthan, Suriani Suratman, Elaine Ho, Ethan Quek, Wong Meisen, Lim Yung Tzen, Audrey Chye, Gerald Yip, and Daniel Tan. Parts of this book were written during a brief summer stay with Jiwook Jung, Eunmi Mun, and Sammi Jung. Thank you for your kindness and much valued friendship, and for feeding me remarkably well.

At Cornell University Press, I owe my sincere thanks to editors Sameena Mulla, Kevin Karpiak, William Garriott, and Ilana Feldman for their collective editorial stewardship of the series Police/Worlds: Studies in Security, Crime, and Governance that has given this book a home. In particular, the professionalism and kindness rendered from Sameena have made the process all for the better. Jim Lance played a key role as acquisitions editor. He definitively steered the manuscript to the finish line in a more than unstinting manner, for which I express my appreciation. Two anonymous reviewers for Cornell generously offered their endorsement, important suggestions, and gainful critique that further strengthened this work. Karen Hwa and Alfredo Gutierrez Rios have been pivotal in facilitating the production and marketing aspects of my journey with the press. My thanks also go to Radhika Mathrani Chakraborty for her crucial help and finesse in preparing the manuscript for production, to Jack Rummel for his copyediting adroitness, and to Wu Yuanzhe for constructing the two maps for the book. My appreciation goes to Freddy Chong, whose editing skills made it possible for images to be included in this book, and also to Rachel Lyon for preparing the index.

Analyses presented in chapter 1 of this book originally appeared as "Migrant Warriors and Transnational Lives: Constructing a Gurkha Diaspora," *Ethnic and Racial Studies* 39 (5): 840–57, https://doi.org/10.1080/01419870.2015.1080377. Discussions on the experiences of Singapore Gurkha families pertaining to belonging presented in this book first appeared as "Belonging and Not Belonging: Experiences of Nepali Gurkha Families on Returning from Singapore," in *Global Nepalis: Religion, Culture, and Community in a New and Old Diaspora*, ed. David N. Gellner and Sondra L. Hausner, 163–87 (New Delhi: Oxford University Press, 2018). Material from these publications have been substantially reworked, expanded, and updated for incorporation into this book.

A study that has brought me to different countries over a sustained period of time also requires a timely combination of funding support and research assistance. For their varied and invaluable assistance provided across the different parts, phases, and periods of research carried out for this book, I duly acknowledge the work and contributions of Sanjay Sharma, Tan Junbin, Farhan Musa, Josiah Berlian, Cybil Kho, Alexandra Galvez, and Woo Wee Meng. Academic grants that have supported my research include the Start-up Grant, together with a few ODPRT Grants for Research Excellence, all of which come from the National University of Singapore (NUS). In addition, a collaborative Tier 2 grant from the Ministry of Education led by Tim Bunnell as principal investigator made multiple overseas research trips possible. A subvention provided through the NUS HDRSS, together with the NUS Excellent Researcher Award, have also channeled the necessary funding to publish this book.

Staff members at various archives where I conducted research were of utmost help and immense support. I thank these individuals who serve with resolute professionalism at the Gurkha Memorial Museum (Pokhara), the Gurkha Museum (Winchester), University of Hong Kong, the British Library (London), the National Archives of Singapore, the National Library Board (Singapore), and the National Archives at Kew. I have benefited as well from the feedback, critique, and endorsement from several scholars for earlier ideas that culminated into this book. They include Joanna Pfaff-Czarnecka, David N. Gellner, Sondra

L. Hausner, Naveeda Khan, Koh Keng We, Wyman Tang, and Siumi Maria Tam. I also express my appreciation to participants who have attended my talks and shared their ideas and comments on this project when we crossed paths at Seoul National University, University of Bielefeld, and University of Oxford.

If this book reads any better than its earlier drafts, I have Noorman Abdullah to thank. His forbearance, astute reading, and sage critique of my work have only improved my earlier ideas and presentation. I cannot but firmly find him culpable for the better parts of the book. Finally, my loved ones have constantly stood by me. Their quiet yet unyielding support and strength have enabled me to stand tall and forge ahead.

Abbreviations

AIT	Asylum and Immigration Tribunal
AFC	Armed Forces Concession
AFPS	Armed Forces pension scheme
BCG	British Council of Gurkhas
BGWS	British Gurkha Welfare Society
BGAESO	British Gurkha Army Ex-Servicemen's Organization
DSP	diplomatic service procedures
ECHR	European Council of Human Rights
ECO	entry clearance officer
GAESO	Gurkha Army Ex-Servicemen's Organization
GCSPF	Gurkha Contingent Singapore Police Force
GOTT	Gurkha offer To transfer
GPS	Gurkha pension scheme
IDI	immigration directorates' instructions
ILR/E	indefinite leave to remain or enter
IR	immigration rules
MAS	married accompanied service
MOD	Ministry of Defence (UK)
MP	Member of Parliament
PMSC	private military and security companies
PR	potential recruit
NESO	Nepal Ex-Servicemen Organization
SPF	Singapore Police Force
TACOS	terms and conditions of service
TPA	Tripartite Agreement (1947)
UBGEA	United British Gurkha Ex-Servicemen's Association

INTRODUCTION

Gurkhas and Bracketed Belonging

> **As a former Gurkha, I am eligible for a full UK passport. My friends there have asked me to go but I said "No, thank you." I prefer to return to Nepal. The climate and food in the UK is [*sic*] not good. The weather in Nepal is nice. The money is better in Hong Kong. I have to support one sister who is unmarried and living in a village in Nepal. Our son lives in the U.S., but, with Mr. Trump, he may have to come back. Two daughters are married, one in Nepal, and one lives with us in Hong Kong. Over the next year or two, we plan to return to Nepal. We have a small plot of land there. As they say, join the British Army and go around the world—what I have done.**

Captain Nam Sing Thapa Magar, a retired Gurkha who served in
Hong Kong, cited in Mark O'Neill and Annemarie Evans,
How South Asians Helped to Make Hong Kong

How and why does the military as an institution of empire recruit migrant soldiers and police and influence their shifting senses of belonging? How does this multiscalar relationship in its various permutations connect across the different domains of citizenship, intergenerational flows of migrants, and the formation and sustenance of diaspora? In engaging closely with these various processes, this book addresses how nations and their governance of security determine social constellations and shape sociopolitical and legal assertions of belonging and allegiance. I examine the contours and limits of belonging that underlie the complex social contract (Jenkins 2014; Ngai 2004) between mobile migrants and nations in the context of a global military-security market (Chisholm and Ketola 2020). I interrogate these core themes through the case of Nepali Gurkhas and their families as military and paramilitary migrants—such as that of Captain (Ret) Magar's own familial experience mentioned in the quote that opens this chapter. Recruited to serve in the military or police force (see figure I.1 for recruitment centers across Nepal), Gurkhas are trained in jungle warfare skills that other police groups do not possess (Chong 2014). There is thus the professional link to military training and the formation of a unique paramilitary police force with

FIGURE I.1.   Map of Recruitment Centers in Nepal. Source: Map by Wu Yuanzhe and Marshall Hopkins.

the backdrop of colonialism (cf. Chisholm and Ketola 2020). In these contexts, this book offers fresh perspectives on studying global security, migration, and diasporic lives. It sets a new agenda by analytically bridging empire, military, and security maneuvers, and migratory pathways and options. The broader aims of this study are to analyze migration and belonging vis-à-vis structures of colonialism, militarism, and security interests, and to comprehend the experiences of military/security contractors and their families through migratory mobility and varied notions of belonging. This twofold analytical approach is one that is seldom broached in policing scholarship and on security contractor families. In undertaking these intersecting lines of inquiry, it is my hope that this book serves as a novel contribution to current scholarship on migration and transnationalism, and on police and security studies. Adopting a migratory perspective in policing and security studies, the book discusses how a global security infrastructure that unfolds across nations is enacted by the echoes of empire (Ware 2012) and contemporary security and migratory agendas.

The Gurkhas—whose history of migration and movement from Nepal to Southeast Asia and other regions date back to the period of British colonialism—have established themselves in the former British colonies of Singapore, Hong Kong, and India, as well as the United Kingdom itself. Although Nepal was never a part of the English colonial empire, the Gurkhas were first recruited by the British Army in 1815 in the middle of the Anglo-Nepalese War of 1814–16. This was because the British were impressed with their bravery and hardiness (Banskota

1994; Golay 2009; Ling 1999; Parker 1999). During World War I, more than 200,000 Gurkhas fought for Britain, and these numbers climbed up to more than 250,000 in World War II (Chudal 2020b; O'Neill and Evans 2018). In certain contexts of military labor migration, they are allowed to bring their immediate families to settle down and receive education. Over the last two centuries, Gurkhas and their families have registered a palpable global presence working in the police and armed forces. The transnational circuit of recruitment, training, and deployment also includes the Gurkha police and soldiers' second career within the wider landscape of labor-security migration. Recruit training for these police servicemen takes place over a period of nine months, where they are drilled in infantry soldiering tasks and skills comprising trench digging, camouflaging, and firefighting exercises. Their training takes place in different countries across Malaysia, Singapore, and Hong Kong. Select top trainees are also sent to Jamaica and Belize to undergo a jungle warfare operator's course. These Gurkha police servicemen therefore strike an arduous balance between developing proficiency in paramilitary tactics and handling police and guard duties. To accomplish these, they would have to meet stringent fitness requirements that go beyond those of normal police units. As differentiated from regular police officers, these Gurkha police servicemen are well-trained in operating weapons including submachine guns, shotguns, and rifles. The best among them would form a sniper platoon and who serve as sharpshooters in securing key events and to protect VIPs (Chong 2014). Their police and security roles have concomitantly expanded over time to include overseas deployment in Timor Leste, Cambodia, Australia, and other places both for peacekeeping and security maintenance, as well as to train new recruits in basic policing skills (Chong 2014).

The Gurkha police and soldiers, both in active service and their subsequent second-career pathways serve in the global security market. Specifically, they form part of the group of security contractors hired by private military and security companies (PMSCs) as a military-experienced and cheap source of labor (Christensen 2017).[1] These PMSCs constitute a multibillion-dollar industry that supplies security contractors such as the Gurkhas as well as logistical services to various governments, nongovernment organizations, and commercial groups (Chisholm and Stachowitsch 2017). This industry has therefore opened up platforms through which state and nonstate actors assemble and practice security governance today (Leander 2013). Such assemblages occurring on a global scale would also mean a denationalization of national military, police, and security forces (Uesugi 2019a). The Gurkhas' second-career jobs include being private military guards in Iraq and Afghanistan (Bhandari 2021; Dixit 2017), the Bruneian sultan's special guard force (De Vienne and Jammes 2020; Kershaw 2018), and working for security agencies in the Middle East. Where Gurkhas work therefore highlights the various transnational points or networks of the global security sector. Overall, they work and reside not only in the countries for which they serve in the army (United Kingdom, Hong Kong, India, Brunei, and Malaysia) or police force (Singapore), but also in other contexts where they have retired or embarked on a second career overseas in the private military and security industries (Bharadwaj 2003; Chakrabarti 2008; Davis 2000; Francis 1999; Gurung 2009; Low 2020; Maxwell 1999; Uesugi 2007), cruise tourism (Jackman 2009; Wood 2002), and manual labor (Yamanaka 2000).

Gurkhas and their families' migrant lifeworlds and aspirations, however, have seldom been comprehensively addressed in the wider scholarly literature, notwithstanding a few scattered exceptions (for example, Bellamy 2011; Des Chene 1991, 1992; Pariyar 2018). Other works based on Gurkha experiences include popular historical writings by British writers (or former British-Gurkha officers; see, for example, Bolt 1967; Bullock 2009; Smith 1973), Gurkhas themselves (Gurung 2020; Rai 2020), and various other sources (Chudal 2020a; Crew 2004; Cross and Gurung 2007; Karki 2009; Laksamba et al. 2013; Parajuly 2013; Sharma 2017). In regnant studies of migration and transnationalism, and the various reasons and contexts under which people move, the military as an institution has often been neglected in accounting for how and why people—such as the British Gurkha soldiers or the French Foreign Legion—relocate to foreign lands. Studying the Gurkhas and their varied mobilities arising from the British military as an organ addresses not only this lacuna. It also raises different perspectives with which to rethink belonging as liminal and time-bound with tenure limits. These are crafted in relation to the specificities of military and security structures that conjugate with the immigration policies of nation-states. I examine the Gurkhas' positions that lie between citizens and noncitizens— similar to "civil-military entanglements" (Uesugi 2019a)—as they police and protect local order and borders. I do so by addressing their everyday lives and their diasporic mobilities and practices of bracketed belonging. These points of engagement crucially pique renewed conceptualizations of how social actors approach, experience, and negotiate migration and various idioms of belonging on several fronts. Gurkha experiences of belonging that are simultaneously self-constructed and externally imposed substantively differ from those of other migrant groups such as refugees, expatriates, labor migrants, asylum seekers, long-term residents, and various other actors. Addressing the migratory lifeworlds of the Gurkhas and their families therefore offer hitherto underexplored focus on and access into the lives of diasporic security forces that have fallen out of view in the broader literature. Migration, mobility, and contrastive sentiments of diasporic belonging are apprehended through the lens of empire building, military recruitment, and deployment structures as an original contribution to extant scholarship.

I also consider the expansion of policing space and changing relations between nation-states and internal and external security. The transnational nature of security work in the Gurkhas' case add to existing police scholarship that touches on the expansion and redefinition of policing space (Marenin 2005). Such space coexists with state security infrastructures at the transnational and local levels concurrently. In this sense, security frameworks of nation-states are not only a matter of domestic governance, but include social contracts with external third parties (Marenin 2005) such as Gurkha police as an alternate security composition via PMSCs. Another point to raise here is the expansion of policing space that calls for a rethinking of state-centered policing that Marenin (2005) further mentions. A broader argument arising from this call is that studying the Gurkhas as police and soldiers also unveils shifting configurations and relations transpiring between the state, the military, and the police in different transnational axes as I demonstrate in this book. The close-knit relation between the Gurkhas as a military force and a police force blurs the demarcated lines between military security to protect nations from external threats, and police security to manage domestic unrest, which is a key feature of the modern nation-state (Kraska 2021). In some ways, the Gurkhas as a case of police militarization par excellence provide renewed perspectives to think about police militarization (Kraska 2021), police paramilitary security structures, and their attendant transnational circuits of security work. The transnational aspects of Gurkha police and military work thereby render them a unique security force on the one hand that cuts across nation-state boundaries under the frame of security and peacekeeping. Furthermore, this also shores up pertinent issues related to limits of belonging as a diasporic security force and as circumscribed by individual nation-states on the other hand. Together, these experiences and parameters make them a distinctive force for investigation vis-à-vis the wider scholarship on contemporary policing in articulating forms of global security circuits based on Gurkha mobilities.

In order to comprehend their global dispersions, and more pertinently, to query the migratory processes and their implications for both Gurkhas and their children, this book engages with notions of "belonging" and "not-belonging." These are terms that have recently been taken up in the scholarly literature on migration and transnationalism (Hölzle and Pfaff-Czarnecka 2023; Jones and Krzyzanowski 2011; Pariyar, Shrestha, and Gellner 2014; Pfaff-Czarnecka 2022; Rottmann, Josipovic, and Reeger 2020). I take belonging and not-belonging as coconstituted rather than mutually exclusive. Belonging is comprehensively explicated across the four countries where research has been undertaken—Nepal, Singapore, the United Kingdom, and Hong Kong.[2] Fieldwork and archival research in these four countries were carried out from 2011, comprising interviews with different generations of active and retired Gurkha servicemen, Gurkha families, and other individuals such as filmmakers, artists, and entrepreneurs. I have met with and interviewed more than seventy ex-Gurkhas and their family members. The age range of retired Gurkhas and their wives span between those in their early to mid-forties, and earlier generations of retired Gurkhas, with the oldest who is now in his nineties. The ages of Gurkha children range from six to forty-five. The wide age spans make it useful to compare the diasporic experiences of different generations that would shed light on diverse sentiments of belonging and displacement. I also attended a variety of public events hosted either by these families as a broader Nepali community, or by the armed forces in the United Kingdom as part of my research. This book thus presents an unprecedented scope of inquiry in exploring the Gurkhas as part of a wider South Asian diasporic community within a globally militarized and mobile world. I deploy belonging as an analytical lens to examine the lifeworlds of Gurkhas and their families as migratory experiences. I use the notion to problematize and unpack the lived experiences of different generations of Gurkhas and their family members across the four countries of inquiry. Furthermore, I interrogate the extent to which belonging is mobilized as a political and legal resource vis-à-vis rights to remain, citizenship issues, and compensation policies.

Building on archival research, ethnographic fieldwork, and interviews conducted (2011–20) across these four sites, this study scrutinizes transnational ties and establishes further discussions pertaining to diasporic networks and post/colonial armed forces connections. I complicate notions of multiple homes/hostlands (cf. Beckles-Raymond 2020; Han 2019; Shams 2020) by employing Nepali Gurkha families as a historical and contemporary case study. In doing so, the aspirations of migratory Gurkhas at a transnational level can then be more critically engaged. This is achieved by analyzing their biographies in different urban milieu and temporal contexts in association with the backdrop of military historiography.

Conceptualizing Belonging

Belonging is a political, sociocultural, legal, and moral concept. At one level, I am interested in unraveling the different modulations and notions of belonging from the standpoint of Gurkhas and their families. These include addressing their experiences across different generations and the location they are emplaced within—Singapore, Hong Kong, Nepal, or the United Kingdom. Feelings of belonging and how they shift and transform are contingent on temporality, institutional structures, and policies, as well as the different cycles or steps of migration. These depend on the social actors and the migratory routes undertaken.

I therefore explain how belonging is enacted at two scales of analysis; the local context, and via transnational connections across borders within and beyond the Asian region. On another level, assessing how belonging transpires requires a closer interrogation of other social actors, including the state and other institutions. These other actors and their policies on belonging cut across broader structural levels and processes. Taking both dimensions concurrently, investigations into the breadth and depth of belonging and not-belonging then engender a broader discussion and deliberation on what it means to conceive of a Gurkha diaspora.

In interrogating the migrant–nation-state relation, three central research queries foster my analytical thrust: (1) What is belonging, and what is its character? (2) What are the politics of belonging, and how do such politics shift over time, within and across generations, and through changing sociopolitical climates? and (3) What are the limits and/or possibilities of belonging? The first question can be answered by comprehending what belonging (and by extension, not-belonging) means to individual Gurkha family members. The second, then, deals with what is at stake for those families, contextualized within the constraints and the freedoms that social actors exercise as they assess their own contexts of not-belonging. In short, I am interested in exploring what belonging looks and feels like personally (or at the individual and social group level), as well as what it means in political and structural terms (or at the collective level).

The distinction between the first two queries corresponds with Yuval-Davis's (2006) differentiation of belonging and the politics of belonging. For her, the former refers to tangible dimensions of belonging that include emotional attachment and a sense of "home" that one experiences. The latter has to do with how belonging is connected to collectives in particular ways, dovetailing discourses on nationalism, citizenship, and rights. Antonsich (2010) makes a very similar distinction between belonging as "place-belongingness" and personal and intimate sentiments of feeling "at home," and the "politics of belonging" as a "discursive resource" that is related to claims or resistance revolving inclusion and exclusion (see also Guibernau 2013; Prabhat 2018). His typology comprises five factors that elucidate belonging as felt and experienced: autobiographical, relational, cultural, economic, and legal. These five elements will provide the necessary scaffolding for analyzing my data, resembling what Yuval-Davis includes as "social locations; identifications and emotional attachments; and ethical and political values" (2006, 199). Such discourses on belonging need to be framed within a set of specific historical and contemporary conditions (Teerling 2011) that confront Gurkhas and their families. For instance, one major difference between working for the British Army and the Singapore Police Force (SPF) is that while both British and Singapore Gurkhas took their families to live with them in their respective country of service, the latter is not allowed to remain in Singapore on retirement, as compared to the former. Such conditions of employment and domicile therefore influence and shape both sentiments and structures of belonging that conjoin the two interrelated queries outlined above.

The third dimension of belonging pertaining to limits or possibilities are contingent on how *bracketing* takes place. Where belonging and not-belonging as a lens is useful to exemplify how social actors feel neither here nor there, as well as here *and* there (e.g., feeling a sense of belonging to both Singapore and Nepal), I go a step further. I propose the notion of *bracketed belonging* based on three interrelated emphases. The first is to signal how belonging is both actor- and action-oriented—running the range of social actors from individuals, communities, to state actors and their accompanying legal infrastructure, immigration rules, and others. Signaling belonging as such also highlights the intersubjective dimensions of not-belonging. The second has to do with analyzing the limits of belonging. Such limits are either placed on oneself, or nation-states and other structures constrain aspirations or hopes to belong. Third, bracketed belonging as a conceptual framework points not only to definitive belonging or not; it also indicates what or who would be both included and excluded simultaneously. Concomitantly, it unveils the varied motivations underlying these processes of inclusion and exclusion. Such bracketing is either self-constructed, or imposed on the self (cf. Guibernau 2013) by other actors including the nation-state. For example, bracketing belonging as self-constructed may be exemplified by a Gurkha police serviceman telling his daughter to not get too used to life in Singapore as she had recounted to me. This is because the family would have to return to Nepal once his service comes to an end. By way of doing so, the father consciously sets the limits and extent to which his children may experience a felt sense of belonging. Albeit having been born and bred in Singapore, the children's felt sense may not be (allowed to be) enduring. Knowing that mandatory repatriation to Nepal comes at the end of one's service thus explains and motivates the Gurkha father's conscious and cautionary act of bracketing. In essence, he suspends if not limits her belonging. The character, rationale, and felt senses of belonging and not-belonging therefore continue to take shape, bend, and respond to wider circumstances. These depend on how the actor locates him or herself (and/or the family) at any one biographical point in the broader migratory schema. Therefore, the notion of bracketed belonging as an analytical tool makes visible a variety of contours and loci of affinity for different members or generations of Gurkha families. These are contingent on time, place, history, and culture as I demonstrate in this book.

As an instance of bracketed belonging that is imposed on the individual, one may refer to legal structures that place some social actors at the edge of belonging.

In certain cases of adult Gurkha children, the First Tier Tribunal in the United Kingdom has ruled that some of them are not granted an Indefinite Leave to Remain (ILR) in connection with immigration policy. This outcome also arises owing to the lack of sufficient evidence to prove family connectedness and potential disruption to family life (see chapter 5). By delineating when and how one may belong, with limits and boundaries put in place, bracketed belonging holds the potential to showcase the criteria and range of how belonging, not-belonging, and partial or limited belonging transpire. The brackets that govern belonging, either through self-construction or external imposition, thereby frame the extent and degree of not-belonging at any given point in time and within a specific sociopolitical context. Crucially, "belonging is never entirely about migrants' subjective feelings of 'fitting in' or not, but also relates to how (powerful) others define who belongs" (Ralph and Staeheli 2011, 523). Furthermore, to belong is not merely about articulating felt experiences but to also translate these as a moral right or resource (Mustassari, Maki-Petaja-Leinonen, and Griffiths 2017). Arising from this translation, social actors may argue for certain citizenship provisions or entitlements. Therefore, belonging is deployed as a moral and political tool in negotiations for rights to resources such as improved pension arrangements, among others.

Bracketed belonging goes beyond mere identification of belonging and not-belonging as neatly defined categories. Through bracketing as a form of framing, the concept also distills the limits, contours, and negotiations that are spotlighted beyond belonging and not-belonging as coterminous. How far can an individual claim for oneself or others to belong only in particular ways that are at the same time accompanied by limits and boundaries? These constraints and contours are contingent on spatiotemporal experiences, as well as structural frames that nation-states operate with and that institutionally bracket who does or does not belong. To bracket is to draw up or delineate boundaries that both include and exclude as exacted by an array of institutional gatekeepers. To bracket also means making delineations as a thought or felt experience at the back of one's mind that is not usually foregrounded. In Lamont and Molnar's (2002) discussion on acts of boundary making, they point out that such processes involve boundaries that are drawn up in less outwardly manifest ways. Paying attention to bracketing in these ways therefore make visible multiple frames of belonging and not-belonging that are usually concomitant rather than distinct or lucidly kept separate. In approaching belonging through bracketed terms, therefore, I consider belonging as multiple (Freyer 2019; Gellner 2015; Jones and Krzyzanowski 2011; Pfaff-Czarnecka 2020), intersectional, and derivative from shifting contexts across different nation-states.

Bracketed belonging as a key conceptual anchor broadens the cartography and analytical scope of belonging in studying migrants, mobility, and nation-states.

It is about the experiences, options, choices, and constraints that people and countries manage and negotiate within a migrant–nation-state nexus. I consider their various shifts, permutations, intergenerational similarities and differences, among others. Furthermore, one needs to think about temporality, inter- and intragenerational lived experiences, calibrations, and changes in how belonging is asserted or not. It would be a mistake to assume intergenerational difference and intragenerational sameness. A similar point is noted by Jones and Krzyzanowski (2011, 43) who contend that migrants should not be reified as a "coherent [and] internally consistent group." There exist wide-ranging possible sources and repertoires of identification, experience, and allegiance arising from military or police and security service and diasporic phases. Different cohorts of Gurkhas and their children may therefore adopt similar or contrastive views about where and how they belong. Together, these dynamics thereby raise further differentiation in how bracketed belonging transpires across time, generations, and locales. They also importantly reflect the heterogeneity and fluidity of experiences in the wider Gurkha diaspora.

I briefly discuss the point on intergenerational difference and sameness by returning to the context of Gurkha police service in Singapore. While Gurkhas themselves are subject to contractual terms with the SPF that determine the length of their service, children of Gurkhas are by association affected by these terms. As mentioned, once their Gurkha father leaves the SPF, the entire family has to go back to Nepal. However, it is interesting to consider the experiences of Gurkha children in relation to "return migration"—for which the term needs to be problematized. This is because the children are, in a manner of speaking, not really "returning" to Nepal since they were born and educated in Singapore. They are second-generation children, not migrants themselves (Brocket 2020; Graf 2017; Haikkola 2011). They are returning to their parents' birth country and not their own. This has consequences for the way they relate and adjust to living in Nepal, having spent close to two formative decades of their lives overseas as Singaporean-born Nepalis. This is unlike their parents' biographies, which include their birth and a substantial period of their youth in Nepal. The notion of "return migration" is therefore more applicable for the first generation, that is, Gurkhas and their wives. Teerling's explanation concerning second-generation migrants and "return" is instructive:

> For the second generation, the term "return" is ambiguous; it is not a return in terms of birthplace statistics, but rather an emigration to another country. Nevertheless, these migrants often do have a sentimental relationship with the parental homeland. Hence the "return" has empirical meaning even if it breaches the logic of migration statistics. (Teerling 2011, 1080)

In this regard, what then is the significance of "return" for both generations? How do they differ in terms of their capacities for engendering a sense of belonging or not-belonging given their respective exposure to contrastive linguistic, cultural, and national contexts? Ostensibly, migration as well as experiences of belonging are not static or consistent when we compare across the different generations of Gurkhas and their families. They change over time, contingent on how social actors choose or have to lead their lives over different periods and in response to options presented to them, or changes at the structural level based on the rules and regulations of varying nation-states. I echo Des Chene's (1998) point on addressing the nexus between structural arrangements and contingent circumstances in my interrogation of belonging. Such circumstances refer to "contingent happenings of daily life," which intertwine with structure. These work concomitantly as "people think through their positions and act from within a host of structured but also contingent circumstances" (1998–40). After all, belonging is "something that emerges from a lived experience" (Allwood 2020, 40). Employing the metaphor of bracketing, and how it modulates over time, expands on newer imaginaries or felt senses of belonging. Consequently, notions of home are then constructed and rationalized accordingly. These are dependent on one's biographical phase, aspirations, constraints, and possibilities. It follows that social actors routinely assemble, disassemble, and/or reassemble what it means to belong or not over the course of their life and migratory routes. It is therefore pertinent to examine the degree and extent to which social actors continually craft and carve both belonging and otherwise through the act of bracketing.

As a corollary, processes and acts of bracketing are impermanent. With shifts in temporal and sociocultural contexts, such bracketing may transform or realign accordingly. The process of bracketing one's belonging as a multilayered construct is contingent on specific circumstances, one's biographical phase in the migratory runway, rather than based on a fixed or static sense of belonging (Antonsich 2010). Belonging is therefore an ongoing, constant project in the making—corresponding with what Thapa (2009, 97) calls as a "process in continuum." It also highlights the various struggles and negotiations that social actors navigate in finding their own footing on how, where, and when to belong across experiential, spatial, temporal, and legal terms. Every act of bracketing requires or intersects with varying social formations that may either be easily enacted or encounter contestation as I explain in this book. Such fluidity brings to the fore, how belonging vis-à-vis attachments and affinities transpire on multiple fronts and over a range of social constellations (Röttger-Rössler 2018; Pfaff-Czarnecka 2013). In sum, I deploy the notion of bracketed belonging that intersects with three dimensions of analyses. First, I demonstrate how bracketed belonging instigates renewed interpretations of colonialism, empire, and security studies in terms of the migratory movements of diasporic Gurkha communities across the globe. Second, the notion illustrates how belonging is continually negotiated, contested, with time-bound limits exacted across vastly different political, legal, and social contexts and by different social actors. Third, bracketed belonging makes visible multiple and bracketed frames of belonging and not-belonging, which transpire in different contexts and temporalities. Probing the varying subtleties and transformations of belonging across shifting time periods and through these three dimensions reflect deeply the relationship that migrants share with nation-states in the wider diaspora.

Scheme of the Book

This book ethnographically documents how Gurkhas and their families negotiate transnational interfaces in relation to their migrant experiences of work, everyday life, and interpretations of "home." It addresses how the Gurkhas and their families as transnational actors are situated in regard to citizenship, belonging, rights, and entitlements across the four countries in which they work and live. The book fleshes out and deliberates on such processes in these different contexts. Overall, it interrogates the transnationalization of Gurkha security and armed forces work and their familial lives in documenting the far-reaching effects of the British Empire in colonial and postcolonial temporalities. At the heart of the book lies how Gurkha families as a transnational diasporic community live their military and police lives in different places as well as grapple with their predicaments of belonging and not-belonging. All of these arise from global military networks and security structures that govern where and how Gurkha family lives unfold in ways that are simultaneously constraining and enabling. On a broader level, the book critically unveils how nation-states and military migrants articulate, circumscribe, and assert varying rights over different time periods within the locus of state-diaspora relations.

In order to conceive of the Gurkhas not only as soldiers but as military and police migrants, the next chapter explores the conceptual and empirical parameters of a Gurkha diaspora. I do so by assessing their military- and police-migratory flows. These flows are explained against the backdrop of armed forces service and how Gurkhas have been deployed globally since 1815. By deliberating on the connection between military and police service and migration paths, I construct a Gurkha diaspora in the context of Asia and map out their diverse phases and routes of migration. I articulate their regional if not global dispersal that has been contingent on military vicissitudes and security requirements as well as nation-specific structures in terms of citizenship and political rights. Through acts of transnational bracketing, I analyze how a Gurkha diaspora is made (with reference to military/police recruitment of Gurkhas and their right to remain in a particular context, among other things), and how this diaspora is experienced (with reference to one's sense of home and belonging in different contexts).

Based on my close reading of military autobiographies, military documents, archival materials, media reports, popular history books, social media posts/discussions, and other texts, chapter 2 focuses on how the Gurkhas form an imagination for the British and the wider public as "warriors." Additionally, I analyze military handbooks that stipulate recruitment criteria of Nepali soldiers in both historical and contemporary contexts. This approach adds to constructions of the warrior Gurkha. By explaining the different ethnic compositions of Nepali society that have been consigned as "martial races" (cf. Imy 2019)—Limbu and Rai (from eastern Nepal); and Gurung and Magar (from western Nepal)—and how the Gurkhas are associated with bravery, courage, and valor (Dhakal 2016; Stirr 2017; Streets 2004), this chapter documents and problematizes the image of the Gurkha as a warrior. The discussion therefore serves as a foil to the succeeding chapter. Acts of bravery and willingness to die for the crown are juxtaposed against the everyday life narratives of the Gurkhas that at times bifurcate from such extant discourses. I reflect on stereotypical constructions of the warrior Gurkha, contrasted against how they have lived their (military and police) lives and what this reputation might imply for their children, known otherwise in Nepali as *bhanja* (male) or *bhanji* (female).[3] Such constructions of the Gurkhas as a martial race thereby articulate the workings of imperial knowledge and power that conjugate ideas of nation and race (Imy 2019; Rand 2006).

Chapter 3 conveys the Gurkhas' own experiences of enlistment as well as military and police service by tracing their lives as diasporic security forces. It extends information given in earlier chapters that structurally depict the Gurkhas' recruitment process and service. The discussion comprises how they reconstruct their biographies and talk about their varied mobilities and experiences of military and police service. I draw on primary data in the form of my interviews carried out with retired Gurkhas living in Nepal, the United Kingdom, and Hong Kong, and present their narratives as migrant actors. Tapping into a wide range of oral history accounts shared by Gurkhas, including my examination of other secondary sources, I provide an overall background to the enlistment, posting, and military and other experiences of the Gurkhas. After enlistment and initial periods of military training, they traveled across and lived in multiple places around the globe during different phases of their lives. By laying out the processes and obstacles toward being recruited as a Gurkha police or soldier, including their overseas postings and life thereafter, this chapter serves as a corollary to the previous discussion. It charts the different routes that young Gurkhas first took as they leave their home in Nepal. Given the recent turn to possibilities of enlisting female recruits into Gurkha service for the British Army, I also address issues related to gender positionings. I critique how plans for the recruitment of Nepalese women have been debated and received. In so doing, I take "Gurkha" as a gendered category of analysis beyond well-debated notions revolving around masculinity and bravery among Gurkha men. This discussion thereby amplifies earlier discourses presented in chapter 2.

Furthermore, I trace the Gurkha culture of emigration (Yamanaka 2000) that threads across the different generations of Gurkha families. I also explicate how this culture has shifted valence over time. I note as well that older generations of Gurkhas and their wives went through different experiences compared to younger Gurkha cohorts. Variations across generations are therefore teased out and compared. Such comparisons are useful to unveil shifts and attendant transformations in what it means to be a Gurkha over contrastive periods of historical and contemporary contexts within which they are emplaced. Over and above popular constructions of the Gurkhas as fearsome warriors (see Chapter 2), their multifold work and life trajectories have extended beyond national boundaries (Pries 2001). These include recruitment to overseas regimental postings, and how the Gurkhas build families across borders. The chapter therefore elucidates their lives as migrant warriors and how they grapple with bracketing varying sentiments toward the country or countries in which they have trained and lived.

For retired Gurkhas and their wives, the variegated ways in which belonging occurs will be explored. The aim is to present their strategies as returnees to Nepal after a few decades of Gurkha service abroad. How they make themselves relevant and contribute to Nepali society in such cities as Kathmandu and Pokhara through various initiatives will be documented and analyzed. Their forms and practices of belonging are subsequently evaluated in terms of their identities both as retired Gurkhas and as Nepali citizens. In order to illustrate how Gurkhas and their wives' generation differs considerably from their children's generation, the notion of bracketed belonging is deployed. Where the former consigns Nepal as their place of origin, the latter does not necessarily relate to Nepal as "home."

Where Gurkhas are clearly mobile based on their military service and accompanying vicissitudes, their wives and children are, in a manner of speaking, bound to the various cycles of military postings and security service. How did their wives cope with life at home in Nepal or other places while the Gurkhas continued to work for the British Army elsewhere? How and why were these children taught Nepalese customs, language, and religion—for those who were born and bred in Singapore, the United Kingdom, or Hong Kong? How are Nepali children who have not left Nepal compared to Gurkha children who first lived "abroad" before they gather a sense of what Nepal is as a country and as their parents' country of origin? These key inquiries constitute the core of chapter 4. Stemming from their nonrecognition of Nepal as home, Gurkha children are caught in a conflictual position: they feel a sense of neither belonging here nor there. These children are those who have lived their early and adult years elsewhere. While the Gurkhas may regard Nepal as their homeland, the same sentiment cannot be applied to their children whose birthplace is Singapore, the United Kingdom, or Hong Kong. The latter's connection to Nepal is perhaps only realized through their parents' inculcation (Espiritu and Tran 2002; Kananen 2020) rather than by their own recognition of Nepal as their country. In this sense, the bifocality of homeland/place of residence requires further examination. While the children attempt to make sense of Nepal and Singapore based on their Gurkha father's return back to Nepal after his police service concludes, they are also aspiring to move elsewhere either for further studies or for work. These places include the United Kingdom, Australia, and the United States, among others. Conceptually, I show how the migratory pathways of the Gurkhas and their offspring diverge and thus illustrate the "different turning points" (Berg 2011, 46) for each diasporic generation. In doing so, I return to my notion of bracketed belonging. I demonstrate how this idea captures the divergent sentiments and senses of belonging for different generations of Gurkhas and their families through a close reading of their migrant biographies. Examining these biographies will illustrate how these diasporans traverse between structural arrangements and contingent circumstances (Des Chene 1998).

Belonging is explored as a legal trope in chapter 5 as I shift gears here to examine broader sociolegal and structural processes. I interrogate the legal aspects of citizenship, pension issues, and other rights that different cohorts and groups of Gurkhas lobby for. The key question here is: To what extent and degree are the Gurkhas and their families allowed to belong in legal terms? I expand the conceptual utility of bracketed belonging to illustrate how states and their legislative behavior place the Gurkhas and their families at the edge of belonging in the United Kingdom. Such state behavior in effect reveals the threshold of belonging; juridical lines are drawn between citizenry and Gurkha "foreignness" that thereby block the "doorway to belonging" (Morrice 2017, 600). I suggest that in terms of legal aspects, the Gurkhas and their families stand at the margins of belonging. This is so, given that various laws and policies appear to be discriminatory in manifold aspects. The chapter covers and expands the range of Gurkha settlement policies, compensation packages for retired Gurkhas and/or Gurkha widows, pension issues, indefinite leave to enter (ILE), citizenship and rights to remain, and tribunal adjudication, among others. The discussion is accomplished by carefully scrutinized official documents from the UK Ministry of Defence and other sources. I account for how immigration controls of the

Nepalese Gurkha community as meted out by the British government signal legal structures of rights to belong based on previous Gurkha service. I also address how the legacy of such service impinges on the rights of children in terms of entry and/or citizenry, as well as other issues. In doing so, I critically examine the legal-political approaches to and implications of bracketing belonging to demonstrate how inclusionary and exclusionary mechanisms intersect with legal manifestations of belonging or otherwise.

I provide a consolidated analysis of manifold and contextual notions of belonging—deliberated across different groups and generations of social actors to include the Gurkhas, their wives, and their children by way of conclusion. As a concept and as enacted in practice, bracketed belonging and its attendant registers are summarized in order to explain its broader analytical and explanatory use in the fields of security migration, diaspora, and transnationalism studies. I reiterate the conceptual linkages between diaspora and its transnational connections, belonging and not-belonging, as well as generational difference and sameness. I recapitulate how the Gurkha experience reflects migrant mobilities and aspirations couched within specific temporalities and structural possibilities and/or constraints. These dynamics together articulate the workings of a global military-security landscape wherein the migratory flows and mobilities of Gurkhas and their kin transpire.

The many facets of transnational ties, linkages, and senses of belonging are realized over time due to the global dispersion of these migrant warrior families since the imperial period. Such webs of transnational connectivity are enacted with social actors operating along different axial and kin ties occurring between, inter alia, Singapore and Hong Kong, the United Kingdom and Nepal, and Nepal and Hong Kong. Taken together, the differentiated senses of bracketed belonging elucidate the robustness of belonging as an analytical tool. I use it to comprehend the features, composition, and lived experiences of the Gurkha diaspora. The concluding chapter therefore weaves together a broader abstraction of how one may approach diaspora and belonging by considering military-labor social actors as a migrant category alongside the spectrum and depth of bracketed belonging. This would thereby depart from the extant inventory of migrants that existing studies have routinely examined. In the process, the book unveils new aspects of colonialism and security infrastructures that continue to wield enduring influence in the present. More pertinently, I address and reiterate the key inquiry of how to more generally grapple with and problematize the relation and social contract between migrants and nation-states in the wake of empire and global security networks.

CONSTRUCTING A GURKHA DIASPORA

Gurkhas are dispersed all over the world as military and police forces working in the global security market. I investigate the trajectory of Gurkhas as migrants and explore the Gurkha diaspora in terms of different migratory flows. I construct a Gurkha diaspora in the context of Asia by delineating both empirical and conceptual parameters of their military-migratory dispersions and diasporic mobilities. Through historical articulations of the connections between military and police service and migration paths, I map out the different phases and routes of migration that Gurkhas and their families embarked on over time. Broadly speaking, military and paramilitary service served as recruitment structures that led to the placement of Gurkhas in different parts of Asia and elsewhere. This outcome has implications in terms of the various migratory cycles that they take, including their children who may or may not "return" to Nepal upon the completion of their Gurkha-father's career. Furthermore, immigration controls and residency rights of different countries likewise determine where they (are allowed to) settle down. By addressing these issues, the Gurkhas and their families are then viewed as migrant actors whose mobility is largely determined by regimental waged labor (Des Chene 1991).

The term *diaspora* typically invokes the prototypical Jewish, Armenian, and Greek cases (Vertovec 2009). These cases represent diasporic experiences in relation to isolation, exile, loss, and displacement with a yearning for a return to the homeland. The implication is that homeland needs to be territorially specific. Living away from it is not desirable (Ang 2007). The "classic" or "victim" diasporic approaches are however necessarily limited in today's context of intensified mobility and which takes place under different conditions. The term *diaspora* in today's usage is now amplified into a larger semantic domain. It comprises further categories such as immigrants, expatriates, refugees, ethnic minorities, overseas communities, exile communities, and guest workers (Ang 2007; Brubaker 2005). I expand this vocabulary by including the Gurkhas as a category of military-labor migrants. Overall, this chapter rests on two key trajectories (Parreñas and Siu 2007)—how a Gurkha diaspora is *made* (with reference to military/police recruitment of Gurkhas, their right to remain in a particular context, among other things), and how this diaspora is *experienced* (with reference to one's sense of belonging and notions of "home" in different contexts). By analyzing the latter, I contend that instead of looking at diaspora as a bounded entity and therefore succumbing to problems of groupism, we should think of diaspora as a "category of practice." It follows that diaspora encompasses a range of claims making, the formulation of expectations, as well as the mobilization of energies (Brubaker 2005).

I interrogate as well notions of return- and step-migration vis-à-vis Yamanaka's (2000) "culture of emigration." This is done in order to theorize the notion of diaspora in relation to different generations of Gurkha families. Where some of the retired Gurkhas have shared with me that Gurkha service runs in the family—comprising their fathers, brothers, or uncles who have served as Gurkhas in both the British and Indian armies—such a culture of emigration overtime has ceased to influence the aspirations of or migratory decisions that Gurkha children undertake. In comparing across generations, I shed light on diverse sentiments of belonging and displacement. This would be similar to what Berg (2011, 46) has termed the "different turning points" for each diasporic generation.

Building on the foregoing conceptual vectors, I establish the connection between Gurkha military service and diasporic experience. I seek to map their regional if not global dispersal (see figure 1.1) that has been contingent on military vicissitudes as well as nation-specific structures in terms of citizenship and political rights. In this manner, it is not so much that the nation should be jettisoned per se (Wimmer and Glick Schiller 2002). Instead, the focus should be recalibrated to shed light on how the flows and mobilities of Gurkhas and their families are enacted through these institutions and structures across time and space. Varying forms of transnational history include connections, transfers, circulations, and entangled or shared history. These are undergirded by the stance that "historical and social processes cannot be apprehended and understood exclusively within customary, delineated spaces or containers" (Struck et al. 2011, 573–74). What is important here is how peoples, institutions, and ideas interact and circulate across the boundaries of nation-states (e.g., Kananen 2020; Uesugi 2007). Such interactions and circulations thereby point to entanglements

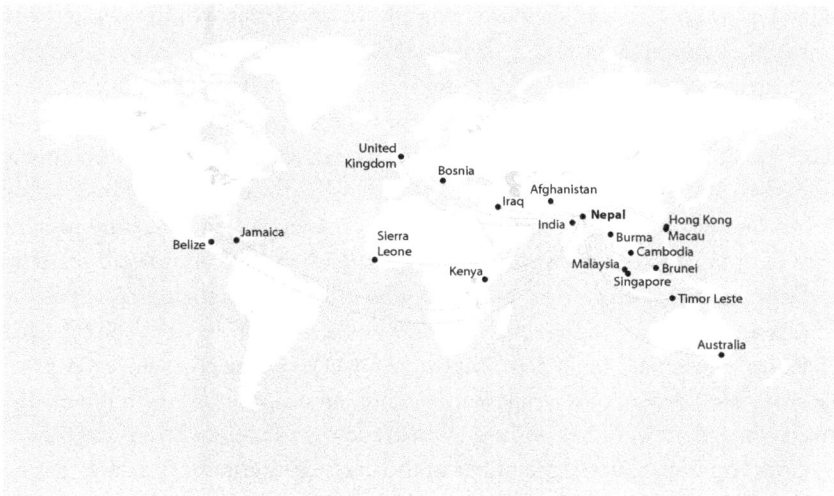

FIGURE 1.1.   Map of the different countries where Gurkhas have trained, served, and lived. Source: Map by Wu Yuanzhe and Marshall Hopkins.

between and the mutual influencing of nation-states. A transnational approach admits and engages with a plurality of cultural symbols and codes which transcend the nation-state. This approach also comprises notions of "home" as multiple, and which is not only about geography, but ideology and emotion as well. My aim here is twofold: to empirically ground methodological transnationalism, and to utilize the transnational history approach toward studying the Gurkhas and their families' migratory and transnational experiences.

Diaspora Theorizing

Diaspora has been theorized across a wide-ranging spectrum of scholarly research and various disciplines, including sociology, anthropology, cultural studies, area studies, literature, and queer theory. Beyond the archetypical Armenian, Jewish, and Greek cases that are invoked in earlier discussions on diaspora that stand for negative diasporic experiences (Rai 2014; Sahoo 2021; Vertovec 2009), diasporic groups and how they regard what constitutes as "home" has altered considerably. Homeland as predicated on territory only reveals a methodologically nationalist orientation (Brubaker 2005). Furthermore, there is a weakening of the "hold of modern nation-state on the identities and identifications of the populations who have come to live within their borders" (Ang 2007, 286–87). Diasporic groups today no longer perceive themselves as ethnic minorities within nation-states. Rather, they regard themselves as transnational subjects. Instead of pledging allegiance to a particular nation-state, these actors' senses of loyalties and affiliations occupy the interstitial space between nation-states (Ang 2007). It follows that diasporic cultures and politics today have very much to do with transnational flows and connections brought about by intensified processes of globalization and technological communications via social media. We are therefore moving from diaspora and trauma, or "victim origin" (Cohen 2008, 4), toward diaspora as the condition of dispersion and continuity of ties across nations. Such a shift reflects an expansionist project to "reimagine the idea of *diaspora*" (Jung 2016, 77; italics in original). In tandem, Nieswand (2011) contends that since diasporas do cross the borders of a single nation-state, an examination of migrant life-worlds that go beyond the confines of methodological nationalism is expedient.

Works on transnational mobilities in the fields of migration and cross-border studies have critiqued the paradigm of methodological nationalism and its nation-centered lens and bounded parameters (Amelina et al. 2013; Wimmer and Glick Schiller 2002). As an "ideological orientation that approaches the study of social and historical processes as if they were contained within the borders of individual nation-states" (Glick Schiller 2010, 110–11), it places migrants inside one nation-state (Weiss and Nohl 2013). If such an orientation is limited in analyzing flows and belonging, I adopt instead, the perspective of transnational history. To comprehend the dynamics of international migration and its flows, migration research is a "transnational undertaking." This endeavor requires analytical toolkits that may be deployed to maneuver beyond the nation-state as a container (Castles 2007). Furthermore, the transnational history perspective is to be differentiated from that of global history, where the former "looks at individuals in various contexts, including nations" (Iriye 2013, 15). Therefore, my selection of transnational history as an approach arises as a result of scale—or what Struck et al. (2011, 574) call a "sub-world scale" in terms of focusing on a region. Moreover, as I show below, the history of Gurkha recruitment and service necessitates the adoption of a transnational lens in contextualizing colonial times as well as present-day global security and policing circuits. This is selected so I can situate the social mechanisms that have produced a Gurkha diaspora. By extension, I also address how Gurkha families settle in different parts of Asia and the United Kingdom. Such an approach is interested in flows and movements of people, as well as border crossings and diaspora. I bring forward extant criticism of methodological nationalism into an empirical realization of methodological transnationalism (Faist and Nergiz 2013; Khagram and Levitt 2007; Low 2015). As a conceptual approach, methodological transnationalism includes both historical and empirical accounts of migration that expose transnational processes and forms. This approach encompasses observations and evidence from new types of data that better capture the realities of transnationalism (Khagram and Levitt 2007; Schrooten 2012).

My use of military and policing histories below represents a source of data that furnishes the construction of a Gurkha diaspora. Closer attention is paid to transnational connections, thereby operating with and beyond the national box (Siu 2005; Wimmer and Glick Schiller 2002). Additionally, subscribing to methodological transnationalism implies that the idea of diaspora is not only about the binary of home/hostland (Beckles-Raymond 2020; Parreñas and Siu 2007). My treatment of diaspora instead acts as a critical inquiry into, inter alia, what constitutes homeland for both the Gurkhas and their children? I mentioned previously that while the Gurkhas may regard Nepal as their country of origin, the same sentiment cannot be applied to their children whose birthplace is Singapore, the United Kingdom, or Hong Kong. The latter's connection to Nepal is perhaps only realized through their parents' inculcation rather than by themselves to regard Nepal as their homeland. As a consequence of Singapore's management of the Gurkha police contingent and their contractual service, both Gurkhas and their families would have to return to Nepal on the completion of service, early retirement, or when the Gurkha serviceman reaches the age of forty-five. In this sense, the bifocality of homeland/place of residence requires further interrogation. Similarly, Safran (2009) suggests that while diaspora is space-related, such a spatial feature ought to include a consideration of not one but several hostlands. I add to this the possibility of more than one homeland as well given that diasporans today inhabit an "intersectional position" (Siu 2005, 5). Diaspora studies and a more nuanced unraveling of home- and hostlands are therefore useful in challenging certain calcified assumptions about identity, belonging, and citizenship that are usually associated with territory.

At this juncture, I open a discussion on how to conceive of the Gurkha diaspora vis-à-vis extant works on South Asian diasporas. Mass migrations from South Asia in the last three centuries have taken place during two broad periods (Jacobsen and Kumar 2018; Vertovec 2000). The first occurred under imperialism with large numbers of South Asians serving as indentured laborers in various colonies, and the second phase (also taking place currently) has involved migrants of South Asian descent in various occupations who travel freely to Western countries and the Middle East. However, the South Asia diaspora that has been studied by scholars tend to eclipse the mobilities of Gurkhas and their families. This notwithstanding, I avoid using the rubric of South Asian diaspora in discussing the Nepali Gurkhas. This is because the Gurkhas' experience of military/police work and migration has taken place under somewhat different circumstances in relation to regimental service. Besides, the term *South Asian diaspora* implies a "regional political identity" (Koshy 2008, 9), which should not be unreflexively conflated with being a Nepali or a Gurkha. Additionally, Brown (2006) questions if it is appropriate to speak of one South Asian diaspora given the vast diversity of migrants from the region (see also Sinha 2019) who are of different religions, linguistic backgrounds, and nation-states. The case of the Gurkha diaspora therefore differs from other South Asian diasporic groups such as the Sindhis (Cohen 2009), the Sri Lankan Tamils (Orjuela and Sriskandarajah 2008), or the Indians in South Africa (Lemon 1990). The difference is due to regimental structures as compared to different labor migratory circumstances of these other groups. Furthermore, I take heed of Siu's (2005) position that "living in diaspora may not be a choice," and instead diasporan networks and cultivated senses of belonging are engaged with and worked at as ongoing processes (cf. Al-Hilo and Marandi 2020). Following Brown (2006), I propose that the Gurkha diaspora is one of the many strands of South Asian diasporic formations that needs to be contextually analyzed.

Constructing a Gurkha Diaspora

Extant works on the Gurkhas as a "martial race" (Caplan 1991; Rai 2009) address their military experiences in colonial contexts, or draw attention to their rights to remain in the United Kingdom (Carroll 2012; Ware 2010). While these are important issues that I take up in other chapters, it is also pertinent to examine Gurkha biographies as migrants in the larger structural scheme of migratory flows both in historical and contemporary times herein. What are the streams of Gurkha recruitment and military mobility that build up to what we may delineate as a Gurkha diaspora? These streams are accompanied by shifting notions and ties of belonging, self- and national identity, and also the various migration cycles. I focus on transnational connections between the British and Asian countries. In doing so, I flesh out the migratory interpellations that structurally determine Gurkha security mobilities and where their families settle down.

The Anglo-Nepal war of 1814–16 was where the British first "discovered" the Gurkhas (Caplan 1991). Resulting in the defeat of Nepal, this war led to the discovery of Nepalese military prowess. Since then, Gurkha soldiers have served under the British crown with the East India Company as their first employer. Subsequently, they worked under the Indian Army after the Mutiny, and then with the British Army and the Indian Army following India's independence (Uesugi 2007). In a way, Gurkha recruitment served as the beginning point from which Nepal subsequently became incorporated into the global capitalist economy (Shrestha 2018). When India achieved independence in 1947, a full-fledged "contract migration" between the employers, the British and the Indian Army, and the "supplier of Gurkhas, Nepal" was formed (Uesugi 2007, 386). The Gurkhas have since been regular soldiers in the British Army, where the 1947 Tripartite Agreement (TPA) "provides the basis for employment policies until today" (Uesugi 2007, 386). Under this agreement, the employment of Nepalese citizens by the British and Indian armies was governed. The agreement called for similar wages and conditions of service for Gurkhas serving in both the British and Indian armies (Bullock 2009). Bellamy (2011) notes that 176 out of around 11,000 applicants are selected annually by the British Army to serve as Gurkhas. India recruits about 2,000 candidates yearly, although the number varies based on need.

Dhakal (2016) points out that the Gurkhas were the earliest Nepalis to migrate to India in large numbers, dating back to the Nepalese War of 1814–15. The recruitment of Gurkhas for the Indian Army was made possible through the 1815 Treaty of Sagauli signed between the East India Company and Nepal (Bammi 2009). Prior to that, the author also mentions that some of these Gurkhas were recruited by King Ranjit Singh of Punjab. There is however no clear indication of the recruitment volume in the king's army. Singh records that this Sikh king had praised the Gurkhas' agility when they fought against his Punjab army in 1809 (Singh 1962). When the Indian Rebellion broke out in 1857, Gurkhas fought on the British side and became a part of the British Indian Army (Farwell 1984; Purthi 2011). Gurkha units began to gradually expand between 1857 and 1900. They were recruited into the Assam Regiment and the Assam Military Police. The 1st Assam Rifles was raised at Changsil in the north Lushai Hills in 1889. Due to some problems of recruitment of Gurkhas from Nepal compared to other races who were serving in the British Indian Army, each regiment was allotted a "home" located in the hills of northern India.[1] The plan was that at least "some of the men might settle down with their families" and use these locations as their base to which they could return from active service in either Afghanistan or other places (Bammi 2009, 78). After retiring from the police forces and the army, the Gurkhas regarded the Lushai Hills as their homeland (Purthi 2011). Other "homes" or "stations" were established at Dharamsala, Dehra Dun, Almora, and Bakloh, where Gurkha wives and children began to settle.[2] Subsequently, many Gurkha pensioners took up residence in the vicinity, thereby forming a number of Gurkha communities in India. From these communities, many young, Indian-born Gurkha sons also enlisted into their fathers' regiments (Bolt 1967).

Owing to an increase in Gurkha strength in the British Army, a Gurkha Recruitment Depot was established in Gorakhpur and Ghoom in the 1880s (Bammi 2009). The years between 1901 and 1906 saw a renumbering of Gurkha regiments from the 1st to the 10th, and they were then redesignated as the Gurkha Rifles (Purthi 2011). They were regarded as the "gold standard of Indian soldiering" (Callahan 2007, 33). By 1908, the regiments came to be known as the Brigade of Gurkhas, comprising twenty battalions that were organized into ten regiments (Bammi 2009; Purthi 2011). In order to maintain the battalions at full strength containing approximately 26,000 Gurkhas in 1914 (Bolt 1967), about 1,500 recruits were required annually (Farwell 1984). By the end of the First World War, many Gurkhas retired, but only a small proportion had returned from India to Nepal. Out of the 10,932 Gurkhas who were discharged, only 3,838 have been recorded as having returned to Nepal in 1919. For those who chose to stay on, they had hoped to secure better employment opportunities in India, which was lacking back in Nepal (Banskota 1994). This aside, soldiering continued to be considered an honorable profession. Gurkha families often had their members serving in the same regiment. Sons followed the footsteps of their fathers into the same soldiering profession.[3] For example, Kulbahadur Gurung had enlisted in the 5th Gurkhas in 1898. In 1921, he retired as an honorary captain. Thirty years later in 1951, he had gone to a recruiting depot at Lehra, India, to speak with one of the recruiting officers. He might have lost two sons, but he was "quick to add that he had two grandsons who would soon be old enough to enlist" (Farwell 1984, 77). Since India's independence in 1947, the original ten Gurkha regiments were split between the British Army and the newly independent Indian Army. Four were transferred to the former, and the remaining six to the latter. This reorganization arose from the TPA inked between the British, the Indian, and the Nepalese governments in August 1947 (Izuyama 1999; Rathaur 2001). The Gurkhas have subsequently fought in many of the post-1947 conflicts that India had faced, including the wars with Pakistan in 1947, 1965, and 1971, as well as against China in 1962 (Purthi 2011). About 32,000 Gurkhas serve in the Indian Army over seven Gurkha Rifle Regiments today.[4] Chakraborty (2018, 34) observes that it was "technically easier for the young Gorkha men from Nepal to recruit themselves as soldiers in the Indian Army," as compared to young Gorkha men from Darjeeling wanting to be recruited into this army. This was due to the Indo-Nepal treaty, and where the eulogization of the *Bir Gorkha* (Brave Gorkha) (Chakraborty 2018, 34) meant that they would have received preferential treatment when it came to army recruitment processes. The inflow of "Nepali/*Gorkhas*" to Darjeeling, mostly occurring during British times, also meant triggering ethnic sensitivities in the region of northern Bengal in terms of interests to protect cultural and linguistic identities (Chakraborty 2018, 33; cf. Sharma 2022). In concert, these factors add further to an understanding of the presence of the Nepalis in India in subsequent times. One should note also that there are native Nepali-speaking people in India who subscribe to a self-defined ethnic identity via Gorkhaland, Darjeeling (Chakraborty 2020). Such self-definition, the author argues, is connected to claims to belonging to the martial race of the Gurkhas or Bir Gorkha, enacted through literary sources including poetry and plays. In the present-day context, the Indian Army recruits approximately 1,300 Gurkhas annually.[5]

In Singapore, the first Gurkha Contingent (GC) of the Singapore Police Force (SPF) was assembled on 9 April 1949 (Kiruppalini 2016; Rai 2009). Prior to this, 144 Gurkhas, who were due to be discharged from the army in Malaya, were recruited to set up the force, as they were willing to stay on (Gould 1999). The GC was raised to take over a Sikh unit that had operated throughout the Second World War and formed an important contingent of the SPF (Rai 2009). The GC of the SPF recruited service personnel in Nepal through the agency of the British Army (Gould 1999).[6] By 1952, the GC grew to a total of 300 Gurkhas (Leathart 1998). When race riots broke out in Singapore in the 1950s and 1960s, the Gurkhas were looked on as a neutral group to maintain order (Bellamy 2011). Elon Thule, a former Singapore Gurkha wrote in Nepali about his Gurkha experiences.[7] He explains in his book that the Gurkha Contingent within the Singapore Police Force is maintained and respected as a neutral force that has contributed to maintaining peace in several riots in Singapore (Thule 2011, 6–7). Such outbreaks included the 1950 Maria Hertogh riots, the 1955 Hock Lee Bus riots, and the 1956 Chinese Middle School riots (Nedumaran 2017). As the following media article summarizes:

> "You have, in the Gurkha Police—although they are from another land—very great friends," Mr. Lee That, Officer in Charge of the Gurkha Contingent in Singapore, said in a talk over Radio Malaya last night. "They like Singapore and they like its people, and they dislike anyone who plots to disturb or destroy your way of life, your homes or your property," said Mr. Lee That. "They may not be able to converse with you fluently but they understand when you want help and they will give you that help to the best of their ability," he added.[8]

Throughout riotous moments in Singapore's history prior to independence in 1965, the Gurkhas "proved their ability to perform as dispassionate keepers of the peace, who being untarnished by communal or sectarian bias, carried out their duties without fear or favour" (Nedumaran 2017, 279). The loyalty of these Gurkha police was broached through their children's generation, seen in a media report: "This little lad [referring to a photograph of a Gurkha's son] is the son of a Gurkha policeman in Singapore and a member of the Gurkha police camp in Cantonment Road, where thirty-seven families live. They are intensely patriotic and the youngster above has already been taught to salute."[9]

In 1958, the British, Nepalese, and the new Singapore government reached an agreement concerning the terms of Gurkha service. One of the items agreed on was that the Gurkha contingent was to be led only by British and Gurkha officers. The intention was to sustain "political impartiality essential in a para-military unit of a police force" (Leathart 1998, 261). Over time, the security duties of the Gurkhas also expanded. An elite Gurkha unit known as the Prison Gurkha Unit was formed in 1978. This unit comprised Gurkhas who worked as prison wardens serving in Changi Prison and Moon Crescent Centre (Lim 2009). In 1981, the unit was absorbed into the GC, and subsequently underwent six months of basic police training. This marked the beginning of their duties in the prison as policemen and no longer as warders.[10] In addition, they also perform guard duties that continue until today, and Gurkhas in Singapore secure important facilities in the country, and also guard the residences of top politicians. They function as a paramilitary force in maintaining internal security, comprising approximately 1,850 officers (13 percent of the total police force). In neighboring Malaysia, Gurkhas form a substantial portion of those who work in security businesses (Low 2020). Perumal (2018; cited in Low 2020) estimates that about 150,000 out of half a million Nepalese workers in Malaysia were hired as security guards. They also work in the manufacturing sector. The majority of foreign labor stems from Nepal, totaling almost 51 percent of the total foreign labor force in 2015 (Samsi, Abdullah, and Lim 2020).

The GC recruits eighty Gurkhas annually (Bellamy 2011). Gurkhas and their families reside in a camp (Mount Vernon camp) in central Singapore. The camp serves both as a training and a self-contained residential complex that is out of bounds to Singaporeans and other non-Nepalese. In 1950, the camp was described as a "little Nepal in Singapore" as "Gurkhas keep to themselves [within it] and speak nothing but Gurkhali."[11] Facilities in this complex include a Nepali Hindu temple, a clinic, a minimart, an officers' mess, and a family welfare center. Further to these outfits, the camp also comes with a wide range of sports amenities that include a gymnasium, basketball court, soccer field, a large swimming pool, track and field stadium, and some playgrounds. There is also a Gurkha Children School, known as *bhitra* school ("inside" school), as well as a GC Boys' Club and Girls' Club where "*bhānjās* and *bhānjīs* can interact and organise dance, games, and cultural shows" (Kiruppalini 2016, 264). In order to remain as a neutral force, Gurkhas are discouraged from integrating with locals. They are also not allowed to marry Singaporeans. It is for these reasons that they are permitted to bring their wives and family from Nepal to Singapore. Most of the children, however, are born and educated in Singapore. A majority of the children attended school at Bartley Primary, where about one-third of its student population were constituted by the children of Gurkha policemen. In 1985, it was reported that there were 121 Gurkha children who schooled at Bartley, coming from the 650-strong Gurkha contingent.[12]

Although the children go to school in Singapore, both wives and children are forbidden from seeking employment locally. Given expectations that the Gurkhas will "exercise impartiality in the event of a racial riot," such a logic underpins the requirement that Gurkha families "reside as a gated community" within the perimeters of Mount Vernon camp and not take up Singaporean citizenship (Kiruppalini 2016, 260). The condition of impartiality is recorded in a teleletter dated 2 May 1980 issued by J. D. Hennings Esq CMG to the SEAD, Foreign and Commonwealth Office in Kathmandu. It states: "In a civil disturbance the PGC (Police Gurkha Contingent) will be used as an impartial and deterrent force to patrol riot-torn areas, to search and flush areas for trouble-makers and to escort postal vans, oil tankers, ambulances and fire-engines."[13] Expectations of their neutrality have also been raised by Singapore's first prime minister, the late Lee Kuan Yew: "When I returned to Oxley Road, Gurkha policemen (recruited by the British from Nepal) were posted as sentries. To have either Chinese policeman shooting Malays or Malay policemen shooting Chinese would have caused widespread repercussions. The Gurkhas on the other hand were neutral, besides having the reputation for total discipline and loyalty" (Lee 2000, 21–22). Upon their Gurkha father's retirement from service at the age of forty-five, the whole family would have to be repatriated to Nepal. Overall, Singapore state policies ensure that the Gurkhas and their families remain as insularized "sojourners . . . ironically treating them as an exquisite and yet dispensable and renewable source of labour" (Kiruppalini 2016, 265). According to the Ministry of Defence, UK, website, the plan was to recruit 140 Gurkhas for the GC in 2021 and 2022.[14]

Gurkha presence in Brunei began in 1962 through defense arrangements that led to their postimperial security of the Brunei Sultanate (Menon 1988). Prior to this, Brunei was a protectorate of the British Empire based on the September 1959 Brunei Constitution. The United Kingdom was responsible for handling Brunei's foreign relations, defense, and security (Lim 1976). In December 1962, due to dissatisfaction with the prospect of the British Protectorate of Brunei becoming a part of the then-proposed Federation of Malaysia, which was to include Singapore (Lim 1976), the Partai Rakyat (Brunei People's Party) staged a revolt. The revolt was put down with the aid of British Gurkha troops—the 1st/2nd Gurkha regiment—who were "flown in from British bases in Singapore" (Lim 1976, 159). They had arrived "into Brunei Town in the darkness of the night of 8 December" (Nedumaran 2017, 283). The sultan of Brunei and his family were "quite literally saved from physical harm . . . [as the Gurkhas] arrived at his palace in the nick of time and successfully rescued both him and his family" (Nedumaran 2017, 280). Ever since the revolt, the Gurkha battalion has remained in Brunei on the basis of a bilateral defense agreement with the British (Hamzah 1989). The sultan had remarked that since young Bruneian men were too occupied with studying to take up arms, it was thus "desirous" to form Brunei's security forces by recruiting Gurkhas.[15] The upkeep for the Gurkha battalion is paid from Brunei's oil revenues (Kershaw 2003). This arrangement has since been renewed every five years and also continued after the handover of Hong Kong to China in 1997, thereby providing the British Gurkha troops a permanent base in Southeast Asia (Kershaw 2003).

Throughout the 1960s, the Gurkhas were involved in Brunei, fighting against guerrillas and also guarding oil installations (Dutt 1981). They also used to work alongside the Royal Brunei Police and the Royal Brunei Malay Regiment in securing essential buildings as well as government and private sector installations (Gurung 2020). As the sultan of Brunei wanted to fortify the security of the country, he later recruited retired British Gurkhas to form the Gurkha Reserve Unit (GRU) (Croissant and Lorenz 2018; Kershaw 2003) or Unit Simpanan Gurkha (in Malay; Nedumaran 2017). This provided a platform for what is known as a second career for Gurkhas who have retired from service to continue as economic migrants. Yamanaka (2000) estimates that about 2,200 former Gurkha soldiers serve as the Bruneian sultan's security guards. They safeguard the royal families and royal palaces as their main duty (Gurung 2020). At present, the British Army in Brunei comprises one infantry battalion of Gurkhas, in addition to an Army Air Corps Flight of Bell 212 helicopters.[16] A Jungle Warfare Division serves at the army's jungle warfare school where courses such as Jungle Warfare Instructor and Operational Tracking Instructor are held. The resident Gurkha Battalion—the 1st Royal Gurkha Rifles (1RGR)—resides at the Tuker Lines, which is also where the garrison headquarters are located. Once every three years, 1RGR and 2RGR arms rotate between Folkestone (Kent, England) and Brunei.[17] Gurkha presence in Brunei comprises connections between the United Kingdom, Brunei, and Singapore, their entanglements have been explained using a transnational historical approach (Struck et al. 2011).

Haaland and Gurung (2007) note that as a result of Gurkha service with the British Army since the 1800s, descendants of these Gurkha settlers may be found in parts of India such as Assam, Sikkim, and Darjeeling, as well as Myanmar (Burma). During the colonial period, the Gurkhas in Burma constituted part of the larger process of Nepali migration. They were recruited into the Military Police Force, which was raised in 1886, enlisted in the four battalions of Burma Rifles in World War I, the Burma Frontier Force in the 1930s, and fought in the Burma campaign of World War II (Gurung 2016). After retirement, pockets of Gurkha settlements were formed as they were permitted to reside near the military headquarters and outposts. The census of 1901 recorded in the Myitkyina district in Kachin State of Burma that almost 10 percent of the population comprised so-called "others," where a majority of this group was composed of settled pensioned Gurkha soldiers and their families (Gurung 2016). These retirees found that settling in Myitkyina was an attractive alternative compared to the densely settled valleys in Pahad (hills of Nepal) or the malaria-infested Tarai (lowlands of Nepal) (Haaland and Gurung 2007). These retirees practiced Hinduism and carried out "ritual forms current in the home country" (Haaland and Gurung 2007), representing diasporic connections maintained with Nepal. Prior to 1935, family arrangements for the Gurkhas were very limited. Major Rakamsing Rai recalled the limited family welfare avenues during time spent in Maymyo with the 1st/10th Gurkhas in which his father had served. His child-hood anecdotes provide a glimpse into early Gurkha family life in Myanmar:

> Before 1935 family arrangements only existed for the barest essentials. There was a room and a kitchen for each family. There was no family hospital, family welfare room . . . or *dhai* [nurse]. So if the women and children were ill or dying, or babies were being born, it all took place in the one room. As there was no *dhai,* the women had to get together and help one another. (cited in Forbes 1964, 189)

In terms of household sundries, however, there was always an abundance:

> There was no shortage of food and drink or clothing. In order to make the fire in the cooking place husband and wife had to go out into the forest and cut firewood. The women sat at home all day long knitting stockings and scarves. Their chief responsibility was cleaning the house, caring for the children and helping their husbands prepare the curry and rice. (Forbes 1964, 189)

In 1941, an estimated 200,000 Gurkhas were domiciled in Burma (Gurung 2016). This figure comprises a mix of both military and civilian Gurkhas. Not only did they serve in the armed forces, they were also vegetable growers, dairy-men, and miners employed in the Bawdin mines and the Mawchi mine in Karenni (Gurung 2016; Tinker 1967). There were some among them who married Bur-mese women as well (Gurung 2016). Although there was relative peace between the Nepalese and other ethnic groups in Kachin hills under British colonial rule, the situation changed after independence in 1948. The state-controlled economy ended in a state of high inflation. Movements organized by students and ethnic groups soon took place as a critique of the government. With these periods of unrest and following the Kachin Independence movement, as well as the student movement of the 1970s and 1980s, many Nepalese left Myanmar and looked for opportunities elsewhere. Where some of them returned to Nepal, others went to India (such as to Manipur and Assam) and some also went to Thailand (Haaland and Gurung 2007).[18] These various vicissitudes, representing both colonial and local contexts of empire and governance, set the stage for non/return migration and also step migration. These different cycles and routes of movements further explain how the Gurkhas and their families and descendants are dispersed in the region.

British imperialist presence in Hong Kong commenced after the Opium War of 1841, when Hong Kong was transformed into a colony. Gurkha troops were stationed there since 1948 (Rai 2009). When the Chinese Communist Party took power in China in 1949, masses of refugees from China went to Hong Kong. There was also a fear of the Chinese communists taking Hong Kong back by force. It was then that the first battalion of Gurkhas—the 2nd/10th Gurkha Rifles—was transferred from British Malaya[19] to Hong Kong on 17 March 1948 for a two-year tour (Gurung 2020). The Gurkha engineers built the border that stood between mainland China and Hong Kong (Bellamy 2011). Tim I. Gurung (2020), a retired Gurkha who previously served with the British Army notes that while the battalion was initially stationed at Whitfield Barracks (the Kowloon Park of today), they were later moved to a horse stable located near the Beas River, New Territories.[20] After having cleaned up the stables and with the horses removed, the Gurkha battalion had to make way for the 1st Middlesex Battalion of the British Army. They then relocated to a tented camp near San Wai, which was unfortunately hit by a typhoon:

> Once the tented camp was up, it was hit by a severe typhoon, and they had to take refuge in the nearby camps. Thankfully, the small group of Gurkha families was safe back at the Whitfield barracks . . . the brigade had no ready-made camps for the troops during their first stay in Hong Kong, and the Gurkha battalions had to do with the tented camps in the open grounds of the New Territories. . . . The daily routines mostly involved guarding frontier police stations, training recruits, army training, sports, maintenance of the camps, inter-battalion competition within the garrison and ceremonial parades. (Gurung 2020, 138)[21]

Where the first wave of South Asian migration to colonial Hong Kong comprised different Indian ethnic groups such as the Parsis (who did business with China), Sikhs (who filled up security posts), and also Muslims from Punjab who worked as policemen and prison guards, the second wave occurred when the Gurkhas were moved from Malaya to Hong Kong (Law and Lee 2013). The independence of India from British colonial rule meant that employing Indians in the police force in Hong Kong became problematic for the colonial government. Moreover, it was easier for the British to recruit Gurkhas since they had an agreement with Nepal. Consequently, the introduction of Gurkhas into Hong Kong changed the demographic landscape of South Asian minorities in the colony (Law and Lee 2013). The primary policing duties of the Gurkhas were to protect the population of Hong Kong and to deal with illegal immigrants (Suen and Rana 2020). The Gurkhas patrolled the British Hong Kong–China border in the 1950s and 1960s when massive streams of Chinese immigrants left China due to famines and economic calamities. Security duties were also carried out by the Gurkhas during the Chinese Cultural Revolution (1966–76), when they formed boat troops in order to manage refugees attempting to enter Hong Kong by water. By the late 1970s, the British had deployed five Gurkha battalions along the border in order to round up illegal immigrants. Where the Gurkha engineers constructed barbed-wire fences that laid across the border, the Gurkha signals provided the necessary radio and communications systems, and the Gurkha transport supported with supplies and logistics (Gurung 2020). Over a two-year period, 27,500 illegal immigrants were caught by the Gurkhas. The numbers peaked in 1979 "when 90,000 flooded across the border" (Parker 1999, 214) into the already overcrowded British colony. Apart from handling the influx of illegal immigrants from China, the Gurkhas had to manage another group, the Vietnamese boat people. In this context, they were involved in building and operating new refugee camps, and in assisting the police and providing requisite security reinforcements (Erni and Leung 2014; Gurung 2020).

Apart from these security tasks, Hong Kong also served as a training center for the Gurkhas. They supported with crowd control during the Star Ferry riots of 1966 (O'Neill and Evans 2018). Arising from the Hong Kong Leftist riots that broke out in 1967 (initially over a labor dispute that later escalated into a "full-blown civil disobedience and unrest movement" Gurung [2020, 139]), four Gurkha battalions were deployed in the country. The military camps were mostly located in the New Territories of Hong Kong, housing approximately eight thousand Gurkha troops (Gurung 2020). Barracks were located in the areas of Jordan, Shek Kong, and Yuen Long (Erni and Leung 2014). Similar to the British soldiers, the Gurkhas lived in camps apart from the local community as they had their own temples, restaurants, sports grounds, kindergartens, and schools among other facilities (O'Neill and Evans 2018)—which are mirrored in the Singapore Mount Vernon camp context as mentioned above. There were but limited opportunities for them to learn Cantonese or to mix with the local Chinese population arising from cultural differences and language barriers (Suen and Rana 2020). Furthermore, there was a British Military Hospital situated at King's Park, Kowloon, meant for Gurkha service personnel and their families and at which "the mothers enjoyed excellent pre- and post-natal care" (O'Neill and Evans 2018, 145). There was also a Gurkha high school housed in Shek Kong camp. Gurkha children from all the military camps were ferried by bus on a daily basis to attend the high school (Gurung 2020).

Before Hong Kong was due to be handed back to China in 1997, it was the main home for the Gurkhas, the "last major area of traditional Gurkha deployment in the Far East apart from Brunei" (Parker 1999, 239) with numbers then standing at eight thousand (Law and Lee 2013). Gurkhas were able to have their families live with them in the married quarters of the military barracks in Hong Kong. Their children were born in Hong Kong, but families were allowed to stay with the Gurkhas for no more than three years. They would have to return to Nepal thereafter (Law and Lee 2013). Accordingly, children of Gurkhas born in Hong Kong before 1983 were able to attain Hong Kong residency. Based on the 1984 Sino-British Joint Declaration, local-born babies automatically acquired Hong Kong citizenship (Tang 2009). From the 1990s onward, these children were given a "right to abode" status, thereby enabling Gurkhas to bring their spouses and children as their dependents to become residents in Hong Kong (Rai 2009). Interestingly, this provision generated not only substantial migration numbers to Hong Kong by children of Gurkha soldiers, but also by many non-Gurkhas who managed to obtain fake Hong Kong birth certificates. Many youths over the age of sixteen moved to Hong Kong.

Many second-generation Gurkhas went back to Hong Kong (their birthplace) after the mid-1990s.[22] For instance, Rana Ray, a second-generation Nepalese, returned to Hong Kong in 1994 in pursuit of better job prospects after spending fifteen years in Nepal. While overseeing a construction company, Ray took evening business courses. His wife joined him in Hong Kong in 1997 and began working in grocery store management. By 2000, the couple converted the construction company and started their New General Bouddha Store as a response to demands for a grocer's in Yuen Long (Erni and Leung 2014, 164). In the post-1997 Hong Kong context, Britain drastically reduced its Gurkha Brigades. With the collapse of the Berlin Wall in 1989, and the disintegration of the Soviet Union in 1991, many Western countries including Britain no longer needed large armies (O'Neill and Evans 2018). Consequently, the British regiments lobbied aggressively to be saved. They "argued that foreign soldiers like the Gurkhas should be laid off before British ones" (O'Neill and Evans 2018, 46). About six hundred Gurkha retirees now work in the security industry in Hong Kong (Yamanaka 2000). Notwithstanding the decrease in Gurkha numbers in the context of Hong Kong, Yamanaka (2000, 70) notes that as a result of Nepal's culture of emigration in which Nepalese young men follow their fathers' footsteps to become Gurkhas in foreign lands, this tradition has fostered the "construction of extensive information networks—often called 'the Gurkha connection'—throughout the Asia-Pacific region where troops were stationed." The center of these networks, according to Yamanaka, may be traced to Hong Kong, which was once home to more than ten thousand Gurkhas and their families.

Many Gurkhas who were born in Hong Kong could therefore return there from Nepal as civilians and found work as security guards, bodyguards, drivers, valets, and on construction sites (Gurung 2020; O'Neill and Evans 2018). Compared to their grandfathers, they did not have to go back to farming and were about to seek out "opportunities from various nations" (Gurung 2020, 149). As Gurung further explains, Gurkhas had concerns for the future of their children. Hong Kong was deemed to be an ideal as well as familiar country where they "felt comfortable [in] establishing their new home" (2020, 149). According to Adhikari (2007), most of the Pokhara citizens who work outside of Nepal are found in Hong Kong. Many of the Pokhara youths are able to work and live in Hong Kong because of being "born there while their fathers were working in the British Army" (2007, 33). As for those who were not born in Hong Kong, they had no right to stay, even if they had already lived in the country for more than seven years. This is a prerequisite for foreigners prior to being able to obtain an identity card for taking up permanent residence. Given that the Gurkhas were not required to go through Hong Kong immigration either on entering or exiting the colony, there was therefore no record of how long they had lived in the country (O'Neill and Evans 2018). At that time as well, Britain had not yet offered the option for retired Gurkhas to live in the country that they had served for almost two hundred years. Thus, those who were not eligible to stay in Hong Kong and who were not able to secure work in other places had to return to Nepal. It was only in 2004 that the Gurkhas were allowed to settle in the United Kingdom, owing to the British government's policy of allowing this option for those who have retired after 1997. A further concession was provided after the Gurkha justice campaign led by actress Joanna Lumley (the daughter of a Gurkha officer who served as a major in the 6th Gurkha Rifles) successfully won the right for Gurkhas to settle in the United Kingdom in 2009 (Gellner 2018; Seeberg 2016). The British home secretary announced on 21 May 2009 that Gurkha veterans who retired before 1997, and with minimally four years' service would be allowed abode in the United Kingdom (O'Neill and Evans 2018; Purthi 2011).

While I have presented national contexts where the Gurkhas are located, the above accounts also unveil local and transnational configurations. Different sets of cross-border relations and institutional arrangements among these countries in the context of colonial and postcolonial vicissitudes led to the subsequent diasporic dispersal of the Gurkhas and their children in the region over time. These include security and cooperative policies, military recruitment and agreements, residency rights, and second-career options. A diasporic community of Gurkhas has therefore emerged under such entangled historical circumstances and contract migration, which determine their country of sojourn and/or settlement.

These varied diasporic routes have inadvertently created multiple host/home countries for Gurkhas and their families, which I shall now address.

Gurkha Connections and Diasporic Features

If the preceding accounts illustrate the imbricated dispersal and migratory routes of Gurkha families, how is this diaspora experienced in terms of their everyday practices, their further/future mobilities, and their identity construction? As a preliminary overview, I examine here, the lives of Gurkha diasporans by disrupting the home/hostland binary. Further data and analysis on diasporic experiences will be presented in subsequent chapters. Drawing on my narrative interviews generated over the years, along with secondary materials from print and online sources, I also locate newer platforms of diasporic connections and practices through such online media as Facebook and blogs. Three themes are employed for analysis: (1) notions of return/step migration; (2) notions of home/land; and (3) e-diasporic connections. Overall, the data that I analyze below are useful in empirically realizing methodological transnationalism as well as shedding light on how bracketed belonging transpires across a spectrum of social actors. The analyses to follow illustrate the practices and strengths of transnational links and differentiated meanings of "home."

Return/Step Migration

I first met Muna in Kathmandu in 2012. She grew up in Singapore and later married at the age of twenty-one. Having spent a few years in Nepal after her father's retirement from the Singapore GC, she presently lives in the United Kingdom with her husband, with plans for further studies. When asked as to why she opted to study nursing in Singapore, she replied:

> Because [I] heard from others that for nursing, you have a lot of job opportunities overseas, so [it was] easier for you to go abroad. . . . Because once you come back here [Nepal], it's difficult if your subject, your diploma, is based in business or other areas. It's very difficult for you to get a job and everything. . . . Eventually you cannot go abroad. So it's mainly [because of] the job opportunities that you are forced to take the subject that you don't like.

Muna's return and later onward migration shows that going back to Nepal was not her settlement destination. Marriage has brought her to the United Kingdom where her husband is working, illustrating how return migration does not necessarily imply that the migratory cycle is completed (Cassarino 2004). There is instead a "perennial openness to further movement at distinctive passages in the life cycle" (Ley and Kobayashi 2009, 134). As with the experiences of other Gurkha children, Muna's case shows how some diasporans were considering step migration, which thus influenced the discipline of studies that they selected as a stepping stone for the next migratory path. Her friend, Ganga, now based in Kathmandu, is likewise thinking of furthering her studies in Australia for a nursing degree.

A parallel example may be found in Sirish's biography. Born and bred in Singapore, he returned to Nepal when he turned seventeen and currently works in the fashion industry. Having been back in Kathmandu for four years at the time of our meeting, he planned to pursue overseas studies:

> I knew it was going to happen. But leaving Singapore was still so hard for me. It was so depressing. . . . I remember, before flying off, all my friends were messaging me, "goodbye bro," "take care" . . . and I felt like crying . . . Then when I came here [Nepal], it was like, "ok . . . new lifestyle." But from a positive point of view, what one of the good thing is that coming from Singapore and then coming to Nepal, staying in these two countries balances out . . . the high life and then the village life, and everything. So now that I've lived in Singapore and I've lived in Nepal, send me wherever and I'll adapt. . . . If I can adapt in Nepal, I can adapt anywhere. . . . In Singapore it is [a] small country, there wasn't much problem. In Nepal, we have to be more careful as well. . . . That's why, after coming here . . . actually in a way Nepal has prepared me for the future. So wherever country I decide to go, I know that I will handle it well. . . . That's why I say it's a blessing in disguise. There's good and bad. . . . That's why I feel that Singapore was chapter one of my life, Nepal is chapter two. And in the future, I am sure that US or somewhere is going to be chapter three. That's why these two chapters have prepared me well for the next chapter of my life.

Looking toward "chapter three" of his life, Sirish sees return migration as being more relevant to him than his parents, whose country of origin is Nepal. Nepal is a "place of transit" (Laguerre 2009) before Sirish relocates later on. Overall, narratives of return of Gurkha children illustrate that they are transitory in their outlook and have plans for onward migration. This is especially so given that return migration for children of Singapore Gurkhas is not voluntary but enforced. Such repatriated return was not always understood by the children, especially those of a tender age. Mandatory repatriation—as a form of imposed bracketed belonging to Nepal—constitutes part of the state's transnational policies that thereby inform migrants' life strategies (Uesugi 2007) and plans for their families.

Arjun opted for earlier retirement from the Singapore GC, as he was concerned about whether his two young children—aged eleven and nine—would be able to cope with life in Nepal. He joined Gurkha service when he was twenty years old, and decided to retire after serving seventeen years. Not only were his children reluctant to leave Singapore, the same sentiment was also shared by his wife.

> They [the children] were not so very clear of what is wrong and right. I just try to make understanding, Nepal is our motherland. Now I know . . . Singapore is better. But you cannot continue your study here. Finally, you must stop your study, and then you have to go overseas Australia or US something like that and you need very big amount. And at that time, and also . . . you go back to Nepal, you know nothing in Nepal at that time. So if you go now, you have basic there, you have sufficient time to acclimatize, mix with the Nepal environment, Nepalese society, so that easy for you and next time you can get the job also. But if you, because if they complete O Levels there, they come to Nepal, they have no job. . . . That's the problem, because they have no Nepali, because our office need Nepali subject in their certificate.

Arjun's narrative points to return migration in lieu of the children's long-term welfare, indicating that Nepal was "motherland" after all. At the same time, he is concerned about onward education migration for his children. His own onward migration was enacted through an attempt at a second career in Brunei in the security industry. This stint, however, lasted five months before he returned to Kathmandu again. Having saved money from his Gurkha service in Singapore, invested in land and built a house there, Arjun's migratory biography—a case of moving back and forth between home and host countries (Berg 2014)—is an example of how early voluntary return was planned in such a way so as to also pave the future steps for his children.

Meanings of Homeland

The relationship between home- and hostland is a key feature of diasporic theorizing. I problematize this relationship by arguing that both categories may be multiple instead of singular. Moreover, shifting meanings of both may be discerned among Gurkha diasporans. These meanings are also to be considered, ostensibly, from different vantage points, or through the perspective of different social actors. For example, Hindu festivities are celebrated in the context of Hong Kong where Gurkhas serve.

> Important Hindu festivals such as the Dashain festival that falls in October, and Tihar, the five-day festival of lights in Nepal, would be formal regimental affairs. The whole idea of making it so formal and regimental was because the Gurkhas had for many years been stationed in foreign countries during the First and Second World Wars in battle-field areas. . . . So, by ensuring that they could celebrate their festivals together, *the military could give them a sense of being at home and mitigate the homesickness* of not marking these festivals in their native Nepalese mountains. (O'Neill and Evans 2018, 160–61; my emphasis)

Similarly, in Singapore, Kiruppalini (2016, 264; my emphasis) argues that the government has "made concerted efforts to foster a Gurkha-family-oriented policy." In order to make Gurkha families feel "at home,"

> they celebrate various festivals such as Dasaī, Tihār and Maghe Sankranti inside the camp so that *they will always remember Nepal.* . . . During the festive occasion of Vijayā Dashami, special arrangements are made so that rituals such as the sacrificial slaughtering of the goat can be observed within the premise of the Camp. There is also a Brahmin from Nepal who works as a priest in the temple of the Camp.

Given such various concerted efforts of the Singapore GC, Kiruppalini's (2016, 265) interlocutors shared with her that "we never forgot home [Nepal] while we served in Singapore . . . we celebrated festivals to remember our homeland," and "at the Camp, you are within your Gorkhāli community and ironically, most of the time you will not even realise that you are in Singapore." In both contexts of Hong Kong and Singapore then, "home," or Nepal, is re-created through the overseas celebration of festivals as a way to maintain transnational ties for Gurkha families. Additionally, Gurkha soldiers were discouraged from marrying foreigners before the handover of Hong Kong to China in 1997. This was done to sustain the cohesion of the Gurkha community in the colony on the basis of cultural and national homogeneity (Uesugi 2019a). The regimental desire for such cohesion and homogeneity thereby illustrate further the institutional view on ensuring bracketed belonging to Nepal by maintaining tradition and regulating endogenous marital ties.

Similar policy approaches in ensuring such homogeneity may already be traced back to the 1800s in the context of Gurkhas serving in the Indian Army. According to a letter sent from Maj. Gen. W. Galbraith, C.B., Adjutant (General in India) to the Secretary to the Government of India, Military Department, in 1891, a proposal was drafted in order to encourage marriage in the Gurkha regiments in India. To facilitate this, Maj. Gen. Galbraith had indicated that "free railway passages" ought to be given to Gurkha women to "immigrate to India."[23] He explains:

> Our policy with respect to Gurkhas is undoubtedly to encourage the immigration of Gurkha women from Nepal in every way. From the Resident in Nepal, and on his behalf from the Foreign Office, come reports of such conduct on the part of the Durbar towards Gurkha soldiers in our service that the day may come, and at no distant date, when the return of Gurkhas into Nepal, on furlough, may have to be stopped. They would then have to throw in their lot with the Government of India for life, and, once enlisted, make their home in British India. The wife makes the home; therefore, if we are to keep the men, the Gurkha womankind should be encouraged to come freely and settle down in India.[24]

Given the stated preference for Gurkha soldiers to be married, such encouragement needed to be in line with them marrying "a pure Gurkha woman, a Native of Nepal."[25] In so doing, encouraging marital unions of this type would attain the military policy of disciplining Gurkha soldiers, and of maintaining the homogeneity of a Gurkha community in India:

> The object of encouraging matrimony is—first, the Gurkha when unmarried is often of a restless disposition; apt, if the whim seizes him, or if he thinks he is hardly treated, to take his discharge and go back to Nepal; whereas if he is married, he thinks twice about it. Again, on discharge, many unmarried Gurkhas return to Nepal, whereas married ones often settle in India. If more did so, the nucleus of a Gurkha reserve would be obtained.[26]

The plan was to target at least 20 percent, or the equivalence of 160 men per battalion, for such marriages. Married servicemen would be given double hutting allowances, along with a family allowance amounting to INR two per month. Free passages would also be sanctioned not only for families from Nepal but also "families of deceased men who may wish to return there."[27] Covering ten Gurkha battalions for this marriage proposal, the amount invested into this scheme came up to INR 50,000 annually.[28] The scheme was first piloted with the 1st Battalion, 3rd Gurkha Regiment, at Almora. The government of India's understanding was that "the hutting and family allowances will be passed only in the cases of marriage with women of pure Gurkha extraction."[29] A year later, in 1892, a follow-up letter by Maj. Gen. Galbraith sent to the Secretary to the Government of India,

Military Department, noted that the matrimony proposal was a success. This was measured by "a great diminution in the number of admissions into hospital for venereal diseases, a result which in itself is highly satisfactory, and the conduct of the battalion has improved, no court martial having been held during the past fourteen months."[30] Insofar as military policies such as the above have been enacted in terms of both biopolitical and matrimonial disciplining toward ensuring cultural and national homogeneity, I make a case for this as an example of bracketed belonging. Even if Gurkha women had been allowed to travel to India for marriage, the larger point of this proposal was to precisely bracket the Gurkha community in an overseas context. In this sense, bracketed belonging is consciously structured if not mandated in the military in order to orchestrate Gurkha boundedness in a manner of speaking. It is also noteworthy that brackets of belonging may contract or expand, depending on the social actors who are involved, including the decisions they take and the contexts in which they occur that would have consequences in sociocultural and geopolitical terms.

Aside from festivities discussed above, including military policies on marital ties between Gurkha men and women, military employment policies of the British in the same manner further facilitated and ensured transnational connections between Gurkhas and Nepal. These instances of bracketed belonging "thus helped form a Nepalese community and a sociocultural boundary between the Gurkhas and the British servicemen in the camps of the British Army" (Uesugi 2015, 18). British recruitment of Gurkhas was based on the 1947 TPA signed by Britain, India, and Nepal. Uesugi highlights that one of the main aims of the TPA was to "authorise and maintain transnational ties between Gurkha soldiers and their society of origin in both formal and informal affairs to prevent Gurkhas from being despised as mercenaries" (2015, 17). The British operated with the TPA up to the middle of the 1990s. Based on the agreement, Gurkhas are supposed to be both recruited from and discharged back to Nepal. Furthermore, retired Gurkha servicemen at that time were neither granted UK citizenship nor working visas. As earlier iterated, families were only allowed to accompany the Gurkhas in the army barracks depending on the latter's rank and only over a limited period of time. With this limitation in place, the Gurkhas remitted money, wrote letters, or called home and sent gifts back to Nepal in maintaining their transnational familial ties (Uesugi 2015), as I also elaborate in chapter 3. Moreover, the brigade had always operated with a cultural policy of "symbolically reuniting Gurkhas with their country of origin, Nepal" (Uesugi 2007, 388) by focusing on Hinduism, which is the national religion of Nepal. There are Hindu religious teachers employed in the capacity of civilians who hold Hindu ceremonies on a daily basis, in addition to formal holidays observed by the camps during times of Hindu festivities as discussed earlier. Specifically, these dates are synchronous with Nepalese time. Camps follow the calendar as used by the Almanac Commit-tee in Kathmandu (Uesugi 2007). These various ritual and custom orchestrations in effect foster a "Nepalese consciousness" (see Ragsdale 1989, 49–50) for the Gurkhas and their families.

In essence, while Gurkhas were transported out of Nepal for military recruit-ment, training, and service, there was no equivocation about how Nepal con-tinued to be regarded as home for these servicemen, and as the final location in which the Gurkhas (and their children) ought to return.[31] Such affective-religious belonging to Nepal as home also extends to political belonging. While the Gur-khas would have sworn allegiance to the British crown, they were permitted to remain loyal to the king of Nepal (Uesugi 2015). It was also economically favor-able for the British Army to continuously pursue the policy of maintaining close ties between the Gurkhas soldiers and Nepal. By justifying that their family lives in Nepal meant considerably lower costs of living as compared to the United Kingdom, this rationale was therefore the basis on which Gurkhas received lower salaries and pensions (Uesugi 2019a). In the post-1990s period and with the rights for Gurkhas and their families to settle in the United Kingdom and Hong Kong, such changing circumstances further add to how home is constructed based on a host of internal and external factors and conditions. Home as felt by individuals and as determined by military structures are both parallel processes. These processes are subject to change vis-à-vis wider sociopolitical conditions that intertwine different countries as demonstrated above.

In the following focus group interview that I held in Nepal, Ganga, Riju, and Dipesh (all in their twenties) discussed how the notion of home is complicated as they possess an outlook of what they call "neither here nor there":

> GANGA: Very funny you know, when we were in Singapore we used to tell people that we are from Nepal. You know, that we are Nepali, so proud of our, you know, our country. And when we come here, we. . . . [*laughs*] . . . tell them that we are from Singapore.
>
> RIJU: In Singapore, they ask you where are you from, and you are, "I'm from Nepal." You don't look like you're born there. Then when come here, "Where are you from?" "I am from Singapore." Oh my god it is so confusing.
>
> KELVIN: Why so?
>
> DIPESH: Aiya, we are from neither here nor there.
>
> RIJU: Yeah, we are from neither here nor there.

The group interview suggests that the issue of home/hostland needs to be rethought in terms of diasporans' territorial and affective senses of belonging.

As Riju remarked, they are "neither here nor there," illustrating how the home/host binary transcends its bifocality to indicate ambivalence as to where one felt at "home." Such ambivalence denotes the "transnational struggles" (Wolf 2002, 257) that interlocutors such as Riju and Dipesh have expressed. They continue to grapple with differing notions of which country or culture they belong to—a query that persists in their minds and lives. Correspondingly, Berg (2011) recommends that it would be less productive to think of home- and hostlands in singular terms, especially when different generations of a diaspora possess heterogeneous experiences. Ganga's and Riju's responses reflect how both Nepal and Singapore can be referred to as their homeland, depending on the context. Another respondent, Manisha, told me that she has gradually gotten used to life in Nepal, having returned there from Singapore when she was sixteen. The home/hostland distinction does not apply in singular terms. Instead, both Nepal and Singapore simultaneously qualify as "home." At the same time however, she shared that she was constantly reminded by her father (while living in Singapore) to know that she is Nepalese despite getting the "whole Singapore experience." She was thus cautioned not to "blend too completely" in Singapore society. Learning the Nepali language is therefore an important aspect of their Nepalese identity. Such language acquisition applies to the different Gurkha families that have resided in Singapore, Hong Kong, and the United Kingdom. In Singapore, for instance, Gurkha children learn Nepali from their mothers or other Gurkha wives when they return home from school as the language is not part of the curriculum in Singapore schools.

Furthermore, where identity and diaspora consciousness are place based, such awareness is also tied to a set of sociocultural practices that diasporans are most familiar with. Renu mentioned: "I don't know, because from the time I came from Singapore, and ever since I started to live here [Nepal], everything I come across I just. . . . Everything is about comparing it with Singapore. Whatever it is, Singapore never goes out of the picture." Singapore is to her, the place of "origin," as she grew up there as opposed to Nepal. As such, Renu identified more with her Singapore experience. This therefore begs the question of the notion of "origin" in the larger scheme of Gurkha mobilities, including identification with the country where she was residing as compared to disidentification with her current experience in Kathmandu.

Another Gurkha interlocutor Ram was recruited into the British Army at the age of nineteen. He spent five years training in Hong Kong, and first arrived in England in 1994. He has three daughters. The first two were born in Nepal, and the youngest was born in England. He said this of his youngest child, Sumira, when I asked how often they returned to Nepal: "My little one [Sumira] says 'I'm born here, I'm English.' Then we keep asking her, 'Where are your parents from?' then she say 'Nepal obviously.' Then we say, 'Ya, then you are Nepalese,' but she says no she's English. It is hard." Sumira has identified herself as English in association with her birth country. Although Ram and his wife make a point of teaching the children Nepali, and to "encourage children to wear our culture dress, and dance or perform," Sumira preferred to speak in English. She was also not very fond of Nepalese food. Ram further shared that while he and his wife plan on returning to Nepal once their children are independent, they would let their daughters "decide wherever they want to go."

Evidently, these varied experiences point to a need to transcend the home/hostland relation that is homogeneously applied to members of a given diaspora. Where Nepal is Arjun's "motherland," the same does not apply to his children. A parallel is observed in the case of Ram and Sumira. In these instances, and by interpreting the experiences of Gurkhas (and their children) as migrants, mandatory return migration—as in the case of Singapore Gurkha families—thereby wields influence over what is home and how sentiments of belonging shape the identity of these individuals vis-à-vis their transnational affiliations and comparisons. Retired Gurkhas such as Arjun and Ram, as with many of my other interlocutors, make continued and deliberate choices. These are elected to ensure that their children learn the ways of Nepali culture while living abroad—either through mastery of the language, cultural performances through song and dance, or through food and foodways. Collectively, these stand for elements and practices of "symbolic transnationalism" (Espiritu and Tran 2002) as efforts to maintain cultural and transnational links with Nepal. As bracketing efforts, these features collectively represent Nepali tradition and culture that are meant to be instilled in the second generation. This is done in order for them to be positioned to "remain connected to the homeland of their parents" (Kananen 2020, 172). Perhaps more so for the children of Gurkhas, they are "simultaneously involved in two different narratives of being and belonging" (Kananen 2020, 182). This is contrasted with their Gurkha parents who have spent a significant part of their lives in Nepal as their country of origin. Such duality of narratives and exposure to at least two different cultural schemes as experienced by the children can fall onto different axial configurations—that between Nepal and Singapore for Arjun's children, or that between Nepal and the United Kingdom for Ram's daughters. In these differentiated links of diasporic distance, then, the meanings of home/hostland wield different import for inter- and intragenerational diasporans. Such meanings largely depend on where they live and grow up as well. Pertinently, the roots and routes of different generations of the Gurkha diaspora are thus to be carefully differentiated. In so doing, I offer further critique and engagement with diasporic theorizing and how notions of "home" are bracketed and experienced.

E-Diaspora

Since diasporic communities have always relied on networks (Yamanaka 2000), the internet "is now the central framework for such networks, so that observing online structures can provide insights into diasporic community characteristics" (Kissau and Hunger 2010, 246). The growing use of the internet—email, Skype, Facebook, Twitter, TikTok, Instagram, blogs and others—has provided a different platform through which transnational communities connect to each other. These online avenues provide an interesting source whereby everyday diasporic life in terms of memory-making, transnational connections, information networks, participatory channels, and others may thrive regardless of territorial position (Adzmi and Bahry 2020; Witteborn 2019). Interdiasporic ties are thus evident where some of my Hong Kong-based respondents maintain contact with their Gurkha relations in Singapore through Facebook, while those in Nepal keep abreast of news and the lives of their relations and friends living in Singapore through Facebook and other social media forms. Following the exchange of information on these online media therefore accords a glimpse into how members of the Gurkha diaspora enact intradiasporic experiences. These experiences may include the retention or reawakening of identities and imagined homelands, sharing information about job opportunities, and updating members on Gurkha-related issues. Studying online communication also facilitates overcoming problems of methodological nationalism and groupism. Internet users do not work within boundaries at the national or group level. These online networks are instead grouped around similar interests and topics (Kissau and Hunger 2010).

The topics that I identify through e-diasporic channels indicate diasporic connectivity as a feature of migrant transnationalism. They include sharing memories of growing up in Singapore, connecting with Gurkha children of different cohorts, and building information networks for job opportunities. Memories of migration and sojourn are pivotal for both individual and group identity formation. They also have bearings on experiences of belonging to a particular place or home. The excerpts below, posted on the Gurkha Contingent Singapore Confessions Facebook page point to recollections of growing up:

> Playing 7stones, shooting, baseball from 4pm along the pathway of Pokhara Garden and Everest Heights has got to be the best childhood memory for the 90s kid. (14 May 2013)

> Remember that one time during the old GC days. There was always some sort of a trend. One does it and then everyone's into it. Rollerblades, kite flying, skippy caps, digimon, kang catching (Feed your kang saliva rampart Horip huncha) haha, fighting fish, go Bartley longkang explore . . . Miss those golden 80s days man. (14 May 2013)

The entries above have generated further posts from other Gurkha children who also join in by reminiscing about their days in Singapore through such online dialogues, which represent relatable good days of the past. There is a sense of online togetherness where these posts serve as nostalgic expressions that contribute toward shared imaginations and group solidarity (Schrooten 2012). This would form an important aspect of their migratory lives and how they view "home" through such experiences.

Such collective behavior is further reflected through an assumed shared experience of identification, as the next post demonstrates:

Every bhanja and bhanji's conversation with outsiders usually start like this:

> OUTSIDER: Are you Malay or Chinese?
> GC KID: I'm Nepalese from Nepal.
> OUTSIDER: Oh. How long you stay in Singapore?
> GC KID: I was born here.
> OUTSIDER: Oh, so you're Singaporean, ah?
> GC KID: No.
> *GO KUNA CRY;("
> (17 MAY 2013)

This post reveals a number of issues pertaining to self-identification and identification by others in the context of multiracial Singapore. "Outsider" is employing two out of the four official race categories (Chinese, Malay, Indian, and Others) that the Singapore state endorses as part of its multiracial ideology, in an attempt to classify "GC kid." When "GC kid" replies that s/he is Nepalese, the next answers are unexpected since being born in Singapore for Gurkha children does not qualify them for citizenship. This is an issue that has been heavily criticized and lobbied among the Singapore Gurkhas and their adult children. While outsiders may be trying to "place" Gurkha children in the local context, the latter are facing identity struggles concerning their legal rights.

Where information networks are concerned, the following two posts (from the Gurkha Contingent Singapore Confessions Facebook page and the Gurkha Reserve Unit [Brunei] Facebook page, respectively) show how different cohorts of Gurkha children are connected, and how e-diasporic channels may serve as a job network platform:

> Good to know that there are so many bhanjas and bhanjis who are living a successful life as a doctor, nurse, etc. Why don't you guys share the difficulties and the sacrifices that you had to make to reach this stage? I guess it can help the younger bhanjas and bhanjis who are clueless to

be prepared for what they are going to face in the coming days if they want to be successful like you guys. Particularly the life after GC because this is where most of the bhanjas and bhanjis get lost.

i like to say that gurkhas in brunei happy new year 2013 my name is hum bdr.jhendi magar i am ex police in singapore i just want request [*sic*] how to found [*sic*] the gurkhas job in brunei at the moment i am in macau thanks my contact no XXX.

Diasporic experiences of migration are reflected not only through narrative interviews but also online social media presented above. Despite limitations such as lacking face-to-face interaction, ascertaining migrants' location, and anonymity that makes it difficult to link web phenomena to social groups or individuals (Kissau and Hunger 2010), online connectivity is a feature of contemporary transnational realities and should be included in diaspora studies. If research on migrant transnationalism is about flows and connections, it is then crucial to add e-activities to the inventory as newer forms of migrant transnationalism (Nedelcu 2012).

Taking a closer look at military and police histories, the patterns and mechanisms of Gurkha dispersal across a range of Asian countries demonstrate that the transnational history approach is useful toward grounding methodological transnationalism. Studying military histories here mean delineating how colonial-local webs of entanglements, military aggression, conquests, and defeats collectively account for the dispersal of different Gurkha units and their families in Asia and beyond. Empirically realizing methodological transnationalism translates into tracing the transnational military/police-migratory routes of Gurkha families. This approach also involves analyzing the transnational connections and practices that they maintain while living overseas. I have shown that interrogating diasporic formation is about unpacking the logic of dispersion in terms of how the Gurkha diaspora was created, resulting from military and paramilitary contexts of service and retirement policies. The historical connections between the Gurkhas and Britain hold implications in terms of their countries of settlement, including the next cycles of migration for those who have chosen not to remain in Nepal.

State-oriented/military policies and efforts maintain the Gurkha families as "sojourners" (Kiruppalini 2016). Through these efforts, they sustain continued ties with Nepal by organizing festivities celebrated overseas (Kiruppalini 2016; O'Neill and Evans 2018)—all of which converge in two ways. First, these empirically demonstrate how methodological transnationalism is enacted by different actors. Second, such efforts are also indicative of bracketed belonging—such as that transpiring through the TPA (Uesugi 2015) in limiting possibilities of belonging. In the process, multiple meanings of home emerge as I have documented. However, it is not merely about identifying how the notion of home is regarded differently. Through pinpointing both institutional and individual acts of bracketed belonging that intersect with transnational practices, my discussion further highlights how home is also determined by if not imposed on diasporans in the context of Gurkha military service and postservice policies. This would also cohere with my earlier argument about how belonging can either be self-constructed or imposed externally (e.g., GCSPF and Hong Kong, which make it regimentally official to celebrate festivities).[32] These dynamics likewise map respectively onto what Espiritu and Tran (2002, 386) term as processes of "self-making" and "being made."

Home and belonging in the diaspora culminate from an interplay of transnational practices and acts of bracketing carried out by a variety of social actors. Transnational practices are not merely about maintaining ties with Nepal, but looking ahead to the future (Uesugi 2007) when diasporans (may have to) go back to Nepal. Symbolic transnational practices (Epiritu and Tran 2002; Kananen 2020) prepare children to be able to fit into Nepal subsequently. In tandem, Uesugi (2007) points out that until 1998, Nepali teachers taught the children of Gurkha in Nepali, and followed Nepal's national curriculum that was mapped onto Gurkha schools in the camps. Such preparation is therefore further highlighted when analyzed from the perspective and process of bracketing as I have done so. Bracketed belonging aids in revealing the intent or motivation behind the transnational practices that actors carry out across different domains of enactment. For Gurkhas and their families, these processes are to be comprehended under military structures and state policies. These may either facilitate rights to a place or denial/curtail such rights through bracketing that confers temporary status as military migrants. The former transpires in the contexts of the United Kingdom and Hong Kong arising from colonial and postcolonial circumstances. The latter emerges in the case of Singapore given the nation-state's stance on multiracialism under which the Gurkhas' policing neutrality is prized, and no more than that. The GCSPF and its various state policies are installed by way of bracketing the limits of how Gurkhas and their families are not allowed to settle down in Singapore by the end of Gurkha service. As temporary diasporans, Gurkha men gain employment and their children are granted education. Getting too acquainted with the locals is however not permitted for the two main reasons of security-neutrality, and of eventual repatriation at the end of one's service from the force. These reasons therefore account for how the nation-state brackets and limits affective and other forms of belonging for Gurkha families in Singapore as an example.

Constructing and experiencing a Gurkha diaspora through these lenses thereby pique a rethinking of historical and contemporary mobilities subject to various forces, structures, and the choices that diasporans make. Under these institutional frameworks then, the home-host binary is further complicated to address these Gurkha experiences and transnational realities in the wider diasporic space. In this process I have argued with a critique of the home/hostland binary by not only tracing migratory routes of Gurkha families, but outlining how home continues to be an imaginary that is not merely reducible to territory. The idea of "home" does not necessarily have to refer merely to place (Wolf 2002). It can as well stand as a "concept and a desire" (Espiritu and Tran 2002, 369). Subscribing to methodological transnationalism goes beyond the assumption of the nation-state as the central social context within which migration takes place (Amelina and Faist 2012). This perspective thereby aids in reframing the singular binary of "home" and "host" country and account for subsequent experiences of belonging and not-belonging. Identification with home/hostlands may be multiple and simultaneous. There is more than one binary that Gurkhas and their family members relate to in the present and the future, between what counts as "home" and from where they are based. Consequently, this reflects a departure from territorial limitation (Wimmer and Glick Schiller 2002).

Paying attention to the turning points of different generations of diasporans is also important. This analytically engenders a further nuanced layer of how to problematize and approach home as a multifaceted notion in wider diasporic discourses. There are, of course, differences among different generations. Examining the Gurkha diaspora and their varied sense of belonging further throws light on the different migratory aspirations or turning points of these actors. For most of the retired Gurkhas, interest in a second career is perhaps the last stop before they return to Nepal to settle down. The younger generation of Gurkha children, however, possess a more transnational outlook given the fairly early stage of their lives. Embarking either on the pursuit of higher education or work mobility contrasts against the Gurkhas for whom Nepal as homeland wields more significance. Cumulatively, these varied turning points reveal where home is intended, rejected, or reimagined by different actors based on their varied biographical experiences and aspirations.

Diasporic consciousness and formation are not static processes but undergo modification alongside subsequent cycles of migration for different members of the diaspora. Where some Gurkhas and their wives may persist with their transnational connections to Nepal while they live overseas, their children may think otherwise and look elsewhere for their further mobilities. In short, there are "some immigrants who feel very strongly about being transnational," and there are others "who want nothing to do with it" (Jones-Correa 2002, 232) in terms of connecting to an ancestral homeland that is Nepal. Transnationalism and acts and sentiments of belonging are unevenly experienced for Gurkhas and their family members. Different diasporic members, due to their contrasting migratory biographies, therefore elucidate the extent to which transnational outlook and mobility may vary considerably. This would then relate back to how we ought to examine diaspora as a "category of practice" (Brubaker 2005) and not as a static, homogeneous collective.

Gurkha transnational lives are closely connected to reterritorialized dimensions of home, identity, and belonging. Beyond the limiting binary of home/hostland in earlier diaspora discourses then, my case of the Gurkhas lends newer perspectives with which to grapple with modulating notions of home. Ostensibly, these changing notions are contingent on entangled military/police, colonial, postcolonial, and national histories. These insights thereby exemplify the transnational history approach in both constructing a Gurkha diaspora and how diasporans consider their own transnational experiences. Such experiences are apprehended in relation to where home is and where and how belonging is felt. My bricolage of intersecting transnationalism, bracketing processes, and multiple meanings of home therefore further illustrate the uniqueness of the Gurkha diaspora per se that cannot be subsumed under studies and discourses surrounding the South Asia diaspora as iterated at the outset. The intensity and frequency of transnational connections across the Gurkha diaspora may also be found, as my data has shown, through the e-diaspora platform. This digital space serves as a virtual meeting point for different diasporic members who are in their own ways and through varied memories connected both to Nepal and their country of settlement or sojourn. The potentials of an e-diaspora and its "digital diasporic practices" (Alinejad et al. 2019, 39) therefore enhance the transnational connections of migrants. These connections include mobilizing sentiments of belonging, supporting causes such as pension issues and the right to remain for the Gurkha children, among other agendas of the Gurkha diaspora that I further discuss in the following pages.

THE WARRIOR GURKHA

> Here, I can say one thing about the Gurkha, that he is in many ways
> the most delightful person. He has all the nicest characteristics of
> the British race, i.e., he likes playing games, he likes drinking, he
> likes women, he likes gambling. However, in my experience he has
> little feelings for the dead, either the enemy or his own comrades . . .
> no feeling of sadness and certainly none of remorse when they'd
> killed the Japanese. Hence the attitude they took when I told them
> to stop it and put their *kukri*s away. At the time they were elated.
> And it's a very interesting fact that Gurkhas when they are going into
> action at close quarters become bloodshot in their eyes and are a
> very fearsome adversary.
>
> John Parker, *The Gurkhas*

Michael Marshall was a commissioned officer of the 5th Royal Gurkha Rifles. He was posted to Burma in May 1943 and was involved in the fight against the Japanese in the paddy fields of the Arakan region located on the west coast of Burma. The mission was to cut Japanese supply lines to the south of the Mayu River and to eventually capture Buthidaung in Rakhine State (Parker 1999). Marshall had witnessed "at close quarters" the Gurkhas using their kukris on the Japanese. They were moving "very briskly and mostly went for the throat" (Parker 1999, 136). His characterization of the Gurkhas as recounted by Parker (1999) above raises a number of queries pertaining to the image of the warrior Gurkha. What were the Gurkhas like as soldiers? How were they associated with such traits of bravery, fearsomeness, and loyalty? What lies beneath the depiction of Gurkhas as "small in stature and mighty in battle"?[1] How might an investigation of martial race theory avail an analytical complication of and more nuanced understandings of the Gurkhas and their global image as gallant fighters?

To start with, the term *Gurkha* requires unpacking as a historical category arising out of "military imagination" (Caplan 1995b, 10). They were designated by British officials as a martial race (Purthi 2011; Roy 2013).[2] In the eighteenth and nineteenth centuries, Nepal was at that time referred to as the Kingdom of the Gurkhas, Goorkhas or Gorkhalees. This reference was made in connection to a small territory called Gorkha, which was situated in the hills west of the

Kathmandu Valley. The Gurkhas today are therefore taken as the descendants of the fighting men of Gorkha, who played pivotal roles in taking the Kathmandu Valley under King Prithibinarayan Shah of the Gorkha Kingdom. He had unified the three independent political principalities of Kathmandu, Lalitpur, and Bhaktapur, which subsequently paved the way for the creation of the modern Nepalese state (Banskota 1994; Caplan 1995b).

Caplan (1995b) suggests alongside Pemble (1971) that to take the Gurkhas as descendants of Gorkha fighting men was a misconception. He clarifies:

> Gurkhas exist in the context of military imagination, and are thereby products of the officers who command and write about them; outside that setting, it can be argued, there are no Gurkhas, only Nepalis. Besides, in Nepal, no group or category of people refers to itself or is referred to by other Nepalis as Gurkhas. The term most commonly used for a soldier who serves or has served in foreign armies is *lahure*, a corruption of Lahore, the city in Punjab. (Caplan 1995b, 10–11)

It follows that the figure of the Gurkha is but a fictive category, borne out of "military ambiance in which he assumes his persona," as well as that arising from military writers who represent him (Caplan 1995b, 12). As Gould (1999, 1) notes in tandem, regimental histories are "simultaneously records of fact and repositories of myth." I trace such regimental ambiance and also the works of authors, including the Gurkhas themselves (see for example, Gurung 2020; Limbu 2015, 2021; Rai 2020). They have together sustained this category that has been built on martial race theory over the centuries. In my discussion, I align with and also extend from extant scholarship revolving around discourses on the Gurkhas in the past and present. For instance, Chisholm (2022, 12) contends that the Gurkhas are perceived as "racialized contractors," given that martial race histories persist in defining them, and through which they are able to continue gaining labor access to the global security market. Studies such as this critically appraise ideological constructs and diverse representations of Gurkhas that concurrently reflect the enduring effects and influences of colonial histories (Bhandari 2021; Chisholm 2014; Streets 2004).

Constructing a Martial Race

> When the newly arrived recruits reached the Centre after the first train journey of their lives, the majority of them had never before seen a train, motor car, clock or even worn a pair of boots. They were like a cheerful shaggy crowd of half-grown puppies; they laughed when they should

have stood silent, chattered freely in the ranks and spoke openly to the NCO about anything that interested them. For those first days they were all like our shepherd boy, Manbahadur Limbu, showing the basic qualities of the Gurkhas, their love of life, a natural warm sense of humour and an unconscious but fearless pride in their race. (Purthi 2007, 129)

From "half-grown puppies" to warriors, the ways Gurkhas were regarded say a lot about the building of martial race, only to be fulfilled by the British themselves through their training and guidance. Martial race theory and its stereotypes include soldiers who tended to come from rural areas, and who were "hardened by harsher climates," "relatively uneducated," and "could be counted upon to be reliable on and off the battlefield" (Peers 2007, 34). The assumption was that such individuals possessed a warlike predisposition and therefore were "better suited to military service" (Peers 2007, 34). That said, however, martial race notions also predated colonial military cultures (Caplan 1995a) and beyond those derived by the British to include other empires. They comprise examples drawn from the contexts of Africa (Kirk-Greene 1980; Osborne 2014) as well as Ireland (Denman 1996), among others. Similarly, the key assumption was that these groups presumably possessed an aptitude for war (Enloe 1980; Peers 2007), as such individuals were both socially and economically less advanced, and as they come from hostile environments in which they inhabit. A widespread concept of a martial race has therefore to do with the idea of natural qualities, with an inherent inclination toward military occupations traced to a particular ethnic community (Enloe 1980). Warlike qualities as assumed to be in the "blood" of Gurkhas also meant that such a trait could be passed on through the generations, thereby deeming them as "natural soldiers" (Vansittart 1906) or a "born soldier" (Northey and Morris 1987, 98).

The Gurkhas were thus one of such groups assumed to possess martial fiber, alongside others such as the Punjabis (Mahmood and Khan 2017; Singh and Singh 2020; Streets 2004) or the Scottish Highlanders (Roy 2013). They have also been compared to these other soldiers, having been recognized as being second to none: "Their fighting qualities, whether for sturdy, unflinching courage, or daring elan, are *nulli secundus* amongst the troops we enrol in our ranks from the varied classes of our Indian Empire" (Vansittart 1906, 64). Not only were the Gurkhas marked as possessing the requisite physical and mental capacities to be recruited and trained as good and loyal soldiers, which together constitute what Enloe (1980) has termed as a "Gurkha syndrome," army officers were also playing a critical role in how such cultural and ethnographic information was gathered and analyzed. Thus, they were not merely "consumers of colonial knowledge" but were as well "producers," positioned as such in the recruitment process (Peers 2007, 36). Importantly, as Peers observes, "What constituted a Gurkha or a Sikh was largely the product of these efforts at identification and classification, and the end result was a series of categories that were as much the product of imperial imaginations as they were the result of indigenous development" (2007, 36). Imperial constructions of these famed warriors consistently highlight their physical abilities and attributes alongside their weapon, the kukri. As Vansittart describes:

> The Gurkha, from the warlike qualities of his forefathers, and the traditions handed down to him of their military prowess as conquerors of Nepal, is imbued with, and cherishes the true military spirit. His physique, compact and sturdy built, powerful muscular development, keen sight, acute hearing, and hereditary education as a sportsman, eminently capacitate him for the duties of a light infantry soldier on the mountain side, while his acquaintance with forest lore makes him as a pioneer in a jungle almost unrivalled. His national weapon, the *kukri*, has, in Burma and other places, proved itself invaluable. (1906, 62)

Another interpretation of the kukri comes from Gould (1999, 1; see also Purthi 2007, 124) who talks about a joke in order to demonstrate how the weapon is a "rich source of mythology": "The Gurkha's legendary prowess with the curved knife which is his trademark weapon is celebrated in a wartime joke. Locked in close combat with a large German, a Gurkha takes a swipe at him with his *kukri*. The German says, 'Ha, missed!' To which the Gurkha replies, 'Shake your head.'"

For Gould then, the kukri functions "more often as a kind of billhook than as a lethal weapon" (Gould 1999, 1). To further his critique of the kukri as imbued with more mythical prowess exacted by the Gurkhas, Gould (1999, 195) cites MacDonell and Macauley (1940, 375) who paint a hyperbolic picture (Gould terms these as "lurid tales") of the Gurkhas and their knives (presumably the kukri):

> It was stated that they could progress uphill on all fours at a greater speed than a horse could run on the level; they carried a large flat knife in their mouths and without faltering could fell the undergrowth, even large trees, and so cut their way through the forest. At times, it was said, they would hang head downwards from the branches of trees and slash off the heads of the enemy with this formidable knife; at other times they would throw the knife with such accuracy as to kill their man immediately, and would then rush forward and regain the knife. As they

did these things they would laugh with glee; the scowl of a Cossack was nothing to the smile of a Gurkha.

If anything, such "wild and exaggerated stories" revolving around the kukris serve to function as an "excellent propaganda weapon" for which "even if untrue . . . helped to inspire fear" (Purthi 2007, 124).

The instilling of fear was not only undertaken by British writers. Kailash Limbu (2015), who was a Gurkha serving in Afghanistan, related a story about Gurkhas and their kukris to the locals, with an intention to strike fear in their hearts. Limbu told of Gurkhas and the British who were fighting against the Pashtun tribesmen in defending the North-West Frontier in the 1930s. When one of these tribesmen captured and decapitated a British soldier's head and put it on display, the British *sahib* gave out orders for the Gurkhas to also capture and behead a tribesman. After they did that, the sahib called the local villagers to watch a football match together. In place of an actual football, the players were using the decapitated head of the tribesman. The sahib later explained to the elders of the village that if any one of his soldiers were to be attacked again, he would instruct the Gurkhas to "go out with their *kukri*s and cut the heads off every single male over the age of fourteen" (Limbu 2015, 78). Limbu stated that he did want the Afghans who had heard this story to be frightened of the Gurkhas. Indeed, the account of the kukri and decapitation, whether authentic or not, worked as the Afghans had "listened to this story in silence" (Limbu 2015, 78). One of them later asked if the blade of the kukri was very sharp. The formation of this embellished image along with the kukri has been disseminated through the various avenues listed above. These various platforms thereby illuminate analytical light on how Gurkha martiality was both manufactured and circulated with particular motivations in mind.

Comparing across Nepali Groups

Martial race theory and classification, while broadly applied to Gurkhas, also differed across the various groups or "tribes" of Nepal. Caplan (1995b) suggests that Hamilton (1819, 19) was probably the first European to use the term "martial tribes," while Hodgson classifies specific groups as "martial classes" (1833, 220). Heterogeneous appraisal of their group-specific traits by British writers stemmed from orientalist constructs of Nepalese. Recruitment classification and comparisons were also made through these constructs as part of the imperial imaginary. Nepal was divided up into different ethnic or "tribal" units, each accompanied by a set of defining characteristics (Caplan 1991). In the process, a handful of British officers ended up becoming "avid ethnographers" (Caplan 1991) in producing military recruitment handbooks (for example, Leonard 1965; Vansittart 1906). These handbooks, among others, underscored ethnic differences across the different groups in Nepal in systematized and exaggerated manners. Eden Vansittart, who was lieutenant colonel of the 2nd Battalion, 10th Gurkha Rifles, notes in the preface of his handbook: "The classification of the various races of Nepal is almost entirely my own . . . [and for which] the Magars, Gurungs, and Thakurs are, I believe, fairly complete and correct" (1906, i). As for the other groups comprising the Khas, Limbus, Rais, Sunwars, and Murmis, their classifications are "undoubtedly incomplete, and perhaps in parts incorrect," but for which "a full and true list of their tribes and subdivisions, can only be done after years of incessantly putting down on paper, each fresh tribe and each fresh clan of the same, at such time as a member of it presents himself for enlistment, and then by checking its accuracy over and over again" (Vansittart 1906, i–ii). Vansittart's account broadly reads akin to what is known as "verandah anthropology" through which natives are summoned to the ethnographer's verandah. This is so that the latter may study the culture of the former (see Jarvie 1977; Malinowski 1922). In tandem, Enloe (1980, 28) calls the establishment of militaries an "ethnographic enterprise" in which the Gurkhas have become "ethnic soldiers" (Enloe 1980) recruited vis-à-vis British predilections.[3]

These preoccupations of the British also meant that these enlisted Nepalis would only be able to realize their combat potential under the training and control of British officers (Northey 1938). Not unlike colonial discourses and practices of civilizing natives then, the recruited Gurkhas were assumed to be able to reach their military might through the guidance of the British. This view is articulated by J. P. Cross, a retired colonel who had worked alongside the Gurkhas for almost four decades: "Where many a British soldier got bored too easily and so disregarded basic rules, the Gurkha was very good when properly led" (2009, 144). This seems also to be the case in contexts where Indian officers and Gurkha soldiers are concerned. The former have indicated that even though Gurkhas have obeyed orders, they would convey "explicit obedience" but not necessarily that they had understood these orders (Bammi 2009).

Gurkha recruitment typically centered on four main groups—the Magars, Gurungs, Rais, and Limbus (Farwell 1984), although the latter two groups had been regarded as too fractious, headstrong, and undisciplined (Banskota 1994). Hence, they were initially recruited for paramilitary forces such as the Assam Rifles and Burma Military Police (Bammi 2009). Even if the British typically take and represent these groups as a "uniform category" by and large, there certainly are substantial overlaps vis-à-vis inter- and intragroup characteristics (as

I indicated above), and not to mention the same in comparison to other groups who are usually not recruited (Caplan 1995b). Magars and Gurungs are deemed to be the "*beau ideal*" of what Gurkha soldiers ought to be like. They are assumed to be "fond of soldiering," very "hardy," and are thought to be "intensely loyal to each other and their officers" during times of danger or trouble (Vansittart 1906, 77). There are also differentiations made between Gurungs from central Nepal as compared to those coming from eastern Nepal. Those from central Nepal are thought to be "magnificent" with "splendid physique" whereas the others from eastern Nepal are considered as "very much inferior" in "physique, appearance, and in all respects." This was because of their intermarriages with other groups of Eastern Nepal which meant that they had through miscegenation "deteriorated in physique" (Vansittart 1906, 81; see also Roy 2013). Vansittart argues that instead of recruiting an "average Magar or Gurung of Eastern Nepal," others such as a "good Limbu, Rai, or Sunwar" would be more desirable as soldiers (Vansittart 1906, 81). Among the different clans of the Magars, there are some who stand out for military purposes. They range from the Ales being the "most desirable" men to recruit, followed by the Burathokis who were "very desirable" men to enlist (Vansittart 1906, 87). As a contrast to the Magars and Gurungs, the Newars were regarded as potentially "good soldiers," even if they were "not a warlike or military race" (Vansittart 1906, 93). As for the Thakurs, those who belonged to good clans and who possessed good soldiery qualities could be recruited in small numbers, since they were quite comparable to the "best Magar or Gurung" (Vansittart 1906, 65).

The Limbus live in the easternmost areas of Nepal, working in the main as shepherds or cultivators. Even if their physique was good and their appearance resembled that of Magars or Gurungs, they were not thought to be as good soldiers compared to them. They were shorter, fairer, and stockier as compared to the Magars and Gurungs. With a quarrelsome nature and headstrong character, the Limbus were thus not as martially comparable to the aforementioned two groups. That said, however, Gurkha regiments which consisted chiefly of Limbus and Rais (namely the 10th Gurkha Rifles and the 8th Madras Infantry) proved that they were just as "amenable to discipline" as Magars and Gurungs. They were thereby to be recognized as well, as Gurkhas deservedly (Vansittart 1906, 101). Limbus and Rais consider each other "equal in all respects," where their habits and customs according to themselves are identical (Vansittart 1906, 128). What these various physiognomic, cultural, and linguistic differences that Vansittart (1906) and others have recorded concerning the various groups show is that the term *Gurkha* as a single moniker was far from that of a homogeneous categorization (Roy 2013). In her discussion of British resident Brian Houghton

Hodgson (1823–43), Des Chene (1991) notes that Hodgson has queried the idea of "genuine Goorkhas." Where he concluded that even if the Khas, Magars, and Gurungs emerged as "military tribes" in Nepal, these groups were differentiated from other categories including the Brahmans, "aboriginal tribes," and "broken tribes" that Hodgson discussed elsewhere (Des Chene 1991, 62). Furthermore, Des Chene (1991, 83) also notes the wide-ranging spectrum of characterizations that depict the Gurkhas from being "fond of flowers," "hate being nagged at," to being "a simple soul," "light-hearted and cheerful," and "exceedingly supersti- tious." As the "Brigade of Gurkhas may typify the martial classes of Nepal but is far from representing typical Nepalis, or even Gurkhas" (Cross 2009, 192), there is therefore no such tribe called Gurkha, and that not all Nepalis are entitled to be called Gurkhas as well (Banskota 1994). Ostensibly, martial race theory and its various constructivist perspectives that these authors deliberate on raise "inherent contradictions" (Des Chene 1991, 74) that underlie the category of the "Gurkha."

Similar to Vansittart's group differentiation, Gurung (2009) uses such terms as *military castes* (2009, 262) or *the best fighting castes* (2009, 265) in talking about how some Gurkhas were recruited to work as coal mining colliery laborers in Assam in 1923 and 1924. Such labor was considered "trivial jobs" that wasted "human resources," aside from the ill-treatment of colliers (2009, 265). Regarding castes such as Magar, Gurung, Chhetri, and Thakur as the fighting castes, recruit- ing them to work at coal mines would "lead to a drain of the manpower and the physique of Nepal . . . [and] would affect recruitment by cutting into the supply of Gorkhas into the colonial armed force" (Gurung 2009, 265). More important, as Gurung (2009, 268–69) observes, such a process of recruiting Gorkhas to work as colliers

> brings to light interesting aspects of how migration of labour to the region was conditioned by the interests of the colonial state. The issue of Gorkha recruitment also brings into focus the wider and an impor- tant aspect of colonial thinking or representation on "race" and "martial castes" which was assiduously propagated and cultivated from the late nineteenth century to justify colonial rule. . . . The exploitation of a mar- tial race . . . especially in coal mines would be pernicious in its effects on the manpower and physique of Nepal. . . . Eventually the colonial state had to intervene which prevented the recruitment of certain categories of the "martial race" to industrial services like in the coal mines.

In summation, the British recruitment policy derived from the subscription of martial race theory meant that only particular castes or tribes can be Gurkhas. In adhering to the quadrant recruitment template of Gurungs, Magars, Rais, and

Limbus, some applicants were actually "forced to lie and change their surname to any of the four" so as to realize their hopes of Gurkha recruitment (Gurung 2020, 24).

Encounters between the British and the Gurkhas

If there were handbooks in the early 1800s and 1900s that guided the Gurkha recruitment process by differentiating among the various groups, then there are also handbooks in the present-day context that offer guidelines for British military personnel as to how they ought to interact with the Gurkhas. Their interactions are shaped based on prior knowledge about Nepalese culture, religion, and customs. For example, it is "taboo to touch a Gurkha's shoulder or head especially from behind, during 'stand to,' because at that time the Gurkhas believe that God is present on his shoulder or head." Another cautionary item reads: "Gurkhas get very upset if a British Officer/soldier talks to other people in their presence about their country in derogatory manner. This must be avoided."[4] Drawing from encounters such as these and others below, I elucidate on the various instances of cross-cultural encounters and interface between these two groups of military actors. The analysis therefore highlights essentialist racial discourses that revolve around those social actors who toil for the British Army, including the power relations built into their interactions.

Through months of recruit training, Gurkhas enlisting as "young boys" later became "fully trained soldiers" (Purthi 2007, 129). But while these young Nepali soldiers were changing, their growth was also accompanied by British officers who likewise had to adapt to regimental life with the Gurkhas (see also, Darnell 2012). Apart from learning Gurkhali, the lingua franca of Nepal (Farwell 1984), they also played games with them, spent leisure time with Gurkha officers after parade, and gradually learnt more about these seemingly tractable men they were to lead. Purthi (2007, 129) describes these British officers in an almost paternalistic position:

> The stocky, slant-eye children of Nepal had now become trained recruits; their officers could see how they had changed from shy, unspoilt boys into seasoned riflemen, expert with their weapons and trained in many of the complexities of warfare that were to face them in the jungles of Burma, the deserts of North Africa, or in the mountains of Italy.

The Gurkhas' martial traits of unsurpassable courage and feats of daring were oftentimes juxtaposed alongside their childlike qualities (Caplan 1991; Chetri 2016), given for instance, the description above that points to them as "stocky" and "slant-eye children." Such narrative alignment of two opposite sets of characteristics further feeds into the power dynamics between the British and the Gurkhas. The British-Gurkha relation of power and hierarchy may be interpreted via two subjectivities of the "protective Gurkha officer father" and the "grateful and dutiful Gurkha son" (Chisholm 2022, 83). Such a relationship is therefore never premised on "equal footing," but that it will "continue to be haunted by the colonial structures and gender hierarchies" that are found in related histories (Chisholm 2022, 83). Beyond these two subject positions, the "warm relations" that they share extend to officers developing further connections with their troops at a "personal level." British officers would visit the homes and villages of the Gurkha soldiers to meet with their families and relatives. Arising from such personal ties and intimate knowledge, the British were therefore able to both inspire and discipline these Gurkha soldiers (Barkawi 2017, 46). Where military thinkers assumed that the Gurkhas were simple-minded and uncomplicated, this also translated into further presumptions that they would therefore be both apolitical and unquestioning in their allegiance (Caplan 1995b). In these respects, the British continues to wield control and discipline over the Gurkhas. The latter relied on the former to develop their warlike skills, only to be accomplished based on their docility, obedience, and presumed lack of intellect and maturity (Bolt 1967; Caplan 1995b; Chetri 2016).

Power relations between the British and the Gurkhas may be that of the latter being subordinated to the former, as routinely reflected in regimental histories and accounts of wartime. However, Des Chene (1991) makes an interesting if not obverse observation pertaining to the supposed loyalty of the Gurkhas for these white officers. Far from actually possessing "qualities of dog-like devotion" that were oftentimes implied in the accounts of British officers, the Gurkhas instead regarded these officers as incompetent and therefore in need of protection:

> The many British tales of faithful Gurkhas shadowing their officers across battlefields or seeing that they have hot meals or rest are read differently by *lahores*. When I recounted these stories men explained that because the British are likely to be killed due to their incompetencies they must watch out for them. These remarks are not meant to be insulting. Gurungs do not expect wealthy, white, urban people to have such abilities, as they are not the ones they acquire through their lifestyle. This distribution of the abilities required in the army was important to *lahores* in retaining a sense of their equality with their officers. (1991, 317–18)

It is therefore pertinent to consider both narratives of such presumed loyalty, as well as what the Gurkhas actually thought in terms of their relationship with and regard for the British. For example, Gurkha officers were known to be tactful during moments where they pointed out and corrected the faults of junior British officers. Without encroaching on the latter's confidence, then, these young officers also learned to respect the Gurkhas' experience and knowledge without feeling that they had relinquished their authority over them (Farwell 1984). Probing into these divergent perspectives makes it useful to reconsider the British-Gurkha relation of power and hierarchy. This relationship has also routinely been characterized as a special bond, a form of "spiritual companionship" (Farwell 1984, 129), or even as a love-romantic relationship (Gould 1999).

Besides these aforementioned narratives of concurrent strength and docility, including the Gurkhas' sometimes pitying take on the British, there are other narratives as well that read as problematic. This has to do with assumptions of the sportive life that Gurkhas were involved in. Take for instance, the account below that stretches the athletic abilities of the Gurkhas:

> Gurkhas delight in all manly sports—shooting, fishing, etc, and are mostly keen sportsmen and possess great skill with gun and rod. They amuse themselves in their leisure hours, either in this way in the field, or in putting the shot, playing quoits or foot-ball, and they are always eager to join in any game with Europeans. . . . As compared with other orientals, Gurkhas are bold, enduring, faithful, frank, very independent and self-reliant; in their own country they are jealous of foreigners, and self-asserting. (Vansittart 1906, 60)

Caplan (1995b) notes that even as military writings on the Gurkhas repeatedly highlight their love for sports, sportive life in Nepali society was next to nil, as also corroborated by Allen (1976). Furthermore, it was only from the 1950s that sports began to be developed in Kathmandu (Singh 1980). Apart from wrestling, which was Nepal's most popular sport before the 1940s, other modern games including football, cricket, and hockey were "practically non-existent" until the mid-twentieth century (Singh 1980, 76).

Given accounts of the Gurkhas' martialness, including other accounts that decry such image production, how can one then further apprehend both narratives and counternarratives revolving around Gurkhas and their lives that intertwine closely with the British? How are we to make sense of contradictions, gaps, convergent as well as divergent stories of how the Gurkhas are talked about, including their own perspectives?

Domains of Martiality: Narratives and Counternarratives

Narrative constructions of the marital race ideology that typify Gurkhas as brave, fierce, and inherently suited for warfare are on the one hand disseminated across varying domains over time. On the other hand, counternarratives of martiality are also increasingly evident in stories, autobiographies, and histories of Gurkhas. Where constructed narratives are necessarily selective in maintaining the portrayal of these global warriors as indomitable, counternarratives accomplish the opposite and reveal aspects of their physical and mental strain and fear that are seldom articulated. One domain of constructed narratives is traced to British constructions of these Nepalese soldiers' bodily comportment and skills that render them as a warrior group. As one among numerous examples, Farwell (1984, 51) writes of the Gurkhas perceived through British eyes:

> Discipline in its finest senses is the cheerful obedience of orders. This perfect discipline the Gurkha has always possessed, for he knows how to be obedient without being servile and he loves soldiering. . . . The Gurkha characteristic which most astonished Britons was his quick adaptability and his acceptance of strange people and extraordinary circumstances. Few young soldiers in any army, facing battle for the first time, are prepared for the noise, muddle, blood, horror, and their own fear, nor are they fully aware of the physical and psychological attrition resulting from cumulative filth and fatigue, but even the newest Gurkha recruit appeared to accept with equanimity war's horrors and physical hardships, remaining cheerful, able to emerge from battle—even defeat—with his morale unimpaired.

Where the British had constructed martial races such as the Gurkhas who presumably love soldiering and thereby highlight their allegedly innate and "untamed" warrior characteristics (Kochhar-George 2010; Laubenthal and Schumacher 2020), such racial stereotyping enacted by the British in turn allows them to construct themselves as sophisticated "masters" by contrast (Golay 2009). By extension, then, martial values are connected as well to "an ethos of discipline, loyalty and self-sacrifice" (Ware 2012, 120; see also, Enloe 1980, 27). I note here contradistinctions to the disciplined trait of the Gurkhas that the British assume. A different way to look at discipline that stems not from innateness but obligation is seen in Rai's account of having to be the "first target of the enemy" (2020, 95). He says:

> Somehow, I was disheartened. I did not know why only our section always had to take the role of leading section to face the enemy's first

firing. Everybody dearly loves their life. A volcano of resistance gravely grew inside me. I looked at the obliged section commander. His appearance wore gloom. Who could stand against the order? Military life is always governed by order and discipline so, we had no other options other than putting ourselves under the yoke of order. (95)

As an example of a counternarrative to discipline and obedience then, Rai's own experience at war indicates clearly how discipline arose instead out of regimental obligation.

Apart from the perspectives of British officers regarding the Gurkhas, Indian officers likewise shared similar views, even if these are usually not as visible compared to the British point of view in the wider literature. Bammi (2009) interviewed a number of retired Indian officers who had served in Gurkha regiments of the Indian Army. He found that the Gurkhas were similarly lauded by these officers. Gurkha troops followed military orders to the tee, were not afraid of hard work nor fatigue, were "fierce in hand-to-hand combat," and also preferred using their kukri rather than the bayonet (Bammi 2009, 453). They were also known to possess unshakeable loyalty, "provided the officer was as brave and dedicated as them" (Bammi 2009, 454). What is interesting here, as we see clear overlaps in both British and Indian officers' regard for the Gurkhas, is that the British had deliberately kept the Gurkhas away from the Indian military. Bammi (2009, 454) contends: "Till Independence the British had kept the Gorkhas away from Indian officers and troops, primarily to serve their imperial motives, but that myth has been broken as now the Gorkha soldier mixes very well with the Indian troops and perform exceedingly well under their Indian officers." Such separation was borne out of the British's construction of several martial communities in the Indian Army so as to prevent an "amalgamation of identities between the Nepal army's soldiers and the Gurkhas of the Indian army" (Roy 2001, 132). Moreover, constructing martial races by the British would also enable them to "play off different communities against each other," in an effort to prevent any possibility for a "unified anti-British sentiment amongst the colonized" (Roy 2013, 1325).

Some British officers were also known to look down on Indian officers of Gurkha regiments (Caplan 1995b; Izuyama 1999; Rathaur 2000). It was a commonly shared view among British officers that Gurkha soldiers would not have Indian officers commanding them, as the Nepalese as hillmen "had the highlander's usual aversion to the men of the plains" (Caplan 1995b, 69). To the Gurkhas, therefore, the "idea of military service under Indians [would be deemed as] unacceptable" (Tuker 1950, 626). This view, however, was a misrepresentation, as substantial numbers of Gurkhas had chosen to serve in the Indian Army in 1947, as opposed to moving to the British Army (see Caplan 1995b, 117–18). As Bammi also asserts through his interviews with Indian officers of the Gurkhas, these two groups would establish a "family bond." Gurkhas had expected a "genuine life-long friendship on [a] reciprocal basis" (2009, 456). The reciprocal relation that these two share can be seen from the Gurkhas having visited both serving and retired Indian officers in Nepalese villages. How the Gurkhas experience and recount their military worlds are apprehended somewhat differently from those who write about them, such as British chroniclers or Nepalese intellectuals (Caplan 1995b). This difference would therefore map onto the productions of martial race communities, where the dissonance between representation and experience form part of the story of martial mien and its constructions (Streets 2004).

The trope of bravery continues to dominate in martial race discourses revolving around the Gurkhas (Caplan 1991). These various war stories, penned either by British officers or Gurkhas themselves, all highlight the extraordinary prowess, bravery, and valor of the Gurkhas—culminating toward articulating the figure of the warrior Gurkha over time. With their famed motto,[5] "kafar hunne bhanda morno ramro" ("better to die than be a coward") (Bishop 1976; Vansittart 1906), Caplan (1991, 585) makes an observation that there exists "no printed work on the Gurkhas which does not refer to their toughness, strength, ferocity, courage and bravery."[6] I add to Caplan's observation that such tropes also successively surface in a variety of contemporary sources or write-ups about the Gurkhas, be it through print or social media across different countries as I discuss below.

British military writings are replete with the extraordinary valor and strength of the Gurkhas. Some of these narratives center around a spectacular Gurkha soldier, who seemed to have extraordinarily persisted against all odds. For example, we learn of Havildar Gaje who had fought in the battle against the Manipuris in 1891. Despite leading his platoon and having sustained severe wounds from a grenade, Gaje was still able to sprint through machine-gun fire to not only come face to face with the enemy, but to "cut a swath through them" using his kukri. Only when his commander ordered him to dress his wounds did he eventually relented (Bolt 1967). Having already destroyed two tanks, Rifleman Ganju Lama went forward on his own. Despite being wounded at his wrist, arms and legs, he ploughed on for a good thirty yards to the next tank and also destroyed it single-handedly. Subsequently, both Lama and Gaje were awarded the Victoria's Cross (Bolt 1967).

Another account conveys not only the superb resilience of a Gurkha warrior, but that his stoic sense of loyalty also comes across simultaneously. Motilal Thapa was lying face down in a ditch, with his "shattered arm hanging by a thread of flesh" (Farwell 1984, 93). He was joined by Captain Hartwell who was also wounded and who took cover in the ditch next to Thapa. After moments when no medical aid came to these two, Hartwell had fallen asleep owing to exhaustion.

When he awoken later, Hartwell saw that Thapa had somehow managed to prop himself up and leaned against one side of the ditch. He used his other good arm to shield Hartwell's face from the sun by holding his field service cap over Hartwell's eyes. In a melodramatic moment, Thapa had muttered: "I must not cry out. I am a Gurkha," and died before he could reach an aid station (Farwell 1984, 93). While these are historical examples in the main, such famed warrior figures continue to be constructed martially in the current-day context, which is the subject of the next section.

Cross (2009, 275) notes that it would be "wrong, stupid and unrealistic to consider all Gurkhas 'supermen,' 'heroes,' or 'ten feet tall.'" Instead, he observes that "Gurkhas are intensely human people, with strengths and weaknesses like everyone else," and that the Gurkha's "strengths are the ones the British Army needs and his weaknesses not so intrusive to be an encumbrance or a liability" (2009, 275–76). Ganesh Rai (2020) fought in the Falklands War in 1982 when he was twenty years old. His views on war, including those of his fellow Gurkha soldiers, demonstrably evince senses of fear and dread as they prepared to go on the battlefield:

> We all were physically prepared to go to the war, however, making ourselves mentally prepared was even harder than we ever thought. Psychological terror kept on haunting us. Nobody definitely would smile and step out of door to go to fight the enemy in war. Some senior soldiers . . . would miserably say, "I should really be pensioned off, but they didn't let me retire. Now, I have to go to the battlefield." (43–44)

Clearly, soldiers who are recruited to fight will either have to kill the enemy or be killed, as Rai (2020) further notes. His introspective questions—"Who doesn't love his or her life?. . . Who would be ready to die in the world?" (Rai 2020, 44)— speak volumes about what Cross (2009) had also pointed out. Over and above the popular image of Gurkhas as ready to kill or ready to die, there are indubitably many senses of uncertainty and fear of death in contexts of war that therefore reflect the emotional "weaknesses" of these famed soldiers. These weaknesses, which run contrary to martial bravery, are seldom broached in the wider literature on Gurkhas. In contrast to the portrayed stoic heroism of Motilal Thapa, Rai's (2020, 94) close brush with death points toward his sense of hopelessness: "'Death is sure to claim me today,' I gave up my hope of being alive by looking at the dropping bomb. Unexpectedly the bomb changed its direction after falling around fifteen feet. . . . I was astounded. Thank god! I survived despite my hopelessness."

In tandem, Caplan (1995b, 143–44) interestingly decries the assumed martiality of the Gurkhas and their courage, querying if their courageous acts stemmed from fearlessness, or fear itself. For him, the Gurkhas' display of courage is mainly physical and where such display stems from "emotion rather than the intellect" (Caplan 1995b, 148). Gould's (1999) suggestion differs from that of Caplan's (1995b). He proclaims that for the Gurkhas, war—even though it might be a "grim business" and was a "matter of kill or be killed"—was "approached in a lighthearted manner" and through which they would "extract what fun they could," looking on war as "a kind of sport, or *shikar* (hunt)" (Gould 1999, 114). Gould refers to a soldier's (James Hare of the British 60th Rifles) notes on the Gurkhas to substantiate such a hunting approach: "Yesterday, a sepoy had gone into a hut and was shooting out at the door, when two little Ghoorkas set out to catch him. They sneaked up, one on either side of the door, and presently the sepoy put out his head to see if the coast was clear, when one grabbed him by the hair, and the other whacked off his head with his cookery" (Gould 1999, 114). That said, Gould (1999) makes further pronouncements about courage where the Gurkhas are concerned. He had served as a young officer with the Gurkhas in the 1st Battalion, 7th Gurkha Rifles in the late 1950s. Gould planned on brushing up on his Nepali four decades later in the 1990s, when he wanted to revisit Nepal. He was then put in touch with Lieutenant (QGO) Khembahadur Thapa, who was senior Gurkha officer at 28 Army Education Center in Church Crookham. Gould learnt from Khem that the "two fundamental virtues of the Gurkhas were trust and loyalty" (1999, 400). According to Khem, these virtues had developed from the hilly environments that Gurkhas had lived in prior to enlistment. Khem had said to Gould: "If somebody says to a goatherd that he will bring food on such-and-such a day and fails to do so, it may well mean the goatherd starves to death" (400). Honoring one's promise is therefore "sacrosanct to a Gurkha" (400). When Khem had sworn allegiance to the crown, it was therefore of utmost importance to keep his words. For Khem, says Gould, British military authors who had rep-resented the Gurkhas as "*kukri*-waving little supermen," and by "extolling their bravery," only served to dehumanize them (400). Adding to Caplan's (1995b) discussion of courage and the Gurkhas, courage for Khem was interpreted as such: "Courage, or the lack of it, was an individual, not a racial, trait and if it was indeed more common among Gurkhas than in some other peoples then that was a product of the harsh conditions of their life, not some mysterious, innate force" (Gould 1999, 400). Martial race theory, taken as contingent on the basis of European biological determinism (Caplan 1995b; Seeberg 2016), then, ought to consider the climate and environment in which Nepalis have lived which thereby fostered their senses of morality and the cultivation of their values. While this might at a glance be similar with Caplan's (1995b, 90) indication concerning the "climatic-environmental element," it was not so much about such an element having organically produced the "best soldiers" (1995b, 90). Rather, it was due more to the adherence to a set of values and norms by the Nepalis/Gurkhas, as shown by Khem's perspective.

Another way to conceive of courage among the Gurkhas has to do with tradition and history. Limbu (2015, 143) proclaims that Gurkha heroism is not about the self:

> To us Gurkhas, our history is very important. It is how we keep our tradition alive. We remember and honour the great deeds of our ancestors, the men who have gone before us. When, today, a Gurkha does something heroic, he does not do it for himself, but for his comrades and in honour of these ancestors. For us, there is nothing greater a man can do than act courageously in battle, and we take enormous pride when one of our number is commended for bravery.

Aside from history and tradition, another interpretation of bravery, fear, and courage is contingent on the "consequence of certain conditions" (Gurung 2017, 111). It is clear that Gurkhas were also fearful of death and underwent numerous moments of uncertainty. In these varied contexts, the bravery of the Gurkhas "appears only when there is fear and when person sense [*sic*] a less or no surviving option" (Gurung 2017, 111). For Gurung (2017), the Gurkhas' bravery is attributed not to their fearless fighting, but rather, to life-threatening situations that compel them to be nothing but brave in order to survive. Placing these different interpretations alongside one another, the above narrative examples therefore further confirm the constructivist aspects of martial race theory and suppositions of the Gurkhas' traits. Courage can at once be mediated through bravery, fear, humor, and tradition and history, depending on who is the one talking about it and for what reasons. Be it for the self or for others, courage and how it is narrated has to do with divergent motivations and intentions that are unveiled through both narratives and counternarratives as analyzed above.

Apart from the aforementioned military and war stories of the Gurkhas' ardent courage and tenacity, their roles and presence as a part of the police force in Singapore also register similar "martialness" (Ray 2013). The GCSPF (Gurkha Contingent Singapore Police Force) celebrated its seventieth anniversary in the year 2019. Singapore's then prime minister Lee Hsien Loong visited the GC on this occasion and also took to Facebook to register that visit as well as his appreciation to these Gurkha policemen.[7] In his post, Lee highlighted the Gurkhas' "well-deserved reputation for toughness, alertness, mental and physical resilience." To continue such traits of martiality, Lee further noted that they were "totally dependable, highly self-disciplined, loyal, and fearless in executing their duties."[8] Even as the nation last saw these Gurkhas on security duty at such events including the DPRK-US Singapore Summit in 2018, or the annual Shangri-La Dialogue, the Gurkhas were previously pivotal in "restoring order and confidence" in the riot history of Singapore—the Maria Hertogh riots of 1950, the Hock Lee bus riots of 1955, or the communal clashes between the Chinese and the Malay in 1964, as Lee listed.

The lauding of the Gurkha police in Singapore by its political leaders is not a new phenomenon. The late Lee Kuan Yew, who was Singapore's first prime minister and who had served in the role for three decades, said this about the Gurkhas in the context of the Japanese invasion of 1941:

> There were some who won my respect and admiration. Among them were the Highlanders whom I recognised by their Scottish caps.... And the Gurkhas were like the Highlanders. They too marched erect, unbroken and doughty in defeat. I secretly cheered them. They left a life-long impression on me. As a result, the Singapore government has employed a Gurkha company for its anti-riot police squad from the 1960s to this day. (Lee 1998, 55)

Lee's account is resonant for two reasons. The first is that he makes a firsthand comparison between two martial races—that of the Scottish Highlanders and the Gurkhas, and thereby arrives at his conclusion that they were very similar in terms of their martial deportment and military integrity, which further reify colonial logics. The second points to the deployment of the Gurkhas in the Singapore police force to maintain social order given their neutrality, which works well in the country. Local news dailies similarly reiterate the indomitable bravery and hardihood of the Gurkhas. They have been routinely described as being well-known for their "extraordinary physical and mental robustness, resourcefulness and dependability,"[9] "never-say-die commitment," "athletic prowess," "total impartiality," or personified as "loyal soldiers," "warriors on their battlefield," "unsung heroes," "gutsy Gurkhas," "sinewy Nepalese warriors wielding wicked *kukris*," "small men with great courage," and as a "little tough soldier."[10] Ostensibly, characteristics of their martiality continue to be emphasized across a variety of media reports and attention placed on them, even if they remain a "visibly invisible community" (Zainal 2012, 93) in Singapore.

Quite apart from straightforward and augmented accounts of bravery and courage, and appellations of fearlessness, there are also expressions of confusion, mixed feelings, and constant fear that Gurkhas at war experience but which are not always explicitly articulated as counternarratives to martiality. Limbu (2015), who had gone through four tours of active service in Afghanistan, in addition to operations in Bosnia and Sierra Leone, expressed his constant fear, uncertainty, and ambivalence while preparing for an operation:

> Did we have enough ammunition? How long would it last if there was a big contact on landing?. . . What about food? How many days could we go if we found ourselves cut off and no resupp could get in?. . . What if one of the vehicles waiting for us was hit? What if the vehicles weren't waiting at all? What if one of my riflemen got hit? The possibilities were endless. (Limbu 2015, 27–28)

If anything, the only factor that Limbu did not have to be concerned with was the loyalty and reliability of his men: "As some officer *sahib* once said, the Gurkha is a pack animal. We work together and fight together as a team. Everyone helps everyone; that's how we operate. We'd be fine just so long as we remembered what we'd been taught" (Limbu 2015, 29).

I further demonstrate through excerpts from two poems, how Gurkhas and their senses of uncertainty of war and potential death constantly consume their thoughts.[11] Such articulations importantly serve as a foil or counterpoint to the routinely embellished or hyperbolized accounts of registering if not celebrating Gurkha gallantry which tend to dominate literature on Gurkha and war experiences (cf. Bhandari 2021; Seeberg 2016). The first is a poem that talks about senses of vulnerability and preoccupations of death that a Gurkha experiences vis-à-vis an enemy.

Me, The Point Man
When I walk through the ploughed field
When I step on the rough paths
When I jump across the ditch
When I run between the walls
When I go through the tree line . . .
Every step that I make
has a potential explosion.
Enemy might find me first
Enemy might see me first
Enemy might judge me first
Enemy might shoot me first
Every time when they shoot
I am the first sand bag to block bullets
—Run!
-Move fast
-Slow down

-Go firm
-Halt
Every step I make
Death will always be with me
    —Mijash Tembe, *Gurkha War Poems*

The second poem, "War," expresses in tandem the unpredictability of attacks, and of dancing with death that continues to be an ongoing and incontrovertible threat to one at war:

War

An armed soldier am I
Blowing the siren of war.
Ready to explode
.   .   .   .

Playing hide-and-seek
With bullets and gunpowder.
Awaiting the foe-men
.   .   .   .

I am celebrating
A festival of death
Barely aware of the darkness
Looming over me.
    —Devendra Kheresh, *Gurkha War Poems*

Expressions of the unknown, potential threats to life, the constant worry about one's enemy are recurrent motifs in both of the poems above. These forms of uncertainties reveal the magnitude of the Gurkhas' inner sense of fear, seldom the thematic foci of war literature and regimental histories that routinely celebrate their martiality and which elide their vulnerabilities.

Aside from vulnerabilities as a foil to martial traits, Gurkhas have also stood on the opposite side of discipline and orderliness. Gurkha police in Singapore have over the decades garnered media attention, these times not for their reputed loyalty nor impeccable standards of duty and discipline. Rather, they have also been guilty of "disorderly and boisterous behaviour."[12] Such unruly conduct or criminal offences cover the range from stealing, reckless driving, and assault, to kidnapping, desertion, armed robbery, participating in a mutiny, involvement in unlicensed cross-border money transfers, and manslaughter and murder.[13] Quite clearly, I am not making a claim that Gurkhas are imperfect social actors. Instead, the above examples exemplify different sides or characteristics of Gurkhas who may have fallen on the wrong side of the law, but pertinently demonstrate contrastive attributes that are at clear odds with the tenets of martial race theory. This point is crucial for two reasons. The first is to reiterate the gaps or shortcomings of martiality as constructed and reproduced by different actors and sources, for which blanketing Gurkhas as martial figures becomes problematic. The second is to draw attention to the Gurkhas not only to be comprehended as warriors in the main, but also as fallible and vulnerable social actors who were confronted in their lives with economic difficulties, the dangers and risks of wars, as well as the challenges of leading their and their families' lives as migrant actors given the scheme of military and police service.

Martial Race Expositions or What Comes Before and After the Warrior Gurkha

The image of the Gurkhas as gallant soldiers is also utilized as a resource by retired Gurkhas themselves in reproducing the "rhetoric of martiality" (Caplan 1995b, 101), both for pre-enlistees as well as those who have retired from Gurkha service. By this reproduction I refer to training academies that prepare aspirant Gurkha recruits, as well as security companies that have been established in different countries around the world. These academies and companies have deployed the image of bravery and refrains of martiality as a marketing tool to project and sustain the prowess of these Gurkha men. Such imagery is strategically used to promote conformity to the martial bearing for trainees, as well as to connect with the Gurkha history and branding for security employment. By expanding such constructionist approaches, I develop critical appraisals of different presentations and how tropes of courage and strength are being leveraged by various parties in different temporal contexts. If the Gurkhas are depicted by British military authors as larger than life (Caplan 1995b), such depictions that I have discussed heretofore can also be constitutive of what Gould (1999, 1) terms as "supertruths"—which refer to "permissible exaggerations of real and defining qualities." These exaggerations are not without cause, for they "perform a vital function in military lore" where the fearsome reputation of the Gurkhas have been established (1999, 1). Similarly, I argue that the function of the celebrated Gurkha figure in the contexts of training centers (Piya 2020) and security services (Chisholm 2014) has to do with promoting the very same reputation in order to convince trainees and clientele who require martial training as well as security services.

As an instructive case in point, Piya's (2020) study comprises an investigation of two training centers in Pokhara that guide young Nepalese men toward projecting themselves as possessing "normative virtues of a Gurkha soldier" (2020, 327). Calling this inculcated projection as a new form of governmentality as it regulates the bodily comportment of these young aspirants, the author suggests that the enduring legacy of martiality continues to hold firm in shaping how these youths adopt the different registers of Gurkha virtues. Young men who go to such training centers exemplify the learning of martial techniques. Interactions between the technology of the Gurkha self takes place with the technology of domination of the British (Piya 2020). As intermediaries, training centers now have taken over from a group of middlemen called the *gallās*, often ex-Gurkhas who were remunerated by the British to conduct a preliminary stage of Gurkha recruitment in different villages. These gallās were therefore a complicit party in reinforcing martial race ideology (Piya 2020).

In the training and preparation programs that these centers offer, trainees are evaluated on the basis of their physical, mental, and social and interpersonal competencies (Piya 2020). Stamina, knowledge, and character basically map onto these three avenues. Through such training, grilling, and assessments, these young trainees thus develop and come into their "own understandings of what it means to be a quintessential Gurkha soldier" (Piya 2020, 335; see also, Chisholm and Ketola 2020). In particular, specific Gurkha narratives are told to these trainees, who later then present them as "appropriate answers" at the actual recruitment process (Piya 2020, 336). These trainees therefore learn to memorize questions, including standard answers. In the process, they "internalize what it means to be a Gurkha" when interviewed by British and Nepali officers subsequently (Piya 2020, 336). Instructors, otherwise known as gurus or masters at these training centers, coach young men to remember ideal answers, including emphasizing one's mongoloid background. One should also state that as one had come from a Gurkha lineage, there was interest from the applicant to want to "preserve that tradition by serving in the British Military" (Piya 2020, 337). Interviewees who relate explicitly to their "ethnic identity and linkage to Gurkha heritage" are therefore considered as having successfully prepared for these assessments. As an outcome, then, this "reified the British constructed martial race categories" (Piya 2020, 337). Apart from these emphases, trainees are also instructed to present themselves at interviews as both outgoing and shy, and who will carry out action and refrain from talking too much. Besides, they are told to carry the virtues of a *lahure* by standing in a balanced way, maintaining eye contact whenever spoken to, and to hold their heads high up (Piya 2020). Gurkha training centers by and large provide the necessary learning processes for trainees to "embody the ideals of a Gurkha soldier" (Piya 2020, 349). In sum, learning through "rigorous repetition" not only produces a certain structure of governmentality. Such learning has also sustained and reinforced martial race theory in the present. This is because these centers are replete with "symbols, artefacts, and myths" (Piya 2020, 350) that persistently echo martiality.

From the phase of training toward aspiring to becoming a Gurkha, we now go to the "after" phase of what happens when Gurkhas retire and look to second career options. In this phase, martial characteristics continue to persist and are harnessed for global security marketing. Portraying ex-Gurkhas as carrying martial qualities serves to bring them "into existence and [make them] intelligible only through the colonial script of martial race" (Chisholm 2014, 356). With such a portrayal, this would thereby bring forth "imaginings of a fierce warrior" and his "physical prowess" (Chisholm 2014, 356) even if Gurkhas have left military service. Where Chisholm's (2014) work investigates Gurkha security companies that are run by white British Gurkha officers who now assume directorships in these outfits, and thus only they can speak for the Gurkhas, my examples here examine companies that are directed by Gurkhas themselves. My first case is Gurkha Security Services, which operates from the United Kingdom with the head office located at Farnborough, and with two other offices in Kent and Birmingham.[14] This company comprises a directorate of three former British Gurkha personnel, including a handful of other ex-Gurkhas occupying the positions of senior/operations manager. To begin with, their accreditation as a security company is first built on the individual Gurkha background of their staff, thereafter to be further confirmed by testimonials that they put up on their website which they obtained from previous clients. We learn that one of the directors, Bishnu Bahadur Tamang, had served with the British Army for more than two decades in the Royal Gurkha Rifles and Parachute Regiment. His vast military experience covered both military and peace support operations, where he has therefore "accumulated vast amount of experience and know-how in organising military activities."[15] Bishnu is further described as possessing an "unyielding work ethic" and as someone who "has a passion for quality and distinction in everything he takes on." These (martial) traits of his have apparently positively influenced the "working culture of his staff in Gurkha Security Services, securing a great service time and time again."[16]

Not unlike the Gurkha-martial depiction that represents Bishnu, the other two directors—also with more than two decades of Gurkha experience under their belt as we are told—have likewise highlighted their military and now corporate valor in largely similarly ways. Hari Kumar Shrestha is versatile and enthusiastic in all his undertakings, and he is able to perform exceptionally under duress. Nabin Kumar Siwa wields "immense military experience" that stands him in very good stead to run "in-house company security training for the officers and potential officers."[17] Other staff members such as operations manager Un Bahadur Thapa have also utilized their years of Gurkha experience and tapped on their martial abilities that are now translated into the provision of security services in the United Kingdom. His biography certifies that "with a strong sense of commitment, loyalty and professionalism gained from his time served in the British Army, Un has built a very comprehensive set of skills that he uses in his day to day role as the Operations Manager."[18] Clearly, the invocation of one's Gurkha-martial abilities, certified through decades of military expertise and experience, are built into both the management and training of security services as a company makeup. Their biographies are further bolstered by a tab on the company website that provides a brief "History of Gurkhas," which predictably underscores the various colonial logics of martial traits as I have analyzed above. "As gentle in daily life as they are fearless and tenacious in battle, they are a digni-fied people and ideal soldiers and security personnel"[19] is how these ex-Gurkhas are being characterized. In their current positions as security directors and com-pany staff, they are together able to traverse seamlessly from their martial capaci-ties, coupled with gentleness, to current security purposes. The following quote on the website echoes quite clearly, the martial race template that British writers have long deployed:

> British officials in the 19th century declared the Gurkhas as a "Mar-tial Race," a term describing people thought to be "naturally warlike and aggressive in battle" possessing qualities of courage, loyalty, self-sufficiency, physical strength, resilience, orderliness, the ability to work hard for long periods of time, fighting tenacity and military strength. . . . Gurkhas are famed for carrying a khukuri. It is the national weapon of Nepal, but it is also used as a work tool in the Hills. Each Gurkha carries two khukuris, one for every-day use and one for ceremonial purposes. Their famous war cry, "Ayo Gorkhali" translates as "The Gurkhas are here," their motto, "*Kaphar hunnu bhanda marnu ramro*" means "It is better to die than to live like a coward."[20]

Taking off from the above martial attestation, the recording and promotion of the Gurkhas' valiant martiality are further attested by client testimonials. Cli-ents similarly respond by referring to such colonial martial descriptions as they endorse the company with customer satisfaction. Clients routinely praise the company security staff's reliability, agility, and being "always with an attitude of helpfulness."[21] In sum, security personnel who are ex-Gurkhas in the main, have been certified as such: "Anticipating threats and handling difficult situations calmly, swiftly and effectively is second nature to them—as is trust, discipline, courage and dedication to duty."[22]

It goes without saying that both parties—the company and clients—utilize and reassert colonial martial templates. These templates transpire from the days of war theaters that the United Kingdom was involved in together with the Gurkhas to the present-day context of providing security coverage and support during peacetime at public events based on clientele needs. This enduring attestation and utility of the martial race attributes of the Gurkhas, both exercised by themselves and those who hire them, reflect crucially on the durability and continued reification of martiality. The reification transfers from military to civilian domains of security needs and also cuts across different temporalities as well. In this manner, my analysis here coheres with Chisholm's (2014) study whereby British colonial histories of martial race theorization continue to persist, influence, and make possible security labor for ex-Gurkhas and those who require martial services.

My second case is taken from another Gurkha security company, this time founded and operating in Kowloon, Hong Kong. Called The Gurkhas Group, this security company was established in 1997 and offers a wide range of security services that run from close protection bodyguards and drivers to security for construction, events, Covid-19, industrial, ports and railway, government, and residential requirements.[23] This range indicates the reach and expanse of military martiality that could similarly and readily apply to nonmilitary security sectors in the civilian world. Like the earlier case, The Gurkhas Group is managed by a mix of former Gurkhas, police officers, and civilians. We are told that the chairman, Pun Tej Prakash, was born in Nepal and served with the British for thirteen years. Another fellow ex-Gurkha, Gurung Bhim Bahadur, takes on the role of Assistant Operations Manager. His military biography spanned more than twenty-five years and has included armed force tours of duty in places such as Afghanistan, Sierra Leone, Kosovo, and Bosnia—typical of a Gurkha's military profile.[24] Where the first case presented testimonials drawn from clients, The Gurkhas Group, or G3S as they call themselves, feature instead, snippets of interviews undertaken with ex-Gurkhas in Hong Kong. One of the interviewees, Ghale Humkumar, comes from a Gurkha lineage in which his grandfather, father, and oldest brother all served in the British Army. Ghale feels proud to be a Gurkha. He found his training in the Falklands to be the most memorable, apart from his military experiences in Hong Kong, East Africa, and the United Kingdom. After retiring from Gurkha service in 2001, Ghale then became the bodyguard for Hong Kong magnate Li Ka Shing for three years, before he subsequently joined G3S.[25] Gurung Thaku, another of the interviewees, responded to a question on what had changed for him after becoming a Gurkha. His reply serves as a standard martial race template. He said that after joining the brigade, many things in his life had changed, pointing especially to a sense of discipline. Such a trait, accompanied with his other military experiences, have thus carried him further into different security jobs where he worked as a surveillance supervisor in the US consulate in Hong Kong as well as a bodyguard, driver, and the current security job offered by G3S.[26]

In another news segment that G3S carries, one write-up provides a quick list of who the Gurkhas are. Predictably, martial characteristics are foregrounded across the "10 Quick Facts" section that represent the Gurkhas. They are "well known for their loyalty and bravery" and are "fearless in combat but will never leave one behind."[27] Moreover, when a Gurkha "draws his *kukri* in anger, he must also draw blood."[28] Finally, "when you know you're with the Gurkhas, I think there's no safer place to be," says HRH Prince Harry when he was on a military tour in Afghanistan.[29] The message here, as with the case of Gurkha Security Services rings clear. Hire the Gurkhas for security needs, as they are globally known for their bravery, discipline, courage, and invincibility. These martial attributes are routinely verified not only by the Gurkhas themselves who manage and form such companies, but by those who have had close encounters with them, from clients to royalty. One can therefore not go wrong with the martial race template, both in military and civilian contexts.

My third and fourth cases showcase how security companies in different Southeast Asian countries also extrapolate the Gurkha reputation and appropriate their credibility for their security services. The third case is taken from the company Gurkha International Security Services Co. Ltd, located in Thailand. The company's brief write-up indicates a combination of staff who are not only ex-Gurkhas, but recruited from various other security personnel all over the world:

> GURKHA International Security Co., Ltd. is a standard security company with more than 7 decades of experience in security and law enforcement and our people have been part of the British fighting Army and British Royal guard for almost 202 years, still serving as Singapore Gurkha Police contingent, Brunei King Sultans palace guard & bodyguard, UAE Royal guard, Hong Kong coastal guard during British time and still operating various security duties in Malaysia, Saudi Arabia, Qatar etc.[30]

The same global security services of the company reach out to various countries beyond Thailand to include Iraq, Afghanistan, Singapore, Malaysia, India, and Nepal.[31] Although materials pointing to martial race theory are not as evident as the aforementioned two examples in this case, the company, in foregrounding their branding as that of "Gurkha International" among other security personnel and their varied experiences, deploys the Gurkha name to attract clientele. An example that reflects martial traits can be read from such service as "Bodyguards and VVIP Escorting Team Guard Force." This unit comprises bodyguards who are "ex-military or special forces with unique skill sets that allow them to provide exceptional security services to their clients."[32]

The fourth and final case is known as Chico Force (M) Sdn Bhd, based in Malaysia.[33] As a company that provides security management services by deploying handpicked "ex-senior police officers," Chico Force also collaborates with ex-Gurkhas as part of their company makeup.[34] They have obtained the approval of the Ministry of Home Affairs to bring in ex-British Army Gurkhas to serve as security guards in Klang Valley.[35] Appropriative mentions of these ex-Gurkhas' martial staples include pointing out their "bravery, integrity and loyalty." Having served across the globe to include Hong Kong, Brunei, and other locations, these former soldiers are now "re-employed internationally" as security guards, or take up security-related roles in Miami, Los Angeles, and Europe.[36] In gist, Chico Force confirms that as these martial soldiers are able to adapt to any new environment, this ability in addition to their military experience and other martial mien thus explain why they are sought after internationally.[37]

Martial qualities interweave a Gurkha soldier's trajectory, both before one attempts to qualify for recruitment as gleaned from Piya's (2020) work, and after one's Gurkha service and into a second career in security as I have examined. Both phases, indeed, are geared toward subscribing to the martial warrior image, and seeing that through in another career after regimental service. All four examples bear the sinews of martial race theory and take on similar and complementary forms. Not only are the Gurkhas and those who manage them complicit with upholding martial traits (see Chisholm 2014), clients in need of security labor also form another party that endorses such martiality in the production, consumption, and deployment of martial framing. In the end, what is enduring here over time is not only the tenets of martial race theory that continue to construct the image of the Gurkhas in their military and postmilitary milieu. More important, my examples here confirm the multiple functions of the theory, exemplified not only in military and political ways that the British had intended (Streets 2004), but also in influencing current-day security industries that, not unlike the British or SPF, look to Gurkhas and ex-Gurkhas for maintaining order and social control for commercial needs.

Martiality that governs both the "before" and "after" phases of the warrior Gurkha figure signals if not confirms the enduring role and function that the theory serves. These encompass a variety of cognate security needs that characterize both historical and contemporary times. While the tapestry of martial race theory threads through different times and varying purposes, the reach of this theory is also clearly transnational. This transpires through my examples of security companies owned by and operated with ex-Gurkhas (if not to merely use the Gurkha brand), which are located in different parts of the world and include the United Kingdom, Hong Kong, Macau, Thailand, New Zealand, Cyprus, as well as Nepal among many others.[38] Indeed, the relics and colonial logics of empire, to paraphrase Des Chene (1991), are far-reaching in terms of both temporality and locality.

Beyond Martial Race Theory and the Warrior Gurkha Image

Just as different versions or constructions of stereotypical if not apocryphal portraits of the Gurkhas abound, then so too would the same apply to the different groups of Nepalis who were singled out as a good fit for military life. Martial race theory blends both reality and imagination (Roy 2013), as I have demonstrated in this chapter and with further examples to follow in subsequent chapters. There are two main strands of representation where constructions of the Gurkhas are concerned. The first clearly speaks to the global image of the Gurkhas' valor, gallantry, and loyalty, which stems in the main from British military writings, postcolonial discourses, and of late from ex-Gurkhas themselves. The second has to do with the exact opposite. In Nepali modernist and literary narratives (Bhandari 2021; Seeberg 2016), literary texts about the Gurkhas focus on contrastive themes that depart from the first strand. Instead of further highlighting martiality, unconditional loyalty, and bravery, these texts construct Gurkhas in terms of their licentious nature,[39] lack of patriotism, moral corruption, as well as their varied experiences of personal loss and separation (Bhandari 2021; Hutt 2012).[40] As an important corollary, Paudyal and Baral's (2021) study of Nepali war poetry over two centuries highlights important shifts in how such poetry—some of which are written by Gorkha soldiers themselves—has moved from valorizing the soldiers' martiality and participation in war, to a denouncement of such violence. This arose in part due to the realization that the Gorkhas' aggrandized bravery was an outcome of colonial design and fabrication in the main. Martial race stereotypes, then, in connection with present-day Gurkha recruitment continue to "rankle purist nationalists across the political spectrum" (Stirr 2017, 188) as Gurkha service for the British imperial power continues to be read as an embarrassment to the sovereignty of Nepal.

The diverse constructions and representations of what Gurkhas were and are like seemingly point toward specific discourses that are either hyperbolized, silenced, or deployed as a means toward particular ends. When hyperbolized, Gurkhas are portrayed as martial soldiering heroes and painted as such in order to facilitate strategic recruitment (Enloe 1980), and to mimetically form the mirror image of British officers themselves and thus to be "embraced as honorary Europeans" (Caplan 1995b, 155). The basic premise here is to reinforce their outstanding military prowess (Bhandari 2021) so as to achieve both military and political goals (Streets 2004). Discourses that are silenced by both colonial and postcolonial constructs of the Gurkhas include disruptions to family life owing to military theaters and also general feelings of damage, loss, alienation, and meaninglessness as a Gurkha who participated in British military undertakings

(Seeberg 2016). As Tim I. Gurung (2020, 2–3), a Gurkha corporal who retired in 1993 vividly puts it:

> All the books regarding the Gurkhas so far were mostly written from the Western point of view, mainly by writers with military backgrounds. No matter how much diversity they may have claimed . . . it was still a one-sided work. . . . One was the bravery of the Gurkhas, and the other was the self-aggrandizement of the parts of British officers had played in making the Gurkhas world-famous. . . . The other side of the Gurkha story is unfortunately still not being told . . . It's the main reason why the Gurkhas are only known as the bravest soldiers to the world, while forgetting the fact that they were also humans like the rest of us.

Importantly, Gurung continues, the "Gurkha story is not only about bravery, but it's also the story of tragedy" (Gurung 2020, 2–3). Apart from the other side of the Gurkha story, the deployment of traits of martiality in the present-day context as exacted by security companies and agencies thereby also demonstrate how such characteristics make ex-Gurkhas as potential security guards work for clients as a convincing and reliable narrative. Essentially, they are positioned favorably in the labor-security market where a "Gurkha security package" both markets and commoditizes them (Chisholm 2014).

I return to Marshall's experience posted at the outset of this chapter here. He had fought alongside the Gurkhas for four years and reflected on his time with the Gurkha battalions:

> British officers who served with Gurkha battalions as regulars before the war became rather unbalanced and starry-eyed about the virtues of Gurkhas. One got the impression that some thought the Gurkha could do no wrong. This of course isn't so. The Gurkha, I think I've indicated earlier, had many of the same vices and virtues of the British tommy, which is probably why they get on so well together, but, also, there was absolutely no doubting their courage. (Parker 1999, 143–44)

Clearly, the Gurkhas as courageous and indomitable continue to remain as the core image of those who have had close encounters with them on the battlefields of their lives. The image of Gurkhas as brave, undefeatable, and indefatigable has also traversed onto their next generation, the *bhanja* and *bhanji*—or at least so from the point of view of others. In the focus group interview that I held in Kathmandu, Ganga and her friends shared stories of how their teachers used to make fun of their Gurkha heritage. These teachers assumed the same competencies in their fitness levels and strength if not stereotypes about the Gurkhas or Nepalis as a whole given "centuries of hill-climbing ancestors" (Bammi 2009, 86).[41] Ganga and Dipesh each recounted what one of their teachers in Singapore had said to them on separate occasions:

> GANGA: You children . . . you all go back to Nepal and climb mountain. You know? She said that to the guys. Then to the girls right, she'll say you children, you go back to Nepal and get married.
>
> DIPESH: I was sick lah . . . I was sick for three days. Then I was coughing, coughing. Then you know what she said? You're [a] Gurkha son right [to her friend], how come you get sick?

Ganga further told me that her group was probably the first to enroll as Gurkha children in a Singapore school. Right after their first day at school, the athletic team called the Gurkha students for a meeting—"just because we are Gurkha's [children]" and "they want us to run track and field and everything." The experiences of Gurkha children such as Ganga and Dipesh, among others, is telling of how notions of martial race, first attached to the Gurkhas in military and the police force, have now trickled down into their offspring. Just as the Gurkhas have been perceived in terms of their supposed innate military might and prowess, then so too would that be expected of their children's physical abilities and capacities. This goes to show how the biological deterministic view of martial race sustains and assumes currency from generation to generation in the eyes of others.

Over and above their brave image, the Gurkhas have also been talked about as being "gentle and compassionate."[42] In 1988, it was reported that more than 600 out of the 760-strong Gurkha contingent in the GCSPF had volunteered to sign up as organ donors. Thus, despite being "renowned for their toughness in battle," they are also deemed as compassionate and gentle, arising from this voluntary participation.[43] In the words of Vansittart (1906, 60), the Gurkhas "are domestic in their habits and kind and affectionate husbands and parents." Interestingly, a 1973 press report in Singapore carried the following headlines: "Gurkha Wife Helps Mellow Warrior Image." In that report, readers are told that a Gurkha housewife, Mrs. Parwati Thapa, was awarded a Public Service Star by the Singapore Government:

> A Gurkha housewife in a dark purple sari helped to mellow the traditional warrior image of her community on Thursday night. It happened when stately Mrs. Parwati Thapa, wife of a Gurkha officer with the Singapore Police Force, strode gracefully to President Shears to receive her Public Service Star at an investiture ceremony. . . . She was the first Gurkha women to win such high honour from Singapore Government, and one of the only three women to win the Public Service Star in the 1972

National Day honours. A voluntary welfare worker, she teaches Nepali, reading, knitting, sewing and generally serves as a problem solver to families of the Gurkha contingent with the Singapore Police.[44]

Mrs. Thapa came to Singapore in August 1953, which was her first trip out of Nepal. Dubbed a "heroine in her community," she "won her status not on the battlefield in true warrior tradition but by helping the policemen's wives and children."[45] It is interesting to see this example of Mrs. Thapa, who was accorded high recognition by the Singapore Government for her contributions to the Gurkha community. More important, she has been singled out as a foil to the warrior persona of the Gurkhas, reflecting a different perspective with which to regard Gurkhas and their families.

Orientalist discourses that depict the Gurkhas as quintessentially brave and loyal come with a "very strong sense of consensus and continuity" and which are usually "monolithic and timeless" (Caplan 1991, 573). Such portrayal relies in the main on stereotypes and which seldom consider either the historical or political context. Even if Gurkhas have been positively caricatured or portrayed as larger than life (Caplan 1995b), these constructions have over time become reality given the constant repetition and replication of aligned martial race characteristics produced through a largely unified and integrated narrative (Caplan 1995b; Des Chene 1991). It has also been suggested that these martial soldiers have similarly found resonance in martiality, where they have accepted or even relished such an identity (Streets 2004). Specifically, even if Caplan points out that how these discourses are being produced has to do with the issue of power (since it is usually the British officers who produce "peremptory knowledge about their military subordinates," [Caplan 1995b, 2]), I add to this line of argument the observation that the Gurkhas themselves have also articulated such similar discourses in order to benefit their post-Gurkha service endeavors in the security industry. The crux here lies in how an examination of texts about and by Gurkhas need to take into consideration those particular contexts through which they were written (Caplan 1995b).

When Rai (2020, 170) returned to England safe and victorious from the Falklands, he and his band of Gurkha soldiers were once more praised and lauded for their "utmost bravery and loyalty." They had also received many letters of invitations as well as appreciation coming from different parts of the United Kingdom. Having participated in some of such events, Rai had met with some local residents. He says this of their understanding of the Gurkhas, which forms the kernel of what I have examined here:

> Despite their considerable knowledge about Gurkhas, we found they didn't usually know about the etymological meaning of the word

"Gurkha." They had understood the word "Gurkha" as synonymous with courageousness, bravery and fearlessness. That may not be the precise etymology, but I am happy and proud for them to make that link in their minds with my brave people. (Rai 2020, 170–71)

Although Rai has pertinently pointed out some limited understandings of the term *Gurkha*, he has in a way also imbibed if not solidified martiality ("with my brave people") as Streets (2004) has suggested of martial soldiers. My cursory discussions about the category of "Gurkhas," martial race theory, and its various expositions in this chapter provide but only a brief treatment and examination of the vast corpus of Gurkha literature that continues to be produced and circulated widely.[46] Suffice it to say that where Caplan (1991, 590) raises an interesting line of analysis about how depictions of the Gurkhas by British officer-authors reflect "the essential characteristics of those very officers," (see also, Bolt 1967; Gould 1999; Leonard 1965), my contribution here concerns how the Gurkhas themselves have as well absorbed and appropriated elements of martial race theory in their self-depictions.[47] They do this in order to utilize the warrior image for their varied purposes. In this way, it would be jejune to assume that Gurkha literature by and large is to be read only through "crude orientalist" agendas (Caplan 1995b, 3). Instead, I depart from Caplan's three-decades-old narrative (and the plenteous genres of writing on Gurkhas that continue to proliferate through print and social media), to contribute toward a rethinking of how martial race theory has also been brought into advantageous deployment by the Gurkhas themselves. In so doing, the Gurkhas are, in somewhat equal measure with their British counterparts, complicit in building and sustaining the image of the warrior Gurkha. The main point therefore is not so much about unveiling the ins-and-outs of martial race theorization. It is rather about critically engaging with how and why such framing is put into place; by whom and for what purpose. Scholars have rightly pointed out the constructedness of martial race theory in which the British had deployed vague ideas about martiality and which changed over time and through different perspectives (Des Chene 1999; Gurung 2011). Moreover, others such as Gurung (2017) have contended that the bravery of the Gurkhas is not so much about martiality, but rather, "conditional" where the author's notion of "conditional bravery" (2017, 105) points toward "becoming brave under certain conditions" (2017, 105). Problematizing Gurkhas as a martial race through examples of narratives and counternarratives is an exercise in exploring how identity claims (Chetri 2016) are projected. Such projection thereby underscores the social, political, and economic utility of the famed image of warrior Gurkhas across history. The constructed nature of martiality and valor of the Gurkhas are therefore made evident, and such constructions are shown to be utilized purposefully by different social actors.

The next chapter foregrounds other aspects of Gurkha lives that transcend the martial race and warrior constructions that I have attended to. If they are "made to appear larger than life" (Caplan 1991, 586) vis-à-vis their invincibility and ferocity, I address the migratory and familial experiences of Gurkhas from the time they leave Nepal, right up to their retirement years. These varied experiences are narrated and analyzed with the backdrop of military and nation-state governance of social actors. Chapter 3 therefore resumes my discussion on bracketed belonging. I spotlight the Gurkhas' migratory and transnational encounters beyond what we know publicly of their traits as spectacular regimental figures in Gurkha military expositions. Such encounters remain fairly inchoate in the wider migration and transnational literature when relatively compared, and thus warrant attention.

I close this chapter by quoting an excerpt from the poem "The Buddhas Inside War" by Daya Krishna Rai (2013).[48] The following lines in a nutshell lend resonance to martial race theory as a construct and as a myth. The bravery of Gurkhas, if not deemed innate, are brought out through encounters with war and in various military contexts—the underlining principle for which select groups of Nepalis are classified as suitable for warfare; for war gave birth to Gurkhas who are brave:

> Had war never existed
> Peace wouldn't have so much importance
> Buddha wouldn't have been Buddha today
> Hadn't war been there
> Gurkhas would have never been Brave Gurkhas
> War gave birth to Brave Gurkhas
> Buddha gave birth to peace

THE MIGRANT GURKHA

"It's like a culture to join the British Army, to be a Gurkha," Chapal told me during our interview in March 2014 where we met in Hong Kong. Chapal was recruited into regimental service in 1980 in Dharan, which was one of the main Gurkha recruitment camps in Nepal.[1] The eldest of three sons, Chapal was the only one in the family who joined the Gurkhas. While his father was not a British Gurkha, his grandfather used to work for the Nepalese Army. When he said that it is "a culture" to be recruited as a Gurkha, Chapal is referring to a culture of emigration (Yamanaka 2000) in that his (extended) family and relatives included some kin who joined as Gurkhas. Parker (1999) writes of his interview with a retired Gurkha officer, Major Dal Bahadur Gurung, who had served in the 6th Gurkha Rifles for the entirety of his military career. Both of Dal's great-great-grandfathers were part of the East India Company. His great-grandfather, grandfather, father, and two elder brothers all enlisted as Gurkhas in their respective times:

> When I was seven years old, my brother enlisted in the Gurkhas in 1942, and my second eldest brother enlisted a year later, leaving myself, my sister and younger brother at home. When my brothers came home in their uniforms, it was a true family occasion. Everyone was very proud, and my grandfather said I should enlist as soon as I could. The next year, when I was only fifteen, the recruiting officers came as usual looking for young men to join up. I was one of the boys selected, but my mother said: 'No, you are too young.' Next year when I was sixteen, the recruiting officers came back again and I ran away with them. (Parker 1999, 203–4)

Similarly, another retired Gurkha soldier, Ramesh, explained to me: "I [am] meant to be a Gurkha because I have to follow my generation" in referring to his father-in-law who served as a Gurkha in the 2nd Regiment. In Chapal's case, he was posted to Hong Kong right after recruitment, and has since been living there for thirty-five years at the time of my meeting with him.

Having had two children who were born and who grew up in Hong Kong, Chapal's wife works as a waitress. Chapal is now a bodyguard-driver (as a second career). He said that he has visited the United Kingdom a few times. He has also thought about returning to Nepal: "Maybe I go back home my country [Nepal] . . . my birthplace." When Chapal was still active in service, he traveled back to Nepal about once every three to four years. Now that he is retired and a civilian, he makes more frequent trips to Nepal, which average once a year. Both his children are presently studying in Nepal. Throughout the course of the interview, he talked about how much the Gurkhas have contributed to the British, and for which the former ought to be remembered through memorials and other forms. He opined:

> As I said before, Gurkhas start[ed] . . . in Hong Kong in 1948. And they put on duty, and all the Gurkhas move here, all the Gurkhas move before the 1971. All the recruits, everything. So we then fifty years of time, fifty years of time, all our three generation of people, like me. I said, three generation, you know what I mean, we spend all our time, many of our time, almost minimum time fifteen years in Hong Kong, and that's if we work here. Everything from Hong Kong. At that time, ruled by British and the colonial government. Ya. But is still, the things what we did was the governmental, the ruler is gone, the British left already. But still the things we did, we made, is still here, continue, is still here. But, I need to say though, if the things is still used to, is still good for everyone and good for people, then why not us? There is nothing else, no, if you go find something, you want to know, you can go museum, you go somewhere else, or somewhere far, you cannot find anything . . . . What I meant to say is, there should be something there. . . . If you know, if you visit Nepal, you go to Pokhara . . . [they are] trying to start, there is a Gurkha monument [they are building].

Putting aside Chapal's importunity for the need to remember the Gurkhas, he also shared later that Gurkhas were not always well regarded. He noted: "In Hong Kong, but now, there is some Chinese guys, they're hired but maybe they don't like, but maybe when you talk to kids, they don't like some Gurkhas, Nepalese." This statement is indicative of the different extent and degree to which Gurkhas in Hong Kong (and elsewhere) are welcomed or otherwise, depending on the country of residence that Gurkhas are situated in. Such reception is likewise contingent on particular structural frameworks, including policies revolving around multiculturalism, rights to remain, citizenship, and ethnic majority-minority relations among others.[2]

Another Gurkha, Manjul, has been to Bosnia, Yugoslavia, Kenya, Brunei, and East Timor as part of his battalion's varied postings over the years of his Gurkha service since 1994. He enlisted into Gurkha training in Pokhara at the age of nineteen—which was his second (successful) try after his first attempt undertaken a year before in 1993. Unlike most other Gurkhas, Manjul was married eight months prior to recruitment. He was already a father of a two-month-old son before he joined the army. Nine months of recruit training formally commenced in Hong Kong two weeks after he was enlisted. Manjul was aware of this overseas posting (and for which most Gurkha recruits are not made privy to), having learned some information from his brother who was previously in the British Army and who has now retired in the United Kingdom. Manjul's next stop after Hong Kong was the United Kingdom, and thereafter to the aforementioned countries in following his battalion's deployment.

After recruitment, the next time Manjul saw his wife and son was four years later in 1998, given that the first long leave for new Gurkha soldier-recruits was allowed after about three-and-a-half years of service. As Parker explains somewhat similarly:

> British officers faced an even longer journey if a visit to England was on the cards, and a system of long leaves evolved whereby they took six months every three years. For the Gurkhas, this suited the parents of new recruits who, on returning home after their first three years, would find their bride waiting for them for a prompt marriage and hopefully, before the leave was over, the bride would be pregnant, and the child would be three the next time he or she saw the father—if indeed he came back. (1999, 65)

Manjul recounted somewhat bemusedly to me: "It's, the interesting thing is four years after I've seen my wife, and four years after my son is running everywhere, and I say that your dad is finally home . . . 'Who are you?' He say like that you know." As a result of Gurkha service, Manjul noted, some Gurkhas' plans for raising a family were interrupted. Manjul explained in detail:

> You know they married, example, when they married recruiting time. Then their family promotion to the twelve, thirteen, fourteen years after, then that long gap. Then some of the, didn't make the chance in their baby. That's why the you know the they hurt the baby you know,

> forever. They lose the baby. Then, just one husband and a wife. Because
> of the separation. They want a baby but, they can't.

The reference to twelve or more years by Manjul is made in relation to the number of years that Gurkhas had to fulfil before they were allowed to have their families join them in the married quarters of their army barracks. Permission to have their family members live with them was also contingent on their respective rank in the army (Ku et al. 2010). Given these various military regulations and other accompanying structural constraints, raising a family for some Gurkhas was not always easy due to many years of separation and differentiated rank-and-file treatment in the regiment. In Manjul's case, he was only allowed to bring his family to the Gurkha barracks in Brunei in 2005—just over a decade after he was enlisted. This was because he was promoted only then and was therefore allowed to bring his wife and children to Brunei where he was based. Fifteen days later, however, he received news that he was to be posted to Afghanistan for six months. This left him with a mere two months since his family first joined him in Brunei, before he was to depart for Afghanistan thereafter. While based in Brunei, Manjul also took the chance to travel with his wife to nearby countries, including Singapore, Thailand, and Malaysia. In Singapore, he visited the Gurkha camp of the Singapore Police Force, where his sister and a fellow Nepalese Gurkha were based.

Manjul is now working in the United Kingdom. Though his wife and he are eligible to apply for British citizenship, both are not keen.[3] His wife and children, however, do hold the "indefinite leave to remain" (ILR)—which means eligibility for settlement in the United Kingdom. Although he noted that the children would be better off in the United Kingdom than Nepal—"when they came here then they study English in school. Then they have all English friend[s]. . . . If they going to Nepal, there's nothing. You know. They don't study in Nepal, they don't know the Nepal. . . . They have a future in here, they don't have future in Nepal"— Manjul himself would prefer to return to Nepal. When I probed him about how much longer he plans to stay in the United Kingdom, he expressed his quandary given the political situation in Nepal at the time of our interview:[4]

> Is the dependent on situation you know. In Nepal is the now, very difficult. You know the, I love my country. I love my village. I love my com- . . . you know the community. But there is now very difficult. There's you know, some of this, is the politics and is you know, no good for Nepal. . . . I thinking I'm back to Nepal. Because I am born there, you know. If, if the politics is good, then I'm not going to stay here. I back to Nepal. [*laughs*]

Experiences relating to regimental recruitment, notions of home, belonging, Gurkha children and their education and future, transnational Gurkha or kin ties, among many others, are replete and recurrently raised by my interlocutors throughout the course of my fieldwork. I provide an overall background to the enlistment, posting, and military and other experiences of the Gurkhas who have traveled across and lived in different places around the globe during different phases of their lives. I draw on a wide range of narrative accounts shared with me by Gurkhas and their family members, including my examination of other secondary sources, which I analyze in this and the next chapter. The varied experiences and perspectives of Chapal, Manjul, and many others constitute my analytical focus. By laying out the multiple processes and obstacles toward being recruited as a Gurkha, including their overseas postings and life thereafter, I extend my previous discussion by mapping out the different routes that young Gurkhas first took as they leave their home in Nepal. Given the recent turn to possibilities of enlisting female recruits into Gurkha service for the British Army, I also discuss issues related to gender positions and how recruitment of Nepalese women has been debated and received. In so doing, I take *Gurkha* as a gendered category of analysis beyond well-debated notions revolving around masculinity and bravery among Gurkha men.

Over and above popular if not stereotypical constructions of the Gurkhas as brave warriors, their multiple work and life trajectories have clearly extended beyond national boundaries (Pries 2001) within the wider global security network. These trajectories and movements include the periods and contexts from recruitment to overseas regimental and other postings as security contractors (see for example, Chakrabarti 2008; Chisholm 2014; Coburn 2018; Thule 2011; Vines 1999) and building families across borders. Acknowledging and analyzing these cross-border movements and settlements will therefore shed light on their lives as migrant warriors. I am interested in addressing and problematizing how they assess varying sentiments toward the country or countries in which they have trained and lived, and how these together reflect the different ways to approach bracketed belonging beyond their military and police experiences. In sum, the dynamics of leaving their villages or other towns in Nepal, and heading for early days of military and police training in Singapore, Hong Kong, Malaysia, or the United Kingdom in their first years in service pertinently illustrate and illuminate the beginnings of their different or multiple migratory paths. These in turn affected the timing and ways in which they settled down and started having children, and where they later would choose to retire. These are among many other issues that are, with some exceptions, seldom deliberated on in earlier and current literature on the Gurkhas. As a response to Gould (1999, 4), who proclaims that the "void at the centre of all histories of the Gurkhas is the voice of Gurkhas themselves," I therefore address these important themes in this book.

What are their aspirations as they embark on a Gurkha career, and subsequently a second career in the security and tourism-related industries in the region and beyond? Where do they regard their homes to be, and what remembrances of the Gurkhas and of Nepal do these warriors possess? What considerations come to their minds as some of them choose early retirement from service, to return to Nepal with their children, or to think about retiring in Nepal in their twilight years after a long period of stay outside of their homeland? How can one make sense of these varied decisions and pathways, routes and roots vis-à-vis the wider literature on migration, home, aspiration, and mobility? As I systematically engage with these interpellated queries, I show how their lives as migrants and not merely as soldiers in the fore are affected by a host of both military and paramilitary vicissitudes. My engagement also considers the varied roles of nation-states and their accompanying governance structures that determine Gurkha mobilities. Together, these contexts and rules provide the backdrop that render them as a crucial category of para/military-labor migrants within the wider diasporic literature. In sum, I discuss the lives of Gurkhas and their families beyond their global reputation as warriors. In doing so, I therefore indicate how the Gurkhas' life history experiences and their aspirations—the multiple layers, convergences, and divergences—and manifold mobilities or immobilities may be conceived and interrogated through the lens and conceptual apparatuses of migration, bracketed belonging, and other cognate scholarship.

(Do) I Want to Be a Gurkha

Manjul's first encounter with Gurkhas took place when he was a little boy of about five or six years of age. The figure of the Gurkha as a strong, fit, and successful migrant was poignantly carved in Manjul's memory. He described the initial encounter to me:

> Yeah it's the why I'm join the Gurkhas is the Gurkhas is when I born, like the . . . I'm, my age is five or six years, then I heard in the Gurkhas that time there is this some of the senior person is the, he is the British Army . . . In my village. Then he say that I'm the captain. He said the Gurkhas' captain. And he looks very handsome and good man! Then the becoming one of the villager another senior than me, he join also the army, lots of the British Army, we have in that village.

This "culture of emigration" as earlier iterated refers to the tradition of young Nepalese men who follow their male kins' footsteps—be they their fathers, uncles, brothers, or cousins—in taking up Gurkha service as a form of livelihood.

Naveen, who was recruited into the British Army in 1991, noted: "Initially those who were serving in Gurkhas, their family background completely Gurkhas, you know. Like my father who was in Gurkha before, and when he retired, and my first and second brother." Consequently, such a tradition of Gurkha enlistment and service has fostered a culture of emigration whereby "Gurkha connections" have been formed over time. These connections generate extensive information networks that both inculcate the positive aspects of serving as Gurkhas, as well as shore up other stories of their migratory-military experiences. Badal, whose grandfather was a Gurkha, had this to say where recruitment is concerned:

> Even there are army family around and all. So they always have this mindset that okay, as a son of a Gurkha, a grandson of Gurkha, at least you should try [to be recruited], at least you should try to. . . . Luckily for me, maybe you know I was fat, and they always thought I'll never be a Gurkha? But I was good in study, so they never force me.

Notwithstanding Badal's family history and how he did not (have to) follow in the footsteps of his grandfather, such networks and tradition of Gurkha recruitment and emigration that my interlocutors have shared are broadly similar to other migratory niches and occupations. Occupational provincialism, coupled with economic motivations to migrate, are consonant with other similar studies on overseas migration. These studies examine how and why migrants seek to better both their personal situations as well as familial circumstances (Des Chene 1992; Kumar 2004; Low 2014).

Being a Gurkha, and serving in countries such as the United Kingdom, Singapore, Hong Kong, or elsewhere proved to be economically favorable stints. For one, their service helped construct the figure of the successful migrant. This figure was embodied in Gurkhas who returned to their villages over the period of their long leave. Manjul illustrated this in detail:

> We grown up like seventeen or sixteen, and that time my brother also he join the army. That's why the, when they come back, they're late you know. Three years after they can take leave then they say I think you, you also join in the British Army, and they say like that then why? And if you, they say that it's not good. At least you have the job. That's why you can survive. So we have a good history, the Gurkhas' history, now around 100 year plus. 150 years now, mostly say like that. Then it's still I'm you know the just quite, the not very interesting, just little bit of dangers there, then when I grown like eighteen years then I decide ok, and I've seen lots of the not my village or the village of there, there is also all the British Army, and the they have the huge, huge houses they

build themselves. That's why he got the job, he got lots of money, then he afford to build their house. A nice house and nice building it looks very good. And but we don't have job that time then how do we build that?

Apart from having encountered the figure of the Gurkha as a child, and in addition to his own brother's experience of serving in the British Army, Manjul saw that Gurkhas who had returned in-between their service had accomplished a fairly good life in owning property. This was registered through the huge houses that they could afford to build, along with "lots of money" that only being a Gurkha could earn in a situation of limited job prospects in the country. Jishnu claimed to be the first Gurkha in his family. He enlisted in 1980. He explained that although he did well in school and sports and that his teacher had dissuaded him from joining the army, he enlisted in any case because he had to support his family:

> Frankly speaking, I'm the first, I was the first generation to be a Gurkha, to be enrolled in the Gurkha. And my teacher asked me, requested me many time not to go to the Gurkha because I was very good in the study, and I was the school union leader, and I was good in sports, so my teacher asked me not to go there. Because with my situation, not very good, I cannot go into university, so after high school, I just wanted to join the army. That's all, there. Because of my family situation. . . . I have a big family. I was the youngest one, and so I had no choice but to make a quick money, support my family. I could join the army.

His decision to join the army was also prompted by his remembrance of Gurkhas who had gone before him, and who, not unlike that of Manjul's recollection, were successful when they returned:

> They told me, you have very bright future here. But you know, the young Gurkhas, they used to live and show off everything. It's really I think one of the attraction that attracted us in the village. . . . Not that kind of chance to have the watch, have new clothes and anything. Anything, you get it. . . . And the radio. . . . At that time, Panasonic. . . . And Kelvin, because I joined the army, that really helped a lot, a lot to my family's situation at that time, financial situation.

Calling the current generation as "rich young Gurkhas," Jishnu compared them and his generation. He saw that while he was not always able to visit home as frequently, the current Gurkhas are able to do that more often. This is due not only to changes in regimental rules concerning leave cycles, but also attributed to the somewhat improved affluence of Gurkhas today. Such a context again adds to the image of the successful migrant, of which Gurkha service has been able to produce over time. Jishnu's own experience as a migrant who has done relatively well is seen through the material goods that he himself had been able to bring home on his visits—a Panasonic radio, a Yashica camera, and a Seiko watch—for which he felt "proud." At that time, the ability to buy these commodities and to bring them home either as possessions or as gifts for their families was seen as rare. Similarly, Lakshan's view aligns with the image of the successful migrant:

> Main, main impression is because you must have seen people coming back happy. Happily coming back to see the family with the money, nice clothings, nice personal equipment, like radio. Oh, nowadays you think, oh very easy. So you think you have a lot of money, you can earn a lot of money. So that's why they become very attracted and eager to go.

These material objects therefore constitute a marker of success after the Gurkhas leave for service, and then return to Nepal on short-term visits. In Kumud's words: "There's different style . . . There's different style, different environment, different feeling, different image." Dervla Murphy, Irish author and touring cyclist, crafts a vivid description (for which I quote at length) of the transition from Nepali youth to Gurkha serviceman who had done well as a migrant:

> Sometimes one sees scared, barefooted youths from remote hill villages coming to the airfield, carrying battered little tin boxes of meagre possessions, on their way to join those elder brothers, cousins and uncles who are "doing well" with the British Army in Hong Kong, Borneo or Malaya. Then one often sees Gurkhas returning on six months' leave, after three years' service, and invariably they look sensationally spruce among their welcoming family. The grimy stay-at-home wear unwashed, fraying garments, while the well-scrubbed soldiers are attired in starched, neatly-creased khaki shorts, flowered bush-shirts and broad-brimmed straw hats. And instead of the modest little tin box with which they departed from home they now possess at least four huge padlocked trunks. These, of course, are left for their wives, mothers or sisters to carry . . . while the Returned Hero strides importantly ahead, an expensive camera slung over his shoulder and a raucous transistor screaming in his hand as he chats with those male relatives who trot respectfully beside him, carrying light pieces of hand-luggage. Usually at this stage the hero's pocket is full of newly-acquired rupees, for he will have paused long enough on the airfield to sell a selection of excellent Swiss watches and Japanese pocket-transistors at incredibly low prices. (Murphy 1967, 59)

Over time, however, the capacity to purchase these items have now become the norm rather than the exception.

That said, and even if Gurkha salaries were and are relatively meagre as compared to their British counterparts (Uesugi 2019a), successful recruitment into Gurkha service not only offered a better economic livelihood for Nepalese men. To be enlisted into the Gurkha brigade was also regarded as an achievement and thereby brought pride to the family. Such pride is evident in the case of Dhruba who proclaimed, "As a Gurkha, it's hard work and if, because you don't get the promotion. You get good name, if, cannot, so get nothing. Name of Gurkha also, let it be. [laughs] . . . our ancestors was very great and very good name and [I] want to effort [strive] to keep that name." Furthermore, Badal also noted how he and his family were regarded, especially when people around them knew about their Gurkha lineage. He said, "And, growing up in a Gurkha family was kind of good in a way. Because the thing was, especially if you look at Nepal, and the people look at you different. Then oh, you're the grandson of Gurkha. Like you know how they talk—like maybe it's the financial status."

Being proud of one's Gurkha ancestry or lineage and thereby to serve as one is however not always the case for some of the other Gurkhas I spoke with. Manohar, as an example, shared that he was compelled by his father to join the service as a Gurkha—"My dad forced me to join"—as their family was poor and there were no other better economic options. He lamented, "Actually before, when I was young, I, I was uh, very upset. But there is no choice. Because my family is very poor." In a similar way, Ujesh explained that at the time of his enlistment in 1969, there were simply no other opportunities to consider apart from potential livelihood as a Gurkha arising from economic necessity. Without a foreseeable future in Nepal itself, Gurkha recruitment was in fact a palpably feasible option. It need not necessarily stem from his family's or his own choice per se: "We are actually compel[led] to go ourself, outside Nepal. Because there's no future in the country. No jobs. So, it is everyone, in everyone's mind they want to leave the country and go somewhere to do work. No matter what other job they get. . . . And they enjoy that." Correspondingly, Kamadev shared that "mainly in Nepal, people are unemployed, that's why we liked to join the army . . . that was a decision to survive." Ujesh further explained that while some families continued with a tradition of Gurkha service, others did not: "They, some are, some have none. But some have link to, their forefathers, grandfathers. Because they all, one person used to be up, by the Gurkhas." He later pointed out that there was a family in his village where out of eight siblings, six were working as Gurkhas in the British Army. His friend and colleague, Lakshan, who was also at this interview with us followed up on this point. Lakshan considered it a fortunate situation where finances are concerned: "Yes, more than six. Very lucky. Some you know, they got all their sons in the army. And they very lucky because financially they in very good health for the family."

Lakshan was speaking as someone from a Gurkha lineage that threads through a few generations in his own family. As the only son, he recalled, "Ya, but people do get the forefathers in the army. My father was in the army when my grandfather was in the army. But after my grandfather, my great great great grandfather was in the army." Such a lineage proved to be helpful where the British officers were concerned, as Lakshan later elaborated:

> But again, also those reporting officers and British officers, they do actually trust people or rely or they relate those close people in the army before. So I say my grandfather was in the army. "Oh really?" . . . Ya. So they do actually, what you call, respect. Ya. So if you have a father in the army who has done very well, then it's a good opportunity for you, even nowadays, to be you know, be high rank. But if your father, your father was a very bad guy, then you are most not likely [*laughs*]. "Oh, I know him! Oh, he's your father? I know him!" [*laughs*]

The Gurkha reputation—both of tradition and lineage, as well as of their standing in the army—therefore engenders not only recruitment for some families in following the footsteps of their various male kin. Such reputation is further enlarged precisely because of others who have gone before them. Lakshan's narrative exemplifies the importance and usefulness of having a Gurkha "family line," which led the British to hold him in good regard given his family history. Keeping the good name of the Gurkhas, as Dhruba mentioned above, is thus a pertinent practice that has lasted over time as well in the culture of Gurkha service with the British. During the time of his Gurkha service, Vasava had trained and worked in Hong Kong, Brunei, the United Kingdom, Fiji, Australia, Malaysia, and Singapore. He explained why he was amenable to Gurkha recruitment:

> In that time, our country, no transportation, only train, no motor, no roads. . . . When my children hood [*sic*], I didn't see any car, any taxis, any buses. . . . Then that time, then my father and my grandfather told us because the Gurkha is good, if you die, die. . . . If you survive after the pension, you get pension, they will give you pension so I will get benefit too. Then my concept, when I join the army, pension is from Hong Kong.

For Vasava, being a Gurkha in the context of retirement and the ability to provide for oneself through the pension motivated him to enter the army. Having a grandfather and father who both served as Gurkhas, he later shared with me that joining the British Army was akin to "heritage, you know . . . Yeah, family heritage." Tradition, lineage, heritage, and the culture of emigration based on the above accounts stand alongside one another in illustrating the continuity of Gurkha recruitment among Nepali youths and across different generations.

What is interesting about Yamanaka's (2000) "culture of emigration" in this context is that over time, Gurkha recruitment was no longer the preferred route of emigration. This is precisely because of Gurkha recruitment and service over the past several generations that led to better lives for their offspring and subsequent generations. With each generation faring better due to Gurkhas and their service that generated sufficient funds and resources for improving their livelihoods, and opening up educational paths for their children, the later generations are therefore much more highly educated. The need to be enlisted as Gurkhas subsequently becomes less exigent. This view is shared with me by Uttam and Parijat. Where Uttam pointed out that he would not mind being a Gurkha all over again, he also noted that the current younger generation would not consider joining the army as an option. Similarly, Parijat opined that the younger generation would plan their studies according to whichever field is more marketable. This for him was very different from his generation, in terms of plans to join the army for their future. As Parijat related to me: "Somehow it's come to my mind, like everybody is going to join the British Army, why don't you try? I have a goal that I can meet, that was it. My father, me, is two generations [of Gurkhas]."

Parijat and Lagan both joined as Gurkhas in 1973, and subsequently retired in 1999. Parijat's father used to serve in the British Army, and had retired back in his village: "He loves his property, enjoy living in the village. He is seventy-nine now, he is still going strong." In Lagan's case, his grandfather served in the Nepalese Army, while his father was a soldier in the Indian Army. But the sons of both these respondents did not follow in their footsteps to undergo Gurkha enlistment. At the time of my meeting with them, Parijat's son was pursuing his bachelor's degree in Sussex, while Lagan's two sons "sadly" did not wish to join the army, and therefore "the tradition is stopped" as was recounted to me. Parijat further reminisced, "In our time, when I joined the British Army and I come back home, in the village, oh! Ex-British Army having a good time. You can have few things where the people in the village don't have. So we'd done proud, but not anymore [laughs]."

Although Parijat's account above leans toward an example of what successful migration and returning home would look like, such a mentality, according to him, is no longer as desirable. This is because the "young generation have a different mind" about Gurkha service and military labor, as Parijat later opined. As commanding officer of the Catterick camp where Gurkha recruits are sent for training, Capt. Anderson notes that "in the past joining the British Army was definitely the only way out of Nepal. That's not true now."[5] In gist, "they're all educated now and they prefer to all go to the other industry, not the military," remarked Nishad, another of my respondents. Nishad's response is indicative of some measure of upward mobility for the younger generation given that they are "all educated now" as compared to earlier Nepalis who received little education during their time.

I suggest that while there are still practices and aspirations to be elsewhere for educational pursuits and thereafter for work, the culture of emigration therefore still exists. However, it operates in a different form in a newer context of many decades of Gurkha service and the expansion of the wider job markets in the region. For many years, Gurkha service with the British have provided crucial sources of income for the subsistence of their families back in Nepal based on cattle herding and terrace farming, coupled with pensions that Gurkhas receive (Yamanaka 2005). Gurkha service has also brought about some forms of horizontal if not upward mobility and (aspirations for) higher living standards for the next generations (cf. Lan 2020; Tran, Lee, and Huang, 2019). The latter are able to pursue higher education, unlike their Gurkha fathers, uncles, or brothers. In place of the Gurkha pathway are such other options or aspirations, including pursuing a degree in nursing in Australian universities (as is fairly common among the daughters in Gurkha families; see for example, Pariyar 2019), or further education elsewhere, including the United Kingdom as an option since some of the Gurkhas have worked there and have obtained the IRL as mentioned in an earlier chapter.

In problematizing the culture of emigration, one acknowledges and appreciates the concatenation of a number of factors that lead young Nepali men to join Gurkha service borne out of necessity, tradition, or volition. Aside from family tradition in which a Gurkha lineage exists and persists in some families in Nepal, economic conditions and the lack of any other desirable opportunities for work and for sustaining families are also reasons why young Nepali men aspire to be Gurkhas. These reasons are further conjugated with the image of the returnee Gurkha who seems to be doing well, and thereby explain why Gurkha enlistment has persisted for more than two hundred years. Even if enlistment figures may have seen their fair share of highs and lows over time, and even if retired Gurkhas and widows have lobbied tirelessly over the years to obtain more substantial pension funds, Gurkha recruitment continues today. In fact, female enlistees have begun to join as well.[6] The change in recruitment direction to include women came in the wake of the election of Nepal's first female president, Bidhya Devi Bhandari in 2015. This itself is unprecedented, given especially the context of Nepal as a traditionally male-dominated society. Beyond this new direction in welcoming female applicants, the change is also enacted as a result of recruitment crisis in the British Army. As the UK defence secretary Gavin Williamson notes:

"The Gurkhas are renowned as one of the best fighting forces in the world with a proud history of serving Her Majesty, and it is right that women have the opportunity to serve in this elite group."[7] In order to manage the lack of enlistees, the army had in 2016 lifted its ban on women holding frontline ground fighting positions.[8] At present, there are about three thousand Gurkhas in the British Army. By opening the doors to women, the army hopes to add another eight hundred Gurkhas to the fold. New female soldiers will form a new infantry battalion as well as new units of communication experts and engineers.[9]

The British Army had earlier floated the idea of recruiting female Gurkhas in 2007, but the plan was later rescinded, citing reasons of impracticality.[10] This notwithstanding, a few Nepalese women have joined the force by relying on their British Overseas National passport privileges. The move to now include female applicants is also welcomed by some members of the Gurkha Army Ex-Servicemen's Organisation (GAESO) in Nepal. The president of GAESO, Krishna Kumar Rai (a former Gurkha), says that it is a "matter of pride" and an important departure from an earlier belief that the presence of Nepalese women in the brigade would "destroy its comradeship."[11] The president of GAESO's Kathmandu District Committee, Sunita Gurung, states: "It's a moment of happiness for many Nepalese women aspiring to be the part of elite British Gurkha soldiers whose selection will be conducted in Nepal." Furthermore, she adds that "it's a big opportunity for Nepalese women to get a prestigious job and earn a handsome income in the United Kingdom."[12]

While the foregoing discussion and reportage have portrayed positive reception of female recruitment, female hopefuls themselves are somewhat hesitant to let others know of their intentions given the unconfirmed news.[13] They are also fearful of being ridiculed. As reported recently in the *Kathmandu Post* in February 2019,[14] some women have already begun training in preparation for recruitment selection (see also, Stanik 2019)—training under the same set of criteria that men are expected to fulfill. Training centers such as the Salute Gorkha Training Center in Kathmandu, a branch at Basundhara, has admitted female trainees for the first time. Although some of the aspirant females come from nonmilitary family backgrounds, there are others whose father or elder brother was/is a Gurkha. Tsheden Lama, who commenced her training since early January 2019, has yet to inform her relatives about her Gurkha aspiration. Instead, she told them that she was enrolled in some preparatory classes before beginning her university studies. The reason for not telling them was because she was afraid they would "look down on her choice to recruit in the military."[15] Another trainee, Riya Shrestha from Budol, Kavre, said: "I came to know that the British Army is recruiting women through social media, after which I googled for the training centres where I can prepare myself for the competitive recruitment process and this is how I ended up here."[16] Interestingly, the Indian Army has recently begun to recruit women. Vacancies are available for Nepali women to join the Military Police. Nepali youths have been recruited into the Indian Army's Gurkha Regiment since 1816, traced back to the rule of the East India Company. To date, more than 3,200 Nepali nationals are serving in the army, with many thousands of veterans who have since retired and are presently receiving pensions.[17] Online applications were opened in July 2020 to eligible Nepali women, following an announcement made by the Indian Embassy in Kathmandu.

The new drive for female recruits to join as Gurkhas under the British shores up two broader points of contention in terms of Nepal-UK relations, and of gender relations in Nepal. On the one hand, public discourse on Nepalese young men being drafted into Gurkha service for a foreign power has been somewhat frowned on. In 2013, a parliamentary committee of the Nepalese government had put in a recommendation to the government to slowly reduce and end Gurkha recruitment into the British Army.[18] On the other hand, however, the Gurkhas' global reputation as brave and loyal soldiers persists in wider Nepalese discourse and is still harnessed as a source of pride and continued legacy. Furthermore, while growing numbers of women aspire to join Gurkha service—and which is an important step forward in Nepal's traditionally patriarchal society— their hesitation to talk about such aspirations openly simultaneously serves as a reminder that Nepal might not as yet be ready to comprehensively rethink military service, a male-dominated industry, as an avenue for female participation.[19] This is in spite of the Nepali Army, which has included women in general service roles since 2004. Plans for female recruitment have garnered negative reactions from Nepali lawmakers. Some senior Nepali politicians point out that as the current treaty with the British government only stipulates the recruitment of male Gurkhas, the female recruitment process should be stopped immediately. Additionally, the House of Representatives noted, "The government must review the treaty on the recruitment of Gurkhas and implement Nepal's foreign policy and ensure that it is in the spirit of the Constitution of Nepal and its democratic system."[20]

In March 2019, the Nepali Parliament canceled recruitment plans for female hopefuls to join the British Gurkha Brigade.[21] It cited the reason that the timing was not right owing to ongoing issues revolving around pension and other compensation issues affecting ex-Gurkhas. It was later reported in March 2021 that talks about Gurkha female recruitment were ongoing, as noted by the British ambassador to Nepal.[22] These notwithstanding, plans for female recruitment if eventually approved might in the longer run result in a repositioning in Gurkha families from split- to dual-wage earning household. Such a change on household income would also depend on whether female inductees are married to Gurkha husbands, or if rules regulating the prohibition of (non-Gurkha) wives of Gurkhas to work while living with their husbands in the army barracks might be revised or not. The scenario for retired Gurkhas is somewhat different. Among my interlocutors, most if not all Gurkha wives hold either full- or part-time jobs alongside their husbands who have embarked on their second post-Gurkha careers. This group of retired Gurkhas and their families, therefore, constitute dual-income households as opposed to some of the active Gurkhas I spoke with, or Gurkhas who used to be in service prior to their retirement.

In these varying contexts then, the trajectory and role of the male sojourner also shifts (cf. Seo 2019; Werbner and Johnson 2011), depending on the point of his career in the armed forces. The case of Gurkha families (both during active service and after retirement from the forces) therefore serves as an important intervention and critique of the image of the sole male sojourner. In their case, being the sole male wage earner at the beginning of their Gurkha career does not simply imply that women are not able to work outside of the home on their own. Neither is it a case of clear gendered division of labor that attributes men as contributing to the public sphere as waged laborers while the women reside within the private or domestic realm of family life. Instead, it is due to the military rules of prohibiting women from joining their Gurkha husbands at first, and then prohibiting them from taking on a job after joining them, that bring about split-labor households for younger Gurkha families at the outset. Wives of retired Gurkhas I have spoken to hold jobs as teachers, museum staff, cleaners, and other occupations in the food and beverage industries, among others.

In sum, one may approach an analysis of Gurkha as a gender category to consider beyond masculine physical traits of strength and resilience other broader structural resonances and gender positionalities. As discussed above, the varied dimensions of gender-resonant issues revolving around Gurkha recruitment, military and legal domains of interest, and migratory trajectories demonstrate how one can and should maneuver beyond the staple figure of the indomitable and loyal Gurkha. Approaching "Gurkha" as a gender category reveals and sheds further light on male-female relations across different spheres of social life. They include (1) British Army and the recruitment process and guidelines of whether females should play a role in frontline combat positions; (2) how potential gender discrimination as preempted by the British Army illustrates the involvement or invocation of the law that intertwines with military policies and practices; (3) Nepali gender relations in a country that is traditionally steeped in patriarchal outlook and everyday life; and (4) how gender relations and the image of the male sojourner lend further analytical avenues to rethink shifting forms of split-labor and dual wage households resulting from Gurkha service, and at different points of a Gurkha's career path.

The Recruitment Process: Criteria, Experience, and Pathways

Manjul talked about recruitment and overseas posting, which determined the Gurkhas' future trajectory and (migratory) circumstances and where he would serve and live:

> MANJUL: I mean, the Singapore police. In Nepal, selection at the same time. That's why the Singapore police trained by in Singapore. They have their recruit company in Singapore right. But very easy you know we split the British soldiers here, the Singapore police here. Then they announce the same time . . .
>
> KELVIN: Same time?
>
> MANJUL: Yeah, say the number-wise, like 2116, go here, 2117, go here, Singapore. 2118, British, 2119, go to Singapore.
>
> KELVIN: Ah okay, okay. So your friend didn't end up at the Gurkha side.
>
> MANJUL: Yeah, my friend is gone to Singapore [Police Force]. And I go to . . . split yeah.
>
> KELVIN: Right, right right. Okay.
>
> MANJUL: Yeah and that's right and we are separate. He went to Singapore. He said, "You know, you have a good life in the UK. I never good life in the UK [*laughs*], you have a good life . . . you have thirty-two years, forty years in Singapore, funny, he said. You know can't I do these thirty-two years, we don't have thirty-two years, at least we have twenty-two years in Singapore." And how long they doing? Maybe twenty-two years? Maybe thirty years?

This interview segment illustrates how military service and the initial posting after recruitment essentially determined the longer-term trajectory of where Gurkhas could eventually work and live. In a way then, bracketed belonging—here based on recruitment trajectories—would have already been fostered from the outset of a migrant Gurkha's career. As I have iterated previously, being posted to Singapore meant that Gurkhas had to, by the rules of the SPF, retire at age forty-five or earlier. Accompanying their retirement is a mandatory rule that all family members and the Gurkha himself would have to return to Nepal. They would not be allowed to continue their residence in Singapore after the Gurkha's police service concludes. In contrast, those who were posted to Hong Kong or the United Kingdom faced different pathways of settlement. Due to changes in the rules in each country over recent years with the former providing the right to abode, and the latter the right to remain, or the IRL, these respectively meant that Gurkhas who have retired can exercise the option to remain in either of these two countries.

I would also add that while earlier generations could not exercise any option pertaining to which country they would be posted to, Hiresh—who was posted to the Singapore Police Force in 1978—pointed out that one could now state his preference in regard to postings:

> KELVIN: So only after recruitment then you know where you are posted to. UK or Singapore.
>
> HIRESH: Those days. Now . . .
>
> KELVIN: Now you can say your preference.
>
> HIRESH: Not preference. Yeah, now it is a preference.
>
> KELVIN: You can indicate yeah? It is a preference.
>
> HIRESH: No, because they have a problem here, in the recruitment you know? In fact, nobody wanted to go. Like that, if they don't use the current procedure, nobody like to go Singapore. That was the problem. Because of the salary, because of the privilege, those things. Who wants to go now?
>
> KELVIN: So people know now?
>
> HIRESH: People, after selecting, I don't know this year, few wanted to go. The following year they changed the rule. And what they did is, the first, the very beginning they are asked to fill up the form, that where you want to go.
>
> KELVIN: Ahh, that's what they introduce.
>
> HIRESH: The system they introduce. You want to go to British Army or you want to go to Singapore? Ok, now it is much more clearer.

In any case, both military and paramilitary institutional structures govern the locales of residence after retirement, including where Gurkha children are allowed to continue their education or not, or to find a job in whichever country that permits their stay beyond their Gurkha father's service. Resultantly, sentiments and constructions of "home" and of belonging are therefore contingent on these aforementioned circumstances. These different contexts provide a range of varying experiences that lend analytical fodder toward unraveling and critiquing the binary of home/hostland in more nuanced and concrete manners as earlier discussed.

Gurkha recruitment is an arduous and physically strenuous process that takes place over a few rounds from registration to regional selection, and central selection. As explained on the British Army's Ministry of Defence website, Gurkha recruitment comprises "free, fair and transparent" selection for enlistees for either the British Army or the Singapore Police Force between the ages of eighteen and twenty-one.[23] For 2021, the targeted number of recruits was 218 for Britain's Brigade of Gurkhas, and 140 for the Gurkha Contingent of the SPF (GCSPF). For 2022, the respective targeted recruitment numbers stood at 196, and 140. In the following year, 200 potential recruits were targeted for Britain's Brigade and 144 recruits were targeted for the GCSPF.[24] Over the decades, recruitment numbers have shifted; in 2005 for example, 230 positions were available for the army and 77 for SPF,[25] while in 2014, 126 places were available for the army.[26] Applicants first register either at the British Gurkha Dharan (BGD) Old Ghopa camp for those from districts in Eastern Nepal (including Jhapa, Sunsari, Morang, Dhankuta, and others), or the British Gurkha Pokhara (BGP) camp for those from districts in Western Nepal (including Tanahun, Gorkha, Kaski, Lamjung, and others). Current selection rounds will conclude by December 2024 for recruitment into the GCSPF, and by February 2025 for the British Army.[27]

Part of the grueling Gurkha recruitment process involves applicants completing a series of physical tasks. These tasks are differentiated for those interested to try out for the British Army or the GCSPF. For the former, PRs (potential recruits) are to complete six heaves and to carry out a mid-thigh pull test at registration. As for the latter, PRs are required to complete eight heaves. For both groups, failure to carry out these tests successfully results in PRs not being able to register.[28] Successful registrants will then move on to the next round, the regional selection, which is held either in Pokhara or Dharan. The physical assessment criteria for regional selection (as of 2020) includes an eight hundred meter run under two minutes and forty seconds, a "Repeated Lift and Carry" test in which one carries a twenty kilogram weight for thirty meters and then runs another thirty meters without the weight in under one minute and fifty seconds. Further tests require a minimum of twelve overarm heaves, a medicine ball throw of over 3.1 meters, and a mid-thigh pull of one hundred kilograms. The third task is only applicable for those applying for the GCSPF, and the last two tasks are applicable only for those applying for the British Army. An interview with a Nepali and a British Gurkha Officer forms part of regional selection. Both officers will ask candidates questions, including knowledge of the Gurkha brigade, notions of commitment and teamwork, resilience and integrity, among others. Successful candidates from the regional selection will then move on to the Central selection round, which again contains a series of physical, educational (English and mathematics), and medical assessments.

Gurkha recruitment comprises as well the famous *doko* race in which one carries a twenty-five kilogram basket on his back while running uphill on the hilly terrains over a course of five kilometers.[29] The term *doko* refers to a traditional wicker basket.[30] The race, according to one of the British recruitment officers,

Col. James Robinson, is "a test of stamina, character, and commitment. . . . And it separates the men from the boys."[31] The doko race has been described as follows:

> At 7am, the assembled young men are given the off and they push and jostle each other as they make for the best route across the paddy fields. Some lose their balance, fall over, their *doko* baskets pulling them to the ground, but this is a frantic, momentous race and they scramble back to their feet. They move up steep steps, avoiding the buffalo droppings that pepper the route, up through the morning haze, past the clouds to the point where the crisp white peaks of the Annapurna massif and the sacred mountain of Macchapucchre are visible. Many of the applicants, thanks to a lifetime on these mountains, have powerful calf and thigh muscles, but for some it is a terrible struggle. The torture of the route and the pain of such weight on their shoulders is cut into the PR's (potential recruits) sweat-sodden faces. Families and friends gather at the side of the pathway, clapping and shouting them on. At the finishing line, exhausted and drenched, the young men must wait in line to have their *doko*s reweighed. Each basket should contain exactly 25kgs of rocks—any less and the runner is out. Only after the weigh-in are the PRs given a drink and a blanket for warmth.[32]

One of my respondents, Gopan, recounted this race. He compared this requirement during his time with present-day expectations:

> Yes, doko race, that's right. So our time is tough then now these guys. Cos' ours was like twice we have to do. But now only once, and they finish in half then come back. But our time, you have to start, go up, down, up and down hill then you have to go twice, come down and then again. So our time were tough times. I respect those guys who join the Gurkhas because . . . [really tough].

Given these stringent rules and criteria for Gurkha recruitment, it is no wonder that private training academies have sprung up over the years that offer training programs for interested applicants to prepare for the selection process. During one of my fieldwork trips to Pokhara, I noticed a couple of such training academies promoting their programs to attract potential recruits. Apart from the Gurkha Fitness Centre & Golf School (see figure 3.1) and the Gurkha Army Training School (figure 3.2) that I saw along the roads in Pokhara, Coburn (2018) likewise talks about these academies, where he had encountered a center called Gurkha Strength. Nepali youths would pay about twenty-five thousand Nepali rupees to join these programs. Training centers are also located in Dharan and Bhutwal in addition to other parts of Nepal (Coburn 2018).[33] According to Piya (2020)

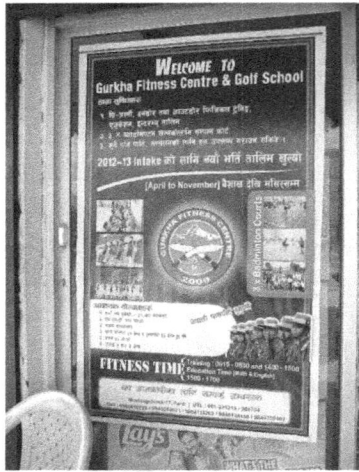

FIGURE 3.1. Gurkha Fitness Centre & Golf School, Pokhara. Source: Photo by author, 2012.

FIGURE 3.2. The Gurkha Army Training School, Pokhara. Source: Photo by author, 2012.

who had researched similar training centers in Pokhara, these centers serve as "cultural intermediaries" given that Gurkha aspirants are trained to acquire a particular comportment and set of virtues associated with a Gurkha soldier. Such training comprises coaching aspirants to emphasize their links to Gurkha heritage in their family, or demonstrate their sense of discipline by adopting particular embodied behaviors and interview protocols, as I have discussed previously.

The Gurkha recruitment exercise is not only about individual applicants. Rather, it is a family event, whereby loved ones are as well vested in hopes for a positive outcome of selection. As Chong (2014, 10–11) describes:

> On the day of the final selection, anxious family members wait outside the gate of the British camp, hoping not to catch a glimpse of their sons walking down a long stretch of road to the exit. To see their son take the "walk of shame" would mean failure in being recruited. Many of the young men, some still in their late teenage years, are on the brink of tears by the time they exit the large metal gates, having come agonisingly close to a life in the military and a chance to leave a country where unemployment stood at forty percent.

Those youths who did not make the cut would either return to schools that they had previously left because of their Gurkha aspirations, or they would look for jobs in Kathmandu. Most, however still harbored dreams of securing work overseas. While some have ended up working in Malaysia, others have gotten jobs in Gulf countries (Coburn 2018). As for those who were successful in the Gurkha recruitment drive, these young Gurkhas would then be sent off to different countries depending on their individual deployment. While clear pathways were assigned to them in terms of being a Gurkha soldier or a police officer, their initial periods of recruit training and subsequent deployment took place in several different places, including Brunei, Hong Kong, Singapore, Malaysia, Cambodia, Belize, Jamaica, and the United Kingdom among other countries (Chong 2014). Already from the beginning of their career, the Gurkhas' mobility was facilitated by military and police security training regimes that brought them to a range of different locations. It is to these varied experiences of life as a migrant Gurkha that I next turn.

Life as/Being a Gurkha

Uttam joined the Gurkhas in 1961, following tradition and the footsteps of his father who was at that time still serving as a British Gurkha. He explained:

> And he was still serving while I was with them. You see? Wherever he went, we followed, because of course, being a part of the family. And I joined the army while I was in the army, with my parents. . . . It was a tradition during those days. I never thought I was going to be soldier because I was thinking of studying and looking for. . . . But in those days, your parents say you go for this and you go for this. And so I didn't know when I was supposed to join the army. I just . . . They said, ok son, your name is put forth to the army, and you go! And I had to go.

He recollected his early training days in Malaysia, where he was posted to Sungei Petani, Kedah, for nine months of recruit training. The next stop was Hong Kong for a duration of three weeks, before he returned to Malaysia where he spent a subsequent half a year in the jungles of Sarawak:

> Since our battalion was in Sarawak, after three weeks we went to Sarawak and it was all in jungle . . . for six months . . . From time to time we had to go although they had a basecamp which was quite far away from the border, from the Indonesian and Malaysian border, Sarawak. And from time to time we had to go over the border to kill the Indonesians. But if you went into the jungle you just cannot talk. . . . All camouflaged. Cooking was only done during the daytime. And no noise, you cannot make any noise. If you had to talk over the radio, you had to get . . . [*inaudible*]. . . . Everything was hand signal. For cooking, daytime then you cook, you cannot cook outside. . . . Maybe daytime was okay, with some foliage or branches. But night time, because if you put on your light, it can be seen. Very difficult . . .

Uttam's account of field discipline (sound and light discipline to avoid raising enemy attention) above is one of many training narratives of hardships that depict how life as a trainee Gurkha commenced. As another example, Hari Bivor Karki joined the Gurkha Engineers (Malaya) in 1961. He recalls his recruit training days at Sungei Petani Camp where he "had a very hard life there" (Karki 2009, 140). He used to wake up at four in the morning every day in order to be ready for bed inspection, followed by breakfast at five thirty. Throughout the day, he had to attend physical training drills, regular parades, as well as jungle training. As a recruit, Karki also had to do twelve-hour shifts for guard duty as well as in sentry posts. Having met the recruitment expectations meted out by the British Army, successful Gurkha enlistees are then faced with a whole host of training regimes, depending on where they would have been posted to—Singapore, Hong Kong, Malaysia, or the United Kingdom, and elsewhere. Through the manifold accounts of training, survival, and hardships that Gurkhas undergo, I highlight stories of difficult moments and periods in their service career. I elucidate on narratives that depart from extant discourses and reportage in the wider literature and media, where stories of heroism and bravery abound in furthering the global reputation of these brave warriors. As Ram confided in me over our first interview: "When I was in the training I was shock, and sometimes I would cry, but my eldest brother he was there sometime in the week, and he would come and see then I was alright, but not too bad I was quite fit, I was all the time running." Over and above extant accounts of gallantry, Gurkhas such as Ram have experienced different moments or periods of despair and tough training, given especially that the training routines meant they were usually not able to return home for a visit until after a few years.

Kumud described broadly, the different types of training that he had to undergo as a Gurkha: "Wah, so many training. How to kill enemy, how to hiding, how to save . . . [to] camouflage, how to save . . . people, how to treatment, how to first-aid. Disaster for the country, how to save these people, how to save people, all the people, anyone. And in Malaysia in general . . . so many snakes, so many have." Where Kumud spoke of his experience in broader terms and where there is a hinted sense of danger, for instance, having to deal with snakes, Manohar furthered similar precarious and uncomfortable conditions he encountered in greater detail. Manohar has experienced both the Malayan Emergency (1948–60) and the Indonesian mass killings (1965–66) since his enlistment in 1959. He vividly narrated his memories of the tough conditions he faced, although it was not made clear as to which context he was referring to:

> And, and then, they actually the already when we have a rotation. . . . Sometime we go to that Malaya place . . . since 1947, I went there as well. And then we all collect passport to Brunei, in Sarawak. And there was an Indonesian . . . in 1965 till 1968 like this. . . . Quite difficult. We have to stay and patrol at least, all these things. For a month, no change. Ah, you believe or not? Very heavy raining. And all leeches biting. And all the insect attacking. The mosquitoes, sandflies. You cannot do anything. And there was very difficult to get the drinking water. So we have a filter of the back of, made of like the cloth, to put the water. . . . And the bottle, something like that. And we boil it and drink. Otherwise get some sickness. Very very bad. At that time, the hospital, Malaya is many problem.

Arjun, whom I introduced in chapter 1, was recruited into Gurkha service at the age of twenty. The youngest among four brothers and five sisters, Arjun was the only one who enlisted as a Gurkha. His second brother did attempt to enlist, but was not successful. Two years earlier, Arjun had made several attempts to join the Indian Army. He had never harbored any plans to join the British Army, nor did he expect to have gone to Singapore subsequently. Upon Gurkha enlistment, Arjun was sent to Singapore to work in the GCSPF. At the beginning, he found it difficult to adjust to life overseas given that he was a young adult who had traveled outside of Nepal for the first time:

> No family history in the army. . . . So that you know, I went to Singapore, everything new for me, sometimes very difficult to adjust ourselves. . . . I faced a lot of problems, especially discipline wise, you know, because I'm from village, I'm from third country, and also from village. . . . Not

from the Kathmandu. If I'm from the Kathmandu, maybe no problem. I am from the village and I went to the first world country . . . so the system, first world country and third world country, it is very different, so it took time to adjust there so sometimes I got policeman, instructor. . . . But it happened all . . . what is called not intentionally . . . Unintentionally. I used to mistake.

In between adjusting to life abroad and juggling the rigors of training, Arjun made it a point to take night classes as well in order to learn English and to better his educational qualifications.[34] Going to night school at seven each evening for three hours over four years had been difficult as he underwent training during the day before attending classes at night. By the end of those four years, Arjun had completed his GCE "O" levels. However, he had to stop taking classes once he was promoted to the rank of lance corporal. Since then, he had to train overseas, having traveled to such places as Belize for a section commander jungle course, as well as Australia and the United States among other countries.

Apart from undergoing intensive and arduous training, and thereafter to experience military life that at times place their lives in varying degrees of uncertainty or precarity, being a Gurkha abroad also meant having to cope with separated family life. This is because new recruits often have to serve at least three years without leave before they are allowed to go home to Nepal on long leave for a duration of six months. This was Arjun's experience among several other Gurkhas whom I have met over the course of my research. After joining the Gurkhas in 1994, he was able to return home to Nepal three years later in 1997, on a six-month long leave. During this period of leave, these young Gurkhas usually settle down through an arranged marriage. They also consummate the marriage before they next return to service. It was during this leave period that Arjun met his wife through an arranged marriage. In his own words: "It is arranged marriage. . . . It is called. . . . We have no time to love [*laughs*]." Given this cycle of service and home visits taking place per three years, the birth of a first child usually occurs in the absence of his/her Gurkha father.

Hemant joined the Gurkhas in 1991, following the footsteps of his father who had also served in the British Army. Having first completed his basic military training in Hong Kong, Hemant was then posted to the Second Royal Gurkha Rifles, and later to the First Royal Gurkha Rifles. His Gurkha experiences include having carried out peacekeeping operations in Bosnia, Sierra-Leone, and Afghanistan. Where his first son was born in Nepal while he was in Brunei, Hemant's second son was later born in the United Kingdom where he has been based since September 2008. Hemant's account of having missed the birth of his first child owing to his deployment in Brunei illustrates my focus on moving beyond the image of Gurkhas as brave warriors in the wider historical/military narrative. He calls this narrative the "big history of the Gurkhas." When Hemant first met his eldest son, the latter was already a two-and-a-half-year-old toddler:

> There is . . . big history of the Gurkhas you know . . . I think you hear that about this painful, this very painful . . . Very young time when I have to [leave] from the family. It is very painful. Even myself, I join in 1991 and I went for course for up to three years to Nepal. And after three years I met my family. And I met when I went for my first leave. . . . We get five months leave after three years. . . . After three years. And I met in that time. Then, I came over to UK, when I posted to Brunei, in that time my first son is born in Nepal but I didn't get the time. . . . And when I see him, my first son was walking, you know? He was talking and he was walking, imagine you know? It's been a big gap.

Apart from Gurkhas not being able to be present at their child's birth, Gurkha spouses are also not allowed to follow their husbands to their military base until a certain point in the Gurkha's career where promotions and rank determine if wives/families may follow them (Uesugi 2019a).

The case of Lalbahadur Gurung attests to the separated family life that was the norm for Gurkha soldiers:

> Also, I was slightly apprehensive about the prospect of an arranged marriage. When I left Nepal at the age of twelve (to go to Hong Kong where his Gurkha father was based), I had been a shepherd boy. . . . And then my father brought me to Hong Kong and I became a city boy. After that, I had spent three years in the British army, and all that goes with the social side of military life. Suddenly, on my first leave home, I am to marry a girl who had never been away from her village. . . . Now . . . we have been married twenty years, we have four children and my eldest daughter is nineteen. She was born seven months after I had returned to my unit after that first leave, and so I did not see her or my wife again until three years later. She sent me tiny little pictures of our daughter, but when I came home on leave I did not recognise her, nor she me. I was walking towards my father's house and this little child ran past me. My sister cried out, "That is your daughter . . ." and tears welled up in my eyes. (Parker 1999, 235–36)

Lalbahadur's experience, similar to Hemant's, is one among many of his Gurkha comrades. As he put it: "This is how it has always been for the Gurkha soldiers. Most of them married in this way" (Parker 1999, 236). Interestingly, Lalbahadur raised a poignant point by juxtaposing the bravery of Gurkhas as opposed to their sentimentality as a husband and a father:

> Believe me, although our image is one of fierce, fighting men, those occasions when we come home on leave and then have to return, leaving our wives, our children, our mothers at home, we are full of tears. It was very hard on the womenfolk and even now, when I talk of it to my wife—although I am retired from the British army—she cries. It brings back those memories of me leaving the village and returning to continue my duties in the British army. (Parker 1999, 236)

This scenario that Lalbahadur maudlinly described in effect led to a "split-household family structure" whereby "a migrant household maintains two family branches separated by geographical space and a national border" (Yamanaka 2005, 338). What keeps these two connected are the remittance flows, as well as occasional returns by migrant members. In Omkar and Ishayu's case, they would seek help from their fellow Gurkha peers who would be returning home, to send to their families some money and gold. Omkar elaborated: "Every time when a friend goes Nepal, we send some money home and gold . . . She would be happy with that [referring to gold]. They waiting [for] us [to send home] . . . we [also] wrote some letters and send some parcels, like gold necklaces." When I asked Omkar if the presents of gold were meant to keep their wives acquiesced due to their prolonged absences, he replied that such items would achieve that. Furthermore, "that's the way they wait for us," as Omkar added. In tandem, Adhikari and Seddon also point out the different cycles of Gurkha servicemen returning to Pokhara on their leave periods and how they channel their incomes:

> It used to be commonly said in Pokhara that when an army serviceman returned home for the first time, he used to devote his savings to getting married, to improving his house and his status in the village and perhaps to buying land in the village. On the second return, he would buy land in Pokhara; and with the money from the sale of the land, the urban vendor also built a house. On the third return, he would bring money to build a house on the land previously acquired in Pokhara. This, roughly was the pattern of the three decades: the 1960s, the 1970s and the 1980s. (Adhikari and Seddon 2002, 104)

In these contexts, Glenn's (1983) discussion on how it is usually the male migrants who would sojourn elsewhere in order to generate income, while left-behind females remain in the homeland where they are responsible for family functions, including reproduction, child-rearing, or looking after their in-laws and other family members, is germane. However, it remains to be seen as to whether the context of split-household economies in Nepal vis-à-vis Gurkhas families may shift to a "dual-wage earner household" (cf. Yamanaka 2005), given as well the pending possibility of female hopefuls wanting to join Gurkha service that was earlier raised.

Due to the separation of spouses and/or family members of the Gurkhas including young children, not all Gurkha wives would be able to manage the prolonged periods of split-household and separated family lives over time.[35] As Fateh explained:

> I've seen other friends like breaking up sometimes. . . . Bad miscommunication. . . . Hey, you're spending three years here, your wife wanting you there, and you're not there. . . . What do you do? And another three years and another three years . . . Ten, twelve years without husband, without wife, what's the point of getting married?

Omkar shared how he had only spent a total of twenty months with his wife, over his Gurkha career that spanned fifteen years in all. Vasava, who was part of my group interview with Omkar and Ishayu also concurred that having only just over two years' time to be with their wives over close to two decades of military service was unusual and difficult to manage. Where "many wives escaped with other people [or stayed] in [their] home" as Vasava noted, other wives according to Omkar had eloped and had given up on their "difficult marriage."[36] Vasava summed it up: "In Nepal when we [are] out, some [referring to Gurkhas] like Hong Kong or UK, see where you belong to [during your service]. Nepal, you know, some [referring to Gurkha wives] cannot wait too long you know. Young years everybody needs what they need. So they said go, they go. . . . Very, very difficult in that time." The mobile-migratory nature of Gurkha service both in the military and police force renders split-household living a norm rather than an exception. Over prolonged periods of separation and absences, these trying cycles of serving and returning home proved consequential on the married and family lives of these migrant warriors. I elaborate on the absences of Gurkhas in their familial contexts in the next chapter when I foreground the experiences of their wives and children.

Beyond Gurkha Service

Gurkhas usually retire from the British Army or GCSPF at the age of forty-five or earlier, given that this age is the maximum one can work up to till retirement.[37] As this is a fairly young age, retired Gurkhas usually embark on what is known as a "second career" in a variety of industries as mentioned earlier.[38] While most are by then able to stay with their family in the same locale, others have continued to venture out of their homes to work elsewhere. They thereby lengthen the period of their absence away from their kin to take on another job after Gurkha service. They have held security jobs dispersed in several different countries as security contractors. For example, Coburn (2018) talks about the experiences of a few of his interlocutors who had taken on security positions in their postretirement years from Gurkha service. The wars which started in Afghanistan in 2001 and in Iraq in 2003 saw an increase in demand for experienced security contractors. This was when international private security companies turned to the Nepali Gurkhas as an easy solution (Coburn 2018). They were still "young and fit," were "well trained" with "clear military experience," and were "far less expensive than a white soldier from a Western country with similar qualifications" (Coburn 2018, 90).

Some of these ex-Gurkhas in Coburn's (2018) research include—among several others—Jeshwal who worked as a security guard for the U.S. embassy in Afghanistan, or Sanjog who was employed by a private security firm to work as a platoon commander in Iraq. Then there were also other retirees who ran manpower firms that served as brokers in catering to security labor needs. These include the UN and its branches such as the UN Assistance Mission in Afghanistan, and the UN Development Program. A retired Gurkha police officer, Pun, ran such a firm in Kathmandu and recruited fellow Gurkha police officers for the UN, while retired Lieutenant Colonel Gurung managed a similar office that specialized in hiring security for casinos and hotels in Macau and in the Gulf (Coburn 2018). Jeshwal, who retired just before 1997 from the British Army, received a small amount of a few hundred pounds per month as pension. This amount differed rather substantially from those who had retired after that year and who received sums that were equivalent to British soldiers. Depending on rank and years of service, the post-1997 pension amount is estimated to be about a few thousand pounds per month. This amount was a marked increase from those who left Gurkha service in pre-1997 times. Through a broker firm based in Kathmandu, Jeshwal was recruited by Global Security, a company that had previously provided security for the U.S. embassy in Afghanistan.[39] The firm had offered him a monthly salary of US$1,700 to work at the embassy. Living quarters for guards like him were situated near the embassy where occupants were housed based on nationality. As a result, Jeshwal and other Nepali guards hardly interacted with other employees. They mainly hung around one another, and only interacted with their American or European supervisors on a needs basis. In 2007, Global Security lost their contract to another firm, ArmorGroup, which wanted Jeshwal to stay on but with a salary cut of US$600. It was then that he decided to leave, and returned to Dharan to "enjoy his retirement" (Coburn 2018, 98).

Depending on the age and generation of Gurkhas, there are also other more elderly Gurkhas who are not able to work anymore. They are therefore reliant on the support of institutions both in the United Kingdom and Nepal. These include the Gurkha Welfare Trust (UK) and the British Gurkha Welfare Society (Uesugi 2019b). Such support also extends beyond Gurkha veterans to include widows. These institutions are crucial especially for retired servicemen who are not eligible for pension given that they have not served a minimum of fifteen years in the force. For those who do qualify for pensions, they invest their money in both land and housing in Pokhara. There are several thousand British Army ex-servicemen who do so, including business interest in the transport as well as hotel and restaurant sectors, and the establishment of finance companies (Adhikari and Seddon 2002).

Hemant spoke with me about a "resettlement course" that Gurkhas would take at the end of their army service, which would run between five and seven weeks.[40] In the course, these Gurkha soldiers are trained with such skills as chauffeuring, plumbing, driving, among others, as a way of preparing them for life after Gurkha service. As Hemant put it: "It is very challenging for me because I served twenty-two years with the Gurkhas. After that, back to 'civi' [civilian] state is very challenging for me." Resettlement training courses include such topics as agriculture, small businesses, construction, plumbing, and shipping among other trades and skills. Newer courses comprise business code and also civil laws. The main aim of these courses is to train Gurkha retirees to be apprised of how things worked in Nepal. This is given especially that they have left the country at an early age, and only returned in their late thirties or early forties. In sum, the "aim of the course was to integrate Gurkha to the society, make Gurkha known to the legal things as well as to encourage them to initiate investment in businesses" (Mani 2020, 6261). Getting retired Gurkhas acquainted with Nepal when they return indicates as well that the country or homeland from which they had left to take up Gurkha service has transformed over time. This is not unlike themselves as military or police migrant laborers who have similarly changed in their outlook, perspectives, or ways of doing things after having been away for a protracted period of time (Shams 2020).

Community-Building in Nepal

Apart from ex-Gurkhas who have taken on second-career jobs as I have discussed, there are Gurkha initiatives relating to community-building efforts undertaken on their retirement. These efforts take off in different parts of Nepal where ex-Gurkhas decide to return and to settle down. Such initiatives in terms of how they are organized and structured bring out important dimensions of belonging, politics, and what is at stake. I contend that bracketed belonging where community is concerned expresses in-group togetherness and out-group exclusion concurrently (cf. Guibernau 2013; Prabhat 2018), as I explain below. At the same time, pursuing these endeavors with the larger good of the community in mind would enhance the visibility of ex-Gurkhas in the contexts of Kathmandu and Pokhara. The succeeding discussion on the politics of belonging is related to the notion of "cultural citizenship," which has to do with community activism as the main signifier and subjective experiences of belonging and membership beyond legal-political aspects (Pawley 2008; Qureshi and Zeitlyn 2013; Yuval-Davis 2006). To begin with, Banskota notes that

> the British Gurkha soldiers became the first common people to get mass education in the country. They were also the first source of public contact with the outside world. They visited different countries . . . and worked side by side with nationals of different countries. This gave them an opportunity to familiarise themselves with new and progressive ideas abroad with which they compared what they found at home. On their return home from abroad they became the vehicle for spreading among their families, friends and communities the importance of education and development. (Banskota 1994, 166–67)

Moreover, such initiatives related to change in Nepal, among other reasons, were also embarked on by ex-Gurkhas in order to counter stereotypes of Gurkhas as fierce and loyal soldiers in the main (Aryal 2008; Bhandari 2021; Onta 1996; Thapa 2021; Uprety 2011) as my respondents explain below.

The Singapore Gurkha Polyclinic was established in Koteshwar, Kathmandu, in 2012 (see figure 3.3). It later moved to its new premises in Lalitpur, where the clinic was officially opened in 2018.[41] The clinic is an initiative driven by retired Gurkhas from the SPF. When I paid a visit to Koteshwar in 2012, I was greeted by a total of seventeen ex-SPF Gurkhas who have invested in the clinic. Arjun, being one of them, had put in 100,000 Nepali rupees (approximately US$806) as his investment, this being the average amount. I recount this visit using my fieldnotes:

> I was at first quite puzzled as to why 'Singapore' is in the name of the clinic when 'Gurkha' would have sufficed. Upon talking more to Udgam, as well as the Chairman and others, it is really an issue of enhancing the visibility of Singapore-Gurkhas, as they want to (1) show the Nepalese government that they are doing something for their country; (2) to differentiate from British Gurkhas since the British government has no contribution towards this clinic; (3) to encourage current

FIGURE 3.3.   Singapore Gurkha Polyclinic Pvt. Ltd., Kathmandu.
Source: Photo by author, 2012.

Singapore-Gurkha servicemen to contribute; and (4) to eventually liaise with and attract doctors and medical personnel from Singapore to work at the polyclinic. (Fieldnotes, 7 May 2012)

Arjun explained to me that some of the facilities and discount rates offered at the clinic were meant only for the Gurkha community who had served in the SPF. The clinic is therefore representative of the Gurkhas' experiences in and connections with Singapore, where they harness such knowledge and ties in order to contribute back in Nepal. Arjun elaborated:

So I think because we worked in Singapore many years, and then we saw the system, we saw all the offices right? And then we want our clinic also like that, like Singapore. We are trying to do that, but still we are not, because our clinic is still in a loss. So actually we want many things, but still we can't, still we are not doing that. Maybe next time, once our clinic is running properly and running nicely, the patient flow is continued, so that we have many things to change, many things to upgrade.

Taking lessons and experiences garnered from Singapore, the new clinic based in Lalitpur highlights the Singapore connection in its introductory message that also echoes Arjun's explanation above:

Singapore Gurkha Polyclinic is the outcome of the Ex-Singapore Police personnel who have had a high-class medical facilities whilst serving in

Singapore and felt that the same can be achieved anywhere in the world. The only requirement was the "will to do." All like-minded people came together and decided to give the society a different taste that was supported by a few doctors and staff of the organization.

Within a span of 6–12 months a group of Singapore Police Gurkhas decided to open the clinic. They were supported by a couple of good and well experienced doctors and nurses. Later they were joined by other retirees and also by some of the serving men from Singapore. The doors are open for all retires and serving personnel to be members of the polyclinic which is aiming to be a full fledged hospital. Official opening on 2 Mar 2012 was inaugurated by Insp.(Retd) Bhakta Bahadur Pun (91 yrs.) one of the pioneer of Gurkha Contingent in 1949. It was very good to see him feeling proud of what came in front of him after so many years of the retirement.[42]

There are aspirations for the clinic to eventually be developed into a "full fledge hospital" given that the medical costs that other hospitals charge are about "30 to 40 percent" more than what Singapore Gurkha Polyclinic is charging, as Arjun indicated to me. He emphasized that "we are not looking for dividends," and "think maybe our clinic will be for many years" as a longer-term vision. In bracketing the Singapore-Gurkha and Singapore connection, Arjun underlined that investment into the clinic is "only for Gurkhas and also from Singapore. Only Singapore, not British Gurkhas." This example therefore illustrates the limits of belonging in terms of resource contributions (Mustassari, Maki-Petaja-Leinonen, and Griffiths, 2017) to the community, as well as recipients of such resources that are together bracketed. While it includes Gurkhas who have worked in Singapore, it concurrently excludes similar others who had served in the British Army.

Retired Gurkha soldiers traverse different routes in their respective postretirement milieus. Since the 1970s, Gurkha retirees have contributed to the economic life of Pokhara, such as retired Gurung soldiers in Tamu settlements for example. That said, however, the life of a retired soldier is also perceived as one that is of "enforced leisure" (Pettigrew 2000, 16), given limited opportunities for jobs coupled with the high cost of living. In extending from Pettigrew, my interlocutors in Pohkara have organized themselves in different ways after Gurkha active service. Through the auspices of the Annapurna Community, four "institutes" have been established since 2009.[43] These institutes represent efforts toward contributing to community building in Pokhara. They include (1) a cooperative (savings and credit) only for Gurkhas and their families (see figure 3.4); (2) a grocery shop that caters to the general public (see figure 3.5); (3) a Gurkhali Radio Station; and (4) a joint-venture jewelry shop. The chair of the community, Lagan, stated: "This

FIGURE 3.4. The Gurkhas Saving & Credit Cooperative Ltd, Pokhara.
Source: Photo by author, 2012.

FIGURE 3.5. Gurkha grocery store, Pokhara. Source: Photo by author, 2012.

[is] our country, [we] take the challenge, try to do something. . . . We are doing every bit to attract and unite our people . . . to highlight our people's activities. . . . We make our identity here [in Pokhara]. . . not only [as] brave fighters . . . we can prove that we have other ways to contribute to this country." Having served with the British Army for over twenty years, and having traveled to many places

including Brunei and Singapore, Lagan reasoned that instead of "keeping the West with me . . . [I'd] rather expose [Nepal] to all these kind of things." With an interest in harnessing the varied experiences that he had accumulated over the course of two decades of serving in the British Army, Lagan helped establish the four institutes as a way of fostering community bonds through self-help services. He also stated that beyond being Gurkhas, they would have "other ways to contribute to" Nepal, thereby indicating the need to transcend stereotypes of Gurkhas as "brave fighters." Active Gurkhas and retired servicemen may be shareholders of these institutes, regardless of whether they are or were working with the British Army or the SPF. Gurkhas serving in the United Kingdom, or residing in Kathmandu or in Singapore, whether they are in active service or otherwise, all contribute to these four organizations. This differs from the case of the Singapore Gurkha Polyclinic. Their transnational contributions indicate the diasporic outreach and inflow of financial assistance or investment into Nepal, or what Seddon et al. (2002, 34) might term as the "(unrecognised) remittance economy." This would also echo Yamanaka's (2000) contention that as a result of the tradition of British Gurkha army service (to which I add Gurkha Singapore Police service), a remittance economy in Nepal has been created in both rural and urban areas. Given that the Gurkhas are the first foreign economic migrants of Nepal, also known as *lahures* (soldiers who have traveled abroad; Kiruppalini 2013), Thapa (2021) calls them "harbingers of modernity" who have helped shape Nepal's modernity and development.

Interestingly, Lagan delineated four categories of Gurkhas who have retired from active service. The four types of retired servicemen are, in his words:

1. "I had enough . . . I have pension . . . and want to do nothing."
2. "They go for [a] second career." (Usually in the security industry.)
3. "They . . . enjoy drinking, playing cards, gambling . . . womanizing."
4. "[They get] involved with community and social work."

Lagan, together with ex-Gurkhas who form individual working committees of each of the four institutes, belongs to the fourth category of retired Gurkhas, or what Cassarino (2004, 270) would call "actors of change." Lagan explained why he decided to return to Nepal to settle down, despite a recent ruling in the United Kingdom which awarded ex-Gurkhas the right to remain in Britain:[44]

> Having served . . . so many years outside the country, where . . . I think every single person, wish to . . . die . . . do something for everyone. So, my . . . resettlement, right to remain in the UK, I prefer myself not to go because you already spent so many years outside of your country, serve for others, so I decided myself to do something for the community, for

the people, who need our help . . . . I learned something, I gained a lot of experience . . . so I decided to get involved in community, social service work.

Across the four institutes that have been established in the last few years, Lagan detailed the number of shareholders per institute, where he also mentioned the amount that each shareholder has to invest. For example, there are about 278 shareholders for the cooperative, and approximately 128 who have invested in the grocery shop, with amounts ranging between 25,000 and 500,000 Nepali rupees (approximately between US$201 and US$4,030). The minimum share for investing in the radio station, Lagan said, is 10,000 Nepali rupees (approximately US$80). Apart from disseminating local, regional, and international news, Gurkhali Radio 106 MHZ also broadcasts a weekly, one-hour program hosted by Lagan himself (figure 3.6). He interviewed ex-Gurkhas about their individual experiences of serving overseas. As for the jewelry shop (figure 3.7), he explained that Gurkha families would go there to purchase accessories for weddings and other special occasions, where they would receive a discount given their Gurkha background.

The four institutes that Lagan oversees represent a cultivated sense of belonging to Nepal or Pokhara as a way of contributing to the community. These institutes act as a platform for Lagan to articulate and further foster his belonging to Nepal, and specifically to Pokhara, by providing services and opportunities to fellow ex-Gurkhas. However, Lagan also pointed out that such contributions

FIGURE 3.6.   Gurkhali radio station, Pokhara. Source: Photo by author, 2012.

FIGURE 3.7. Gurkha and Barah Jewellery store, Pokhara. Source: Photo by author, 2012.

are bracketed only for Gurkhas and their families, and not non-Gurkha locals (in terms of investments). Comparatively, those who invest in the Kathmandu polyclinic need to be connected with Singapore, either as retired members of the GCSPF, or those who are currently in active service in Singapore. In this latter case, there is also bracketing occurring; not between Gurkhas and non-Gurkhas, and instead between Singapore- and non-Singapore Gurkhas.

With an intention to transcend the image of Gurkhas as brave and loyal (and not good at business), and therefore to demonstrate that they can make contributions to the country, Lagan is however of the opinion that locals cannot be trusted. He therefore managed the four institutes for the Gurkha community exclusively. This then raises an interesting point with regard to the issue of belonging that is constructed on the basis of community services. Belonging as performed after return migration means the reestablishment of boundaries when one is back in the homeland. While belonging seems to be a desirable intention after having served a foreign country for two decades or more, such belonging in Nepal concurrently produces exclusionary mechanisms through bracketing approaches. As we see in Lagan's case, exclusion of those not belonging to these Gurkha initiatives takes place as well. One might argue that, as return migrants, they have also changed in terms of the cultural and social frameworks that they have been exposed and subsequently subscribed to. This thereby leads to the bracketed distinction made between Gurkha migrants and nonmigrants, as well as Singapore-Gurkhas and non-Singapore Gurkhas in the context of Pokhara and Kathmandu respectively.

Diasporans who contribute to community building and who are away from Nepal is also a common phenomenon among Gurkhas living overseas as a form of diasporic engagement (Khanal 2013; Shivakoti 2019; Thomas, Smith, and Laurie, 2020; Van Hear 2015). Gopan, who is currently based in the United Kingdom after retiring from the British Army in 2006, had embarked on what he called the "ambulance project" in 2011–12. In his case, he had made arrangements to fly back to Nepal. He shared in greater detail:

> We had a makeup plan to do something for our work place in our motherland, back in Nepal. And our committee had a word, we had discussed, and what should we do, for better, for Nepal? And everybody can to an idea, saying why don't we buy two ambulance because where we born, it's a small area, like mountain and hill. I used to be, when I was in Nepal, when I joined the Gurkhas, I walked three days to come to town to join in the Gurkhas. You know, three days I walk. My heart, my mind, I mean my everything, I know I have my life here, but I dearly love my country, my village you know? Always I want to do something for my village and for my country. And this suddenly come, wow, and committee says let me to coordinator, to organizing this ambulance project . . . we managed to raise over 50 million rupees, Nepalese rupees. That's like 40,000, 45,000 pounds.

Gopan had earlier explained to me that he was the vice chairman of his district back home in Nepal. He was really very keen to do something for his "motherland," for his "dear beloved country Nepal." He continued:

> So this coming 24 February, I am flying back to Nepal not only meet my team. We already contact Nepali government, the red cross. And then we going back to, and then the ambulance already order in India because has to be come from there. And government also has to write the letter. Takes quite a process and we all done it now. So 24 February we all going back to Nepal, and then going to handing over two ambulance. One is other village and one is my village. So two ambulances we are going to handing over to Red Cross in Nepal.

Not only did Gopan spearhead this ambulance project in contributing to his fellow Nepalese back in Nepal, he is also active in community service in the United Kingdom. He is involved in aiding older ex-Gurkhas who may not be as proficient in English as himself. Part of his volunteer work consists of arranging medical support and resources for elderly Gurkha diasporans, as well as helping to resolve pension issues, among others.

Diasporic connections and ties between Nepal and other countries are also manifested through the provision of aid to the former vis-à-vis a variety of aid channels (Sharma and Harper 2017).[45] For example, Nepal was struck by massive earthquakes in April and May 2015.[46] On 25 April, an earthquake measuring 7.8 magnitude hit near Kathmandu. Out of the seventy-five districts of Nepal, thirty-one were affected and fourteen were declared as "crisis-hit" (Shivakoti 2019). Affected districts, including Gorkha, Dhading, and Lamjung, were areas that Singapore Gurkhas came from. These were locales where they had lost their homes and property caused by the earthquake.[47] Some of these Gurkhas were slated to fly to Nepal as part of a Home Team contingent sent by Singapore to assist with search and rescue efforts.[48] Moreover, humanitarian organizations in Singapore, including the Red Cross and Mercy Relief, had sent relief items, emergency supplies, and disaster response teams to Nepal, on top of appealing for donations to help the cause.[49] Former and present Gurkha children studying in Bartley Secondary School in Singapore also came together with the school to raise more than SGD$20,000 within a week. These funds were sent to Nepal through the Singapore Red Cross to contribute toward relief efforts.[50] The British Army had also responded by sending approximately three hundred Gurkha soldiers in all to Nepal to help with the relief effort. These Gurkhas had made their way to villages and more remote hill areas in order to support current Gurkhas, veterans, and their families, and to construct shelters, and repair infrastructure. Their deployment back home formed a "vital element of the international response" given the Gurkhas' "unique set of local knowledge, language skills and engineering experience."[51] Other Gurkha communities based in the United Kingdom including the British Gurkhas Community Winchester and Nepalese Community Winchester, worked together to raise funds for those in Nepal who have been affected.[52] A report carried by Forces TV, a UK-based television channel that brings news on the British Armed Forces, registered this message:

> For 200 years Nepal has given up the bravest of its young men to Britain—often in the knowledge that they may never return. Some 46,000 Nepalese soldiers having died fighting for the Crown and ultimately for the freedom of the people of the United Kingdom. Now it is time for us to fight for them. Members of the Nepalese and Gurkha community in the UK have been left feeling helpless as they watch endless scenes of their devastated Himalayan homeland. Desperate for information, many have been unable to contact loved ones, especially in the remote hill towns from where the British Army Gurkha Regiments draw their ranks. Nowhere is that growing sense of grief and frustration more keenly felt than in Aldershot. The garrison town is home to many of the 11,000 ex-Gurkhas and their families who have chosen to settle in the UK after completing their military service. There, in an

extremely close-knit community—the like of which can only be forged from men having fought in combat together—people are well-versed in pooling resources, sharing information and providing support. The British political establishment has been quick to respond with word and deed. Among them the Deputy Prime Minister Nick Clegg, who told Sky News "The Gurkhas have done so much for us, we now need to support them in their hour of anxiety and need."[53]

I highlight two key points concerning diasporic ties and belonging. Bracketed belonging has to do with a coexistence of both inclusionary and exclusionary practices that thread across diasporans dispersed in different places. Where inclusionary practices are concerned, these have to do with how Gurkhas and the wider Nepalese diasporic community are involved with diasporic engagement in relation to aid and other forms of humanitarian efforts as I have documented. These practices sustained transnational, affective ties vis-à-vis Nepal as a locale that bring these actors together in collective post-earthquake reconstruction efforts, as one example. In contrast, the rationale that underlies community-building efforts by returnee Gurkhas to Nepal point toward exclusionary mechanisms. In effect, such exclusionary bracketing distinguishes between Nepalese who are part of the Gurkha circuit as an in-group, and those who have not been associated with Gurkha service as an out-group. These dynamics reflect on barriers of or thresholds to belonging (Jones and Krzyzanowski 2011; Lems 2020) demarcated by these retired Gurkhas. As a result, probing into how and why bracketed belonging surfaces based on these contradistinctive practices of inclusion and exclusion thereby flesh out the complexities and geometries of belonging that is felt, parenthesized, and maintained. Different aspects of and approaches to belonging are contingent on the migrant trajectories of the Gurkhas and their present relationship with Nepal. The two examples of community efforts taking place in Kathmandu and Pokhara elucidate as well that migrants should not be taken as an internally consistent group (Jones and Krzyzanowski 2011) in relation to how they have approached bracketed belonging. This is also a point that I have earlier prefaced in the introductory chapter. Where diasporans may intersect in their varied engagements with Nepal, there are also segments of social division taking place between migrants and those who are nonmigrants in pursuits and practices of bracketed belonging.

On Citizenship and Home

While I have discussed ideas of homeland in chapter 1 and shown the differences in interpretations of where home is across Gurkhas and their children's generations, I extend the analysis to now include their varied views on citizenship and the issue of who belongs. This is important especially when citizenship rights or possession are intimately tied to where one feels a sense of belonging as home, including other practical considerations of education, work, living standards, and other accompanying factors. Reading meanings of citizenship through the lens of home, residency, and belonging is an approach that Gurkhas and their families have adopted. A large majority of my interlocutors have noted that while they might be comfortable in their present location of living in Hong Kong or the United Kingdom, the eventual plan would be to return home to Nepal. Several reasons account for this sentiment and how their sense of home is rooted in their bracketed belonging that is traced to Nepal. Ex-Gurkhas who have worked and lived in Hong Kong hold differing views in terms of how long they plan to stay in the country vis-à-vis their residency eligibility. Both Uttam and Lakshan mentioned to me over separate interviews that one is eligible to apply for a permanent identity card on working in Hong Kong for seven consecutive years. For Uttam, his daughter possesses Hong Kong citizenship as she was born there. In his own case, he had worked for four years after Gurkha service in a security company as his second career. After these four years, he decided to return back to Nepal where his wife was, instead of continuing for another three years before he would acquire residency eligibility. In Lakshan's case, he had fulfilled seven years of working in Hong Kong and thereby obtained the permanent ID. He told me that while some ex-Gurkhas who had embarked on their second career in Hong Kong subsequently moved to the United Kingdom (once the right to residency was permitted), he found "life [to be] easier" in Hong Kong. Ujesh agreed with Lakshan and further elaborated:

> And in Hong Kong case, a lot of our people like to stay here rather than going back to UK. Simple is because our relation [referring to family]. We are concerned the relationship here. Another thing the weather. Another thing the food. We would like it here. And very near to go back to Nepal, only four hours. If you fly from UK to Nepal it take seventeen hours. That is the reason people who already established in Hong Kong, they wish to stay here. I know many in Hong Kong, they go back to UK and they are still here. But I always say that, in general, people who are above sixty, they want to go back to Nepal.

For those above sixty, one of the reasons that prompt them to return to Nepal is because of their investments there, including property and other assets according to Lakshan. In Parijat's case, he called Nepal his "ancestral home"; he had chosen to return there from Hong Kong partly because of his farm which he references as his "ancestral property." Ostensibly, ancestral ties (Ho 2019; Timalsina 2019) in the forms of home and property constitute one pertinent reason among others for Parijat to return to Nepal. Some ex-Gurkhas among my pool of informants have also expressed to me that they would wish to stay on in Hong Kong further. During the time of our meetings, at least, they harbored no concrete plans to return to Nepal. Where Nishad preferred to remain in Hong Kong because his children are working there and he was deterred as well by political instability in Nepal, Shahid has lived in Hong Kong for sixteen years. Aside from finding ease of access to public transportation and food in Hong Kong, other reasons as to why Shahid prefers to remain there include full medical coverage given that he possessed the permanent identity card.

In my group interview with Vasava, Omkar, and Ishayu in the United Kingdom, all three of them have expressed their eventual plan to go back to Nepal:

> VASAVA: When the children is [themselves established, they] can stay there [referring to the UK]. So no need to stay we are here. Because that time, we are getting very old, we need to read and thinking only. If you stay here [UK], you need to come and work, come and work, go and work, and pay money everything. Everything, everything. . . . If you go back to our country [Nepal], we have our own home. We can have own land so we can . . . time pass in our garden. . . . And relax. . . . So I'm thinking like that. So that's why I'm not going to keep British passport. My Nepalese passport, I can only stay here, I can use the Nepalese passport no need to keep the British passport. The rest of my family have British, so if you are keep the British passport, our government . . . within five years, if you keep another country's passport, they have limited visit so I'm not going back to my country to be . . . my mother land.
>
> OMKAR: We have a British passport. I have a British passport. . . . Whole family. But I don't think we [referring to himself and his wife] are staying longer.
>
> ISHAYU: Because I'm proud to be a Nepalese even I get a British passport. That is my born, I mean heritage citizen . . .

For the three of them, the United Kingdom does not constitute their home. The United Kingdom is a place of work and thus "I don't need to call it home here," said Vasava. Ostensibly, most if not all of my respondents have shared that they will continue to stay on—either in Hong Kong or the United Kingdom—until their children have completed their education and would have become independent. In this manner, these Gurkhas have bracketed their sense of belonging in two ways. The first is that they are holding off their eventual return to Nepal owing to their children's age and educational pursuits. The second is that political uncertainties in Nepal in the early years of the 2000s also prompted them to delay their going back to Nepal. In the end, Nepal is motherland and homeland for these Gurkhas; however, they do not have any wish to install this sense of belonging on their children, leaving the latter the option to decide what they would desire or aspire toward.

That said, however, Gurkhas themselves would continue to educate their children with Nepalese customs and traditions by way of maintaining links to Nepal, not unlike how the military maintains Nepalese religious and festive celebrations while they are overseas as I have previously addressed. Similar to Arjun and Ram's varied efforts to inculcate the Nepalese language and practices among their children, which I discussed, Ishayu talked about his concern with keeping Nepalese customs alive for the children: "We are very cautious and we are very worried to keep our culture, customs to live. So we must teach our children. That's why we have lots of programs, like cultural programs. So that means we can teach them, what we did." Eknath was equally concerned that Gurkha children would be influenced by "British culture" and hence found it important to "teach them" with "our own traditional culture . . . so that they know what are our cultural values." Resulting from this emphasis on the importance of Nepali culture, it is plausible to suggest that Gurkha children thereby experience dual belonging (Kananen 2020) in a sense where they learn all things Nepalese while growing up and living elsewhere. Gurkhas ensured that their children remain connected to *their* homeland on the basis of conveying and sustaining these different aspects of Nepali culture outside of Nepal as transnational practices (cf. Bose 2021). Engaging with such cultural practices is akin to "'routinizing' Nepaliness in their everyday lives" (Bhandari 2017, 127) in bracketing senses of belonging across generations.[54] The difference between the children and their Gurkha parents is that where the former experienced Nepal vis-à-vis these practices and traditions as forms of cultural learning, the latter thought of their belonging to Nepal in territorial, geopolitical ways in addition to these cultural practices. For the children, what they experienced was usually a sense of being neither here nor there, as I explain in the next chapter. It is important to point these out given that they reflect on and reiterate the differentiated forms and degrees of how bracketed belonging ought to be comprehended—through interconnected practices, time, place, and territory that apply differently for each generation of diasporans. In this way, citizenship and belonging transcend formal status and rights. Rather, they crucially involve diasporans' "everyday practice[s] of engagement" that also highlight the emotional and pragmatic components (Muller and Belloni 2020, 4). These components that are regarded or felt differently by different members and generations of the diaspora would also reflect on diasporic incongruity in terms of the definitions of where and what "home" is.

Belonging across generations also has to do with practical considerations. Gurkha children who learn the Nepalese language and customs do not necessarily acquire proficiency in totality. This is one concern Fateh had when I asked what his postretirement plans involved: "You want to go back Nepal? Wah, they say your kids are study here. They are small, they don't speak Nepali. They're illiterate in Nepali but they can write, what's the point of taking them anymore. You're torturing them, you know, mentally. I said oh, I can't do that." When I met Fateh in the United Kingdom in 2011, he had just retired from Gurkha service about eighteen months earlier. His father served in the British Army at the rank of captain and retired twenty-eight years later. Fateh's two elder brothers were also Gurkhas, and he followed suit and enlisted in 1988. All three brothers were born in Singapore, and all subsequently joined the British Army. From recruitment in Pokhara, Fateh was posted to Hong Kong for recruit training over a period of nine months. After another deployment in Brunei that spanned five months, Fateh eventually came to the United Kingdom in 2000. Upon his retirement, Fateh opened a grocery store there. Given his residency status with the right to remain in the United Kingdom, Fateh was not, at that time of our meeting, concerned about applying for British citizenship.[55] For him, he looked at the United Kingdom very differently from his children:

> I wouldn't say I call it home now, for me. For kids, it's their home. They have their friends all these, schools. They are more . . . in everyday life, they are related here. Ours only the army and the friends we had. Now we finish our army career, we don't have any other friends, no civilian friends. . . . So for us it's difficult for us to say that this is my place, that we are going to serve in the army barracks and then we move on. . . . What about Hong Kong, what about Brunei? There are still our battalion there. What about Brunei? Do we call Brunei home? Do we call Hong Kong home? Or, Singapore I was born there, do I call Singapore my home? I don't know . . . it's a confusing time for all of us.

Contingent on an individual's military and/or police career trajectory, including where one's children were born and bred, the idea of "home" becomes one that is a fluid and contested notion. The notion also intertwines with the different life phases and social ties that one goes through and acquires over time. Together, these set of factors wield influence in how one approaches the shifting and parenthetical ideas of home, citizenship, and senses of belonging, contingent as well on temporality and the role of state and state policies on immigration and rights to abode, as I further elaborate in chapter 5.

The year 2015 marked two hundred years of Gurkha service with the British Army and long-standing bilateral relations between Nepal and the United Kingdom. Many events were held that year in celebration of this, including the installation of a Gurkha "memorial stone" in Riversley Park, Nuneaton, a Mount Everest climb and an Artic expedition at Ellesmere Island, and various regimental celebrations held in India and in Singapore, among many others.[56] These different forms of celebrations come with media reportage reminders of the Gurkhas' history and reputation as fierce fighters and loyal soldiers. Beyond the global reputation and image of the Gurkhas as brave warriors who were steadfastly loyal to the crown and who have been presented as fearless in public discourse, I presented different parts and aspects of their Gurkha career and beyond as migrants. The thematic lines of inquiry articulated herein are pertinent for a number of reasons. The first is to go beyond the popular and global image of the Gurkhas as martial warriors in the larger scheme of military contexts as well as the global security industry. This entails narrating and analyzing their varied experiences from the time that they were being recruited into the military and police forces, through their training and manifold postings across different parts of the world; to how they cope with family life; and their hopes, fears, and aspirations both while in Gurkha service and during the period after which they retire or go into a second career. Seldom have these relational domains of their experiences been comprehensively attended to in the wider literature as I have previously iterated and therefore become an exigent endeavor here in this book.

The second reason pertains to how their individual experiences captured here stand as important foil and counterpoints to the image of their bravery and masculinity contextualized within military environments over more than two hundred years and which I have addressed in the previous chapter. Over and above popular depictions of their varied military conquests, loyalty, and stalwart service, Gurkhas were also confronted with many instances in which they feared for their lives, or missed their families given protracted periods of time away from home and their loved ones. By attending to the above aspects vis-à-vis migration scholarship and other cognate domains of interest, I worked through these migratory experiences and phases of Gurkhas as migrant warriors, including how they approached senses of belonging based on shifting contexts of service, postings, and their postretirement milieu. Their diasporic narratives also characterize how bracketed belonging, from their perspective, is reasoned, planned, negotiated vis-à-vis residency/citizenship aspirations managed alongside the future education and prospects of their children. Where Gurkhas who have retired articulated their "homing desire" with aspirations for "eventual return" (Sinha 2022, 90) to Nepal in their conversations with me, "home" appears to be elsewhere for their children, including some of their wives.

As different generational members of the Gurkha diaspora who are associated with variegated roots and routes, Gurkhas and their wives and children comprehend and experience working and living overseas in differentiated manners. In a way, the Gurkhas made a conscious decision to join the army or police force and to leave Nepal (cf. Bhandari 2017). In contrast, their wives and children are away from Nepal owing to other circumstances of their respective marital ties, birth place, and social contexts of growing up, schooling, and work. While I employ the label of "Gurkha diaspora" as an umbrella conceptual placeholder that is to be differentiated from South Asian diasporas as discussed, I am not however subscribing to a singular Gurkha diaspora per se. This is because diasporan members' lives and migratory routes are clearly much more heterogeneous than homogeneous, determined as well by institutional frameworks.

Given the contrastive backgrounds of Gurkhas, their wives, and children that underlie the mobile and transnational aspects of Gurkha family lives, it should not come as a surprise that belonging is differentially experienced and orchestrated based on their manifold migratory trajectories as this and the next chapter illustrate. The act of bracketing belonging therefore continues to be malleable, negotiated, and shifting over time, and which intersect with individual, familial, and structural possibilities and/or constraints. Just as notions and practices of citizenship and home are complex and nuanced, then so too would variegated ideas and experiences of belonging transpire within the same nexus of Gurkha recruitment, marital relations, and family building in both historical and contemporary milieus. I have examined the lived experiences of Gurkhas since the time of their enlistment up to retirement years; next I address the experiences of Gurkha wives and children.

GURKHA WIVES AND CHILDREN

Characterizations of Gurkha wives and children reflect on their early days of having migrated to Singapore with their Gurkha police husbands or fathers. Two media reports from Singapore described the arrival and presence of thirty-seven Gurkha families living in the GCSPF camp in 1950, a year after the contingent was formed:

> Gurkha women are slavishly obedient. They stay in their little homes, and devote all their time and their attention to their husbands and their children. Brought up in the good old-fashioned Eastern tradition, these women who have all come out to Singapore from Nepal, are seldom seen in town. . . . Most of these women have been in Singapore for nearly a year, and slowly, very slowly they are adapting their costume to our tropical climate. It takes them some time to change, for they are very conservative and they cling to old customs and usages.[1]

> Very, very shy and very primitive were the first Gurkha women and children who came to Singapore two years ago. They refused to see the doctor or have any medical attention. In their homes in Nepal, babies were rubbed with oil, not washed with soap and water, and when they arrived in Singapore their filth and odour was indescribable. . . . Gurkha women love cards. They are terrific card players and they also play car-ron [sic] board games. Sometimes they accompany their husbands to watch football and boxing.[2]

It is clear that they have been highlighted as having migrated from a very different place than Singapore, where they have followed their husbands and in which they have devoted their attention to family life.[3] These characterizations of their migratory pathway are also accompanied by further stereotypical constructions conveyed vis-à-vis hygiene and leisure matters. Yet we see a contrastive narrative in other ways through which these women are talked about as related by British officers: "Gurkha women . . . enjoy a freedom unusual in the East and are well able to stand up for themselves. They smoke and drink only slightly less than their menfolk, and are very outspoken" (Leonard 1965, 48).

Given these dissimilar depictions of Gurkha wives or women, I consider their biographical narratives and how they navigated their lives vis-à-vis regimental contexts along with their soldier/police husbands and children.[4] While I have previously discussed some aspects of Gurkha children's lives and experiences (including narratives from Muna, Sirish, Ganga, Riju, and others), I interrogate further the various forms and sentiments of belonging and not-belonging that Gurkha wives and children experience as they live their lives as military and police families in different countries. The transnational nature of Gurkha security work leads inevitably to the expansion of policing space where national police and security forces have become denationalized. Such denationalization also impacts regimental-family lives within and across national borders. In Hong Kong, the first generation of South Asian women—especially Nepalese—were those who had arrived there following their Gurkha husbands. The second generation included daughters of these transnational marriages, and the third generation comprised younger females born in Hong Kong and who have been seeking education and work there (Tam 2010; Yuen 2020). The children of Gurkha soldiers who were born in Hong Kong before 1983 were permitted permanent residence. According to Constable (2014), many of the Gurkha children had returned to Nepal together with their mothers. They only traveled back to Hong Kong when they were young adults.[5]

In Singapore, it is estimated that there are about two thousand Gurkhas serving in the Singapore Police Force (Chong 2014). Upon the retirement of their Gurkha fathers (usually in their forties), the children have to cease their education in Singapore and return to Nepal as I have earlier indicated. By comparison, Gurkhas and their children are able to remain in Hong Kong and the United Kingdom, unlike those who had lived and schooled in Singapore owing to the completion of their Gurkha father's police service. As Gauri lamented to me in comparing her own situation with other bhanja/bhanji:

> But I think what makes us more frustrated is, that UK bhanja bhan-
> jis they can actually go there and settle down there [in the United

Kingdom], and then we have to . . . come back here [to Nepal]. That's
what frustrates us more. Because when our dad, they get repatriated
right, it's [repatriated] together [as a family].

They are also not permitted to apply for Singapore citizenship (Kiruppalini
2016). For Gurkha retirees and their families in the United Kingdom, the 2004
UK Parliament came to a decision to grant residency to them. This decision consequently saw the highest numbers of arrivals that spanned between 2005 and
2007, where the largest Nepali communities in the United Kingdom settle in
Ashford, Kent, Plumstead (East London), and the Farnborough-Aldershot area
(Pariyar, Shrestha, and Gellner 2014).

What was life like for Gurkha wives as they married these servicemen and left
their birth country in the role of camp followers and more? How did they cope
with regimental-family lives in Singapore, Hong Kong, or the United Kingdom?[6]
Adishree, who is married to Ram whom I introduced earlier in the book, talked
about life as a Gurkha wife in the absence of her husband. This was when he was
deployed to Bosnia. Communication channels at that time were inconvenient if
not scarce:

> So all the wives were actually in the same situation so we get together
> sometimes with friends, like other Gurkha's wives . . . and then that
> wasn't . . . after a couple of years Ram went to Bosnia and that was quite
> hard and that was worrying because he went to Bosnia that was quite
> dangerous situation there, so we didn't have telephones, individual that
> time, mobile phone wasn't. . . . I don't think people were using mobile
> phone in Nepal. We just heard you can have mobile phone but we didn't
> have individual, own telephone. We used to have one telephone in . . .
> it was like a public telephone, not so telephone booth. (Interview with
> Adishree)

Over the course of my several meetups with Adishree and her family in the
United Kingdom, she shared different experiences and struggles in relating her
life as a regimental wife, as she raised three daughters together with Ram. By
engaging closely with experiences such as those of Adishree and others, I query
how belonging is depicted, the bracketed forms it takes, as well as the debates and
discourses surrounding the politics of belonging. Although I foreground Gurkha
wives and children as the main social actors, I concurrently intersperse my discussion with perspectives of ex-Gurkhas who also shed light on their kin's lives
abroad and in Nepal. I do so given that belonging is relational and intertwined
with the family as well. Therefore, I demonstrate how belonging and the various forms of bracketing as well as not-belonging are braided across individuals

and families in relation to wider state policies of immigration regulations among other things. In attempting to account for discernible shifts that have arisen through my analyses of interview material, my approach to and assessment of the notion of belonging points toward its fluidity. This analysis thereby extends conceptions of belonging as an ongoing, multidimensional process rather than as an unchanging, discrete status (Mee and Wright 2009; Pfaff-Czarnecka 2011; Schein 2009; Teerling 2011; Teo 2011).

How do Gurkha families negotiate transnational interfaces (Long and Long 1992) in terms of their migrant experiences of work, education, belonging, and notions of "home" across different countries? How are they positioned with regard to citizenship, belonging, rights, and privileges (Kabeer 2005; Kivisto, and Faist 2007)? What does having to curtail one's schooling years mean in terms of attachment to place, social ties that have been established, and the process of returning "home" to Nepal which at times feels more foreign? By exiting Singapore or Hong Kong contrary to their choice, how do the children adapt to life in Nepal? What are the available opportunities for education and employment as they undergo various sociocultural adjustments (Conway and Potter 2009; Gautam 2013)? What factors influence how Gurkha diasporans choose between living and working in Hong Kong or Nepal? These adjustments and how they transpire illuminate the different meanings and attachments that conjoin belonging and the notion of "home" for Gurkha families across the United Kingdom, Hong Kong, Singapore, and Nepal.

To illustrate what "home" entails, I raise the example of Sejun whom I met in London in 2013. Born in Malaysia, and having grown up and schooled in Hong Kong, Sejun has subsequently lived in London since 1986. Both his grandfather and father were Gurkhas. He shared with me that while he grew up with the concept of "being Nepali," he hardly had any reference point to Nepal as home except for his familiarity with Nepalese rituals and festivals. Therefore, Sejun had grown up feeling "alien" in both contexts of Nepal and the United Kingdom—a case of feeling neither here nor there—since he did not necessarily know what being Nepali meant. When he went back to his family village in Nepal at age fifteen, he felt out of place at first. This was because he did not "know how to live in a village," though he gradually learned the language and customs. In his words: "I kinda learnt what it means to be a [his family name] living in a village." Sejun had also developed close relationships with his grandparents and other relatives in the process. What remained etched in his memory of his grandfather was something that the latter had said to the former, and in English. His grandfather seldom spoke in English, and therefore this was poignant for Sejun. His grandfather had told him: "Don't forget, this [referring to Nepal] is your home." Sejun articulated his response to his grandfather's words: "I've never thought of being someone who had a home . . . concept of home . . . my village, our land . . . [I would] always be welcomed, [they] accepted me as I was even if I was very different." When I queried further as to why he felt this way, Sejun elaborated: "I envied people who talked about their home, hometown. . . . As a teenager, I reconciled with the idea that I didn't have a hometown . . . until when I lived in the village; it was a reckoning [moment that] hey I have a hometown! [So] that was a significant period in my life, my young life."

As our interview progressed, Sejun mentioned that for a long time, he was hesitant to apply for British citizenship for fear of losing his "sense of identity." That said, however, he has found "Britain [to be] the least race-conscious place in the world; but Nepali people can even be racist to their own caste." Identifying himself as a British-Nepali, Sejun noted: "My social circle is not predicated on me being Nepali; maybe that means I am assimilated"? He then went on to say: "I don't feel like a second-class citizen . . . I grew up with European people, I didn't find them to be any better than others." This is in contrast to his mother's perspective, on behalf of whom he echoed: "I'd rather live like a first-class citizen in my country (referring to Nepal), than a second-class citizen in other people's country."

Sejun's brief biography and narrative that I have presented here raise and reiterate my contention on shifting or modified senses of palpable belonging (Hausner 2014). His shifting experiences also reflect intergenerational differences. These have to do with how diasporans approach ideas of home and sentiments of belonging, both of which differ from that of his mother. Sejun was at first unsure of his identity and the notion of home vis-à-vis Nepal. However, the village experience, coupled with what his grandfather had said to him as key "turning points" (Berg 2011), steered him in a different direction where belonging for him was concerned. Through experiencing such idioms of belonging that include kin ties, village life, language, and customs, Sejun later also encouraged his brothers and sisters to pay a visit to Nepal. He himself would make it a point to visit and tidy his grandparents' graves whenever he was back in Nepal. Over time, Sejun had felt and become more connected to his Nepali identity both in Britain and Nepal. His idea and feeling of belonging traverse between these two countries in a transnational and bracketed manner. In contrast, his mother thought otherwise in terms of where she felt she belonged. For her, it was very clear that Nepal was and is home so she could "live like a first-class citizen" as Sejun pointed out. Sejun and his family's take on home, citizenship, and belonging ostensibly illustrate Christou's (2009) discussion revolving around the polyvalent layers of "home" and belonging:

> Home is as much fluid as it is rigid, it is flexible and complex. It seeks to ground and localise, but it is also an integral part of a world of movement,

it is relative and contested, a site of ambivalence and a source of anxiety. Home as a concept that raises issues of belongingness can become complicated and difficult to deconstruct and even to contextualise and situate. It may trigger memories, trauma, indifference and evoke struggles over selfhood and nationhood. (Christou 2009, 112)

How do different members of Gurkha families relate to Nepal, Singapore, the United Kingdom, or Hong Kong as home? How do they talk about and rationalize where home is and how belonging is experienced or not? How are such experiences based on having grown up in different environments owing to their fathers' military and police service for foreign countries?

In engaging closely with the above queries, I first discuss life as a Gurkha wife and mother. I examine narratives of these women who married Gurkha servicemen (cf. Des Chene 1998; Tam 2010) and who looked after the children in the absence of their Gurkha spouse. One such narrative is that of Lila Seling Mabo (2022), the oldest of seven children who married a Gurkha soldier and gave birth to a girl in Brunei, and two more children—a girl and a boy—in the United Kingdom. She writes in her memoir:

> I moved to the UK in 2000 due to my husband Shree Mab's career in the British Army (part of the Gurkhas). I have travelled all over the world with him. . . . When I arrived in the UK, I had to start from scratch. I couldn't use any of my education, my qualifications, or my own language. My husband used to leave me regularly on my own with small children and no one to communicate with or any family support. It was very hard. At the time, those were the worst days of my life. Although I had to face many obstacles being an army [Gurkha] wife, I was determined to work hard to carry on my studies and volunteering whilst looking after the children and the house. (Mabo 2022, v)

Building on these experiences such as those of Lila's, I then deliberate on notions of belonging and not-belonging. These notions are particularly helpful for framing narratives of ex-Gurkhas and their family members who have returned to Kathmandu and Pokhara to settle down after working for the Singapore Police Force (SPF) for at least fifteen years or more, in comparison with Gurkha families based in the United Kingdom or Hong Kong. Although I present discussions on belonging and not-belonging separately, I emphasize that these remain contiguous. Presenting them separately accords empirical clarity but should not eclipse my larger point that these are overlapping and approached and felt concurrently, as earlier iterated. This is followed by my analysis of the politics of belonging in relation to organizational efforts put forward by two groups in Pokhara, namely the Everest Association and the Annapurna Community that

I mentioned previously. I conclude by reflecting on how belonging and the politics of belonging, in the case of Gurkha families, demonstrate on the one hand that Gurkha labor recruitment and migration are intertwined with emotive and affective experience. On the other hand, one also needs to take into view structural issues revolving around legal rights to citizenship and residence.

As a Wife and Mother: Married to a Gurkha

The history and account of Gurkha wives and families is one that is sparse if not fragmented in the wider scholarship and popular writings on Gurkha military history (see, for example, Cross and Gurung 2002; Farwell 1984; Gurung 2018; Seddon 2022; Sharma et al. 2022).[7] In Farwell's (1984, 150) words:

> When the young men joined the army they were exposed to a world of new experiences, but to adapt they had only to do as they were told; the army took care of them. Life was more uncertain and held more difficulties for the young brides coming down from the hills of Nepal to be part of their husbands' lives. How did they feel and how did they react? We don't know. No Nepalese woman has ever written about her life as an army bride.

Seddon (2022), whose study revolves around Nepali women who traveled abroad since the time of Gurkha recruitment, goes a step further than Farwell (1984). Using such terms as "camp brides" or "camp followers" in his brief mentions of Gurkha wives, Seddon (2022) notes that such accounts remain "largely untold and unknown" (2022, viii). Prior to the Second World War, there has been "virtually no record of" the experiences of Nepali men as well as women (2022, 114–15). The memoir of Lila Seling Mabo (2022) that I introduced above is probably the first one written by someone who is married to a Gurkha.

Seddon (2022) provides a brief historical backdrop to the positioning of Nepali women vis-à-vis broader military histories connected to Gurkha service in India and other locations. Life for Gurkha wives was always about hard work and struggle, be it remaining back at home to ensure and look after the well-being of family and the household while the men were employed overseas, or when they themselves accompanied their husbands and/or migrated abroad to both live and work. For example, Gurkha husbands who were employed in the military police or army saw increasing numbers of Limbu and Rai women accompany them to such places as Darjeeling. While they set up "house" over there, some of these women either worked as domestic servants or as porters.

Prior to these family settlements for Gurkha soldiers, the government of India had earlier refused an 1856 request from the Sirmoor Battalion to convert some erstwhile barracks at Dehra Dun into homes for these soldiers' families (Farwell 1984). Gradually this attitude changed, and it was thought to be desirable for these men to have their wives and children with them rather than to be far away in the Nepali highlands. Finally in 1864, each of the first four Gurkha regiments of India (Dharmasala, Dehra Dun, Almora, and Bakloh) obtained permission to set up family quarters. This move marked the beginning of official Gurkha settlements abroad (Seddon 2022). That said, however, there was never sufficient quarters to accommodate families of all married Gurkhas. In some cases, some of the Gurkha soldiers had to wait as long as a decade before their families were able to join them (Farwell 1984). Besides, having regimental homes did not necessarily translate into "undisturbed family life, even for those fortunate enough to have their wives and children with them" (Farwell 1984, 146). This was because men who were in active Gurkha service were for the most part away for long periods of time, ranging from months to even years.

Eknath shared with me the problems of family quarters that were associated with Gurkha families in Hong Kong where he was. Although such quarters have been made available to servicemen who are married, Eknath pointed out that "if you have only one child, one bedroom. . . . One child, one bedroom, no carpet, no air condition." That was the situation he encountered with his wife and child. This was in stark contrast with British servicemen who were allocated much better quarters, whereby "British people, regardless of number of families, numbers of kids . . . They [were provided with a] terrace house. The carpet, if you . . . the rotten carpets [that we had] will be replaced by, not new, by the carpet that was thrown away from the British main quarters." Apart from living together in such quarters wherever possible, there were other measures put in place in order to facilitate visitations and communication between Gurkhas and their wives. From 1885, for example, railway warrants were provided to wives who wished to visit their Gurkha husbands in their stations in India (Seddon 2022; Vansittart 1993). Besides India, Gurkha families were also established in Burma and Thailand since the 1940s. Gurkhas who had retired from service were granted Burmese citizenship when Burma obtained independence in 1948. Many of these ex-Gurkhas brought their wives and families to live with them there. In Thailand, a Nepali settlement emerged in the village of Pilok, which is situated near the border town of Kanchanaburi and along the Burmese border. Most of these Nepali families in Pilok were former Gurkhas who had previously served in Burma with the British Army. After the end of World War II in 1945, these Gurkha families settled in Pilok and worked in tin mines (Seddon 2022).

Seddon (2022) characterizes Gurkha wives as those who "keep the home fires burning," where they were always anxiously waiting for news from "the front." They would cling onto hopes that their military husbands would eventually make their way home with no serious injuries or wounds. Rashid (2020) studies how the military as an institution is affectively linked to families and modern society in Pakistan (see also, Chisholm 2022). Soldiers and families, Rashid argues, form "subjects of militarism who stand at the center of war" (2020, 5). Where "masculine men protect the nation and the women," the women in turn "serve the nation by not only producing these soldiers but exalting and praising the men who die in wars to protect the nation" (2020, 7–8). Rashid's gender positioning of men and women in the context of militarism (cf. Enloe 2014) connects to my work on how Gurkha men and women have to organize their lives in terms of military work/sacrifice and gendered division of labor (via family responsibilities among other things). Echoing Seddon (2022), Aadesh similarly pointed out to me the history of the world wars and how wives of Gurkhas had to confront the uncertainties of war:

> And let's say the saddest part is more over here. Let's say those who join in Second World War and First World War are . . . mostly sixteen to nineteen and they all are married; we have statistics. They are all married. So in these two World War, more than 40,000, 50,000 died. I think most of them were married. So what happened to their wife? Back to the home. Because they don't even know where their husband is. And they, they didn't get any information, whether they're alive or whether they're died, you know. Even till now they don't know anything. That is very saddest part of history.[8]

Lila speaks of similar uncertainties when her husband, Shree, was deployed to Iraq. That was in 2003 when she learned of the news that a missile was dropped in Iraq. She was then "constantly checking to see if [her] husband's name was listed as one of the men who had tragically died." Since Shree left the barracks a fortnight ago, Lila had no contact with him and felt it was "an agonising time waiting to find out if he was OK" (Mabo 2022, 7). Clearly, women fear for the men's safety especially during times of war, which thereby influenced how they perceived soldiering (see Des Chene 1991, 253). The agony of waiting and having to deal with unsettling uncertainty as a Gurkha spouse, daughter, or mother is similarly expressed through the following poem written by Anju Anjali (2013, 7–8). I quote in excerpts, this poem titled "Soldiers, War and My Question":

> No sooner you left for the war
> Another war has germinated inside me
> It's war—
> Of your memories
> Of your affection
> Of your whereabouts
> . . . .

Will you ever return from the war all right?
Or losing some body parts,
You will return with medals on chest
Of the wounds of bravery
. . . .

I am a spouse of a brave soldier
I am a daughter of a brave soldier
I am a mother of a brave soldier
I am proud of being referred so
I take pride in this identity

Anjali's worries clearly demonstrate not only the gaping absence of a Gurkha who has left behind his female kin (in their different familial roles), but also contain myriad uncertainties. They include those relating to possible injury, death, yet also triumph—indicated through one's return, and with medals in recognition of bravery.

Kamadev told me how Gurkha wives, residing in the military family quarters while their husbands were deployed across different parts of the world, were "always thinking about the husband," as "we are always running everywhere." Aside from some cases of adultery (Farwell 1984; Seddon 2022), most wives were "faithful and were prepared to immerse themselves in domestic and farm work, bearing the double burden of their menfolk's absence" (Seddon 2022, 185). Keeping home fires burning as Seddon (2022) indicates was also a recurrent responsibility that Gurkhas and their wives have shared with me, though there certainly are exceptions as well. In Kumud's words: "Only the husband [works]. The wife is stay at home [sic]." The gender division of labor between Gurkhas and their wives is similarly pointed out by Chisholm and Stachowitsch (2017, 380–81) who note:

> In most cases, women stay behind and take on subsistence, domestic and agricultural labour. They are an integral part in the decision to migrate and enable male migration by taking over responsibility for family finances and businesses. The gendered relations imbued in the cultural and legal fabric of Nepal further renders the Gurkha wives in the position of supportive labourers at home. Gendered migration patterns are solidified by legal restrictions and social stigma to women's independent migration. Hence, the private security industry depends on gendered power relations and reinforces patriarchal values in their recruitment sites.

Militarism produces masculine subjectivities that are distanced and differentiated from women subjects. Rashid (2020) makes a case for how the manufacturing of the soldier-subject requires constructions of hardiness, valiance, and discipline (cf. MacLeish 2012). These imply that there is a need to establish "distance from former objects of affection and ways of living" (Rashid 2020, 14), which include women and familial attachments perceived as feminine and thereby as "threats to the soldier's ability to stay in service" (Rashid 2020). Similarly, Gurkha soldiers are separated from their wives and families in their initial three years of service (although such rules have been changed), and where military rules have been enforced to provide family barracks for particular ranks in the army, among other regulations and disciplinary mechanisms. Broadly speaking, then, men and women occupy differentiated "subject position" in contexts of militarism and war (Rashid 2020, 14), which is also resonant in my case. Dhanvi married Tufan in 1973, five years after he enlisted into Gurkha service. Their son was born in Nepal while their daughter was born in Hong Kong. They have two grandsons who at the time of my interview in 2014 were two and four years old. As both their son and daughter spoke only Chinese, Dhanvi and Tufan made it a point to practice Nepali with them. They do the same for their grandchildren, who began speaking in English and cannot speak Nepali. Apart from ensuring that their offsprings and the next generation are able to speak their native language, there are also plans to eventually retire in Nepal. When Tufan resumed Gurkha service after the wedding, Dhanvi bought land and built a house using the money that Tufan had remitted home. The spousal partnership that Dhanvi and Tufan share demonstrates that not only did Dhanvi look after the children and her in-laws when Tufan was earlier away from home due to his military service, she also took it on herself to oversee the building of a family house for them during Tufan's absence from Nepal. The responsibilities that Dhanvi undertook may be conceived as a form of "affective labor" (Chisholm 2022, 43) whereby Gurkha wives would honor and valorize the security work that their spouses engage in by looking after the reproductive work (see also, Des Chene 1991, 253) accomplished at home when the Gurkhas were absent. While Dhanvi shared that it was not easy to manage the construction process of the house, it was something she had to do since her Gurkha husband was away for prolonged periods of time to serve in the British Army. His lengthy absence took place in exchange with him being able to send money home to make this construction possible.

Binsa's experience is another example that illustrates the independence of some other Gurkha wives. Uttam, her Gurkha husband, was posted to the United Kingdom in 1989. Given that he was holding the rank of sergeant at that time, he was not allowed to bring his family with him to live in the regimental barracks. From the United Kingdom, Uttam next went on to Hong Kong, where Binsa visited and stayed with him for two weeks before returning to Nepal. She then established a travel agency in Kathmandu with the help of her brother. It was a difficult task for Binsa to set up this business where there was only a runner and her brother looking after the office, though the latter was usually more involved in other businesses. She had basically handled everything on her own. The agency has since expanded to three offices when I last visited Uttam and Binsa in Kathmandu.

In Adishree's case, her first daughter, Mridu was born in 1995 when Ram was away in Bosnia. She said that although Ram was absent from family life with their newborn, she was fortunate to have had the help of her parents and in-laws in his place in sharing "all the hard times." Adishree made a joke of Ram's responsibility to bring the dough home while her "responsibility was more of children, educate them, look after them," thereby indicating a clear division of gendered labor between them. Ostensibly, there would have been no other way given the transnational scheme of Gurkha work. Over the course of Ram's Gurkha service, the first time where Adishree was able to join him in the family barracks was in 2000:

> I applied and I got three months visa and I left Mridu and Chaha back at home with my mum. Then I came to see him, visited him and he requested for leave and we went back to Nepal together. And he got six months leave and then we stayed six months, six months . . . after that . . . we had family permission from MOD (Ministry of Defence, United Kingdom) and then I came in 2001 February to stay for a couple of years then all the circumstances changed. From MOD so we were about to stay here otherwise I had to go back to Nepal after two and a half years.

That was the maximum duration of time that Adishree was granted to stay with Ram while he was in active service, depending on the husband's rank in the army. Two years and six months was all that a wife was allowed to accompany her husband. However, if her "husband was a colonel sergeant, staff sergeant, then you can stay forever with husband." Adishree had found this rule to be challenging since having a "junior rank husband" translated into the latter not having the chance to "spend time with children or being with family."

The examples of Gurkha couples such as Dhanvi and Tufan, and Adishree and Ram, among other pairs whom I have met and interacted with, reflect varied experiences and practices of gender responsibilities and positioning. The women manage household responsibilities and young family members with their absent husbands out of the picture. Even if wives are seldom regarded as active agents and stakeholders in the context of the broader circulation of global labor (Chisholm 2022), they are no doubt instrumental in facilitating the security work that their Gurkha partners do across different security regimes, locales, and temporalities. The various spheres of work and responsibility that Gurkha wives undertake also contrast with the stereotypical characterizations raised above. As a foil to Gurkha wives who have been depicted as shy and subservient, my encounters with these couples generally align more with Farwell's (1984) observation—where Gurkha men are "generally considered to be kind and affectionate husbands," their "wives were by no means subservient to them" and are indeed "more companionable, more on an equal footing" (1984, 147). Similarly, Forbes (1964) considers Gurkha soldiers to be affectionate and thoughtful husbands and who would carry out their fair share of household chores. Farwell (1984) further notes that Gurkha women were intelligent and bright, and also wielded the gift of repartee and sense of humor that were similar to the men.

As for the gender positioning of the next generation that is Gurkha children, my respondents hold different views on the division of labor and gendered relations. I first met Malashree and Gauri, both returning daughters of SPF Gurkhas, in Kathmandu. I recounted to them one of my fieldwork visits to the United Kingdom where I was invited to a party gathering of a few Gurkha families. Near the end of this gathering, I offered to help with clearing the dishes to bring them into the kitchen. I was told by some of my Gurkha respondents to "let the women do it." Upon hearing this, Gauri explained: "It's more of under the Hinduism culture, that the husband they are the sole bread winner of the house so the wives they would take care of the household." When I probed the both of them further as to whether they would follow suit and "take care of the household," Malashree and Gauri immediately echoed a resounding "No!" in unison before breaking out into laughter. Malashree stated clearly: "No way! Because we are Singaporeans . . . self-service." She further explained: "And we also, because we are educated, we are not like our mothers. So we want our own rights, and own choice to make. So we don't really adhere to society's culture." What is interesting about Malashree's response is this—not only did her statement reflect intergenerational difference where the children are educated as compared to their mothers, she has also imbibed the practice of "self-service" from her time spent in Singapore ("we are Singaporeans") that thereby influence how she now views gender relations. Her position pivots more toward partible standing rather than subscribing to patriarchal practices where women are expected to manage the household.

Experiences of absent Gurkha fathers for regimental families typically reflect how a familial household often is split across two countries. When Ram was not with his family, his eldest daughter, Mridu, was about one to two years old. In response to my query as to how her childhood was like without her father being around, Mridu responded that albeit too young to comprehend the context at the beginning, she gradually began to realize as she grew up that she was starting to miss her parents over the course of their continual absence. Mridu had found it particularly difficult when her mother first traveled to England in 2000. While Adishree's first trip to meet Ram spanned only a few months, Mridu felt it tougher when Adishree's second trip took place over more than a year. Mridu and her sister, Chaha, were left in the care of their aunt. At the time of the second trip, Mridu had turned nine. She recollected that "not having both parents" around was "the hardest thing." Adishree pointed out to me that Mridu and Chaha were in the good hands of their aunt and her family who were very caring toward her girls. She further explained as to why Ram and herself had made the decision to leave them behind in Nepal while they were both in the United Kingdom. This decision was borne out of them prioritizing their daughters' education. Adishree elaborated that they did not want to bring their daughters to the United Kingdom for a couple of years, only to take them out of the school system there and to then place them back into the Nepali curriculum. If they had done so, the arrangement would have been disruptive and would result in "a mess for their education" as she rationalized.

Mridu and Chaha were both born in Nepal. Ram had not been able to be around to witness their birth owing to his Gurkha service abroad. They were eleven and nine respectively when they left Nepal for the United Kingdom. Their third sister, Sumira was born in the United Kingdom. Given that Adishree and Ram's first two daughters had left Nepal for the United Kingdom at fairly young ages, they did not miss life in Nepal as much as that compared to their parents. Mridu acknowledged that part of the "downside of moving away [to the United Kingdom] at a small age [sic]" was that she did not get the opportunity to grow close to her cousins compared to those who had not left Nepal. Even if her cousins were "warm and welcoming" whenever she traveled to Nepal, Mridu revealed that they did not share a close relationship. Furthermore, Mridu explained to me that she felt "a little bit distant" from her grandparents, though this would be different for her parents. This was because they have grown up "in a sort of society where it's not just your mum and dad or your siblings, it's about everyone else," she reasoned. For Mridu then, while she found that "it will be nice to see them more often," she regarded these distant ties with her grandparents as constituting "not a big hole" in her life. The experiences of both Mridu and Adishree moving away from Nepal to United Kingdom represent not only intergenerational differences in terms of what it means to migrate as a daughter or a wife of a Gurkha. Rather, their individual experiences also point toward how social actors as migrants, contingent on their biographies and age of outward migration, relate to their nuclear and extended families in contrastive ways. As Mridu further elaborated:

> I guess it's also because they [referring to her parents' generation] have loads of cousins, they have family all around them and so they miss the family that they don't have whereas we don't have anything like that so

we just don't think about it. We just think, "Oh, my mum's here, my dad's here, my sisters are here," that's all I need. I don't need another cousin and another uncle.

These cross-generational differences that Mridu has pointed out thereby convey how belonging takes on varied significance based on one's familial circle and the degree to which these familial ties—ranging from the nuclear to the extended—are either intimately or distantly experienced.

Adishree shared with me that moving to the United Kingdom meant adjusting to a new life: "I used to remember and my friends away from me, but when I am here [in the United Kingdom], it is a different environment and you are all the time busy, so you don't have much time to think about everybody else." In adapting to a new environment, Adishree found that family members whom she had left behind in Nepal seldom occupied her thoughts as her life was now in the United Kingdom with her own set of priorities to manage. When asked if it was the norm that Gurkha couples would plan to stay abroad until their children completed their education and secured employment (before husband and wife would return to Nepal), both Adishree and Ram's response indicated that they were not entirely sure about this. They had harbored mixed feelings. While Ram said that "it's a long way to go," and he was not sure if indeed they'll retire in Nepal, Adishree's perspective on the matter reflects where home ("here" in the United Kingdom) is tied to one's immediate family:

> It is a dream [to return to Nepal]. Because I used to think, I used to plan that when my children grow up and they have a job. And then Ram and myself we would go back to Nepal and stay there for retired life. But now, I think, I just can't imagine how can we do that because our family is my husband, my children, my family is . . . And *when my children are here, three of them here and get job, get married and get children, everything here and how could we leave without family?* This is a family, our family. Parents are parents and they won't be there when we retire like sixty, sixty-five. But in fact I told my brother, sister, they have their own family and it is not close as children is it? So I don't think it's . . . That would be nice if you can, we would be in Nepal. (my emphasis)

Interestingly, returning to Nepal during one's retirement years is bracketed by Adishree as a dream. This dream or hope, however, is contingent on where the (nuclear) family is. Adishree has chosen to remain with her husband and children wherever they would be as home; now that they constitute "family" aside from her own parents or extended kin. That said however, Adishree also acknowledged that for those who have chosen to return to Nepal, their reason for doing so is to "have a good life." This is because once one joins the British Army, the salary is considered as "quite lots of money [*sic*]" compared to that which one could earn in Nepal. Consequently, returnees to Nepal are able to "buy whatever you like" including a "big house" or to "save money in the bank" or "do some kind of little business." Therefore, it would be possible to have "an easy life back at home," Adishree said.

This "easy" or "good" life would be in contrast to those such as Adishree and her family in the United Kingdom whereby it is essential to have to "work every day to survive," for "to earn pound it's not easy." The experience of another Gurkha couple, Ramesh and Neelam, corroborated Adishree's statement that making a living in the United Kingdom is not easy. Where Ramesh works as a postman, his wife, Neelam, holds a job as a cleaner in an army camp. She takes home about £1,000 (approximately US$1,262) per month for eight-hour work days, according to Ramesh. As Ramesh lamented: "If wife not working, can't survive." Given that earning one's keep in the United Kingdom is "so difficult" in the words of Kamadev, he and his wife Roopali have decided that they would eventually leave the country and return to Nepal once their children have married and settled down. Kamadev had declared to me: "I don't want to stay here [referring to the United Kingdom]. My missus and me, plan to go back home." Life at home in Nepal differs from the experience of these Gurkha couples living in the United Kingdom. Adishree continued the comparison with her brother's family where her sister-in-law looked after their children and did not (have to) hold a job outside of the family. For these reasons, Adishree clarified why "Nepalese people don't like to stay here [United Kingdom] until they get, we get old." For if "we stay here, we have to work. If we don't work, we won't be able to survive here . . . we won't be able to pay mortgage and expenses and that's why people go back to Nepal and have a good life." Clearly, Adishree's views on where home is, including where she and her family would be located when they retire, involved a number of considerations. These considerations reflect a mixed bag of emotive ties connected to Nepal, to their immediate and/or extended familial members, and which were accompanied by other underlying reasons and motivations. In Eknath's case, he told me that he thought of the United Kingdom where he is now residing as "home" with a felt sense of belonging for the following reasons: "We call home here. . . . Because we've got family here, we've got communities here, we've got everything. . . . In terms of safety and security of life, there is no question. Only problem is this country is very, very expensive. The more you want, the more you have to pay tax. Not only us, even the people here they don't like." Both Adishree and Eknath's accounts that indicated reasons where home and belonging were, articulate the different factors—intertwining the emotive, pragmatic, and biographical (cf. Yuval Davis 2006)—that collectively determine how belonging is experienced. That said however, I also contend that one's feeling of belonging continues to shift indeterminately (Antonsich 2010; Pickering 2001). As Ram put it, "I can't really say it now but your whole family is there. I don't know if it will happen or not so . . ." Belonging can be experienced momentarily, which also shifts over time.

Bilhana and Manjul wedded through an arranged marriage when they were both just one to two years shy of turning twenty. Manjul, whom I introduced in the previous chapter, was nineteen when he got married to Bilhana. Eight months later, he joined the Gurkhas and flew off to Hong Kong for training. Bilhana stayed behind in Nepal and lived with her parents-in-law, together with Manjul's younger sister. While Bilhana had initially found it "scary" to live with her in-laws, she gradually became more accustomed to them after several months had passed. They treated her well and she also got along with her sister-in-law.[9] During Manjul's Gurkha service, it was not until eleven to twelve years later that he was allowed to bring Bilhana to live with him at the barracks. That took place in 2005 when he was posted to Brunei. However, just fifteen days after Bilhana joined Manjul in Brunei, he received news that he was to be next deployed to Afghanistan for half a year. While they stayed in touch with each other using the phone, Bilhana was constantly worrying for Manjul given that Afghanistan was dangerous, as she repeatedly told her husband. She was finally relieved when Manjul returned to Brunei after serving in Afghanistan. Now that they are both based in the United Kingdom with their two children, Bilhana works as a shop assistant in a military camp. Some Gurkha wives either did not speak English or were minimally proficient in the language for their day-to-day routines, including shopping for groceries. For Bilhana, she maintained that English "it's not my language! You know, I speak Nepalese!" Clearly, she consciously exercised bracketed belonging to Nepal while living abroad, seen through her assertion of speaking her native language, and with plans together with Manjul to return to Nepal for their retirement years.[10] Overall, this appears to be a recurrent attitude and perspective of what most of these Gurkha wives subscribe to, which are largely consonant with those of their husbands' as I have discussed previously.

Mastering and using English as a language including issues revolving around one's accent, span across generations as I return to Adishree and Mridu's experience. Adishree had learned some English while she was in Nepal. This made it slightly easier for her to pick it up when she moved to the United Kingdom to be with Ram. While it was not too challenging for her to continue with learning the English language, she had found it "difficult to understand [the] British accent [at] first." She recounted an incident where she first visited Ram in the United Kingdom, who had his friend with him who was a "Scottish Joe." Adishree could not decipher his accent, as she narrated to me: "He was a Scottish Joe speaking something else, I said pardon pardon . . . three times! [*laughs*] I didn't understand at all, I said. That's alright. He kept explaining me, I said, sorry I didn't understand."

Adishree further added that apart from initial language issues, families in her neighborhood in the United Kingdom were friendly and "very welcoming." This was despite her being aware that in "some area they don't like the foreign people . . . but we have been lucky to stay in this part." Some of her neighbors were actually more curious if anything and had approached her to write their name in Nepali, as Adishree conveyed to me with amusement. She also mentioned that at times, she was careful not to speak using Nepali in front of the English. This was because she did not want to be mistaken for talking about them. In Mridu's case, she took to living in the United Kingdom fairly well from the outset, given that she went there at a young age and hence was able to adapt quickly. She explained in greater detail:

> I think it was easier because I was younger. So I think it would have been really hard, like I see that it is hard for kids to sort of, a lot of kids come over when they are sort of in their teens, and it's really hard for them to adjust because . . . I guess I don't really know but I think when you are a lot younger, a lot of things were a lot simpler and you can get along with people easily and make friends easily, and adapt easily and pick up the language quicker as well so it wasn't particularly hard. Like at the beginning, it was sort of, the first few months were a little bit challenging, it was a bit like . . . I was on the bus with a friend of mine and because, I mean, I knew how to speak English, but obviously you don't learn it at the same extent that obviously people here, they are gonna speak it quickly and I had a friend who was on the bus and she was telling me all these things and I didn't really understand and I was like nodding and smiling . . . and I couldn't understand what she was saying at all. So it did take a while but, I mean, everyone was certainly friendly and it was fine after a bit. The language came quite quickly, it was just everything else, like the studying, the academic side which was quite hard to adjust to.

When I asked Mridu as to how visits back to Nepal were like, given that she had by then picked up the British accent, she pointed out that her second sister, Chaha, and herself would only "talk in English to each other . . . [but] don't talk in English to our cousins." When her younger sister, Sumira (introduced in chapter 1) went back to Nepal at the age of three, Sumira's command of Nepali was poor. This thus led to "miscommunication between the aunties and uncles and cousins." It was therefore difficult to sustain interactions with their extended family. Mridu and her sisters did not use English in speaking with their aunties and uncles, who were older kin and could not comprehend the language as well, compared to their younger cousins. In Sumira's case, Mridu said that she had an accent, so when she spoke Nepali, that came with a British accent. As a result, some of her pronunciation came across "weirdly," leading to funny scenarios whenever the sisters went back to Nepal together.

In terms of accented English and depending on where one was born or raised, I refer to other respondents who followed their Gurkha police fathers to Singapore and who were schooling there. I return to the focus group interview of Singapore Gurkha children including Ganga, Renu, Dipesh, and Muna whom I discussed previously. One incident that these informants raised was that of taking public transport, specifically the bus. Dipesh pointed out to me that whenever they refer to a bus in Nepal, they would have to pronounce it as "boss." This was something that Riju had also confirmed with me. This was because if they were to pronounce "bus" as it is, the locals would laugh at them. Renu explained why this was the case: "Apparently in Nepali, because 'bus' was in English-Singaporean language. Bus also they don't understand. There was in translation English you know, 'do you . . . bus.' Stupid, 'bus' also they don't understand. I have to say 'boss.' Sometimes you have to make a fool of yourself just to make them understand."

Riju cited another example of language-accent miscommunication upon returning from Singapore to Nepal: "When you say 'twelve,' you say 'twelve' right, then they will be like 'hehehe.' For them you must say 'twelve' (using Nepali accent). Even my teacher laugh at me. I am like, what kind of teacher are you? I mean you don't even respect other people and all that." For reasons such as language miscommunication, different accents, and other factors, Gurkha children have found it tough to adapt to life in Nepal after having grown up in Singapore, as I shall elaborate below in terms of experiences of not-belonging.

On Sumira's second trip to Nepal, she traveled only with Adishree. At that time, Sumira's command of the English language was inchoate. When Adishree and Sumira stayed in Nepal for a month, Sumira had also picked up more Nepalese. Said Adishree about Sumira's communicative approach:

> She used to mix Nepalese and English while she was talking, and one of my nieces, she didn't really understand very good English. She wants to communicate with Sumira so Sumira communicated with her in half English half Nepali, she didn't understand whole sentence, she just walked away. I don't understand your English.

What is interesting through these examples of language learning and use, both in the United Kingdom and Nepal, is that not only were there some discernible differences between the two generations of mother and daughter (Adishree and

Mridu). Differences were also apparent *within* a generation when we compare the experiences of Mridu, Chaha, and Sumira as siblings. Being born in Nepal for the former two, and in the United Kingdom for the latter makes a weighted difference in terms of their linguistic capacities, and how these are utilized to communicate with kin in Nepal, or with neighbors and friends in the United Kingdom. Both inter- and intragenerational comparisons that I raise here therefore illustrate the different "repertory of identifications" (Freyer 2019, 257) that connect to manifold approaches to adapting, returning to Nepal (either from the United Kingdom or Singapore), and one's feelings of belonging. Adishree further recounted to me that aside from Sumira's experience, both Mridu and Chaha had earlier learned Nepalese in Nepal, but also continued to do so through reading Nepali books:

> I used to ask my family to send Nepali books and then we can teach them at home. Chaha used to do until a couple of years ago so now she doesn't. But she can read Nepali and she can write. I mean, I think this is good thing to speak in Nepali and understand it only, nice to read Nepali word, even though you have got British citizen, but that's a second thing. But you are being a Nepali, you should read and write your own language.

At this point, Ram chimed in and reinforced what Adishree had just said: "We have to teach [them] where we are from, what is our background, that's our culture, customs everything we have to teach our children. It is our duty to do that." This duty that Ram takes on himself together with Adishree as parents is indicative of acts of bracketed belonging linked to Nepal. The bracketing involves language mastery that they carry out with their children. As Adishree clearly pointed out, even if their daughters are British citizens, this should take second place whereas being a Nepali translates into an expectation that one ought to be able to converse and write in "your own language," and referring simultaneously to the English language as being not of their own. Adishree and Ram's responses, or their act of bracketing linguistic capacity and belonging, echo what Freyer (2019, 255) talks about in terms of a "compound identity." Migrants and their children develop and express multiple belongings in relation to the children's biographical trajectories as they unfold across different social spaces or countries. These approaches of bracketing belonging as manifold further articulate the different migratory trajectories that each of these diasporans have experienced. These variegated trajectories also include the varying points of departure and return across their biographical arc (similar to Sejun's case) that similarly direct and influence their migratory experiences and positionings of belonging and/or otherwise. For some, such a compound identity or expressions of multiple belongings might be a way to transcend how others feel in terms of being "neither here nor there" as I have discussed in an earlier chapter pertaining to some of the Gurkha children. Such expressions might be read as a way of acknowledging how some respondents may consciously wish to be "here and there" simultaneously, seen in the case of Adishree's views on her children's British citizenship that coexist with mastering Nepali as reflective of remaining connected to Nepal.

While Gurkha wives based in the United Kingdom and Hong Kong have been able to find and take up employment, they are not allowed to work in Singapore (Kiruppalini 2011). Some therefore assumed volunteer work with local schools as part of a pilot project called the "school-home-community partnership" that was launched in 1998 by Macpherson Primary School. This project involved a number of volunteer "Nepalese mothers from the Gurkha contingent volunteering their services to deliver Nepali language lessons during the Mother-Tongue periods." Nepalese students constituted about 16 percent of the entire population at this school. This volunteer scheme enabled these mothers to contribute daily hours of their time and has been described as having reinforced "the importance of knowing one's roots and appreciating one's culture."[11] Such a rationale also sits consonantly with many of my informants' bracketing efforts, including those of Adishree and Ram. Apart from language issues, what other identification or markers of belonging and not-belonging do Gurkha wives and children relate to?

Markers of Belonging

Markers of belonging include the myriad pieces of knowledge and practices of everyday life that one acquires and sustains or recollects. This is concisely expressed by Yuval-Davis (2006, 199):

> People can "belong" in many different ways and to many different objects of attachments. These can vary from a particular person to the whole of humanity, in a concrete or abstract way; belonging can be an act of self-identification or identification by others, in a stable, contested or transient way. Even in its most stable "primordial" forms, however, belonging is always a dynamic process, not a reified fixity, which is only a naturalised construction of a particular hegemonic form of power relations.

In my conversations with ex-Gurkhas, and with their wives and children, narratives of belonging are replete with references to everyday practices and encounters that cover the range of informal and formal contexts of sociality. Senses of diasporic belonging as a Nepalese community in the United Kingdom, for example, is exemplified through Yash's words: "It's nice because we have a lot of Nepalese community. . . . We are very close. We celebrate parties. . . . We say a lot of things, like. . . . what can I say? We have a common tie, we have a good tie, and very good solidarity." As an example of a "common tie" as expressed by Yash, food and foodways appear to be a salient and recurring index that connotes one's sense of belonging, given the familiarity and comfort that they provide. Abdullah argues: "Food and the attendant sensory registers . . . readily become quotidian expressions of multiple belongings and embodied connections social actors have with 'home'" (2010, 157). These expressions of belonging through gastronomic practices also include food and foodways that are consciously left out in order to better articulate group sentiments of collective belonging within a singular cultural framing. In Pariyar, Shrestha and Gellner's (2014) discussion on Dasain, which is one of the most important and biggest religious events of the Nepalese calendar, we are told that the executive committee of the Nepalese Community in Oxford (NCO) prescribes a set of rules that determined how Dasain was to be celebrated. As the authors note: "Food had to be explicitly Nepali" and an "ex-Gurkha was ridiculed at one meeting when he suggested including pasta in the menu" (Pariyar, Shrestha, and Gellner 2014, 142). The authors further elaborate: "Perhaps it might have been acceptable for some other occasion such as the summer barbeque, but it was almost a sin to think about having Western food as part of a Dasain feast. Despite their prolonged work overseas, most Gurkhas remained strictly Nepali in terms of what they ate" (Pariyar, Shrestha, and Gellner 2014, 142).

Beyond strict prescriptions as applied to the menu, the same attitude extended to the choice of music at Dasain. Although Gurkha children have a preference for English and Hindi music, such non-Nepali music and dance music were strictly prohibited as pointed out by the authors. What was emphasized at Dasain and other Nepali celebrations was either Nepali folk or country music. Along with gastronomic and musical stipulations, dress was another idiom of belonging adhered to. At Dasain, attendees should as far as possible, put on the Nepali national dress. The overall aim was to "maintain a distinctive Nepali flavour to the cultural programme, people's dress, and the cuisine" (Pariyar, Shrestha, and Gellner 2014, 142). While most of them had indeed followed these cultural expectations, "at least two young Gurkha daughters incurred their displeasure by appearing in miniskirts" (Pariyar, Shrestha, and Gellner 2014, 142).

These examples indicate clearly that belonging is consciously bracketed and performed at such festivals as Dasain, reflected through food and foodways, choice of music, as well as expected apparels. More pertinently, such concerted bracketing also reveals contrastive feelings of belonging or not across these different diasporans. For the older generation of ex-Gurkhas, it was important to maintain a singular cultural framing. The younger generation of Gurkha children may on one hand participate at such celebrations, but on the other hand, subscribe to non-Nepali cultural framing as seen in their music preferences and dress sense. As is evident, these "young people . . . do not want to be constrained by nationalist considerations" (Pariyar, Shrestha, and Gellner 2014, 155). There are therefore concurrent multiple practices and markers of belonging and thereby not-belonging that are determined and carried out by different generations of Gurkha families, depending on their social and biographical location and experience. They relate simultaneously to similar and different cultural scripts in their everyday lives that thereby serve as variegated expressions of how to or not to belong.

Culinary scripts as they are bracketed above reflect the close connections that diasporans wish to maintain with Nepal while they are overseas in the United Kingdom. Conversely, such connections to belonging *elsewhere* are also articulated through food. The fond recollections that informants articulate vis-à-vis gastronomy indicate their sense of attachment and belonging to Singapore, as the following quotes depict:

> GAURI: I think we all, even me, we are so deeply rooted to the sense that sometimes we just wake up, and then there's that, that smell of carrot cake, no I need to go to a hawker centre!
>
> MALASHREE: I think there's like two of my friends there now. I think they also got married to someone in the Force, so now they are wives, the rest of us we are all here. So when we meet it's like eh Hokkien mee, and then roti prata . . .

Gauri and Malashree, who were both born, bred, and schooled in Singapore, returned to Kathmandu on their fathers' end of police service. They told me that whenever they missed Singapore food, they would troop down to a restaurant in Kathmandu known as Sing-ma Foodcourt. This is an eatery opened by a Singaporean who serves both Singaporean and Malaysian cuisine including nasi lemak, chicken rice, and beef rendang. Both their mothers also "talk about missing Singapore's food [*laugh*]. Char kway teow, hokkien mee and other stuff." Missing Singapore and Nepali food thus form a part of the processes of migration and return migration in the context of transnationalism in the Oxford and Singapore examples above. Where Nepali culinary practices are adhered to in the case of Oxford, returnees to Nepal relive their Singapore experiences through foodways that they satiate in Nepal.

Manisha related how her aunt first felt homesick about having to leave Nepal for Singapore at the beginning of her police husband's service. Later on, the same feelings became apparent for Singapore food when her aunt returned to Nepal on holiday during her Gurkha-police husband's leave. Manisha related her aunt's experience as follows:

> I can't wait to go back to Singapore. When I first was a newlywed I went to Singapore, I was so homesick I missed all my family and all the Nepali food back home. Now I stay in Singapore, I can't wait to have chicken rice and all the hokkien mee. . . . I'm so sick already, I can't wait to go [back] to Singapore. I don't know about the kids but I need to be back in Singapore already.

According to Manisha, then, she believed that her aunt "has a sense of belonging to Singapore, and all the food there." Similarly, Manisha's mother, Sreva, could not imagine how she would have to adjust to life back in Nepal, after having followed her husband to Singapore as he joined the GCSPF. She lamented: "So good here [referring to Singapore], I don't know how I am going to manage it when I go back over there [Nepal]. Or enjoy all these roti prata and bee hoon . . . because you won't be having these things after you return to Nepal." Everyday practices such as food and foodways stand for "the process of incorporating the 'nation' into everyday life" (Christou 2009, 109). That is to say, the yearning for Singaporean cuisine represents returnees' subjective identification with the country, mediated through food and food practices as part of everyday senses of belonging.

Interestingly, the identification of belonging to Singapore through food experiences is taken a step further—transpiring in Nepal itself—by Sirish and Manisha when a Kentucky Fried Chicken outlet first opened in Nepal. Sirish vividly described to me his recollection of the event:

> When KFC first came to Nepal, I was like 'yes!' so happy. . . . Wow. During the opening it was working out very well, but now it is pretty empty. But during the opening everyone went and I remembered during the opening. . . . There was a huge, long queue. I think . . . The photo came out in the newspaper. It was so embarrassing. Luckily I was facing my back. So couldn't see my face. My friends were all shown on the long queue. It's like you can really see this bunch of uniform group of guys which are from my school. So we went it, and I still remember.

Ostensibly excited about the opening of KFC's first outlet in Kathmandu, Sirish was able to recollect his memory of joining the queue there. More pertinently, he said that "I can smell the burger smell. It is like, it's good, it's good to be back. I was so happy. But it is not as good as Singapore but it's good enough though." For Sirish, it helped that a piece of Singapore (via KFC) that he could relive while being back in Nepal alleviated the sense of initial displacement that he felt when he returned there from Singapore. Manisha concurred in tandem: "It just helps you feel more at home. Yeah. But it's not exactly home. I mean, when I miss home, I miss Singapore." Similarly, Gauri told me at our meeting that whenever relatives or friends returned from Singapore to Kathmandu, she would take the opportunity to request that they bring her a burger from McDonald's. That was one of the few things that she had missed about having lived in Singapore earlier on. Re-creating memories of Singapore through gastronomy and the senses as indicated by Sirish, Manisha, and Gauri would thereby mirror Antonsich's (2010, 647) perspective on autobiographical factors relating to one's past as a component of "place-belongingness."

Aside from place-belongingness as part of one's recollection of memories in Singapore, food experiences and other practices including language were also important facets of Gurkha children having adapted well to life outside of Nepal. Shradda Gurung was born in Singapore, and attended school at Woodsville Primary.[12] Her experience in Singapore has been characterized as follows:

> She loves chicken rice and roti prata. And she didn't miss a single episode of the recently-ended Channel 8 drama, The Legendary Swordsman. But wait, she's not a Singaporean. Shradda Gurung, 11, is a Nepalese. Born in Singapore, she is a Primary 5 student at Woodsville Primary School. . . . She's by no means alone. More than 200 of the school's 580 pupils are Nepalese.[13]

In this media report, we learn that Mrs. Gurung, Shradda's mother, finds the local teachers to be "very supportive and warm-hearted towards our children."[14] Furthermore, Nepalese parents have also been welcomed by Singaporean parents to organize school activities, including Racial Harmony Day. It is through such school events as this that "Nepalese mothers prepared Nepalese food like *momo* (which is similar to the Chinese dumpling) to sell to students."[15] The report also notes that the medium of instruction for school children in Singapore is English, which is unlike in Nepal where English is but one subject. Mrs. Gurung also pointed out that these Nepalese children "knows very little about [their] own culture." Given this identified gap, the "authorities at the Gurkha camp were concerned that the children might slowly lose their roots."[16] To address this concern, Nepalese children aged between seven and ten (Primary 1 to 4) learn how to read and write Nepali from volunteer Nepalese teachers from the Gurkha camp, thrice a week. By and large both Nepalese and Singaporean children get along well, according to the report. They had "happily showed off the few phrases of Mandarin and Nepali that they had learned from each other," according to the news team who had visited the school.[17]

This example of Shradda Gurung unveils three pertinent points that high-light how dual belonging (Kananen 2020) transpires among the Nepalese children of Gurkhas living in Singapore. First, they have adapted well to local food such as the iconic chicken rice or *roti prata*, but are also not forgetting their roots in consuming (as well as sharing) *momos*, a Nepalese staple. Second, even as they pick up Mandarin or English as a foreign language in local schools, they are still exposed to the Nepali language so that they do not "lose their roots" according to the Gurkha camp officials. What these examples of gastronomic and linguistic practices indicate is that Gurkha children are concurrently exposed to two sets of cultural scripts. While they are able to adjust fairly well to living and schooling in Singapore on the one hand, they would still have to keep up with Nepalese culture on the other hand, which form their "roots." Together, such dual belongingness reflects social anchors that allow these children to enact a transnational relation between Nepal and Singapore in a bracketed sense. This is because they would have to embrace an eventual and incontrovertible return to Nepal upon their fathers' retirement from the police force. Where some Gurkha children such as Dipesh or Riju expressed to me that they felt they are "from neither here or there" as discussed in chapter 1, this media report seems to convey otherwise; that Nepalese children, represented through Shradda's experience, are *both here and there* in terms of adopting and adapting to both Nepalese and Singaporean practices in their day-to-day encounters as a migrant community. Make no mistake, however, that "she's not a Singaporean"—which arguably thus stands for a form of bracketed and limited belonging to Singapore as well. This leads me to my third point on how belonging and not-belonging are coterminous and overlapping (Gellner 2015; Pfaff-Czarnecka 2020). There is a time limit to (bracketed) belonging since the children's roots are elsewhere according to the authorities, despite children such as Shradda who are born in and very much accustomed to living and schooling in Singapore.

Lalita, who is the wife of a retired Gurkha chief inspector now living in Nepal, told me that she maintains an account with a local bank in Singapore so that they can easily withdraw local currency whenever they were in Singapore. Furthermore, Lalita proudly declared: "Singapore is my country." Similarly, Hiresh, who retired from the SPF in 2005 after twenty-seven years of service, receives his pension from the Singapore government through a Singapore bank account. Beyond the practicality of having monthly amounts transferred into this account, he remarked: "Even though [I'm] retired, my heart is still there [Singapore]." He told me that he continues to keep abreast with news on Singapore, making the reading of blogs and other websites for three to four hours a day as part of his daily routine.

These instances of recounting what Gurkha families miss about Singapore, and what they still retain in and of Singapore, represent feelings of sustained belonging. These feelings are not "reducible to human-focused social interaction but . . . can be derived from relationships with places, objects and ideas" (Kendall, Woodward, and Skrbis 2009, 33). The case of Shradda also points toward how these various material and nonmaterial aspects of life in Singapore that are experienced and reconstructed assume emotional valence for informants and other Gurkha diasporans. These aspects, or what Röttger-Rössler (2018, 257; emphasis in original) would term as the "significance of the *experience dimension*" of migration, are meaningful as they provide a sense of connection to Singapore. They likewise parallel what Hedetoft (2004, 24) calls the "sources of belonging" that include "familiarity, sensual experience, human interaction and local knowledge," which are rooted in place. Together, these elements form the "sources of homeness" (Hedetoft 2004, 24). Home, in this case, is traced to Singapore for my interlocutors as mentioned above.

To be a student in Singapore is to recite the national pledge and to sing the national anthem on a daily basis. To be a Nepali studying in Singapore is likewise to both sing and recite allegiance to Singapore, as Singaporean students do. Gauri, for example, claimed that she felt more Singaporean than Nepali, given that reciting the pledge and singing the national anthem has become her daily routine during her school years in Singapore. In fact, she shared with me that she thought she was Singaporean till she had to return to Nepal at the age of twenty-three. In this respect, her sense of "Singaporeanness" thereby acts as a foil to the lack of knowledge or affective ties to Nepal. This is a point that Manisha similarly raised:

> You know I was just thinking about it this morning, what are the significant dates in Nepal—in Singapore it was always 9 August, you know? National Day is coming! And then there's the Padang, and everything, and then here [Nepal] I don't know anything. I know nuts, you know. It was so funny because I was thinking of . . . I think this morning or the morning before, so in a way that just shows like how Singaporean we really are. But like I said, it's slowly coming to terms with acceptance.

Furthermore, Gauri mentioned that "now home is like wherever my family are. So if they are in Singapore, then Singapore is my home. But now we are here . . . we have to accept the fact that we are here, we are Nepalese, so I guess our home is here."

The idea and felt sense of home for my respondents such as Manisha and Gauri point toward the multiplicity of home and its attached and shifting meanings. On the one hand, home is clearly a physical site that is built on one's experiences and memories. On the other hand, familial and other forms of social ties similarly establish where home lies. When my interlocutors concurrently refer to both Singapore and Nepal, this stance further confirms my analysis that they continue to feel neither here nor there as they straddle two worlds in no equal measure. As Malashree shared with me in the course of our interview: "And then we have our childhood memories, everything is there [referring to Singapore]. So we would still feel Singaporean, but we would also love our country, Nepal. We cannot ignore our parents and our own country." Ostensibly, individuals may simultaneously subscribe to both in relation to Singapore and/or Nepal.

While Gurkha children do feel that Singapore is "home" for them, such sentiments of belonging cannot be translated into legislative and political terms. Singapore is still a host society in which they grew up and spent their formative years as noncitizens. I visited a former Gurkha chief inspector of the SPF in Pokhara, where I spoke with his wife, Lalita (introduced earlier) and daughter as well, about their experiences and memories of having lived and studied in Singapore. When asked about citizenship, Lalita went into the house (we were chatting over tea at the verandah) and subsequently brought out her daughter's birth certificate to show me. It was a certificate issued by a Singapore hospital which explicitly stated that "the child is not a citizen of Singapore at the time of birth." By virtue of showing me the birth certificate that clearly and officially marked her daughter as a noncitizen, Lalita indicated that belonging to Singapore was not possible in legal terms.

Thus far, the various examples both demonstrate feelings of belonging and otherwise. The ease and familiarity with which membership of Singapore society and everyday practices are experienced and recounted suggest that there is a felt sense of belonging to the country in which they were born and bred, which is not Nepal—even if it was not legally so. These senses of belonging should not merely be read as "cognitive stories" (Yuval-Davis 2006, 202). They instead stand for emotional connections and desires for attachment, expressing both individual longings and collective social interactions or initiatives in their migrant biographies.

Some of the Gurkha children in Kathmandu meet occasionally under the auspices of what they have termed the Merlion Club, a reference to Singapore's iconic tourist symbol of a half-fish/half-lion mythical figure. Such attachments relate to what Mee and Wright (2009) coin as the "affective aspects of belonging." Through the Merlion Club, as well as other gatherings, a sense of belonging is bolstered through different affiliative configurations that add to identity formation as collectives (cf. Fortier 1999). Gurkha wives told me that they often get together to reminisce about their time in Singapore; comparisons are made between their country of origin (Nepal) and the host country (Singapore). These examples would also exemplify "everyday membership practices of identification and categorization" (Brubaker 2010, 65).

If those who had returned from Singapore to Nepal continue to experience and/or talk about their senses of belonging to the former, then reverse forms of bracketed belonging may also be discerned from my other respondents who are based in Hong Kong and who continue to talk about Nepal as their home country. There are, however different reasons that account for why such ideas or felt sense of belonging and not-belonging transpire, depending on the context in which they are studying and/or working. Where Singapore does not allow residency of Nepali actors beyond the Gurkha's active term of service, Hong Kong grants the right of abode to Gurkha soldiers, their children, and Nepalese civilians who are born in Hong Kong before January 1983. This is based on the Sino-British Joint Declaration of 1984 (Tonsing 2010). This provision notwithstanding, Gurkha children face a set of difficulties as they live in Hong Kong, which thus forms the backdrop that accounts for how they approach belonging or not-belonging. To articulate this context, I draw from among others, Prakat's biography as I turn to the next section on markers of not-belonging.

On Not-Belonging

Since the time of my first meeting with Prakat in Hong Kong where we chatted in his office at Jordan (Kowloon Peninsula), he had by then lived in the country for fifteen years. Born in Nepal in 1972, Prakat comes from a large family of four boys and three girls. His late father had served as a Gurkha with the British Army and had retired in the mid-1950s. Although Prakat himself had attempted the Gurkha recruitment test twice, he was not able to pass and to join Gurkha service. Besides, he was at that time enrolled in college and had given priority to his studies as opposed to plans for working for the British. By the time he had completed his degree, he had passed the maximum age of twenty-one years of age.[18] For his brothers, as "they're the very short type," Prakat pointed out, they therefore could not meet the minimum height requirement for Gurkha recruitment.[19]

After completing college in Kathmandu, Prakat traveled to Hong Kong in 1996. He was by then in his late twenties, and first began working in the security industry. At the beginning, Prakat was not able to adapt to life in Hong Kong for a number of reasons:

> But our first, in the beginning when we come to Hong Kong, many times people maybe they very feel, very uneasy. Not good. Because we can't, can't match, same time with the local culture, local society. But now we follow all their rules and everything. So we are, we are learning

their culture. We are learning their society. We want to get in their society. So now it's okay. But when we come first time, it's very different.
Language problem, food problem, because Chinese food they give us,
we don't know how to don't eat. And argue. We pay money, why your
food is not like Nepal food? Not, not, not Nepalese taste. What kind of
your food? So maybe that is the, maybe some problem.

A year on, Prakat then changed jobs and joined the hotel industry. He subsequently set up his own business thereafter, first operating a kindergarten for the
Nepalese community over four years. He explained:

> The Nepalese community. I was the first time, that time I established the
> one kindergarten. Because that time so many Nepalese, they born the
> baby here, and they no idea, they don't know how to join the school and
> how to get the kindergarten, something like that. . . . So I set up, I set
> up the one kindergarten school. Four years, maybe four years I run the
> kindergarten. After that, after that I sell.

He had set up the kindergarten after obtaining a teacher's license. After sell-
ing the school, he then opened a company which provided manpower—that of
retired Gurkhas—for jobs including security guards, drivers, and body guards.[20]
As a bhanja himself, he mentioned that these job vacancies were matched with
"Gurkhas, Gurkhas' sons, Gurkhas' daughters" as his priority, since "sometimes
they don't know how to get the job." The difficulties faced by these fellow Nepalis
are also tied to language abilities, which formed a barrier in seeking employment
as Prakat further noted: "Any Hong Kong to give them local job is very difficult. Cause we don't know Cantonese. Chinese language, their local language.
But some of the Nepali people, they, they also don't know English, then they
don't know Chinese. They speak only in Nepali or Indian, Indian language. So
it's very difficult to get the job." Language barriers, among other factors, have
effectively led to experiences of social exclusion and/or discrimination encountered in Hong Kong society, as observed by scholars working on South Asian
communities, Nepalese immigrants and/or specifically the Gurkha community
living in Hong Kong (for example, Chiu and Siu 2022; Sun and Fong 2021; Tam
2010; Valenzuela-Silva and Cheung 2016).[21]

Badal, who I introduced in chapter 3, shared with me that he felt out of place
in Hong Kong and was facing an "identity crisis":

> But also sometimes when I come to Hong Kong, because we already
> have the stereotype come here to Hong Kong, one of the incident that
> really, every time that appears on my mind when I talk about Hong
> Kong when I talk about identity is that . . . once I was on my way to

university, someone asked me like where are you from? Because I was talking different language from the Hong Kongers, I was, "Nepalese." "Oh, you're a security guard." So, that was really something that hit me on my mind. Because something very bad. Because it's not that, true. But then I don't want to shout at them, because the problem is that they [don't] know this one. No one taught them, so it's the fault of the system, not the individual's fault. And I said no I'm not like it. I'm like this this this; I introduce myself. And they say, "oh okay." But then, this is something I would also feel bad because you don't have any identity in Hong Kong, that's what I feel.[22]

Badal's grandfather had served as a Gurkha, but his father and himself were instead encouraged by his grandfather to pursue an education rather than to recruit into the British Army. As he was keen on training to be a doctor, Badal had asked around in Hong Kong as to how to apply to university. He was, however, not able to find anyone who was willing to help him. Subsequently, Badal went to Tianjin, China, to study medicine. Based on my last contact with him a couple of years ago, he and his wife had since moved to Europe to take up a hospital job.

In Tang's (2017) study of Nepali drug users in Hong Kong, and out of which a majority of his respondents are descendants (second and third generation) of Gurkha soldiers, the author points out that these offspring have faced difficulties in securing good jobs. Therefore, they are not able to earn sufficient money in order to remit their earnings back to Nepal. As ethnic minorities in Hong Kong, migrant communities such as the Gurkha bhanja and bhanji face differentiated treatment in both domains of education and employment. Ethnic minorities such as the Nepalese, Pakistani, or Indian migrant populations enroll in designated schools with poor prospects that in turn lead their graduates to take on low-salary jobs, including construction work and as cleaners (Ku, Chan, and Sandhu 2005; Leung 2021). As similarly reported in the Hong Kong media,

> Nepalis have an association with the city dating back to 1969–70, when Gurkha regiments were first based here. The British granted the troops and their families permanent residency in the early 1990s. Then, amid political uncertainty in the run-up to the handover in 1997, many returned to Nepal. The early 2000s, when fears had receded, saw them returning. But given difficulties in finding school places for non-Chinese-speaking minorities, many left their children behind. The lack of Chinese-language support persists, and minorities are often allocated places in so-called lower-band schools, which risks entrenching intergenerational poverty in the community.[23]

One of my informants in Hong Kong also told me that South Asian students there attend ethnic minorities school (either government-based or private if they can afford the latter) given that mainstream schools in the country are concerned that these students may affect their rankings with poor scholastic performance. Moreover, jobs that South Asian communities such as the Nepalese hold often-times require long if not irregular working hours; facing such segregation in employment and difficult working conditions thus pivot some of these bhanja to turn to heroin use as a form of coping mechanism (Tang 2017). It is only in recent years, as Tang (2017) points out, that the Hong Kong government has begun state provision of funds for related programs as an ancillary response to the social needs of these ethnic minorities. One interesting point that the author raises (Tang 2017, 221) is that of intergenerational differences in terms of the economic context and employability that these different actors confront: "The first genera-tion of Nepalis in Hong Kong were usually retired Gurkhas. When they retired from the army, their qualifications along with a better economy then made it easier for them to find better employment. Comparatively, the second and third generations do not have such advantages." Essentially, what these descendants of Gurkha soldiers in Hong Kong are facing now are "a changing economy and social marginalization against ethnic minorities" (Tang 2017, 221). These shift-ing factors and contexts make it comparatively more difficult to attain good edu-cation and to find stable and reasonably well-paying jobs.

That said, however, one of my other bhanja interlocutors shared different views on the matter of drug use among the Nepali community. Aakar's grand-father and father were both Gurkhas and who had served in Brunei and Hong Kong, among other places. Aakar was born in Nepal, followed his parents to Hong Kong, spent three years in Brunei in his early teens, and then returned to Nepal in the early 2000s. It was only in 2007 that he went back to Hong Kong, having first worked as a security guard. His wife was born in Hong Kong. After marrying her, he had come to Nepal as her dependent. Through marriage with his Hong Kong-born wife, Aakar had the rights to stay in the country. In fact, his father-in-law and father knew each other through Gurkha service, where both were friends and occupied the same rank. Aakar told me that "some of the bhanja bhanji children who are suffering with drugs and doing nothing and so on and so forth, they are come from Nepal [sic]." Conversely, those who were born in Hong Kong "are patient and study from the young, those who are born . . . born here [referring to Hong Kong], they are . . . they are not involved by this [referring to drug use]." Brian, who served for a decade alongside the Gurkhas as a British officer, shared similar views with those of Prakat's and Aakar's. After serving with the army for a total of two decades, Brian is now the managing director of an employment agency that arranges security jobs for retired Gurkhas. He has been based in Hong Kong with the agency for twenty years by the time I met him there in 2014. Brian first talked about the difficulty of language that Gurkha children face, not unlike what Prakat said:

> And they have difficulty with Chinese language, and will mean that no, very, very few. We're talking about tiny numbers, of Nepalese children will go to the Hong Kong school system and then go to university. And they'll never get a job in Hong Kong as an office worker. So all of the white collar jobs are pretty much ruled out, because they can't read Chinese.

He then went on to say that Hong Kong society holds a particular view of the children of Gurkhas. He described: "Take drugs, involve in crime. And then they can be quite vicious, when their, things go wrong like. And then, I'm not certain, I think one or two, some people who ended up like that, and this caused a bad name across the whole community." Such a sweeping view of the bhanja and bhanji in Hong Kong society is thus read as problematic by both Brian and Aakar. They held the same view that quite clearly, not all children turn to drugs, yet such is the stereotypical impression that emerges in Hong Kong.

This point resonates with what Tang (2017) says, which is that there are evidently intragroup dynamics, intergroup differences and intragroup differentiations that intersect with intergenerational relations when it comes to the matter of turning to drugs. In this instance, it seems to be the case that the location of one's birth place matters in terms of being able to better adapt to a country that is different from one's parents, as opposed to those who had come to Hong Kong from Nepal. There are also some retired Gurkhas living or who had previously lived in Hong Kong such as Uttam and Nishad, whose views on Gurkha children counter that of the stereotypical assumption that the bhanja and bhanji group consume drugs and constitute a problematic population in totality:

> UTTAM: And some of these children are not decent people, some of these children who grew up they went into bad . . . like drugs. And when they went to Hong Kong a lot of them got caught and the Hong Kong government was frustrated with it.
>
> NISHAD: So some of them are doing really good. But then there are some who are looking for the triads kind and drug addiction and drug abuses and all. . . . Too many children of the bhanja bhanji have been, have spoilt . . . If only one can work in Hong Kong, there's no issue, no problem with the finances, the issue and all. If you can work and make money. But then people are not working; they don't want to

work. *They just—they don't think* [of] *Hong Kong as their own place* and they working. That's why they fall into those kind of habit, company. (my emphasis)

Where Uttam pointed out that some of the bhanja and bhanji had mixed with bad company and started taking drugs, Nishad's response illuminated how these Gurkha children do not regard "Hong Kong as their own place." This positioning is indicative of a sense of not-belonging for those from this generation of Gurkha families. Similarly, a media report in Hong Kong dating to December 1996 reflects some Gurkha children's lack of rootedness. In that report, readers are told of a twenty-year-old bhanja, Thapa Tekendra, who was caught with six kilograms of "ice" (i.e., methamphetamine) during a police drug bust operation. First mentioned as the "son of a Gurkha officer," we learn that Thapa had "committed the crime in an extremely confused state," and for which he was subsequently sentenced to seventeen years' imprisonment for drug trafficking. More pertinently, the cause of Thapa's drug offence was traced to his Gurkha father's constant mobile life that consequently rendered him "rootless":

> Thapa began using drugs *because of his rootless life, brought on by his father's moving from base to base throughout Asia*, the High Court heard. His drug use escalated from cough syrup to a hardcore addiction to ice. On February 12, Thapa was caught by the Special Duty Squad of Kowloon West lifting slightly over 6 kg of ice worth an estimated $2.5 million from the boot of a parked car in Ho Man Tin. (my emphasis)[24]

The struggles of some of these Gurkha children in Hong Kong are clear, interpreted both by themselves and public discourse that broach how they are not able to find their grounding and identity in countries such as Hong Kong. Brian shared with me his understanding of what the barriers to good education, including the nonrecognition of one's Nepalese educational background, in Hong Kong meant for some of them:

> Nobody wants a Nepalese education outside Nepal. Or they stay here they get a bad education. They drop out of school, they have problems. . . . Hong Kong's got a really bad social problem. They're not making [it] beyond security guarding, construction work, and driving . . . Those four areas are the only ones they can take on. So Hong Kong is using its ethnic minorities as a sort of underclass.

Despite such barriers, encounters, and varying experiences of discrimination or segregation in the scholastic or economic industries, Prakat maintained that there are more opportunities in Hong Kong as compared to Nepal. He explained,

> I think the Nepal, Nepal is worse off and no government, police is no good. No system is good. Nepal is I think poor country, because I born there but poor country. The government, police is very poor; everything is very poor there. So, Hong Kong is more a richer, police, everything is. And you have many opportunities for everyone. Even educated or not educated, skilled, not skilled, every people they can get the job in Hong Kong. So we have more opportunities in Hong Kong. So I came to Hong Kong, it's a good. If I was in Nepal maybe I'll be unemployed. [*laughs*] Who knows right?

Nishad shared a similar view. He thought that for his sons, "it's better that in Hong Kong they can at least make a living here. No need to go [to be recruited as a] Gurkha." Brian also noted the better prospects that Hong Kong could offer, problems notwithstanding, as compared to the lack of opportunities in Nepal. That said, however, Brian indicated (as with some of my bhanja/bhanji interlocutors) that the desire to stay long-term in Hong Kong is not there. Rather, these diasporans continued to look toward Nepal as their next or eventual destination:

> They treated this place where they work, and where they're based and it's better than Nepal. And it's safer there [Hong Kong]. They don't treat this [Hong Kong] as a base that they're going to live here forever. And *everything in their eyes is back to Nepal*. They go back there for every reason they could think of. (my emphasis)

Brian was of the view that "this isn't where they clearly belong. They just happen to be here [Hong Kong] at the moment." With eyes trained back to Nepal, diasporans such as Prakat may be said to possess a mental and affective sense of bracketed belonging to Nepal. While Prakat thought that most Gurkha children may not be keen on returning to Nepal, his own perspective on and affinity with Nepal was different and palpable:

> Ah, for the bhanja bhanji, I think they don't want to go back to the Nepal. Because they're allowed to live here, they're allowed to die here, they're allowed to work in Hong Kong. And compared to the, I think more opportunities in Hong Kong, compared to the Nepal. *But Nepal is our country. We born there, we love our country.* The culture and everything, the food, environment—*everything is close in our heart.* (my emphasis)

For Prakat, there are still ongoing problems and issues to do with Nepal's political structure and public infrastructure as well. Moreover, he bemoaned the lack of proper public toilets, political instability, and other problems that deterred an immediate return to Nepal. Prakat and his affective belonging to Nepal, despite dissatisfaction with its politics and infrastructure, represented a form of subscribing to belonging by birth and cultural familiarity. Hence, Nepal is his country and Hong Kong is a place to live and to make a living. I conceive of affective belonging in this instance as a bracketed form of longing to belong, yet discouraged only by unfavorable political and structural circumstances in Nepal. Such longingness is also a reflection of bracketing and reserving belonging until the political situation and livelihood in Nepal changes for the better that in turn flesh out shifting migrant–nation-state relations. As Nepal is not seen now as a place to return to settle down, Gurkha diasporans like Prakat can only parenthesize their sense of belonging to Nepal and suspend this till the situation improves. These particular instances of earning their keep in Hong Kong while looking toward Nepal in the near future articulates an aspirational but suspended sense of bracketed belonging to the latter. In the meantime, livelihoods are better realized and enacted elsewhere, which also includes step migration to another *elsewhere* (cf. Bunnell, Gillen, and Ho 2018). In Prakat's case, he told me that he was preparing to go over to the United Kingdom with his son, to join his wife. In Gauri's case, elsewhere is Australia where she pursued a higher degree after first returning to Kathmandu from Singapore.

Children of the GCSPF are connected both to their birthplace (Singapore) and their place of "origin" (Nepal). The word *origin* needs to be clarified. Gurkha children are, by virtue of their parents' nationality, Nepali. Hence, even if they were not born in Nepal, it is because of their parents that Nepal has to be their place of origin or their ancestral homeland. This then accounts for how Manisha's father constantly reminded her and her siblings that they cannot assimilate too much into Singapore society since the eventual locale of settlement would be Nepal and not Singapore. The sense of belonging that Gurkhas instill in their children links them to their country of origin. As she recounted how her father constantly reminded them:

> I don't know about my friends' fathers, but my father would say, he'll be the one . . . he's a man of a few words, he will be the one to say yes, be grateful that you have a chance to grow up as a Singaporean, and it's taken somewhat like a social experiment, you know, you are Nepali but you get the whole Singapore experience, from birth all the way up, but never forget that actually you are Nepali, so in in trying to blend in here [Singapore], do keep a note at the back of your mind, that at one time you have to leave . . . so while blending in, remember or be careful not to blend too completely to the extent that it becomes a weakness somewhat.

The idea of origin thus takes on different nuances for the first and second generation of Nepalese who worked, studied, or assumed housewifely duties in Singapore. Manisha conveyed what her mother thought of having left Nepal after getting married, and having to return upon her husband's retirement. She described:

> And then I think more than for us she was speaking for herself and the other wives, so, I mean, we stayed there for a good eighteen, twenty years, and then now we're here [Nepal]. It's a very pathetic state for us because for us we're neither here nor there . . . so where do we pick up from, you know, where do we pick up and where did we really leave, leave Singapore or leave Nepal?

For the children of Gurkhas, and in the case of Manisha's mother, there is therefore a sense of displacement (Yuval-Davis 2006) in Nepal (where belonging is meant to naturally arise), as a consequence of having spent many years in Singapore (where belonging was meant to be temporary if at all).

Manisha returned to Nepal after she had completed her O levels in Singapore. Her recollection of first impressions of her return conveyed how little she felt she belonged in Nepal. This sense of distance arose from having been brought up in Singapore. Such exposure instilled mores and social norms that Manisha found lacking in Nepal.

> So when I was taking the taxi ride back home [from the airport in Kathmandu], as offerings we got Mandarin oranges . . . and then we were having the oranges in the taxi, and then you know how Singapore is like, you know, it's a "fine" city, you don't litter, and then, like you always keep your litter in a plastic bag or in your pockets, so I was eating the Mandarin oranges, the peels were on my hands, on my lap, and then I'm looking at my aunt, looking at the scenery, I'm like, "Where's the dustbin?" and my aunt points out of the window, and [says] "That's the dustbin." She pointed to the ground [outside of the taxi]. So I'm like, "No, I mean the dustbin," I'm still looking for the dustbin, and then later I comprehend that the dustbin was the open road, and then she just takes the peel from my hand, then she tossed it out the window [while the taxi was still moving]. And until I get home I was still trying to digest, did that really happen? In front of my bare eyes? Or I am just, that was some crazy dream or something? Because I have never done that in my whole life.

Ostensibly, Manisha is confronted with different cultural frameworks (Wilding 2007) in her experience of "return" migration. For her, the materialities of everyday life in the two countries to which she is connected are markedly dissimilar. Similar, Renu's experience in Kathmandu illustrated her having to adjust to how things are done in Nepal as contrasted with Singapore. She said: "Let's say there's a very crowded place, then you have to walk through. Usually in Singapore, we say excuse me. Over here [in Kathmandu], the best way for you to get through is to push. If you say excuse me, it will just fall on deaf ears. You'll have to push." On top of the orange peel incident, the following "phlegm" experience also remained etched in Manisha's memory. The incident highlighted for her the distinction between Singapore and Nepal:

> Even when it comes to . . . dispelling phlegm, we are always taught to spit into our tissue paper, excuse ourselves to the washroom, and here [in Nepal] people just do it in the open. And I was like, I'm gonna hold it, I'm gonna go home and then I'd gonna go the toilet, and then I talk. Then my aunt was like, 'Why are you so quiet, why are you so quiet?' She was elbowing me, but then I was pointing to my mouth, she said, "Just spit it out the window!" It was a second shock in the taxi ride, so already . . . it was really an eye-opener, I couldn't, I don't think I could get a shocking, more realistic eye-opener than a taxi ride to home [Nepal]. . . [the basic everyday things] that I never in my wildest imagination thought would happen in Nepal. There it was, in front of my eyes.

Having to relocate to Nepal because of her father's retirement from the GCSPF, Manisha's process of relocation may be regarded as a "project of the self." This is an undertaking that includes difficulties and successes that operate in tandem as one relocates to one's homeland.

The enforced relocation from Singapore to Nepal meant having to learn how to adapt in Nepali society even if one was not born there. I have mentioned in earlier parts of the book that most Gurkha parents are conscious of teaching their children Nepali culture and language. To return to the point on language acquisition and use (in connection with Shradda's experience above and as I have highlighted in chapter 3 in terms of Fateh's concern), learning Nepali does not always ensure that it may be put to relevant or good use when Gurkha children return to Nepal. Ganga explained in our interview: "Because for them [Nepalis in Kathmandu] it's difficult to understand our English also. There's some words they pronounce differently, like we say *bus,* they say *boss.* When we say *bus,* they go: 'What bus?' So we feel like we are the fool here." Himalee Pun and Anita Rai, both of whom are daughters of Gurkhas who had retired from the GCSPF, decided to return to Nepal when the earthquake occurred in 2015. They wanted to serve as volunteer translators for the Singapore Armed Forces' medical team in contributing to relief aid. Feeling "almost [like] a stranger in [their] homeland," both of them found language to constitute a barrier between the locals and themselves.[25] Said Himalee: "[Our Nepali] sounds different; it's like how [Singaporeans] speak in Singlish. We have our own slang that the locals cannot understand."[26] In tandem,

Anita noted some communicative issues when she went back to Nepal: "The first few months were very difficult as the environment was totally different . . . Our pronunciation was different and as I'm not fluent in Nepali, I had to converse in English, which many could [not] understand."[27] For these social actors who have found it difficult to adjust to life in Nepal, be it for a short visit as is the case for Himalee and Anita, or for good where Ganga and others are concerned, there are a few other bhanja and bhanji like Manisha who had over time became adapted to living and working in Kathmandu.

From the initial stages of adjusting to life in Nepal, to four years later where she is presently working as a hotel guest relations officer in Kathmandu, Manisha has gone through shifts in sentiments of belonging. She has gradually become used to life in Nepal. For instance, she recounted the story of a Nepali friend who spent her first few years in India, and who came back to Nepal while still a young child. Although Manisha said she does not regard this friend as a "true Nepali," she admitted that this friend is "more Nepali than me because of the years that she's here." However, her friend thought otherwise, as Manisha herself explained:

> And yet she says to me that "I'm amazed by the way you've settled in, because when I look at you I feel like you are now the local and I'm the tourist." So I take it as a positive feedback that I've really put myself out here, and challenged myself to fit in, and learn . . . not by the book but by observation and everything that happens around me, and I haven't just challenged myself, I've succeeded actually. So . . . initially the challenges are there but then it's up to the individual, whether to succeed and just stick it in, or still deny that you are Nepali and still speak Singlish and you know just brag whatever thing Singaporean. Because that's sort of an illusion. You are not really holding that red [Singaporean] passport, you have a green passport and you are here [in Nepal].

In Manisha's own evaluation of returning to Nepal, she realized and embraced the challenges that she had to overcome. On the basis of her friend's opinion among other factors, she arrived at the conclusion that she has in fact managed well in (re)incorporating into Nepali society. Such an admission is then rounded off by way of referring to belonging in official and legislative dimensions, where Manisha raised the bureaucratic distinction between passports that connote the different nationalities in this context. Having said that, one should note also that the politics of citizenship and of belonging "can be distinguished analytically" (Brubaker 2010, 64). In spite of the connotations of "formal state membership" that is granted vis-à-vis citizenship, social actors can still possess a sense of belonging to more than one country, or to a country other than where they hold citizenship. Manisha's biography suggests such a form of belonging. While there is no formal belonging to the Singapore state given that she is not in possession of the red passport, Manisha's narrative nonetheless reflects the presence of substantive or felt membership with Singapore.

Feelings of belonging to both Singapore and Nepal may be discerned from Manisha's account of reminiscing about the "good days" that she and her cousin experienced in Singapore:

> You know, "Oh, you know Singapore won a gold medal in the Olympics, or you know, National Day is coming, and did you check the photographs on Facebook and what they are doing different this year . . ." So it's . . . for me, it's sort of like, I think I'm trying . . . I'm becoming more Nepali, and then just when I feel like I'm working there, I mean I don't force myself to work there but I see it happening. Then something happens that brings me back to Singapore. So it's just I think another loud statement that I can't deny that it will always be a part of me. It will have a . . . permanent space in my heart. Yes.

Concurrent sentiments of belonging to both countries, in the above account, are represented through Manisha's subscription to the Singapore community and its success or celebrations with regard to international sports performance or national day as a mark of the nation's independence. Manisha's account also indicates a shift in belonging, as she felt that she is "becoming more Nepali," and yet acknowledged at the same time that Singapore will hold a "permanent space" in her heart. Belonging to one country slowly modulates into belonging to two. In contrast, Riju and Ganga were both of the view that they do not feel like they belong to either Nepal or Singapore:

> RIJU: We would have belonged somewhere . . .
> GANGA: It's like we don't belong anywhere you know. Not in here [referring to Nepal], not in there [referring to Singapore], just dangling.

Drawing from Gurkha children's experiences such as those of Manisha, Riju, and Ganga above, sentiments of belonging and not-belonging—and indeed multiple belonging or otherwise—ought to be perceived as sharing the same plane on a continuum instead of a dichotomous polarity.

As different generational members of the wider Gurkha diaspora, social actors struggle to belong across different countries, contingent on their specific migratory pathway, location, and familial as well as individual biographical compositions. Their varied struggles to want to or at least attempts to belong and fit in traverse a range of everyday domains. They comprise language, education, employment, as well as cultural practices and values and ethics, among others.

Across these domains, not only have my interlocutors shared their self-identified ways of not-belonging arising from intercultural differences, they have also been externally placed in the category of not-belonging by other social actors. The external placement comes from social actors such as the state vis-à-vis both everyday encounters as well as structural exclusion or discrimination. These parallel threads of identification together demonstrate that belonging and not-belonging are both self-realized and externally or structurally imposed. In comparing these two sections on markers of belonging as well as not-belonging, it is also clear that such markers are similar if not identical; that belonging and not-belonging coterminously traverse the same set of factors and circumstances for diasporans located in different countries. In other words, whether one feels a sense of belonging or otherwise, or for others who suspend belonging as aspirational till a latter time, these varied forms of belonging and not-belonging crucially underline how belonging as a notion and in practice is an ongoing and continual project. As a perennial undertaking, belonging as an endeavor synchronizes with one's biographical encounters and phases in the migratory journey. Apart from articulating and interrogating the manifold expressions and experiences of belonging or otherwise above, my analysis of belonging as a key concept in this book also attends to what is at stake. That is to say, I am just as interested in unpacking the implications, consequences, and politics of belonging and not-belonging, as I shall examine next.

The Politics of Belonging: What Is at Stake?

Where the above biographical examples of belonging and not-belonging relate to affective and everyday practices in the main, I alter my direction here to consider the politics of belonging. Such politics may be examined in two ways: the first, how claims to belonging are rationalized, leads to the second: the ways Gurkha families wish to assert the rights that arise from those claims. Overall, there are benefits and costs of (not)belonging to different constellations, representing the valuing and judging of belonging (Yuval-Davis 2006). These may pertain to economic and medical entitlements, as well as community development in the country of settlement. In other words, when belongingness is created, claims to belonging can then be formulated and put forward, for example, to the Singapore or the Hong Kong government. As such, belonging becomes a resource (Antonsich 2010) that can be mobilized whereby social actors assert the right to stay, or to work in a place (Ervine 2008), among other claims.

The chairmen of the Everest Association and the Annapurna Community in Pokhara have organized themselves as a collective. It was agreed that the Everest Association would press claims in Singapore and the Annapurna Community would concentrate on contributing to the Nepali community in their postretirement years. In my meeting him, ex-Gurkha Hiresh who was chairman of the Everest Association, enumerated seven requests to the Singapore government through the SPF. These seven items demonstrate what is at stake if and when claims (built on belonging) are successfully pursued. They were as follows:

1. A review of retired servicemen's pensions, given that the inflation rate [in Nepal] has not been taken into account.
2. An increase of allowance for current servicemen.
3. Review of existing partial medical coverage that can only be reimbursed in Singapore; different medical coverage for servicemen who retired before and after 1994.
4. Permanent residency [in Singapore] for Gurkha children.
5. Wives and children to be allowed to work in Singapore.
6. Reemployment opportunities for retired servicemen.
7. Gurkha widows' pension.

The above requests were put forward by the Everest Association, crafted on the basis of rights of belonging that thereby engender these claims. As Hiresh put it:

> So, once our group retired in 2004, we think, there is no harm requesting to the government . . . . because we are requesting . . . if we don't request . . . we spent half our lives there, we serve, surviving with the pension given by the Singapore government, where [can] we go [to request]? We are not serving the government of Nepal, we were serving [Singapore] so we should request. I think morally, that should not be any problem. We should request.

The rationale for requesting these allowances is contingent on having served Singapore, and not the government of Nepal. This therefore prompted Hiresh and his group of ex-Gurkhas to make their claim based on moral grounds of service and sacrifice as a kind of "framing device" (Laubenthal and Schumacher 2020, 1139). Hiresh cited the example of an ex-Gurkha who, having retired in 1962, continued to receive SGD$62 (approximately US$45) as his pension. The response to this request from the Singapore Police Headquarters was that every retired serviceman who had served in Singapore could, from 2005, receive no more than SGD$218 (approximately US$158) per month.

Further claims to permanent residence for their children were also raised, given that they were born and bred in Singapore. They would therefore not be able to fit in in Nepal:

> We also request with the government that . . . children who were born there, they be given PR, because they are born [there], they are brought

up there! They studied there, and . . . they come here [Nepal], they are treated by Nepalese government like alien. Because they don't know any rule . . . they don't know any rule, they don't know Nepali, they don't know the system here, here you have a lot of under the table things you know? They don't know, they are very straight, they are like Singaporean.

Hiresh argued that they were brought up the "Singaporean way." Following the rationale that these children would know and therefore could survive and adapt to Singapore society, this meant to him that the children thus deserved the right to remain: "I think, for them, surviving in Singapore, they are qualified also. They studied there, they adapted there, so . . . we requested, if they are given, and then, it will be much more better [*sic*]." As bhanji Riju and Ganga both told me in a larger focus group interview, being born and bred in Singapore ought to translate into a right to studying or working there:

> RIJU: I mean even if you don't give us PR [permanent residence], just give work permit and you know . . .
>
> GANGA: We grew up there, we know Singapore's history and everything. It's like our home there you know? And then we are not granted our work permit and we are being sent back [to Nepal]. But then they [in Singapore] are giving work permit to Filipinos, China. . . . Those who don't even know the history of Singapore, those who doesn't even know the national anthem of Singapore, you know?

Ganga's response reflected her claims toward the right to belong based on one's knowledge of Singapore's history and national anthem, which was to be pertinently differentiated from others who are given work permits. Such knowledge translates into a form of resource pegged onto one's right to belong in close association with rights to education and employment. Having a permanent residence status would then mean that the children could continue to pursue their education and eventually work in Singapore, despite their Gurkha fathers' retirement and mandatory return to Nepal. In other words, their claims to belonging articulate pragmatic aspirations if not opportunities for educational and economic inclusion. Comparatively, and even in the case of Hong Kong where Gurkha diasporans have the right to abode which is unlike that in Singapore, those in Hong Kong are also aspiring for similar inclusionary opportunities as I have discussed above. Hiresh elaborated further as to why permanent residence status ought to be awarded to the children, in part due to their families' ability to finance their education costs:

> The other thing is, one thing is, once the father retires, whole family have to retire you know? We are repatriated. Can't stay on. Problem.

That is a difficult fact. Children don't want to come [to Nepal]. Children want to stay there, want to study there! Also cannot! Not given the opportunity. The amazing thing is, if the people want to go for tertiary education, or somebody want to go further studies, in Singapore . . . they also have money, and they are given the opportunity. But the children of the Gurkhas, they have CPF [Central Provident Fund], they have gratuity everything, so they can support their [children's education], because why? Every parent want to support their children. For their education. Even though they have CPF, they have gratuity, they . . . money accumulated for the children, they want to give them also, it's not given the opportunity you know. That's the . . . very sad . . . and very . . . disappointing fact. So . . . we raised this point also.

Similar stances were also adopted by other retired Gurkha servicemen. They claimed it was puzzling and frustrating that in spite of their children having been schooled and trained as nurses in Singapore, they were not allowed to work as nurses thereafter. Furthermore, these servicemen also pointed out that there are many foreigners in Singapore working mainly as nurses in the medical industry. They come from such countries as China, the Philippines, and India. One ex-Gurkha noted that some nurses from China could not speak English: "But they can't even speak English. We can speak English but [are] not allowed to work in Singapore." Hiresh's frustration, similar to Ganga's, is discernible here:

Singapore [is] employing the nurses from Philippines, from China, and India as well. But the Gurkhas' children, study there, and born there, brought up there, and did the nursing course there! Staff nurse course. But not allowed to work. So they migrated to elsewhere. Some . . . Australia, some in United Kingdom, some in the States. Since their degree is accepted in those countries, why not in Singapore? This is the problem. Because the children are penalized because the father is Gurkha. Very sad case.

Beyond the impossibility of working in Singapore, Hiresh's observations raise another point in the cycles or processes of migration that are associated with not-belonging in this instance. That is to say, although some Gurkha children have earned the relevant qualifications, they are on the one hand not permitted to put their skills to good use in the Singapore medical field.

On the other hand, return migration to Nepal is also not a desirable option. According to Hiresh, they would be regarded as "aliens" in Nepal. Migrating to other countries outside of Asia for further studies or work then becomes the only viable option in their onward migratory journeys. In sum, the politics of belonging, documented through the foregoing discussion, is connected to citizenship and its rights and duties, including "the right to migrate, the right of abode, the right to work and, more and more recently, the right to plan a future where you live" (Yuval-Davis 2006, 208). Hiresh's varied rationale on behalf of the Gurkha children reflected a stance premised on exerting both the legitimacy and deservingness to belong (Blachnicka-Ciacek et al. 2021). In so doing, they could thereby join the "community of value" (Anderson 2013) as good migrants. This sentiment has been echoed by both former Gurkhas and their children who worked and studied in Singapore. What is at stake in the politics of belonging—where belonging translates into a localized resource (Khan 2021) as discussed above—has to do with securing both educational and economic rights and stability.

In order to expand on the varying registers of belonging across different generations, and what is at stake in them, I draw particular attention to the seventh requested item that has to do with establishing a widows' pension. Hiresh mentioned that in comparison to the widows' pension that is made available for the wives of deceased Gurkhas in the British and the Indian Army, there is no similar scheme in the case of Singapore. He then explained why such a pension is important:

> Of course we understand that there's no pension for Singaporean also. We understand. But, the Singaporean widow have [*sic*] much more advantage. They can work. The Gurkha wives, they remain as dependents. Whole . . . whole . . . time, all the way, the husband works there. Can't work. And . . . the time when she can work, time has gone you know! By the time the husband reaches the forty-five, forty-five years, then it's too late. She come back here [Nepal], she has nothing. So that's why . . . we requested the government that the, at least, . . . that's why we have a, one widows' fund. We created our own.

Asking for the widows' pension therefore connects to the other request on allowing Gurkha wives to seek employment in Singapore, through which they can then be economically self-sufficient should their spouses pass on.

While waiting for this request to be considered, the Everest Association has, on its own, initiated a widows' pension. Active servicemen contribute SGD$10 (approximately US$7) per month to this cause. Hiresh cited the case of one Gurkha policeman who was in Chitwan on leave from service in Singapore, and who died when the boat he was in capsized. His wife and children had to return to Nepal with no form of support. The widows' fund was subsequently established as a way to help such widows cope with the loss of their only source of income. In this respect, belonging is counterposed to economic dispossession (Stratford 2009) in the recommendation for a pension scheme for Gurkha widows. In other words, belonging here is transformed into a resource for these widows to obtain economic stability as a "right" to be exercised.

Aside from the varied military, police, and migratory experiences of Gurkha soldiers and police as part of the Gurkha diaspora, the other key transnational social actors in this diaspora are their wives and children, and their experiences, encounters, and aspirations as contextualized in different countries. I interrogated the composition, shifts, rationale, and negotiations associated with belonging and not-belonging. In my attempts to evaluate what belonging means, as well as the accompanying stakes that come into play in relation to not-belonging, I have argued that belonging first needs to be empirically realized so as to draw attention to what it means to belong or not belong to a particular country or countries. By narrating a range of perspectives, motivations, plans, and aspirations across a spectrum of social actors, I demonstrated what it means for these individuals to be a part of the Gurkha diaspora. From the Gurkha to his wife, and his children who were born outside of Nepal, the idea of "origin" and therefore "return migration" take on perceptible differences given contrasting biographical backgrounds and social locations of these social actors. Where the Gurkhas and their wives have left Nepal for Singapore or Hong Kong, their children, as Singapore-born Nepalis for instance, have not experienced the same type of departure. Instead, their departure from Singapore may very well connote this country as "origin"; having to "return" to Nepal, at first, makes no sense. It follows that instead of comprehending return as marking the end of the migration cycle, it must be seen as one of many stages in the migratory process (Cassarino 2004). In the case of Gurkha families in Hong Kong, the three different generations of these diasporans and their diverse phases of traveling to Hong Kong, then back to Nepal, and yet again back to Hong Kong likewise corroborate with Cassarino's (2004) critique of "return" as I indicate above. Furthermore, practices of remigration, contingent on which group of Gurkhas and families we are focusing on, implies a reversal of source and destination countries. This reversal thereby reconfigures what constitutes as emigration or immigration locations (Ho 2019). Given the problematization of "return" as a process and not as an end point in the larger scheme of migration, it remains to be seen as to whether senses of belonging and not-belonging may take on different permutations for retired Gurkhas and their families in varying host-origin contexts and further stages of their biographical trajectories.

Second, belonging and not-belonging should not be treated in a dichotomous manner. Through the narratives that I have presented above, it is clear that belonging and not-belonging may take place concurrently, given the simultaneous subscription to felt senses of familiarity, comfort, and longing for both Nepal and Singapore, for instance, that thread across different phases of informants' lives. For the indicators that my interlocutors relate to and register as reflecting their sense of belonging—comprising foodways, language use, and others—then the same set of indicators likewise applies for their sentiments of not-belonging.

Third, belonging also shifts in meaning and through context. Having a stake in a country means asserting one's rights, such as the claims that have been put forward by Gurkha families with regard to education, medical, and employment entitlements in or from Singapore. Returning to Nepal from Singapore also means organizing Gurkha families as a collective, so as to deliver community-based initiatives as Nepal becomes bracketed as their aspired country of belonging in a retirement milieu. Similarly, those who are presently living and working in Hong Kong have as well bracketed their aspirational longing to return to Nepal only when the political situation takes a turn for the better. This is a country they were born in but for which return has to be suspended for the moment.

The final point to note is that much scholarship has made conceptual distinctions between belonging, identity, citizenship, and other cognate notions within the wider discussion on migration. However, these imbricated categories of experience, be they at the level of the everyday or at the structural or sociolegal level, need to be addressed concurrently. The aim is therefore to provide a fuller, and both empirical and categorical, means of unpacking what belonging, not-belonging, and the politics of belonging connote for different generations of migrants. Diasporans and their similar and different pathways are multidirectional and shift from generation to generation. I have pointed out examples that reflect differences both within and between different generations of Gurkha wives and children. These thereby remind us of how such variation call forth manifold "turning points" (Berg 2011) that influence how belonging is felt or continues to shift for different diasporan actors and which thereby assume different valence, forms, and meaning. As I have also suggested, belonging and not-belonging are not to be regarded as occupying two opposite ends of a dichotomy. Rather, they should be consigned as different points along a continuum. It is therefore crucial to realize why and how migrants of different generations inhabit varying points on this continuum, and how best conceptual notions of belonging and not-belonging vis-à-vis- bracketing can account for the heterogeneity of experiences. The investigation should address the multifaceted makeup of diasporic populations and their generational actors, and engage with types of migrant trajectories that together animate cross-border and cross-cultural encounters within specific sociocultural and political structural milieus.

AT THE EDGE OF BELONGING?

In March 2012, Roshan Ghising, a Nepali citizen and son of former Gurkha Lal Bahadur Ghising, appealed against the decision of the First Tier Tribunal. He had been refused the leave to remain (in the United Kingdom) as a dependent of a former British Brigade serviceman.[1] While both Roshan's parents possess the indefinite leave to remain (ILR) in the United Kingdom, he was not granted the same given a few reasons.[2] As the appellant, Roshan had not furnished sufficient evidence to demonstrate "an interference with family life" due to the refusal of his ILR. According to the tribunal, his "emotional ties were no more than the usual ties which a twenty-five year old student has with his parents," and that he had "lived apart from them for over two years." Furthermore, whereas the spouse and minor children of discharged Gurkhas were allowed to remain, the case for adult children is subject to discretionary judgment. Besides, as Roshan had entered the United Kingdom in 2007 on a student visa "of limited duration," there was therefore no "expectation of settling here permanently." In the end, the "removal" of Roshan from the United Kingdom was deemed justified "because of the public interest in a firm and consistent immigration policy." In legal terms, Roshan possessed no right to the ILR in spite of "public interest to remedy an historic injustice in the UK government's previous treatment of Gurkha veterans."[3]

Earlier, I discussed the everyday narratives and affective experiences of belonging and not-belonging among Gurkhas and their families. I now shift gears to attend to broader sociolegal and structural processes and frameworks herein. Bracketed belonging is explored as a legal process where I employ secondary data

that include examples and records of (court) cases such as that of Roshan Ghising and others, as well as UK parliamentary debates and documents. Examples
of such debates include:

> Surely, given their service to this country and communities across the
> land, Gurkhas deserve better than being forced to survive on the edge
> of poverty. I hope the Minister will make clear just what our Govern-
> ment are doing for all those Gurkhas who gave up so much in service
> to our nation.[4]

> We have always considered the Gurkhas' service to be loyal, courageous
> and skillful. Gurkhas are synonymous with the very best of the British
> armed forces. During the world wars, more than 43,000 Gurkhas lost
> their lives in battle, and since then they have served in just about every
> theatre of war, including the Falklands, Kosovo, Iraq and Afghanistan.
> Ultimately, it is a question of value. How do we consider these individu-
> als? Do we consider them as equal and do we properly value them, or
> are they simply a convenient source of personnel?[5]

By analyzing such secondary data, I identify and discuss different modes of
how legal bracketing takes place through law and policymaking as a useful site
for interrogating and deepening the conceptual dimensions of belonging and
not-belonging. Immigration controls of the Nepalese Gurkha community as
meted out by the British government signal legal structures of rights to belong in
close association with Gurkha service. I also address how the legacy of such service impinges on the rights of children in terms of entry for settlement. To do so,
I examine court cases and appeals conducted in the United Kingdom from 2000
to the present-day, given that legislative and policy changes were enacted from
the 1990s onward. I therefore trace the different shifts and argumentation concerning issues revolving around immigration and citizenship, as well as pay and
pension arrangements as outcomes arising from the changes put in place since
the 1990s. That said, there were indubitably legal proceedings and hearings conducted earlier both in Nepal and the United Kingdom. They include in the context of Nepal, the different parliamentary committees that investigated Gurkha
pension issues in the 1990s. There was also another initiative on Gurkha recruitment vis-à-vis international relations and human rights, given concerns raised
about Nepal's foreign policy for the recruitment of Nepali citizens into foreign
armies. On the UK side, the House of Commons had since 1947 debated Gurkha
issues running the range from their terms and conditions of service (TACOS),
pension arrangements, to immigration matters and welfare (see Laksamba et al.
2013; and G. Sangroula 2019).

In Hong Kong, one needs to consider the extent to which Gurkha families are themselves emplaced within larger South Asian diasporic communities and how they are situated within this hierarchy of foreigners (see for example, Erni and Leung 2014; Yung 2002).[6] In the case of Singapore, mandatory repatriation to Nepal is exacted when the Gurkha fulfills his service up to forty-five years of age, or if he opts for early retirement as I earlier reiterated. While his children are allowed to receive education in local schools over the course of his police career, his wife is not granted permission to work. Upon retirement, the entire family has to return to Nepal. This "use-and-repatriate" policy of the Singapore Police Force in which the Gurkhas serve illustrates yet another example of bracketed belonging in terms of their contributions to security and no more beyond that.[7] Prior to 2004 where Gurkha veterans with at least four years of service with the British Army were eligible to apply for settlement in the United Kingdom, they were often "treated less favourably than other comparable non-British Commonwealth citizens" who were also serving in the British Army.[8] The latter group has been able to adhere to a concessionary policy that lay outside of the immigration rules (IR); both serving and retired members of the British Army of this group could obtain the ILR in the United Kingdom upon their discharge. Gurkhas were, before 2004, not included in this policy.[9] Such imbalanced treatment between these two groups thereby reflects "stratified tiers of belonging for migrants" (Morrice 2017, 606).

The key question here is this: To what extent are the Gurkhas and their families allowed to belong in legal terms? If they are, according to the opening epigraphs, surviving at the "edge of poverty," then how should one conceive of what constitutes equality and what of their "value" per se? I expand the conceptual utility of bracketed belonging to illustrate how the UK government and its legislative structures, though not without exceptions and changes, place the Gurkhas and their families at the edge of belonging.[10] Such state and legislative behavior in effect points to the threshold of belonging; lines are drawn between citizenry and Gurkha "foreignness."[11] In terms of legal aspects, the Gurkhas and their families stand at the margins of belonging until otherwise decreed. This is so given that various laws and policies appear to discriminatorily bracket the Gurkhas' belonging that thereby limit their lobbying for particular rights; what Geeta Sangroula would call them in contrast as "rights-holders" (2019, 15).[12] Although legal bracketing marks both inclusionary and exclusionary boundaries as I show below, these brackets are not always calcified. I pose the title of this chapter as a question given that my reading of legal texts and court proceedings show how the edge of belonging for Gurkhas has also changed over time. Looking further into these different changes would aid in conceiving of bracketed belonging as a mutable practice as enacted through law and vis-à-vis immigration policies.

In other words, the edge or threshold of belonging has shifted over the past few decades, through which Gurkha "value" is then foregrounded and made tangible as I later demonstrate. It follows that the equality of treatment is then debated and worked through in legal and parliamentary domains. It is thus my interest to map out and critique these shifts accordingly through the prism of bracketed belonging.

Instead of discussing court cases on their own individual terms in extenso, I extrapolate and present key thematic discussions of how bracketed belonging is broached in the legal and political arenas. Specifically, I investigate the myriad ways in which bracketed belonging is raised, contested, and redrawn in order to flesh out the shifting malleability of belonging and not-belonging vis-à-vis legal frameworks and immigration policies. Bracketed belonging as circumscribed by the states and legal structures illuminate the boundaries and parameters of belonging and not-belonging and of (in)eligibility. Even if one's legal status or rights to legal inclusion is constrained, however, one could still feel a sense of "partial belonging" (Rottmann, Josipovic, and Reeger 2020, 241) as well. I scrutinize the legal aspects of citizenship, pension arrangements, and settlement rights that different cohorts and groups of Gurkhas and their adult children have lobbied for in the United Kingdom since the 1997 handover of Hong Kong to China, which meant that the Brigade of Gurkhas was then brought back to the United Kingdom.

I divide my discussion into four main sections. The first traces the shifting legal and immigratory contexts in order to comprehend the backdrop of how such changes have impacted the Gurkhas' TACOS. I begin with the 1947 Tripartite Agreement (TPA) that laid out the Gurkhas' TACOS and which explains their pay package and pension arrangements as well. This is followed by my discussion of other key turning points, including the 1997 handover of Hong Kong to China, changes to immigration policy and rights to settlement enacted in the early 2000s, and subsequent policy reviews and further changes that also affected Gurkha adult children and their rights to abode in the United Kingdom. The second section addresses legal case hearings and considers claims and appeals for equal treatment, and rights to settlement in the United Kingdom put forward by both Gurkha veterans as well as their adult children. I approach these through an investigation into the various forms and features of legal bracketing. In doing so, I articulate the process, negotiation, resistance, and shifts of legal bracketing and also address the attendant outcomes and consequences thereafter. In the various legal cases I discuss below, one theme that I identify has to do with how principles and practices of the Gurkhas' bracketed belonging to Nepal as adopted by the British government and Army are constantly adhered to. These are routinely raised in the face of their putting up compensation claims, leave issues, accompanied service, and other issues.[13] Emphasizing such bracketing in these cases is a recurrent way to reject the various claims that ex-Gurkhas put up for tribunal hearing.[14] They are, in effect, placed outside of the brackets of belonging to the United Kingdom, which explains such denial of their claims.

Another way to ensure that the Gurkhas remain at the edge of belonging to rights and claims presented to the British courts is that distinctions continue to be made between Gurkha and British soldiers on the basis of nationality. Such distinctions are thereby deployed as justification that "equality of treatment" for these two groups of military actors need to be rethought.[15] Not only are brackets of belonging and not-belonging enforced on Gurkha veterans, similar processes also determine family lives of Gurkhas and their children. Definitions of the family form a unit of contention in legal terms, debated in view of the European Council of Human Rights' (ECHR) values on protecting family lives. By presenting these various analytical threads in my examination of court cases, I explicate the different compositions and features of belonging in the legal arena. They include the four elements of how bracketing is (1) formulated to edge the Gurkhas out of the parameters of belonging and thereby to reject their claims; (2) being resisted in order to challenge the bounded parameters of belonging and not-belonging; (3) shaped by different sets of qualifying conditions to prompt legal recognition of such (newer) brackets of belonging and thereby rights to their claims; and (4) shifted owing to changes in immigration policies that have to do with rights to settlement in the United Kingdom.

In the third section, I discuss the recent 2021 hunger strike that Gurkha veterans and widows put up in protest against the UK government as they demand for equal pensions. Along with the strike was an accompanying petition that garnered more than 100,000 signatures in support of the Gurkha community. The strike and petition had culminated from a lack of sufficient and suitable responses from the UK government pertaining to equal and fair treatment for Gurkhas who have served the crown.[16] As a corollary to this third section, I then scrutinize a UK parliamentary debate that took place in November 2021, arising from the petition above. In this fourth section where I examine the different advocatory speeches delivered by the different members of Parliament (MP), I show how their advocacy for the Gurkhas also reveal the different ways in which belonging is reconceived and tabled for legislative considerations. Together, all four sections therefore elucidate how debates and contestations over the threshold and edges of belonging vis-à-vis rights to resources and others are being worked out by a host of different institutional and individual social actors.

Legal and Immigratory Contexts

The 1947 TPA signed between the United Kingdom, Nepal, and India was anchored on the principle that Gurkhas were to be both recruited from and discharged back to Nepal, as I have earlier discussed.[17] Issues to do with residency rights or full British citizenship at the end of one's Gurkha service were never explicitly discussed or arranged (Laubenthal and Schumacher 2020). Gurkhas were essentially recruited for service in Asia, where they were expected to eventually return to Nepal (Kochhar-George 2010). Given this context, retired Gurkhas then had no right of settlement in the United Kingdom. Concomitantly, their TACOS were therefore different from those of other soldiers serving in the British Army. As many of the court cases involving Gurkha veterans as well as their adult children have to do with claims to pension arrangements, citizenship, and settlement rights, I note here the legal and immigratory contexts and changes since the 1990s. Pension pay schemes and rights to residence in the United Kingdom were revisited over time. Before the handover of Hong Kong to China in 1997, the former served as the Gurkhas' base, in addition to one regiment located in Brunei.[18] The Brigade of Gurkhas was therefore mainly based in Asia, even if they did serve from time to time in Aldershot, United Kingdom. The Gurkhas' TACOS, including pay, pension arrangements, Married Accompanied Service (MAS), and other conditions were pegged to rates adhered by the Indian Army. There was therefore a substantial pay difference between Gurkhas and those others who served in the British Army prior to 1997, and where pension arrangements were also entirely different for these two different groups of military actors.[19] Under the Gurkha Pension Scheme (GPS), Gurkhas received pension amounts that were considerably lower than those of others who also retired from the British Army, but who were paid through the Armed Forces Pension Scheme (AFPS). The GPS was based on the Indian Army Model and for which it provided an immediate pension for retirees who had served at least fifteen years,[20] awarded based on Indian Army rates (Thurley 2021a).[21] Laksamba's (2012) study on the changing identities of the Gurkhas and their struggles for justice in recent years regarding policy issues includes interview materials from former Gurkhas pertaining to the AFPS and pension-related dissimilarity. I quote at length some of their accounts here to illustrate pension disparities between the British and the Gurkhas in the British Army. The first account is from a former Gurkha who retired prior to 1997, and the second, after 1997:

> I am a retired Rifleman from 6th Gurkha Rifles. I get £215 pounds per month in pension as per the Gurkha Pay and Pension Scheme (GPS). I am not allowed to join the British Armed Forces Pension Scheme (AFPS) as I retired before 1997. Even if they allow me to join the AFPS, I heard, my fifteen years in Hong Kong based service will be counted only 5.4 years for UK pensionable service. I think this is unfair for all Gurkhas. I do not understand why the British Government is not allowing us to join the AFPS? (Laksamba 2012, 118)

I served nineteen years and retired from the Army in 2003 at the rank of Staff Sergeant. I get £285 monthly pension. When I reach sixty years of age, my pension will be transferred to the AFPS where my pre 1997 service will be converted to the proportion of four years being equal to one year. This means that I will get around nine years Staff Sergeant's pension. I am supposed to get nineteen years pension equal to my British counterparts. (Laksamba 2012, 118–19).

Ostensibly, both accounts indicate that the Gurkhas have been bracketed out of the AFPS and/or receive less pension compared to their British counterparts. Gurkhas who were temporarily stationed in the United Kingdom before 1997 had received a supplement to their pay. This arrangement subsequently turned into a permanent fixture for those who continued to be based in the United Kingdom after 1997. Even if this supplementary pay made it possible for the Gurkhas' take-home pay to be equivalent to a soldier of similar rank in the British Army, such supplementation did not qualify as pensionable pay. This was because the assumption was that the Gurkhas would return to Nepal upon retirement. At such a point, Gurkhas who had retired were usually in their early thirties and they would embark on a second career after Gurkha service. To contextualize this, the UK courts pointed out that "the pension of an ordinary Gurkha in Nepal equated with the pay of a captain in the Nepalese Army."[22] The payable pension that retired Gurkhas would receive was deemed as sufficient enough for them to maintain a reasonable lifestyle.

The transfer of Hong Kong to China on 1 July 1997 gave rise to fundamental changes that were enacted in terms of the Gurkhas' TACOS. From then till the early 2000s, newer immigratory regulations and citizenship issues were subsequently promulgated. Now that the three regiments based in Hong Kong were unable to remain there after the handover, the home base of the Gurkhas had by then shifted to the United Kingdom. The Gurkhas had, as time passed, "spent increasingly large amounts of their time in the United Kingdom and developed contacts and roots here [referring to the United Kingdom]; so too their families."[23] In the years leading up to the return in 1997, pressure had mounted on the MOD (Ministry of Defence, United Kingdom) in terms of the Gurkhas' TACOS. This was because it was considered by many that the differences in pay and pension arrangements between Gurkha soldiers and others serving in the British Army would lose justification once the Brigade of the Gurkha would have shifted their home base from Hong Kong to the United Kingdom. Parallel to such pressure were concerted calls for the Gurkhas to possess the right to either remain in or to reenter the United Kingdom after they had retired from service. Owing to such collective insistence, Immigration Rules HC 395 were altered. As of 24 October 2004, any Gurkha who had served for at least four years in the British

Army and who had been discharged after 1 July 1997, was able to apply for what was termed as indefinite leave to enter or remain (ILR/E) in the United Kingdom based on newly introduced Immigration Rules 276E–276K. This point was also earlier mentioned by some of my interlocutors in previous chapters.

It has been estimated that out of the 2,230 Gurkhas who were discharged after 1 July 1997 and therefore eligible for the ILR/E, 90 percent of these retirees have applied for the IRL/E accordingly.[24] As for those who were discharged before 1 July 1997, the courts have estimated that there were about 25,000 Gurkhas who were in receipt of the GPS.[25] Other reviews which looked into the differences between British Gurkhas and the rest of the army makeup were conducted pertaining to the Gurkhas' TACOS as well as the availability of MAS. In January 2005, a review of the TACOS was announced by the Secretary of State for Defence. The outcome of this review was the promulgation of the Gurkha Offer to Transfer (GOTT). The promulgation meant that both serving as well as retired Gurkhas ought to be permitted to transfer from the GPS to the AFPS. For those who wished to remain on the GPS, this option was available but would later close from April 2006.[26] The basis for the transfer from the GPS to the AFPS was that their accrued pension, based on service after 1 July 1997, would then be transferred into the AFPS on a year-for-year credit. Such transfer would imply that what the Gurkhas receive would therefore be equivalent to what the rest of the personnel in the British Army would have accrued for that period as well. As for the years of service registered prior to 1 July 1997, the rights accrued in the GPS would be of actuarial value, for which the total sum would be transferred as a pension credit to the AFPS. This pension credit amount was correspondingly lesser (relative to service counted after 1 July 1997 and pension calculations) as the pensionable pay for Gurkhas before 1 July 1997 was substantially lower than that of other soldiers in the British Army.

As for the MAS matter, it had by then become an "increasingly troublesome issue"[27] given that the Brigade of Gurkhas was now based in the United Kingdom post-1997. The outcome for this review was that as of 1 April 2006, MAS was granted to those Gurkhas who had served at least three years with the brigade, in order to facilitate wives and children of Gurkhas serving in the United Kingdom to join their spouse or father.[28] Three years later on 21 May 2009, Home Secretary Jacqui Smith announced to the UK Parliament that any retired Gurkha who had served for at least four continuous years and who had been discharged from the Brigade of Gurkhas prior to 1 July 1997 was eligible for settlement in the United Kingdom. The landmark ruling came on the heels of a motion put forward in the House of Commons by the Liberal Democrats on 29 April 2009 to offer all Gurkhas the right of residence. Voting results for the motion turned out to be 267 in favor of against 246, constituting a first motion defeat for the government since 1978 (Purthi 2011). Such a scheme, articulated as "discretionary arrangements," indicates a recognition of the "unique nature of the service" that Gurkhas have provided and thus are only offered to them "on an exceptional basis."[29] Following on from the 2004 and 2009 policy changes then, most of the Gurkha veterans who were of pension-age had subsequently moved to the United Kingdom to take up residence, relying on pension credit and housing support (Laksamba et al. 2013).

Arising from these changes, one could argue that where legal recognition and bracketing of Gurkha belonging to the United Kingdom have been enacted, such processes also imply that there will be a shift in the home or family base that Gurkhas and their families occupy. In other words, legal recognition and subsequent provision for living in the United Kingdom would similarly entail a recalibration of how Gurkhas and their family members regard where home and family life would be. Such recognition follows from the assumption that after the Brigade of Gurkhas moved its headquarters from Hong Kong to the United Kingdom, Gurkhas who were discharged either on or after 1 July 1997 would "therefore have had more opportunity to develop close physical ties with the United Kingdom."[30] This constitutes another perspective through which to unpack where home may be and how it is determined once the bounds of legality change, in addition to my earlier discussions relating to feelings of belonging that my interlocutors have shared. Not only did such changes alter where home and its location were, they also extended these discretionary arrangements to other family members of Gurkha retirees. While original settlement arrangements had initially been applicable only for former Gurkhas, their wives, and their offspring below the age of eighteen, the discretionary arrangements had later been expanded to include widows of ex-Gurkhas. In certain cases, such arrangements extended to their children who were above the age of eighteen.[31] The 2009 policy was later reviewed by the Home Office between 2014 and 2015, as it had then considered case law as well as evidence which were provided to the All Party Parliamentary Group on Gurkha Welfare. Arising from this review, discretionary arrangements that were promulgated in 2009 were further calibrated. Adult children of ex-Gurkhas were thereafter allowed the right to settle in the United Kingdom, depending on particular circumstances. This policy was only made applicable for applicants either on or after 5 January 2015, and only available to those applicants who were outside of the United Kingdom. As for those adult children of ex-Gurkhas who were already in the United Kingdom, they were expected to exit the United Kingdom and then to put up an application via this policy from overseas.[32]

Forms and Features of Legal Bracketing

In order to address and attend to the above contexts in which laws and immigration policies shift over time with regard to Gurkha rights as a whole, I interrogate the different components and logics of bracketed belonging that I flesh out hereunder based on my analysis of legal documents. With this backdrop, we are then able to further comprehend the mobility, aspirations of, and legal resources to be made available to Gurkhas and their families over time. Bracketed belonging in legal terms and discourses comprise a range of different dynamics in relation to arguments and responses submitted pertaining to rights and access. These different aspects and contours of bracketed belonging understood in relation to a range of social actors and legal processes attest to the conceptual elasticity of bracketed belonging.

Overall, belonging and its bracketed shifts bring to the fore such legal criteria of belonging, which include but are not limited to affective ties and connections, contributions and sacrifices made, and cultural familiarity. These form among many other attributes, the crux of what it means to belong, including its accompanying resources and politics. Shifts in bracketed belonging thereby also indicate two other related issues. First, that sociolegal structures and policies that govern rights to settlement, citizenship, pension issues and claims form structural components of prescribing belonging through governance. Second, such shifts also point toward the malleability and flexibility of how criteria to belong may change, depending on existing as well as renewed structures of governance. What is significant here, however, is how affective and affiliative ties to different countries can seemingly be pronounced in legal documents (cf. Maunaguru 2019; Navaro-Yashin 2007) in favor of denying rights, or likewise in favor of acceding to rights requests. Such affective and affiliative dimensions are drawn from cases involving Gurkha adult children who appealed for rights to settle in the United Kingdom, which I discuss below. These cases are useful in elucidating how the Gurkha family unit is bracketed not only through UK laws, but in concert with other international bodies and their regulations such as the ECHR.[33]

Bracketing Gurkha-Nepal Belonging

There are two ways to consider how bracketing Gurkhas to Nepal transpire in the legal arena. The first is that where assertions of belonging are connected to claims to rights and resources, it should also be said that belonging is accompanied by *obligations*. The second has to do with how such bracketing sheds light on the idea of deservedness by birth and nationality. I first trace obligations to the 1947 Tripartite Agreement (TPA) that arose after Indian independence and where both the British and the Indians were keen on retaining Gurkha service (Gurkhas were recruited and trained in British India territory). Trilateral agreements included consent for establishing Gurkha units both in the British and the Indian Army. These three parties also agreed on a few further points. The Maharajah of Nepal would agree to his subjects serving with the British Army as long as they were not deployed to fight against Hindus. Furthermore, the Gurkhas would be able to be withdrawn at any time if Nepal was involved in any war so that they could be recalled to defend its territory. It is for this reason that the "Government of Nepal regards retention of Nepalese nationality while its troops serve in the Brigade of Gurkhas as of considerable importance."[34]

The recruitment and enlistment of Gurkhas were allowed to take place in India until recruiting stations were established in Nepal, which did not happen until 1952. Gurkha salaries and terms of recruitment were to be equivalent to rates of the Indian Army. These were put in place so as to not allow the British Army any unfair advantage in enlisting the Gurkhas on more favorable terms and thus undermine the Indians. This set of agreements and consensus reflect how belonging vis-à-vis the TPA and to Nepal for the Gurkhas are closely associated with the Gurkhas' obligation to Nepal even while they serve in the British Army. A key component of the TPA notes:

> Gurkhas would serve in the British Army in a dedicated Brigade reflecting the Nepali language, culture and educational standards. This was not a Brigade in the conventional sense of a deployment of various regiments and military units in a formation headed by a Brigadier, but a specialist Gurkha unit reflecting these unique arrangements and the continuing links to Gurkha culture.[35]

The above is a clearly stated and official endorsement that institutionally brackets the Gurkhas' belonging to Nepal in the interest of the country, even as they serve a foreign sovereign.

There are further ways through which bracketing Gurkhas to Nepal are talked about beyond obligations. These surface in relation to tradition, culture, heritage, and family life. Defense lawyers acting on behalf of the British MOD—in a case in which seven ex-Gurkhas alleged that they were subject to both institutionalized and systemic discrimination on the grounds of their race and/or nationality—noted why bracketing Gurkhas to Nepal was pivotal.[36] Following the enclosed brackets where Gurkhas are to be recruited from and retired in Nepal, defense lawyers reminded the court that Gurkhas "are Nepalese citizens and continue to be so during their period of service to the Crown."[37] Upon their retirement, they "will return to Nepal and resume their place in Nepalese society."[38] These brackets form the basis on which Gurkhas are then expected to be able to carry out their service with the British Army, without any issues in "maintaining their distinct Nepalese identity and safeguarding their cultural, religious and ethnic heritage."[39] I previously discussed similar institutional bracketing of Gurkhas to Nepal as exacted through, for example, celebrating Nepalese festivals among the Gurkhas in Hong Kong and Singapore. Such cultural bracketing is thereby meant to sustain the cohesion and cultural homogeneity of the Gurkha community vis-à-vis Nepal (Uesugi 2019a), not unlike what these lawyers have indicated as well.

In congruity with citizenry and cultural bracketing, another way to maintain these brackets relates to the long leave per three years for which Gurkhas are eligible. In this case, the minister of state for defence Mr. Soames had stated in court, "The present entitlement of Gurkha soldiers to long leave every three years will remain. This recognises the continuing importance we attach to keeping the Gurkha soldier in touch with his home culture and roots."[40] Following from bracketing Gurkhas to their roots, Mr. Soames then said that the initial long leave period of six months would be reduced by a month as communications have improved over time.[41] In addition to bracketing that is rationalized through obligations, citizenship, and culture, the next dimension of such bracketing has to do with protecting the national interests of Nepal. The Nepalese government was "happy to permit them [Gurkhas] to be recruited into a foreign army, provided that they are not treated as mercenaries and the interests of their home country are protected."[42] It follows that "Gurkhas must not be allowed to drain Nepal of talent. They remain Nepalese citizens and will return there upon retirement. Hence the continued importance in 2003 of making special arrangements to maintain their distinctive religious, cultural and ethnic heritage."[43]

The maintenance of Nepali heritage and tradition also extends to how family life in Nepal is perceived to be organized by those outside of it. By this I am referring to suppositions about the gender division of labor and family life while the Gurkha husband or father is overseas during active service with the forces. With reference to a 1997 review of the Gurkhas' TACOS, a press release statement mentioned how that review had to take into account "the need for Gurkhas to maintain close cultural and family links with Nepal" alongside the "modern circumstances of the Brigade."[44] The assumption that follows this reads: "Gurkhas would wish to be accompanied for lengthy periods because there was a long established tradition in Nepal's rural economy that the wives of Gurkha soldiers would remain in Nepal to look after the family property while their husbands served abroad and remitted money home."[45] For the next generation, that is, the Gurkhas' children, an accompanying assumption is articulated as follows: "Any children of the family would remain with their mothers in Nepal and be educated there. That factor is of some importance, given that their adult lives will be spent in Nepal."[46] Assumptions about family life subsequently becomes a point of contention when the issue of Gurkha adult children's rights to settlement in the United Kingdom is broached in the eyes of the law, and as I shall attend to below. In sum, the brackets that we see here essentially have to do with circumscribing Gurkhas to Nepal through such avenues of culture, tradition, legality, and family life—determined in order to bracket their belonging to Nepal and not to the United Kingdom. As an intended outcome, then, this approach places the Gurkhas and their families at the edge of belonging to the United Kingdom, in spite of their long service to the British.

Resisting Brackets of Belonging

Although I have by now made clear the contemporaneous practices of inclusion and exclusion where the acts of bracketing are concerned, I should also point out that bracketing belonging has been critiqued, if not resisted. Such resistance or push back further demonstrates how different social actors interpret inclusionary and exclusionary practices of bracketing in contrastive ways. In *Limbu and others v Secretary of State for the Home Department, Entry Clearance Officer* [2008], the lawyer for Gurkha claimants of rights to settle pointed out that the MOD has adopted a fairly stringent and rigid position.[47] This was in terms of what the TPA has set out or what the Nepalese government expects of its citizens even as they serve as Gurkha troops. He said:

> I cannot fail to note the apparently reliable testimony of a former Colonel of the Brigade and others that Gurkhas were to be prevented by application of military discipline from marrying Chinese women when they were stationed in Hong Kong, or from leaving behind dependants who might have a right of residence in such places on redeployment or discharge. The opportunity to preserve cultural links with Nepal may certainly have been a historic assumption of the TPA *but it is not for the Army to force cultural purity down the throats of Gurkhas irrespective of their wishes*. Within the broad confines of the special arrangements that gave rise to the Brigade including the need to preserve Nepalese nationality during service with it, there is plenty of room for the dignity and autonomy of the individual to make informed choices.[48]

Clearly, even if bracketed belonging to Nepal is encapsulated in the TPA, legal resistance is staged in the form of questioning whether indeed the Army holds the right to insist on "cultural purity" in ways that dislodges an individual's autonomy of choice and action when it comes to where one attaches one's sense of belonging. Either way, the larger implication of these relate back to the politics of belonging as I have discussed earlier. This is where the stakes involved, be it one being bracketed inclusively or exclusively out of a society, illustrate how both contexts are accompanied by consequences that relate to the determining of rights to settling in a country and other entitlements.

The following statement denotes unequivocally as to what would be at stake:

> Far from wanting to be transported back to Nepal at public expense where opportunities for employment may be limited, these veterans who remained comparatively young men with long working lives ahead of them wanted to be given permission to remain in the United Kingdom, and in due course be able to apply for British citizenship.[49]

Such unequivocation thus explains why brackets that preclude access to rights such as settlement in the United Kingdom have been questioned given the attendant consequences of further job opportunities. This is clearly of importance since Gurkhas usually retire in their early thirties if not forties, and thus a longer road lies ahead for further gainful employment, as well as the access to citizenship.

Deservedness by Birth and Nationality

While I have demonstrated how the imposition of Gurkha-Nepal belonging has taken place through legal avenues, not all actors are always in agreement with such imposition, hence my preceding discussion on resistance. That said, I now return to another point on this imposition by focusing on the issue of one's birth and nationality. As a corollary to the obligations that Gurkhas are expected to fulfill to Nepal, bracketed belonging in legal terms does not allow overlaps in nationality, rights, and access to settlement. This is unlike bracketed belonging as experienced or practiced by interlocutors in the domains of the everyday, and the affective where they have shared with me, for instance, that they feel coexisting feelings of belonging to more than one country. The outright rejection of overlaps in nationality is exemplified in the following statement:

> But the position of the ex British soldier and the ex Gurkha soldier on retirement is not analogous. While there will be a few exceptions, the former will have been born in the United Kingdom and will expect to retire in the United Kingdom. He may choose to retire to a more or less expensive country, but in that respect he would be no different from any other United Kingdom pensioner. By contrast, the Gurkha, born in Nepal and a citizen of Nepal, will retire to Nepal. It would be wholly irrational to fail to have regard to the very different circumstances that exist in Nepal and Great Britain when making provision for pensions on retirement.[50]

The assumed country of retirement, traced to one's nationality, was thus the justification provided to rationalize why the Gurkhas and British soldiers ought not to be treated as analogous. Having said this, it is also apposite to point out, on the one hand, that nationality as deservedness or as a basis for differential treatment might have appeared as disadvantageous for the Gurkhas. On the other hand, nationality is also upended as advantageous in terms of recruitment, pension, and leave matters. The solicitor, Mr. R. Singh, acting on behalf of the MOD as defendant against claims made by Gurkhas for reviewing pension arrangements noted:

> The Gurkha Brigade can only exist in its present form if the Ministry of Defence applies a policy of recruitment that discriminates against all nationalities other than Nepalese. Discrimination on grounds of nationality is the founding principle indeed the *raison d'être* of the Gurkha Brigade. Those in the Brigade are also the beneficiaries of treatment denied to others in the British Army which discriminates against those others on grounds of nationality. Obvious examples are the ability to retire after fifteen years with an immediate pension and extended paid leave in Nepal.[51]

The above statement may be interpreted as a case of positive discrimination that is approbatory of Gurkhas and their Nepalese nationality, as compared to other nationalities for which enlistment into the brigade and access to these accompanying TACOS are not made available to such others.

Deservedness based on nationality can thus take on these two forms of either discrimination (from the point of view of Gurkha claimants who canvass for equitable pension arrangements) or advantage (in terms of how only Nepalese can be recruited and benefit from the attendant TACOS). In either form, tracing access and rights to one's nationality, and bracketing these as simultaneously discriminatory or favorable, highlights how belonging and the stakes involved become politicized and made apropos in the legal domain. Mr. Singh furthers his argument:

> So it is that the challenge before the Court, in conformity with those that have come before, proceeds from the premise that any benefit accruing to the Gurkhas from their different treatment (including the very existence of the Brigade) should be secure, but perceived disadvantages should be remedied. The claimants appear to regard discrimination on grounds of nationality as justified when it provides benefits but not when it gives rise to disadvantage. It is difficult to see why that should be so, when all of the differences, whether now of only historical interest

or those continuing to have effect, flow from the unique position of the
Gurkha Brigade in the British Army born of its long history of different
and special treatment.[52]

As shown in the above statement, it is clear that the exercise of bracketed belonging based on nationality avails itself as twofold. This depends on which vantage
point one claims in arguing on this basis. The trope of Gurkhas claimants is that
of discrimination based on their Nepalese nationality. For defendants who exercise rejection of the Gurkhas' claims, the trope utilized, albeit still based on the
factor of nationality, has to do with positive discrimination that has been argued
to work advantageously for the Gurkhas. Such an interpretation adds not only
to my position that belonging and not-belonging dovetail. Bracketed belonging
and, in this case, traced to nationality, comes with both inclusionary and exclusionary mechanisms. These are contingent on which position is being taken up
in the legal process. As said above, it can be approached as a matter of "disadvan-
tage" or "benefits."

Bracketing Gurkha-UK Connections

If the acts of bracketing Gurkhas to Nepal as deliberated on in the previous
section place these migrant warriors in close proximity—both literally and
figuratively—with Nepal, the same domains of interest can be identified in terms
of how Gurkha-UK connections are established through itemizing the different
forms of belonging to the United Kingdom. To begin with, while new immigration rules (IR) for Gurkha veterans were enacted in October 2004 in support of
their rights to settlement in the United Kingdom, there were also veterans who
were denied entry to settle as they were not discharged after 1 July 1997 as per
the requirement of rule 276F (ii).[53] In order to table appeals to reverse such denial
in the court, efforts have been made by claimants and their solicitors in working
through the different aspects through which belonging to the United Kingdom
is argued, this time, with reference to policy discretion. In *Limbu and others v
Secretary of State for the Home Department, Entry Clearance Officer and Entry
Officer*, reference was made to the Diplomatic Service Procedures (DSP): Entry
Clearance Volume 1 General Instructions in outlining chapter 29.4, which laid
out terms for discretionary considerations. Such considerations were meant as a
response to settlement applicants who do not meet the requirements of the October 2004 new IR. The chapter contains the following provision: "Discretion may
be exercised to waive these requirements [of 2004] in cases where there are strong
reasons why settlement in the United Kingdom is appropriate."[54] It is instructive
to quote at length the following factors that discretionary consideration covers
in Chapter 29.4:

- Strength of ties with the UK—have they spent a significant amount of time living in the UK, such as a three year tour of duty pre-discharge or three years living in the UK after discharge?
- Do they have any close family living in the UK? What proportion of their close family are in the UK as opposed to living in Nepal?
- Do they have children being educated in the UK?
- Do they have a chronic/long-term medical condition where treatment in the UK would significantly improve quality of life?

If one or more factors listed above are present, ECOs may exercise discretion and grant entry clearance for settlement in the UK.

Close family means immediate family, such as brothers, sisters, children, parents or grandparents.

The requirements for an applicant to have completed at least four years service as a Gurkha with the British Army and to have been discharged on completion of their engagement should not be waived.[55]

The above factors clearly serve as brackets of belonging for Gurkhas to the United Kingdom. These factors are codified as a set of indicators that provide the basis for an exercise of discretion for claims to settlement in the United Kingdom. Such a basis covers the range from one's demonstrated connection to the United Kingdom (based on years of service), close familial relations not extending beyond their grandparents' generation as an indicator of the need to reside in the United Kingdom, to their own children having received education, and indications of a need for health support and/or treatment that would wield significant impact on one's quality of life. These factors together illustrate how possible indicators of the Gurkha-UK links and thereby rights to belong may be taken into account for legal provision of settlement for select veterans that would in turn circumvent IR rules updated in 2004.

What is interesting is the comparison between the list of factors for discretion laid out above, with what *other* factors that claimants themselves raise, in order to argue for rights to settling in the United Kingdom. In other words, while the components of Chapter 29.4 are legal items that are utilized to measure or gauge the strength of belonging for Gurkhas to the United Kingdom, the Gurkhas themselves have also drawn up their own list of criteria. For them, their own list serves as a key barometer to support their claims to entry and settlement as their way of bracketing belonging and thereby rights, to the United Kingdom. This *other* list of factors includes being wounded in action and being the recipient of awards for bravery, among other things—which all point toward risking one's life and sacrificing one's safety for the crown.[56] The assumption here, for these claimants, is that such sacrifice ought to translate into belonging and thus rights to entry and settlement in the United Kingdom.

Juxtaposing these two sets of factors as (consideration of) indicators of the Gurkhas' belonging and rights to settlement in the United Kingdom therefore pertinently indicate that different social actors, including individuals, the state, and the law, are all involved in the exercise of bracketing belonging. Such bracketing is either exacted to the United Kingdom or Nepal—by adhering to a list of practices and criteria, or what has been termed as "qualifying conditions."[57] Where claimants may mount their own set of conditions, these conditions need first to be legally accepted before any provision of rights or claims may be considered and/or processed. To put it clearly, "Gurkhas were never able to claim indefinite residence in the United Kingdom on the basis of their military service however long and gallant it may have been."[58] Such qualifying conditions then arise as ambivalent areas that the law may not sufficiently be able to admit or quantify as criteria for granting ex-Gurkhas settlement in the United Kingdom. For example, while it was suggested that four years or more of service in the Brigade of Gurkhas prior to July 1997 "could not be sufficient to justify the favourable exercise of discretion"[59] for settlement in the United Kingdom, the court further inquired if (a) service amounting to a decade in the Brigade prior to 1997 would suffice; (b) injuries incurred during active service within these years of service would count; (c) Gurkha service in the Falklands was relevant; and (d) decorations for gallant service including the Victoria Cross would constitute a sufficient and relevant factor.[60] We are subsequently told in this case that the example of the Victoria Cross was not one of abstraction. The court heard that a Hon Lt. Pun was awarded this highest honor for war-time gallantry; a highest accolade that a sovereign can bestow. While he was initially refused admission, his case was subsequently personally reviewed by the Secretary of State, through which Hon Lt. Pun was then admitted for settlement.[61]

Despite the case of the Hon Lt. Pun, it remains unclear as to whether the above identified factors that cover the range from years of service to distinctions in battle would justifiably substantiate the "discretionary grant of settlement."[62] It was also pointed out that the Asylum and Immigration Tribunal (AIT) would not have been able to determine the issue that was not in accordance with IR, with reference to the Nationality Immigration and Asylum Act of 2002. It would be "impossible for an Immigration Judge to determine whether the decision had been in accordance with the law where the 'law' was so unclear as to permit conflicting decisions . . . in accordance with the policy by either granting or refusing entry clearance in an identical case."[63] These legal dilemmas clearly exemplify how identifying brackets of belonging in this case of right to settlement enrolls a number of factors and structural actors including the AIT, IR vis-à-vis qualifying conditions, or criteria before the right to settlement may be legally meted out. Quandaries such as these require striking a "delicate balance between rigidity and flexibility" in order to form "such sensitive policies."[64] Further clarifications of what constitute qualifying conditions or criteria for arguing rights to belonging and hence resources are forwarded as follows: "If factors such as ten years service are to be recognised as weighty along with injury in service, decorations for bravery, service in the Falklands conflict or similar matters, this should be identified by further specific examples *so the parameters of the qualifying class can be identified*" (my emphasis).[65] The "parameters of the qualifying class" here are representative of the very criteria that outline renewed brackets of belonging as aspired to or intended as legitimizing factors. In turn, these factors would translate into rights and entitlements—like those that the ex-Gurkhas are arguing for. However, brackets of belonging, as they are to be determined by the law and other social actors, do not change or are admitted easily. As recognized in the court, the "elements of a rational future policy" are yet to be ascertained. Therefore, a "fresh look seems particularly appropriate in the light of the evidence about the attitude of the Government of Nepal."[66] The "fresh look" here points to careful legal considerations for new brackets of belonging, which would be in alignment with the Nepalese government's stance. This has been recorded as never having "expressed opposition to retrospective settlement of Gurkhas in 2004 or before."[67] If these newer brackets of belonging are to be legally passed, then it might be said that the "honouring of a historic debt" in recognition of the Gurkhas' contributions to the United Kingdom would be realized.[68]

Paying such a debt may also be interpreted in terms of what would qualify as exemplary of British national belonging. Ware (2010), for example, has talked about how such national belonging may be contingent on the patriotism of the soldier: "With a strong national identity the traditional rules are clear: one must be ready to kill and die for one's country, or give up one's children, in exchange for protection from the state" (2010, 323). Seen in this way, then, raising newer conditions would also shed light on the transactional aspects of negotiating belonging between ex-Gurkhas and the UK government. In principle, the transactional or reciprocal optics put forward via these conditions has to do with how if Gurkhas have sacrificed and fought gallantly for the crown, they should in turn be privileged with belonging and thereby rights in this military-transactional relationship. Those who have served the interests of empires have in certain instances been led to an expectation of reciprocity contingent on their service and loyalty; examples being the Nepalese Gurkhas as well as Surinamese from former Dutch Guyana who acquired Netherlands citizenship (Cohen 2022). The question lies in how this transactional relationship is going to be negotiated legally given the stakes involved for both parties. For migrant warriors such as the Gurkhas, the right to citizenship and abode may mean a better livelihood and more economic opportunities when compared to that lacking in Nepal. As for those who are older, the option to migrate to the United Kingdom would mean better living conditions and facilities relative to Nepal. For the British government, the conferment of citizenship unto the Gurkhas would imply a recalibration of patterns of resource distribution (cf. Uesugi 2019a). Deservingness to belong (Blachnicka-Ciacek et al. 2021) thereby includes the transactional and the reciprocal in the legal negotiation of belonging and rights.

Overall, if newer qualifying conditions or criteria would be legally accepted into brackets of belonging, then such new brackets or parameters of belonging would ipso facto translate into rights that the Gurkhas are championing for. The processes of arguing and pushing for legal bracketing to belonging by that means also unveil and bring to the fore what is at stake if such brackets are not expanded or rethought in terms of policy and the law. Amounting to an observation that "the legality of discretionary policies . . . seem in part internally contradictory" and where it is vital that "ECOs [Entry Clearance Officer] know precisely what discretion is being afforded to them, and for the AIT to know when the ECOs are acting in accordance with the law and when they are not,"[69] this goes to show the politics of belonging not only in the sense of what is at stake. More pertinently, legal structures in connection with immigration policies need to in concert determine where the brackets of belonging may be found and instituted in the case of the Gurkhas. In the words of Nick Clegg, the Liberal Democrat leader who had supported ex-Gurkhas for the right of abode in the United Kingdom: "If someone is prepared to die for this country, they must be allowed to live in it."[70] In other words, national belonging and national identity also have to take into consideration, if and how armed forces such as the Gurkhas ought to be rewarded and respected in return or exchange for their sacrifice if not risk-taking (Qureshi and Zeitlyn 2013)—these considerations forming the gist of public opinion on Gurkha veterans' rights to abode and other issues.[71]

When Brackets of Belonging Shift

Brackets of belonging can shift owing to immigrant policy changes that allow Gurkhas and their families to reside in the United Kingdom. This however does not automatically translate into further rights as well, as seen in *Gurung and others v The Secretary of State for Defence* [2008].[72] In this particular case, Gurkhas who were claimants had complained that the new pension transfer arrangements that were enacted in 2007 were "irrational, and discriminate against them by comparison with other Gurkhas on the grounds of age."[73] This was taken to contradict their rights based on Article 14 ECHR as well as Article 1 of Protocol 1 to the ECHR.[74] Specifically, and to demonstrate how shifted brackets may not necessarily lead to the provision of rights where pensions are concerned vis-à-vis living in the United Kingdom, it was stated that although an option was created for the Gurkhas to retire after having served four years in the Brigade, they do not "lose their Nepalese citizenship on doing so and can return there at any age if they wish."[75] Furthermore, that "does not mean that there was an obligation or intention to provide a pension which would enable retirement to take place to the UK, still less to do so in any way which avoided the need to find another source of income."[76] Where the GOTT is concerned, it was stated as well that there was "no internal contradiction in the GOTT, or a giving with one hand but a taking away with another."[77] It was clearly indicated that the "aim of the GOTT was not to allow the Gurkha to retire in the United Kingdom on an Immediate Pension at thirty-three years old free from further labour, nor to allow other servicemen now to do so under the AFPS."[78] It was subsequently proclaimed that the Gurkha claimants had misinterpreted the GOTT of having the "aim . . . to enable Gurkhas to 'retire' in the UK, at some unstated age."[79] These examples revolving around the GOTT therefore point toward how brackets that shift can still mean that access to further pension amounts in order to retire in the United Kingdom continues to be foreclosed.

Another issue regarding the GOTT has to do with citizenship ties. The court returned to the 1997 Hong Kong handover moment where the United Kingdom had by then become the new home base for the Gurkhas. Therefore, the "HMFIR change which also affected qualifying dependents, and changes to MAS would all strengthen [the Gurkhas'] ties to the UK, and weaken those to Nepal." In these contexts, legal discourse has it that "ties of citizenship and other ties remain."[80] This assertion of Nepalese citizenship, despite all the various changes listed, importantly implies that irrespective of shifts in policy related to MAS or ILR, Gurkhas remain as Nepalis by citizenship, and are not British citizens. Even in the presence of shifts in bracketing (in this case, greater Gurkha affinity felt for the United Kingdom through all the policy and political changes), it does not necessarily translate into further or equivalent rights as compared to UK citizens. Similarly, even if Gurkhas were to be granted rights to settling in the United Kingdom, this is not automatically pegged to betterment in terms of pension issues:

> If Gurkha veterans are to be allowed to come in as a matter of discretion because of evidence of compelling links through very long or very gallant service, that does not mean that their pensions based on historic terms of service must be uplifted. Perhaps they will choose to remain where they are and their money may go further.[81]

In this instance, there are many items and issues that Gurkha veterans have raised over the years and based on their argument that they belong (in terms of contributions, service and sacrifice to the crown). Their claims as put forward in the UK courts may be interpreted as well as attempts in pushing the needle toward their rights to recognition and others, labeled in court as a "moral debt" or "historic debt" owed to them by the United Kingdom.[82] Even if not all of these issues may achieve legal success, or if such debts are not repaid in a manner of speaking, the very acts of registering their claims and appeals through the institution of the law and in line with immigration policies show how the brackets of belonging are made malleable. Such bracketing thereby shifts according to broader sociolegal structures and modes of boundary governance.

Redrawing brackets of Gurkha belonging to the United Kingdom by those in favor vis-à-vis the fulfillment of military service and sacrifice does not necessarily mean that Gurkha soldiers and British soldiers are thus to be regarded as analogous.[83] In a nutshell, the key inquiry here, when brackets shift, is captured in the following statement: "What the Government of Nepal wanted and indeed has obtained is that during service in the Brigade of Gurkhas, the soldiers remained Nepalese citizens and the links of allegiance to Nepal were not broken. The issue before the court is how should they be treated *after* they served?" (emphasis in original).[84] When these brackets shift due to larger immigration policies later on, such as that enacted from 2004 with regard to the eligibility of Gurkha veterans and their families for settlement and citizenship, this becomes a turning point. Newer brackets of belonging delineated arising from sacrifice and contributions of these Gurkhas and their families would mean that rights to settlement and citizenship are *now* made available to them. In January 2005, the secretary of state for defence announced a review of the Gurkha TACOS:

> Gurkhas have spent an increasing proportion of their time in UK since withdrawal from Hong Kong in 1997, and *successive amendments to the conditions under which they serve have recognised their changing role, status and personal aspirations.* The most recent of these was their inclusion in the new HM forces immigration rule, which took effect from 25 October 2004. This has potentially *far-reaching effects on the way we recruit and manage the brigade and care for its serving members, families and veterans.* In addition, some public criticism and unease continues about the remaining differences between Gurkhas' terms and conditions and those of the wider Army. We are, therefore, anxious to ensure that such differences are absolutely justifiable as well as fully understood and accepted by our Gurkha soldiers and want to ensure that the MOD's position, both legally and morally, is beyond reproach.[85] (my emphases)

The above statement clearly reflects how brackets of belonging have begun to shift in parallel with amendments to the Gurkhas' TACOS after 1997. The shift is registered first from the point of view of Gurkhas, where their role, status, and personal aspirations have altered and more importantly, have been duly recognized. The UK government, and the MOD in particular, have also had to rethink their perspective on how the Brigade of Gurkhas was now to be managed. Increasingly, such governance both in terms of the military and migration policymaking now extends to not only Gurkhas in active service, but those who have retired, including their families. This nod toward the wider Gurkha diaspora thereby manifest how these different actors form part and parcel of the processes of shifting brackets. It is their varied interests and aspirations that will be affected as a result of changes in legislation and immigration policies.

Following the above statement of the Secretary of State, the MOD in December 2006 later published the outcome of the wider TACOS review. Given the newer context whereby changes were made both to the IR and to Married Accompanied Service (MAS), the MOD review team noted that such changes were accompanied by further amendments to the "traditional assumption that British Gurkhas would retire in Nepal." Moreover, the future ahead now points toward a scenario where "Gurkhas could be expected to increasingly to regard the United Kingdom, rather than Nepal, as their family base." Said in a different manner, Gurkhas, prior to 1 July 1997, were "not in an analogous position to the rest of the British Army." This is because they were mainly based overseas, primarily in Hong Kong and elsewhere. Thus they "had little or no opportunity to develop the close physical ties needed to satisfy the immigration regulations." Such a situation was then altered after 1 July when the Gurkhas became UK based.[86] This statement is telling for two reasons. The first is how 1 July becomes the defining and precise moment of change in bracketing, for which Gurkhas before and after this important date are assumed to lean on either Asia or the United Kingdom as home respectively.[87] The second and more crucial reason has to do with how an exemplification of "close physical ties" form a paramount factor or key criterion in order for Gurkhas to "satisfy immigration regulations." Demonstrating these ties could thereby facilitate rights to residence in the United Kingdom.

Additionally, it was also becoming clearer to the MOD that "the remaining differences between Gurkha terms and conditions of service and those applied to the rest of the Army were increasingly open to legal challenge."[88] There is at this point both immigratory and legal recognition of the Gurkhas and their families, owing to new brackets of belonging that can now be translated into these rights. When the UK prime minister noted that the Gurkhas have "served *this country* with great skill, courage and dignity. . . . They have made an enormous contribution not just to our armed forces but to *the life of this country* and it is important their commitment and sacrifice is recognised,"[89] the home secretary David Blunkett added:

> *Throughout their history, the men of the Gurkha Brigade have shown unquestioning loyalty to the Queen and the people of the United Kingdom . . . I am very keen to ensure that we recognise their role in the history of our country and the part they have played in protecting us. This is why we have put together the best possible package to enable discharged Gurkhas to apply for settlement and citizenship.* I hope that the decision I have made today will make our gratitude clear.[90]

While I have earlier indicated that qualifying conditions (not unlike those pronounced above) as put forward by Gurkha claimants did not shift brackets of belonging, these conditions are in this particular instance now admitted into brackets of belonging as denoted by the prime minister and the home secretary. Such rights to discharge in the United Kingdom and access to citizenship are encapsulated as follows:

> Since April 2007 discharge has been able to take place in the United Kingdom. . . . Gurkhas can now also count military service anywhere in the world towards the period of qualifying residence deemed to be in the United Kingdom, for the purposes of naturalisation, although citizenship can only be granted once they have left the Brigade of Gurkhas. These changes were made without objection from the Government of Nepal, just as earlier they had no objection to indefinite leave to remain being granted to Gurkhas.[91]

Given changing regulations that were promulgated since April 2007, rules and thereby brackets of belonging have shifted and thus renewed criteria or qualifying conditions for naturalization and citizenship, as well as location of discharge, differing from the previous context of Nepal. These changes would, in Laksamba et al's (2013) view, reflect the temporal character of inequality and fairness. For Laksamba and his coauthors, it is not only a matter of dealing with the past, but that "righting things for the present and future should take precedence" (2013, 58). Changes such as these therefore reflect not only the mutable nature of bracketed belonging. They highlight the very temporal transience of brackets that (would continue to) alter in close relation with wider shifts in the legal and immigratory domains of governance. In sum, it can be argued that if brackets of belonging are intimately associated with attendant rights and resources in the case of the Gurkhas, then it remains exigent for brackets of belonging to exist interdependently and compatibly with law and policy in the context of the United Kingdom.

Bracketing Family Life for the Gurkhas

Aside from sociolegal bracketing stipulated between the United Kingdom and Nepal, UK policies and immigration rules have also been meted out in regard to bracketing the family unit for Gurkhas and their adult children. The discussion in this section therefore extends my earlier analysis of how bhanja and bhanji relate to where home is and their sense of belonging in a different manner; now illuminating both affective ties as well as legal and practical considerations where rights to settlement in the United Kingdom are concerned. Arising from the October 2004 IR that permitted Gurkha soldiers with at least four years of service and who had retired from the British Army either on or after 1 July 1997 the grant of settlement in the United Kingdom, the Diplomatic Service Procedures (DSP) was issued at the same time. The DSP Chapter 29 provided a set of operational instructions to Entry Clearance Officers and also outlined policy guidelines with regard to Gurkha dependents who were over the age of eighteen.[92] Although Chapter 29 ceased effect as of February 2009, a further policy, SET 12, was published based on the same set of terms. The key points to bear in mind from para 29.14 of the DSP are as follows:[93]

> It is not the intention to split a family unit solely because the dependant is 18 years of age or over. Applications for settlement from dependants who are 18 years of age or over will be considered and discretion to grant settlement outside the rules may be exercised in individual cases. Dependants over the age of 18 need to make separate individual applications and pay the appropriate fee. In assessing whether the settlement in the UK is appropriate the ECO should consider the following factors:
>
> - one parent or a relative of the applicant is present and settled; or being admitted for, or being granted, settlement in the UK under the HM Forces Rule;
> - the applicant has previously been granted limited leave as a dependant of a member of HM Forces;
> - the applicant has been, and wishes to continue, pursuing a full-time course of studies in the UK;
> - refusal of the application would mean that the applicant would be living alone outside the UK and is financially dependent on the parent or relative present and settled; or being granted settlement in the UK under the HM Forces Rule;
> - the applicant would find it very difficult to function because of illness or disability without the help and support of their parent or close relative in the UK.

If one or more of the factors listed above are present, the ECO may exercise discretion to grant entry clearance for settlement in the UK.[94]

The above guidelines, subject to discretion and therefore which are "not necessarily determinative,"[95] form brackets of family belonging that thereby ought to translate into the right to settlement in the United Kingdom for adult children of the Gurkhas. Bracketing the family unit is not so much just about kin relations. It is rather about permitting Gurkha families settlement in the United Kingdom adjudicated on a needs basis and arising from forms of demonstrable dependency as justification. Only when these criteria are deemed to have sufficiently been met are adult children granted settlement rights. The standout point about such family policymaking lies in how affective and emotional aspects of familial relations become recruited as one of the key criteria for determining if a particular child therefore holds the right to settlement. In principle, this right to settlement in the United Kingdom has been announced by the UK government below:

> The government had made it clear that it wished to acknowledge the role played by the Gurkhas in the history of the UK and had expressed the intention of putting together the best possible package to enable discharged Gurkhas to apply for settlement and citizenship. These statements were made with the Military Covenant in mind and the policy was designed to ensure that ex-Gurkha soldiers would be able to enjoy their right to remain in the UK with their family members including dependants over the age of 18.[96]

Court cases that I have analyzed pertaining to Gurkha adult children and their claim if not follow-up appeal for the right to settlement in the United Kingdom reflect how the DSP was contested and argued in two salient ways. The first has to do with terms of the difference between IR and policies. The second pertains to how a family unit is to be conceived, with ramifications for rights of settlement and dependency. It should also be noted that the purpose of the DSP is "*not* to facilitate the settlement in the UK of adult dependant children" and that it "recognises that such children may be granted leave to enter under rule 317(i)(f) and if article 8 requires it." Adult children are therefore "not granted leave to enter unless there are exceptional circumstances."[97]

Where the difference between IR and policies is concerned, it has been stressed in *Entry Clearance Officer v UR and others* [2010] and *Entry Clearance Officer v KG* [2011] that IR have been elevated to a status that may be read as akin to the law. Therefore, IR "must be construed more strictly than was the case in the past."[98] In contrast, policies are "by their nature"[99] "meant to be applied flexibly" and thus mean that there is some room for the "sensible exercise of discretion."[100]

This would mean that the wording in policies do not have to be "construed with all the strictness of a statute."[101] Such definitional contrast between IR and policies have been invoked in cases where adult children of Gurkha have filed claims and follow-up appeals in pursuit of their right to settlement in the United Kingdom. I raise two examples here. The first is taken from *Entry Clearance Officer v UR and others* [2010], which comprises three conjoined cases.[102] There were three appellants who had put up appeals against an ECO who had refused their 2009 applications as overage dependent children of a retired Gurkha who was granted the ILR in 2006. The ECO acted on the basis of these three appellants who were actually not living alone. They were siblings who were living together in Nepal. This contradicted how the ECO had interpreted the DSP fourth bullet point about applicants who ought "to be living alone outside the UK." Immigrant Judge Gillespie who presided this case allowed the appeals and for entry clearance to be granted. This was given that the appellants were indeed "living alone outside the UK," even if they were technically living together in Nepal. Specifically, the three of them were living in a house that was rented by their father, and in which they shared with three other male cousins. A favorable exercise of discretion was adopted by Gillespie to support the appeals.

Another important point of contention raised in this case example had to do with another of the criteria in order for Gurkha children to obtain the rights to settlement in the United Kingdom. This had to do with an "unusual degree of emotional dependency" between adult children and their Gurkha parent that had to be established before the former could be granted permission to "settle with a parent in this [United Kingdom] country."[103] Such emotional dependency as a key point was the one that led to the rejection of Roshan Ghising's appeal for settlement—the case that I outlined at the outset. Ghising's appeal was turned down as he was not able to demonstrate deep (enough) emotional ties with his parents. Besides, Roshan Ghising had also made evident that he was able to live independently and was able to support himself.[104] For the three appellants here then, it was argued against them that financial dependency would not suffice as a condition to allow their settlement in the United Kingdom, for they would have to demonstrate emotional dependency as well. Senior Immigration Judge McKee who presided over this appeal case of the ECO arrived at a decision to accept the ECO's position. He passed his judgment for the three appellants to apply again to the ECO in order for a "fresh decision to be made" regarding their application for residence rights in the United Kingdom.[105]

The second case example that I raise here to exemplify the legal contention of terminology between IR and policies relates to that of *Entry Clearance Officer v KG* [2011].[106] Fairly similar to the above case where the three appellants were technically not living alone outside of the United Kingdom given that they shared their house in Nepal with other relatives, the present case also saw the appellant, a Miss KG who was living at her father's house. Moreover, the house was shared with her uncle and his children. In her situation then, she did not meet the criterion listed in the fourth bullet point concerning living alone. If so, she could then have been categorized as a "stranded sibling" in need of support—which is deemed to be something to eschew based on this fourth bullet point. In other words, Miss KG had both "support and companionship" from her uncle and cousins.[107] Borrowing from a separate case, the issue of living alone had also been debated as such. The "fact that there may be two siblings in Nepal did not change the fact that both of them would be separated from their family members in the UK; they would remain stranded dependants as much as a single stranded dependant."[108]

That said however, this case proceeded with further illustration of evidence and from oral testimonies provided by both Miss KG and her father. The evidence collectively denoted both emotional and financial dependency of the former on the latter and other family members. Miss KG is said to suffer from mental retardation and chronic seizure disorder. Through the copious bundles of medical prescriptions and doctors' notes accumulated over the years, it was confirmed that there is a "continuous need for medication."[109] Furthermore, not only did Miss KG rely on her uncle in Nepal, she was also supported financially by her father. He had continuously sent "generous remittances" to Nepal "amounting to £1,000 a year for her upkeep and for her medication."[110] Judge McKee who had also presided over this case, noted that Miss KG's father had first wanted to "establish himself in this country" and to be gainfully employed before arranging for Miss KG to be brought over to the United Kingdom. On the basis of these evidences, McKee noted that "there is family life between the appellant and her parent, going beyond the normal emotional ties . . . and that the refusal of entry clearance interferes with that family life in a manner sufficiently grave to engage the operation of Article 8."[111] Article 8 of the ECHR—which was invoked in Miss KG's case—has to do with the situation where if "human rights are argued, they should be determined in advance of any argument based on discretion: if the claimant's human rights entitle him to enter or remain in the United Kingdom, any discretionary power to allow him to do so is otiose."[112] The core premise of Article 8 concerns the right to both one's private and family life, as well as home and correspondence. In the case of Miss KG, McKee had argued that "her mental state renders her dependent on her parents in a way that a normal adult would not be."[113] Contingent on having met the criteria of the DSP, and along with Article 8 of the ECHR, McKee allowed Miss KG's appeal for entry clearance into the United Kingdom.

The above two cases are illustrative of how the bracketing of a family unit transpires in order for adult Gurkha children to be awarded the right to join their Gurkha parents in the United Kingdom to live there. Not only do we learn about the conditions or criteria for how such settlement claims and/or appeals are to be made on the basis of residential arrangements (living alone), financial and emotional ties and dependency, as well as ability (health), the notional tussle of terminology between IR and policies further complicates the matter.[114] Such a tussle sheds light on how such familial belonging and its contours may be resisted, debated, and interpreted in different manners in court that hold import in the consequences of residence for Gurkha adult children and their families in the United Kingdom. The complexity of what a family unit and family life entails is aptly encapsulated in Lord Bingham's speech.[115] His 2007 speech featured at a House of Lords hearing that also intertwined with the core values that Article 8 exists in order to protect:

> Human beings are social animals. They depend on others. Their family, or extended family, is the group on which many people most heavily depend, socially, emotionally and often financially. There comes a point at which, for some, prolonged and unavoidable separation from this groups seriously inhibits their ability to live full and fulfilling lives. Matters such as age, health and vulnerability of the applicant, the closeness and previous history of the family, the applicant's dependence on the financial and emotional support of the family, the prevailing cultural conditions in the country of origin and many other factors may all be relevant.[116]

There is ostensibly a balance point to be mediated if not achieved in weighing both the universality of human rights (as encapsulated in Article 8 for example) as well as the particularity of cultural norms (as reflected in Nepalese customs, for example).[117] Adopting cognizance of the particular—and in this case Nepalese customs—also reflect importantly on the sustained transnational links that continue to formulate Gurkha/Nepalese identities in the UK process of the legal bracketing of family units and familial lives.

Taken from a broader viewpoint then, this process reiterates a concomitant bracketing that is taking place between Gurkha families residing in the United Kingdom, with Nepal, as a part of legal processes that determine if they (Gurkha adult children) are to be awarded the rights to settlement in the United Kingdom as a family. At the level of the individual, Roshan Ghising's case (albeit rejected) included a demonstration of his close connection to the United Kingdom based on the following circumstances—he had arrived in the United Kingdom in 2007 from Nepal to study. By the end of 2010 he had completed two courses in Business Management at colleges in London. At the time of his hearing, he had enrolled since January 2012 for an MBA course at the University of East London, which was to conclude in June 2013. Finally, he has "founded a life here [United Kingdom] . . . and has friends and a social network," and where he has also passed both the requisite English test as well as the Life in the UK test, on top of his driving test.[118] In view of the above complexity and entanglements of various factors, then, bracketed belonging in terms of family units interweave both the sociolegal as well as the affective and emotional. It reveals at the same time the porosity not only of definitions of familial belonging, but those relating to policies such as the DSP where the exercise of discretion is concerned. While the law and immigratory rules and policies delineate how familial belonging ought to be verified, this process also determines where home and family life may be for Gurkha veterans and their families. In the process, there is continuity through legal provision that permits Gurkha diasporic presences across different parts of the United Kingdom as I shall further illuminate below.

To Strike and to Petition

Between July and August 2021, Gurkha veterans and widows staged a thirteen-day hunger strike against the British government in order to demand for equal pensions. A petition was launched with the following statement and signed by 108,290 people:[119]

> We are demanding that the government treats Gurkhas fairly and pays them the same pension as other British veterans of the same rank and service. Many Gurkhas joined the Queen's Gurkha Army believing their pension would sustain them and their families but sadly this has not been the case. Gurkhas served the crown and British yet many Gurkhas and their widows live in poverty in the UK and their relatives are forced into modern slavery in countries like Saudi Arabia. We shouldn't treat our heroes like this. So we are demanding all Gurkha veterans are paid an equal pension to other British veterans. That includes veterans from pre-1997.[120]

Three members of the Gurkha Satyagraha—a group which represents Gurkha veterans—took to staging a hunger protest outside 10 Downing Street.[121] In support of these protestors, about a hundred people also participated in a march.[122] Spokesperson for the Gurkhas, Yam Gurung stated, "The government must listen. We have done so much. Why are they treating us like illegitimate children? We have done so much for them. We don't want anybody to die here. Not a single one. We are human beings. I want to ask Boris Johnson, what is your interpretation of human rights? Tell the world. Tell the Gurkhas."[123] Gurkha Satyagraha had earlier in May 2021 written to Prime Minister Boris Johnson, calling for the formation of a bilateral committee comprising the Nepalese and British government. The purpose was to initiate a dialogue to discuss the issue of equal pensions for ex-Gurkhas. This initiative followed on the heels of the March 2018 "Report of the Technical Committee on Gurkha Veterans."[124] The committee was established in order to "provide a platform to explore options for a long term sustainable solution to grievances which some members of the Gurkha veteran community continue to hold."[125] This committee had provided a forum for which the respective positions of the Gurkha veteran community, and both the governments of Nepal and the United Kingdom were heard with regard to five "major areas of grievance." These areas include (1) pension; (2) state pension; (3) redundancy package; (4) medical support in Nepal; and (5) other facilities.[126] In the end, the committee's report recorded standpoints, discussions, and requests without resolution. As indicated, the report was to "provide a baseline" for both the governments of Nepal and the United Kingdom to consider if each of the matters raised warranted further deliberation and through what means or measures.[127]

Since the 2018 publication of this joint technical report, Gurkha Satyagraha noted that there had been no progress in advancing deliberations on the matters raised.[128] It had therefore asked for another committee to be established. This is so that a basis for dialogue between the two governments can be provided in order to address the demands laid out by the British ex-Gurkha veterans. If these demands were not addressed, three leaders from the group would go on a hunger strike from 1 July 2021 (Thurley 2021b). Following written assurance from the Nepalese government that it would take this up with the UK government, the group then postponed their hunger strike till 21 July. On the next day, Gurkhas had launched a relay hunger strike. One protestor was to hold the strike each day, that was to span thirteen days in all. On 7 August 2021, two former Gurkhas— Gyanraj Rai and Dhan Gurung—and one Gurkha widow, Pushpa Rana Ghale, launched a hunger strike (Thurley 2021b). The thirteen-day strike ended after the UK government agreed to further talks, and also stated that the MOD would establish a bilateral committee to discuss Gurkha veterans' welfare issues. On 8 September 2021, Leo Docherty, the minister for defence for people and veterans announced that a bilateral committee attending to Gurkha welfare issues would be set up, and which would discuss such matters in December 2021. Gurkha Satyagraha then noted, together with the Nepali ambassador, that they looked forward to talks to conclude by February 2022. Recommendations were then to be taken from both the British and the Nepali sides to be implemented two months later by 1 April 2022 (Thurley 2021b).

In June 2022, the British Gurkha Army Ex-Servicemen's Organization and BGAESO Singapore Gurkhas Department jointly submitted a sixteen-point memorandum (via the British ambassador to Nepal) to then British prime minister Boris Johnson.[129] The memorandum was meant to seek redress for "longstanding discrimination and disparities BGAESO Singapore Gurkhas Department has been facing."[130] This is a memorandum endorsed by the president of GAESO, Padam Bahadur Gurung, which raises questions related to human rights and the need for justice pertaining to the Gurkhas, including the issues of citizenship, pay, and compensation. I present extracts from the memorandum in order to illustrate the discourses that reflect interpretations of inequitable treatment:

> The tragedy that we have been experiencing for the past two hundred years of our association with the British Military Services is a painful chapter. We are international citizens if our sacrifice is truly recognized. But we are homeless, our service unrecognized and our status inferior. In conclusion, we are neither Nepali citizens nor British; rather we have been devoid of our natural rights.[131]
>
> The young Gurkhas, from remote Nepali settlements, who were enjoying truly unique lifestyle, were recruited in British military services, trained in British lifestyle and returned back to their homeland after fifteen or twenty years at service. Their sons and daughters, grown in British lifestyle at their early age, could hardly adopt their native culture. This caused internal migration to the nearby towns detaching themselves from their native villages. The salary and pension provided by British government is neither adequate to cover their expenses on health and education nor food and clothing. Inherited properties were sold. They lacked options and opportunities in this miserable condition. For this, the Gurkhas, upon retirement, are forced to roving in third countries for second career. Their children not only ignore the guardianship of their mothers, rather are falling into the ill habits of drug addiction and anti-social behaviours. They can neither be characterized as Nepali or British but have been changed into people without homeland.[132]

Overall, the memorandum pushed for equal pay as well as "perks for Gurkhas serving in Singapore."[133] It indicates that both British and Singapore Gurkhas were recruited under similar terms and conditions, as well as performing similar duties. Therefore, the Singapore Gurkhas ought to receive equal pay and pensions and/or that they should be remunerated using the same pay code as their Singapore police counterparts along with comparable perks and benefits.

Apart from GAESO, which established organizational support over time in order to enact a Gurkha Justice movement (Laksamba 2012, 108), there are other similar organizations that have been formed as well to champion for justice for the Gurkhas. They include the Nepal Ex-Servicemen's Association (NESA), the Nepal Ex-Servicemen Organization (NESO), as well as the Gurkha Study and Research Centre, which was later renamed the United British Gurkhas Nepal (UBGN), and then further renamed as the United British Gurkha Ex-Servicemen's Association (UBGEA) (Laksamba 2012, 110). Other organizations were later formed, and which also championed for equal rights and pension similar to the above organizations. They comprise the British Gurkha Welfare Society (BGWS) and the British Council of Gurkhas (BCG). Processes of legal bracketing which I discuss here, may therefore be juxtaposed with these ongoing campaigns that raise causes and the demand of rights for ex-Gurkhas as organizational responses. In sum, the campaign for Gurkha justice at different levels began in 1990 through the efforts of the GAESO, BGWS, UBGEA, BGAESO, NESA, and BCG (Laksamba 2012, 113) in seeking redress for the Gurkhas in terms of both payment and treatment.

Parliamentary Advocacy for the Gurkhas

There was a follow-up parliamentary debate that took place on 22 November 2021, for the petition that was raised alongside the hunger strike. It is interesting to observe how the Gurkhas have been discussed by different members of the UK Parliament at this 104-minute debate. This is in addition to the two above quotations of this chapter cited from Cadbury and Monaghan—members who were also present at that debate. There are four interconnected tropes that I identify from the various speeches put forward by different members of Parliament (MPs) at this November sitting. They are (1) war heroism and commemoration; (2) individual biographies of ex-Gurkhas; (3) national and communal pride for Gurkhas in the United Kingdom and Nepal; and (4) deservedness of respect and tribute paying. Not unlike earlier sections where I discussed how bracketing and its shifts and permutations transpire in the legal arena, similar approaches toward bracketing the Gurkhas' belonging to the United Kingdom are adopted by these MPs. By deploying brief narrative examples that represent these four tropes, MPs themselves are actually bracketing these veterans' belonging to the United Kingdom, and therefore deservedness of equality and fair treatment by the UK government. These tropes, I argue, provide justificatory evidence and framing for these members to seek such equitable rights. This would include inclusionary policies and socioeconomic access for Gurkhas and their families given their varied conformity to such conditions of good migrant behavior (cf. Hackl 2022).

Where the first trope of war heroism and commemoration is concerned, MPs have in various ways recounted the incontestable risks, sacrifices, and loyalty of the Gurkhas in the many theaters of war that the United Kingdom had engaged in in the past and present as a record of history. For example, many spoke about how the Gurkhas served as a pivotal group who fought in both world wars, and in places including the Falklands, Kosovo, Afghanistan, and Iraq, to name a few countries and conflicts in warfare history. Given such military involvement over the more than two centuries of service with the British Army, the Gurkhas have therefore been extolled as a steadfast source of "service and sacrifice." This was expressed by, among others, Stephen Morgan, MP for Portsmouth South:

> To set the debate in its proper context, I will remind the Chamber of the contribution that Gurkhas have made to the British armed forces. Gurkhas have served in Her Majesty's armed forces for more than 200 years, from the earliest recruits to the East India Company through two world wars, during which more than 238,000 enlisted in the brigade, to the Falklands, the Gulf wars and multiple tours of Afghanistan. They have made an outstanding contribution to the UK through centuries of service and sacrifice. They are rightly held in high esteem by the British Army itself and by the wider British public.[134]

From the recognition of service and sacrifice that the Gurkhas have continuously provided to the crown, comes the following narrative of the UK government having a "moral duty" to accord equal respect and treatment for these veterans.[135] Such duty is also connected to debts owed to these Gurkha veterans, as many other MPs have noted.

MP of Glasgow East, David Linden, for instance made it his point to emphasize that an "enormous debt of gratitude" is owed to "the people who have chosen to serve and sacrifice so much." Despite the fact that "Gurkhas and UK personnel served alongside one another, made the same sacrifices and certainly took the same risks" as attested to by the above recount of history, the British Government seems "set on undermining and dismissing the sacrifice that many have made." Thus, it "remains a massive stain on global Britain's brand that so many pensioners, particularly those who served this country, anguish in pension poverty overseas."[136] Consonant with the point on war heroism and the debt that the United Kingdom owes to the Gurkhas, Matt Rodda, MP for Reading East, talked about honor and gallantry as he paid his tribute to them:

> I would like to spend a few moments paying tribute to the Gurkhas. They have given long and loyal service to this country, and it is worth mentioning some of the military history in a brief form. They were vital in world war one. That is less well known than their service in world war two, in which they played a crucial role in the defence of India.

> And they have taken part in many recent conflicts, defending this coun-
> try and our interests overseas. Those include, obviously, the Falklands,
> Afghanistan and many others in between. We owe a debt of honour to
> these brave soldiers, and I hope that the Minister, who I obviously know
> is a gallant gentleman, will respond in an appropriate way.[137]

Alluding to or invoking heroic war pasts is not only a matter of setting the context of the Gurkhas' deep and sustained involvement in empire and colonialism
from the outset. It is also a case of raising the past as a moral resource in order to
put forward claims in the present-day context (cf. Laubenthal and Schumacher
2020). In doing so, war narratives translate into moral narratives of recognition
and debt accrual.

The individual biographies of ex-Gurkhas, including their varied contributions to public service, community building, and to the local economy, is also a
recurrent theme that constitutes my second trope. We learn from Ruth Cadbury,
MP who represents half of the borough of Hounslow, about the large Gurkha
community who live and work there: "We are proud not only of their loyal service to our country, including in the fight against fascism in world war two, but
of their years of service locally in civic life, through their work with charities and
through the many small businesses that play a huge role in our local economy."[138]
To place a face to such civic and economic contributions, Cadbury raised the
example of Councilor Bishnu Gurung, mayor of Hounslow (2021–22) who had
previously contributed as a Gurkha Staff Sergeant. Not only had Bishnu Gurung
served a good nineteen years in the British Army, he was also awarded a long
service medal and a good conduct award. Upon his retirement from the armed
forces, he then settled down to live and work in Hounslow. He is presently a
full-time London bus driver as well as the chairman of the Gurkha Nepalese
Community Hounslow. In gist, said Cadbury, he is "such a good reminder that a
Gurkha's service does not end when they retire."[139]

Similarly, Maria Miller, MP for Basingstoke, recognized the Nepalese community there as "an incredible asset to the town." In her speech, Miller paid tribute to
Mr. Om Gurung, chair of the Basingstoke Nepalese Community, and Mrs. Poonam Gurung who formerly headed the Non-Resident Nepali Association UK.
Miller also lauded Captain Pancha Rai, who not only fought in the Falklands
previously, but is "one of seven people who opened our Gurkha Grocery Shop in
the centre of town."[140] MP for Brecon and Radnorshire, Fay Jones, spoke of the
Gurkha community in her constituency:

> The Gurkha soldiers I have met in my constituency tell me that they
> love living in Wales, that they have a strong connection and that it
> very much reminds them of life back at home in Nepal. Those in my

constituency are valued members of the community, with many volunteering with the Brecon Beacons national park and many heavily
involved in hospitality.[141]

The invocation of "home," drawn from Nepal to Wales for the Gurkhas, together
with the varied contributions of Gurkhas in volunteer work and in hospitality
are expressions of how socially and civically entrenched these migrants are. Not
only are these varied forms of participation underscored as their deep involvement with and connections to these domains of community life, their culinary
and combat skills are also attested to. Khusiman Gurung runs a New Gurkha Inn
located in Talgarth for which Jones "highly recommend[s] its curry"; Jones also
juxtaposed him with many others who are serving as "active soldiers who work
at the Infantry Battle School in Brecon."[142]

Contributions that Gurkhas and other Nepalese migrants bring to different
parts of the United Kingdom continue to feature in MPs' advocative speeches.
In Reading, Gurkha and other Nepalese people total nearly three thousand
people. Apart from the ex-Gurkhas, Reading is also inhabited by "some highly
skilled migrants from Nepal," many of whom "live on relatively modest incomes."
Together, these Nepalese and Gurkha migrants are found in "crucial local public
services," including the NHS, Royal Berkshire Hospital, Reading bus drivers, as
well as many other forms of public service and local businesses. Rodda declared
that "we are proud to have many small local businesses linked to the Gurkha
community." In particular, Rodda delivered a "special tribute" to former Gurkha,
Warrant Officer Gyanraj Rai. He had played a pivotal role in the Gurkha pension
campaign and hunger strike. Having participated in two hunger strikes in the last
decade, Gyanraj Rai has been depicted by Rodda as "the most gallant gentleman"
who had "conducted himself with the utmost gallantry and dignity in this very
difficult period," "suffering greatly" when "he was outside No. 10 Downing Street
for a number of days" together with the other hunger strikers.[143] Rodda then
concluded his speech by registering council support for these veterans by way of
imploring the UK government to follow suit. Pointing out how local communities such as those in Reading have supported "our British Gurkhas," Rodda listed
a range of support from the Reading Borough Council. They include prioritizing
veterans on the council house waiting list, support for them from charities, and
help for elderly veterans and their families to learn English, among other forms
of communal activities. In sum, there appears to be "huge support and appetite
for continuing" these forms of support that are meant to help "people to integrate
into society in this country."[144]

Clearly, in the area of Reading at least, such avenues of support enfold Gurkhas
and their families into British society. This is so that they may be "integrated," as

Rodda indicated. He also hoped that "the Government will now hear this plea" in support of the Gurkha community to investigate further and to commence a dialogue with the Nepalese Government and the veterans themselves. The likes of model or exemplary migrant warriors and Nepalese people, including Bishnu Gurung, Om Gurung, Poonam Gurung, Pancha Rai, Khusiman Gurung, and Gyanraj Rai, are all taken as deserving figures given their substantial contributions to and immersion in the many facets of British social life. Not only have they contributed to various services, their kin and families have also received endorsements, support, and recognition for their Gurkha past and present, something that MPs are now imploring for the UK government to also recognize and give due credit accordingly.

The third trope has to do with both communal and national pride for Nepal and for the United Kingdom. It represents another if not more abstract level of recognizing and officially paying tribute to these Gurkha retirees, including their family members. MP for Aldershot and the minister for defence people and veterans Leo Docherty painted a statistical picture of Gurkha veterans and widows. In doing so, he thereby indicated the "scale of the [pension] issue" in parliament. Docherty noted that 20,681 Gurkha veterans have been receiving the 1948 GPS, out of which 7,382 are widows. For him, these figures reflect the "magnificent scale of the record of service of the Gurkhas," and to which he added that some "13 Victoria Crosses were won by native Gurkhas."[145] With this context, Docherty stated:

> I am very *proud of the deep local connection* that I have with the Brigade of Gurkhas in my borough of Aldershot. We are very pleased to be the home of the Queen's Own Gurkha Logistic Regiment. Many *thousands of Gurkhas have settled and now make their home in Aldershot, Farnborough and the borough of Rushmoor*, following 2009 changes in status of settlement. This represents a *hugely successful integration and settlement*.[146] (my emphases)

Continuing from the above statement, Docherty further singled out three Gurkha councilors and placed on record his thanks to Jib Belbase, Nem Thapa, and Prabesh KC. He praised them for their "tenacity, civic pride and energy"—in also following from the second trope on foregrounding individual, laudable figures. He then pronounced, out of these tributary and prideful endorsements: "We are fiercely proud of our Gurkha community in the borough of Rushmoor."[147]

In tandem with Docherty's approach, Jonathan Gullis, MP for Stoke-on-Trent North, also spoke unequivocally about not only the Gurkhas but all armed forces veterans "in the highest possible regard."[148] In mentioning some slices of his family history where his great-great-uncle and grandfather had served in the armed forces, Gullis then underlined the importance of dedicated and sustained efforts to also "secure better protection for memorials to our glorious dead."[149] Using this as his backdrop, Gullis further made connections of such public and official recognition of veterans—both present and departed—by extending such a position to the Gurkhas. He said:

> First of all, let me say that I know how highly regarded the Gurkhas are and have been for over 200 years. Their service to the British Crown, both here and overseas, has been marked by excellence and sacrifice. As Roy said to my team earlier, they are some of the most loyal soldiers this country has ever had, and have served on the frontlines of every war that the UK has fought in for the past 200 years. Prince Harry famously served alongside them during his 2007–8 tour of Afghanistan, and commented that "when you know you are with the Gurkhas . . . there's no safer place to be." That record of excellence and heroism goes somewhat under the radar, so I thank Joanna Lumley and campaigners like her for bringing the Gurkhas into the limelight.[150]

In the extract above, not only had Gullis placed the Gurkhas on a pedestal, he had also mentioned them alongside well-known British figures such as Prince Harry and Joanna Lumley. He had consciously related the Gurkhas to them by way of further endorsing and spotlighting these veterans so that they are not "somewhat under the radar." Before broaching the topic of pensions, Gullis concluded his lauding of the Gurkhas by announcing that their "distinguished service is a source of immense pride in both the United Kingdom and Nepal."[151] Clearly, the above statements, while reminding us that Gurkhas come from Nepal, nevertheless form a source of pride for both countries. This recognition also evinces the deep historical ties and connections that Nepal and the United Kingdom together share, thereby indicating the exigent need to resolve pension inequities based on such close linkages borne out of history, pride, and respect. Docherty had made it clear that the Gurkhas have now settled in such places as Aldershot, Farnborough, and the borough of Rushmoor in the thousands. The spread of Gurkhas living across such locales for him pertinently represented "a hugely successful integration and settlement" in the United Kingdom. Gullis similarly articulated the same sentiment. On behalf of the Gurkhas, he called the United Kingdom "their country":

> The Gurkhas have served our country—*their country*—and they have kept me, my daughter and the people of Stoke-on-Trent North, Kidsgrove and Talke safe. It is only right and fair that people who are willing to put their lives on the line for the United Kingdom's safety get the

respect that they deserve. . . . We have a fantastic Gurkhas veterans community across the United Kingdom. (my emphasis)[152]

Such official recognition of the Gurkhas' contributions and service to the United Kingdom, expressed through affective positions of respect and pride, form tributary brackets of belonging in underlining how the Gurkhas are a part of the British. Since this is now *their* country, they therefore ought not to be regarded as foreigners. As Monaghan put it: "It is high time that the UK Government treated non-UK-born veterans and those born in the United Kingdom the same way."[153] In other words, emplacing the Gurkhas in British society where they now live, carries them over the edge of not-belonging, into the brackets of belonging to the United Kingdom.

The fourth and final trope is an extension of the third. Here, the deservedness of fair treatment and respect is instrumental in recognizing and acknowledging the manifold sacrifices that Gurkhas have made for the crown. To begin with, Gullis proclaimed, "We have to ensure that if someone is willing to put their life on the line, they are protected and respected. Ultimately, they are willing to make the ultimate sacrifice; potentially, these are fathers and mothers willing to never see their children and loved ones again. I cannot imagine the bravery that that takes."[154] Gullis further fronted the magnitude of the Gurkhas' bravery and readiness to sacrifice where he reminded parliament that these veterans have "always [been] on the frontline, always the first in and, in many cases, always the last out." For Gullis, this "shows what a tremendous group of individuals they are and what they are willing to do."[155] Although I have earlier through legal documents of court hearings indicated that deservedness through nationality is exclusive and holds no room for any overlaps, the same point was treated differently in the parliamentary debate of November 2021. If anything, the difference of nationality as a point becomes moot in this context. This is advanced in view of the immense sacrifices that Gurkhas have been noted to have brought to the United Kingdom. Monaghan provided clear differentiated treatment bestowed on the basis of those from overseas, such as the Gurkhas. She exclaimed:

> Fair status is not granted to personnel from overseas. An individual with a wife and two children would have to pay £10,000 to try to bring their partner and children here. There are also instances of individuals being refused NHS treatment. . . . We must respect and honour their service. If the Government are serious about their commitment to veterans—all veterans, regardless of their place of birth—we must see pension equality, a waiver of immigration fees and a serious approach to veterans' affairs. That is literally a no-brainer.[156]

The issue here is not so much about deservedness by nationality, but rather by contribution and readiness to sacrifice. The principle of empire (Cohen 2022) which I discussed above remains resonant herewith. Being ready to sacrifice denotes the Gurkhas' loyalty to and bravery for the crown. In return, "fair status" as Monaghan put it, ought to be installed. This is clearly the case since deservedness of respect in this manner has already been earned by the Gurkhas; something that also follows from the first trope.

Not only have the Gurkhas earned such respect, their families by extension are also part of the picture where fair treatment is concerned. For Jim Shannon, MP for Strangford, courage formed a key theme in his speech. Having said that he felt "greatly humbled" to actually be in the presence of the Gurkhas when he met them while doing the armed forces parliamentary scheme, Shannon emphasized their "tremendous courage and bravery" which easily "surpasses and equals that of many others across this great nation."[157] Mentioning that one of the Gurkhas who had participated in the hunger strike received only £47 (approximately US$60) a month upon retirement in comparison with his British counterparts who took home £600 (approximately US$758), Shannon then launched into a series of rhetorical queries in parliament:

> At what stage will we decide to do the right thing by those brave men and their families? It is not just about the soldiers; it is about their families as well. They deserve the pension. They have honoured us. They have delivered and they deserve to have it. How many petitions will it take? How many protests? How many demonstrations? How many hunger strikes? There have already been too many.[158]

As the Gurkhas "have delivered," all they are asking for is "parity, equity and fairness," in Shannon's words. Calling the "same benefits, pensions and welfare" as a "debt that is owed" to Gurkha families, Shannon then further reiterated how the Gurkha community ought to be regarded as analogous to the British. He announced that he is "proud to stand, along with others, with the Gurkhas" because "they have stood for freedom and democracy under the banner of our monarchy, and of our Queen, and before that our King."[159] This statement serves as a poignant example that carries allegiance as pledged both by the British as well as the Gurkhas, thereby making these two groups equivalent under the eyes of the UK government. In the end, Shannon called for "delivery for the Gurkhas" in equal measure with what others get:

> Gurkhas and their families still live in poverty, despite believing that fighting for our Government, our country and our Queen would mean security for their families. What we deliver for the Gurkha soldiers, we must also deliver for the families. They deserve nothing less. The

message from this place, as we have all said, must be that we will settle for nothing less on their behalf. We want for the Gurkhas what other soldiers have—nothing less, nothing more.[160]

By the end of the parliamentary debate, Gullis closed the session by proclaiming it as a "fantastic debate." More important, Gullis underscored that "it is clear that we all respect the Gurkhas and want to see them well looked after."[161]

Collective and assenting voices of these MPs who have together spoken in a concerted quest for and support of equal and fair treatment to the Gurkhas and their families represent their strategic acts of bracketing Gurkha families' belonging to the United Kingdom. For the Gurkha community in different parts of the United Kingdom have contributed not only to the theaters of war in the past, but in the present-day context of community contribution, development, and sociality. Through these past and present domains of contributions, Gurkhas and their families have therefore been seen as valued, good, and deserving migrants who by extension ought to "deserve nothing less."[162] Such endorsement of and support for Gurkha veterans and their loved ones reflect the familiar if not classic trope of the construction of good migrants in the wider migration literature on belonging and deservedness (see for example, Hackl 2022; Ratzmann 2021; Sivis 2022). Issues to do with who rightly belongs to a community of solidarity, and thereby connected to the social distribution of state resources (Ratzmann 2021), are routinely raised, as shown by the UK parliamentary debate of November 2021, for example. As Ware (2009, 59) similarly describes the Gurkhas in the context of the Gurkha Justice Campaign, "Far from being another category of unwanted immigrants seeking to cash in on their tenuous connections to the UK, the retired Nepalese soldiers and their dependants were cast as deserving entrants to the national collective." Gurkha veterans are essentially made tangible, legitimate, and worthy as migrants. This in turn enable justification for proper treatment to be meted out accordingly, with an extended reach to their families as well.

The four tropes are therefore demonstrated expressions of deservedness that provide the rationale and substantiation for taking Gurkha pension and other matters seriously, as advocated by the different MPs. This is given especially that the Gurkhas have now crossed the threshold from foreign warriors from the outset, to living in the midst of British citizens. They have essentially formed and continue to form a part of life in the United Kingdom as a veteran community. In essence, MPs vouched for how the Gurkhas and their families have attained cultural and communal integration, of which such evidence presented in parliamentary discourse could be more weighty than legal policies toward determining subjective belonging (cf. Simonsen 2016). On 31 March 2022, the MOD and Gurkha Brigade Association announced that revisions to the GPS, the Gurkha Service Pension, the Gurkha Disability Pension, and the Gurkha Family Pension would be accomplished as of 1 April 2022. These revisions saw a 7.11 percent increase in pension amounts in view of mounting standards of living in Nepal.[163]

The Legal Politics of Bracketing Belonging

Where belonging may be felt, experienced, desirable, or aspirational, it also needs to be adjudicated on, allowed, or approved within the bounds of particular legal-political, sociocultural, and temporal conditions and contexts. It is only when these contexts and conditions shift or alter that parameters of belonging and not-belonging concomitantly transform as well. These shifts and transformations occur differently for Gurkhas, wives, and children, but also that of nation-states, their legal apparatus, and immigration policies. Together, the broader backcloth of empire and postcolonialism in the case of Gurkhas and their families affect and forge the facets, forms, and flexibility of what it means to belong or not-belong.

Legal bracketing implies both acts of inclusion and exclusion as it confronts issues of recognition and equality of treatment. Inclusionary bracketing would mean that criteria for belonging have been met. One would thus be included for rights and resources. The legal recognition and formulation of belonging, arising from the admission of such newer qualifying conditions is thereby accompanied by the legal provision of rights as I have discussed above. By the same token, then, exclusionary bracketing would therefore mean that such criteria or quali-fying conditions have been legally rejected. One is thereby excluded from rights and resources. Claimants are left outside of the brackets of belonging. In other words, legal bracketing can either block or facilitate belonging and subsequently claims to rights. Similar to affective and aspirational practices of belonging, legal belonging and not-belonging are contemporaneous. My close reading of legal and other texts in this chapter and how bracketed belonging transpires therefore showcase and scrutinize the ways through which inclusionary and exclusionary mechanisms come into play. These mechanisms are closely connected to rights and access to provisions or a change in the TACOS. When such mechanisms come to the fore, this therefore also invites resistance to or rejection of bracket-ing, pointing to the stakes involved. These various stakes comprise what is to be gained as well as what is to be lost in the process of legal negotiation and contestation.

As brackets or edges of belonging shift, renew, or transform over time, the figure of the Gurkha soldier is also impacted, if not latently so. Not only does his public persona change from that of "patriotic hero" to "poor working-class victim" (Qureshi and Zeitlyn 2013, 113) in the broader contexts of income and pension issues in relation to his service to the British Army, he has also traversed, where allowed, from that of soldier to citizen. Bracketing strategies as seen in the legal arena or in the UK Parliament debate as previously discussed also reflect how the contours of belonging are illuminated. Gurkhas and their families have had to demonstrate particular efforts, achievements, and action (cf. Hackl 2022) before they are sociolegally recognized as deserving actors. Evident among these parliamentary narratives and the four tropes are legal, affective, social, and communal contributions as identified from Gurkhas both in their active service and postservice milieus. These different forms of contributing to British society thus render Gurkhas and their families as worthy or deserving recipients of abode. They also include access to uplifted sociolegal and economic provisions in the UK context. MPs were essentially delineating and pronouncing brackets of belonging based on the four tropes. In the process, they have together also underlined the rationale for inclusionary rather than exclusionary responses and policymaking from the UK government. By mapping out the different forms of how legal bracketing are mounted, challenged, reconsidered or renewed, I have not only expanded empirical conditions of how bracketed belonging transpires in law and policy, but also add pertinently toward expanding the analytical girth of belonging as a concept in this book. I have done this by foregrounding the legal and political drawing and redrawing of boundaries (i.e., brackets) between deserving individuals and nondeserving ones in relation to the wider landscape of nation-state policy and demographic governance structures. My analysis therefore widens the theoretical radius of how belonging is approached in legislative and bracketed terms.

CONCLUSION

In the Wake of Empire

> I changed professions a few times before I switched over to the restaurant business in Aldershot, over thirty years ago. Except for a few lads in the British Army this place was unknown to any Nepali desirous of doing business in the UK. I had come to English soil with a lungful of oxygen from Nepal, India, Malaya, Hong Kong and Singapore. I knew exactly when a man runs short of his breath and has to take whatever work is offered. The name of my loved venture was *Johnnie Gurkha's Restaurant*.
>
> Hari Bivor Karki, *Johnnie Gurkha's Is with Me*

Born in 1945 near Okhaldhunga in East Nepal, Hari Bivor Karki enlisted into the Brigade of Gurkhas in 1961. Apart from serving in the military, he had also taken on different jobs. These include him being a boxing instructor in training both the army and the police in Kathmandu, as an assembler with Ford Motors in Essex, as well as having worked in the food and beverage industry. In 1978, Karki opened his restaurant, Johnnie Gurkha's Nepalese Cuisine located in Aldershot. It was the first of its kind in the United Kingdom if not any other Western country at that time. His book tells the story of his and his family's life as immigrants, including contributing to the Nepalese community in the United Kingdom. Indeed, Karki's arrival on English soil, after having trudged across the different countries in Asia, reflects his experiences and tribulations as a warrior and migrant Gurkha. By extension, Karki and his family who have traversed different places since his Gurkha days shed light on these Gurkha families as transnational social actors located within the wider Gurkha diaspora.

Gurkhas as military/security actors and as diasporic actors function vis-à-vis the ambitions and structures of colonialism and empire building, as well as the current needs of modern nation-states in terms of security and policing in relation to global PMSCs. These two intertwining ambits influence how Gurkhas and their families lead a variety of transnational lives, negotiate varied senses of belonging (structural, legal, sociocultural, and aspirational among others) and understand what it means to be a migrant warrior. While Gurkha families such as Karki's may all be a part of the same Gurkha diaspora in a manner of speaking, each individual or family unit inhabits diasporic worlds differently and experiences variegated ways of living. These depend on their Gurkha father's or parents' migratory route, as well as where they were born and bred and obtained schooling or jobs that in effect determine how their varied senses of belonging occur. Given that migrants "live transnational lives," "affective belonging is at the same time local, national, and transnational" (Morrice 2017, 605). Together, these mean that there are uneven diasporic and migratory routes. Such unevenness includes different transnational axes of relations, as well as the stipulations and restrictions of nation-states that either enable or constrain rights to abode and citizenship.

The stories and lives of Gurkhas and their families blend colonial histories, migratory aspirations and failures, as well as the manifold acts and challenges of bracketing belonging depending on the different contexts in which they have lived and worked. Arising from these contexts and conditions, then, how belonging pans out, and how belonging shifts for different members of Gurkha families within the wider Gurkha diaspora become key moments in deciphering Gurkhas and their kin as migrant actors beyond the former's global fame as warriors. The Gurkha diaspora has emerged out of a complex constellation of colonialism, imperialist ambitions, and the confluence of world wars and global security needs that in concert also determine the migratory routes of ex-Gurkhas who enter global security industries as their second-career option. The ambitions, plans, and aspirations of Gurkhas and their families illustrate the broader approaches and strategies that immigrants and the next generations deploy: "Depending on their socioeconomic characteristics, immigrants and their children combine incorporation and transnational strategies in different ways at different stages of their lives. They use these to construct their identities, pursue economic mobility, and make political claims in their home or host country or in both" (Levitt and Waters 2002, 12).

In essence, it is due to the entanglement of history, empire, global political relations, and security demands persisting into the present that routes of movement and mobility for Gurkhas, retired Gurkhas, and their wives and children are sustained. Because of this, belonging and recognition may be interpreted as a "moving kaleidoscope" (Cohen 2022), as has been my endeavor in this book. In studying Gurkhas and how their transnational family lives unfold over many generations, I have also provided different perspectives to rethink how historical and contemporary approaches to security industries and policing are closely tied to colonial and postcolonial structures of governance and interdependency. The transnational lives of diasporic security forces such as the Gurkhas in their second-career milieu in security and policing work today remind us that security work and policing remain transnational. National security requires transnational security labor in the form of Gurkha forces.

Manifold and contextual notions of belonging—deliberated across different groups and generations of social actors to include the Gurkhas, their wives, and their children—form the crux of this study in presenting Gurkhas as a group of migrant warriors. I have reiterated the conceptual linkages between diaspora and its transnational connections, belonging and not-belonging, as well as generational difference and sameness. I recapitulated how the Gurkha experience as a diasporic security force reflects on migrant mobilities and aspirations couched within specific temporalities and structural possibilities and/or constraints. These dynamics together articulate the workings of a global security landscape wherein the migratory flows and mobilities of Gurkhas and their kin transpire. The many facets of transnational ties, linkages, and senses of belonging are realized over time due to the global dispersion of these migrant warrior families since the imperial period. Such webs of transnational connectivity are enacted with social actors operating along different axial and kin ties occurring between, inter alia, Singapore and Hong Kong, the United Kingdom and Nepal, and Nepal and Hong Kong. Taken together, the differentiated feelings of bracketed belonging unveil the robustness of belonging as an analytical tool. I used it to capture and comprehend the features, composition, and lived experiences of the Gurkha diaspora. I have therefore weaved together a broader abstraction of how one may approach diaspora and belonging by considering military-labor social actors as a category alongside the spectrum and depth of bracketed belonging. This would thereby depart from the extant inventory of migrants that existing studies have routinely examined. More pertinently, I addressed and reiterated the key inquiry of how to grapple with and problematize the relation between migrants and nation-states using the Gurkhas as an illustrative case.

In bracketed terms, belonging is therefore an intersectional notion that overlays and overlaps with similarities and differences as synchronous rather than disparate or disconnected. Moreover, the process, experience, and decisions that are made and unmade to carry out bracketed belonging are oftentimes acts of weighing options. These options are also accompanied if not influenced by a whole host of multivalent factors that may work in concert or run counter to one another. In essence, they impact on how social actors as migrants determine how, when, and with whom or where one belongs. Where Gurkhas mainly exhibit more certainty in how they feel about Nepal, their children's generation conveys a weightier sense of ambivalence as to where home may be. It follows that, given its shifting complexities and varied meaningfulness that differ from person to person, and from one generation to the next, belonging is more than Janus faced. One also needs to consider the broader institutional and legal structures, as I have analyzed, toward unraveling how brackets of belonging continue to be fluid and malleable, contingent as well on in situ policies and legislative frameworks.

Conceptualizing belonging in bracketed terms highlights the positional and relational aspects of how social actors anchor themselves (Jones and Krzyzanowski 2011). Teasing out the various nuances of what belonging and not-belonging look like indicates how "individuals have to position themselves in relation to an existing collective or community" (Jones and Krzyzanowski 2011, 44). This thereby adds to a further understanding of the relation and social contract between migrants and nation-states. Methodological ventures in the collation of data have brought me to focus on both primary and secondary sources to include narrative interviews, archival-military materials, websites, as well as legal documents that in concert advance important empirical and therefore conceptual avenues to rethink what belonging means.

Belonging is a multiscalar experience, as evidenced throughout the course of this book. How multiple belonging is experienced and narrated reflects "a mixture of hope and fear, integration and marginalization, and longing and belonging" (Kananen 2020, 182). Furthermore, I have also discussed how belonging relates to the transactional and the reciprocal. Where Gurkha children stake claims on their right to belong owing to their birth in Singapore or Hong Kong, or if Gurkha veterans mount claims and pressure on the UK government for equitable pension arrangements or for rights to abode prior to the change of immigratory policies in the United Kingdom in the 2000s, such negotiations of staking belonging reflect precisely their intentions to initiate transactions and reciprocity with nation-states. As Hausner puts it rightly: "To move is not to leave parts of oneself behind, but to attempt to take all parts of oneself to a new place, sometimes with the conscious knowledge that those aspects may look different against another geographical and cultural background" (2018, 511). Together, such experiences and expressions of (wanting to) belong in the United Kingdom, Singapore, or Hong Kong are represented not only through the domain of legal-political citizenship, but that of cultural citizenship. Ong defines cultural citizenship as comprising the "cultural practices and beliefs produced out of negotiating the often ambivalent and contested relations with the state and its hegemonic forms that establish the criteria of belonging within a national population and territory" (1996, 738). In this respect, then, national belonging and its subjective aspects come to the forefront.

A Security Empire of Diaspora Making

The Gurkha diaspora is one that has been created out of colonial contexts, and which continues to bear the remnants of colonial structures in the present. Such a contextual framing that I have adopted in this book echoes Ware's (2015) take on "sinews of empire"; Gurkha military and police work have been closely intertwined with centuries of colonial history. Even if Nepal had lain "outside the bounds of empire" (Ware 2011, 127), the military and policing agreement that began more than two hundred years ago continues to demonstrate the far-reaching effects of empire and imperialism. These apply both to Gurkhas in active service as well as those who have retired and gone into the global security industry. As a result, unfinished imperialism where the structures of empire, inexpensive labor, and Global North–South relations continue to affect Gurkhas and their families as they work through and navigate their varied feelings of belonging, including their work/life trajectories in the wake of empire.

Britain's colonial past, specifically in the context of its martial constructs of Gurkhas as brave warriors, continue to wield lasting impact and influence. This is one of the reasons why Gurkhas who have retired persistently surface as security labor in present-day global circuits that PSMCs sustain. Kiruppalini (2013, 74) talks about Singapore Gurkhas in the police force and how they are "defined by a British colonial immigration heritage." Chisholm (2016, 139) similarly contends that "constitutions of race and colonial histories continue to play out in everyday practices of security." The aftermath and deep-seated histories of colonialism and imperialism that have endured till the present-day therefore form a long-sustaining backdrop (Laubenthal and Schumacher 2020) to current portraits of the Gurkhas as transnational police and security forces, stemming from their global reputation and famed recognition as loyal fighters. Such recognition was further reiterated by then British prime minister Rishi Sunak who had this to say when invited to the world premiere (in London, September 2023) of a Nepali movie—*Gurkha Warrior*—based on the Gurkhas who fought alongside the British Army during the Malayan Emergency of 1949:[1]

> "I am delighted to know about the film made about the bravery, sacrifices and dedication of the brave Gurkha soldiers. Thank you very much for the invitation. I am unable to attend the premiere ceremony. I would like to wish a success for the premier show and the movie. Thank you for the letter," the British PM said in a reply to the letter sent by the makers of the movie.[2]

It is clear that one ought to bear in mind the relevance and significance of the past to present-day contexts. One could argue that martial race theory, which I have also discussed in this book, serves as one of the "best proofs of just how resilient colonial structures and ideologies can be" (Peers 2007, 52). The remnants comprise the differing modes and extent of bracketed belonging that have affected Gurkha families over the centuries, including the relational consequence of expanding police and security global networks, given their participation in PSMCs and transnational circuits of security contractual work.

This study has been an attempt at crafting new perspectives on belonging through the notion of bracketing. Bracketing processes, ideas, and ideals intersect intimately with colonial and global institutions such as the military, police, together with other political and affective sentiments that both operate within and beyond the parameters of nation-states. I deployed bracketed belonging as a conceptual prism to unpack and problematize the migratory experiences, struggles, and aspirations in the wider Gurkha diaspora and vis-à-vis the historical processes and remnants of empire. In this respect, belonging is as much a project of the self as it is a process of subject-citizen-making for Gurkha diasporans. For the Gurkhas, their subject positioning may have shifted from warrior to working-class victim. This shift occurred in the face of their canvassing for recognition of their contributions to the crown, and thereby to be admitted into the brackets of belonging to the United Kingdom for rights of residence and equitable pension arrangements, among other causes and aspirations. Furthermore, their positionality has also transformed from that of soldier to citizen, at least in the case of the United Kingdom, and in the Hong Kong context where they possess the right to abode. The exception here is that of Singapore where mandatory repatriation remains the order of the day for Gurkhas and their family members. Overall, these processes do not come easily, nor do they mean that belonging is experienced positively and with ease. The different rounds and contours of negotiations, contestations, and recognition in toto go to show how bracketed belonging is valued by both individual and nation-state actors. This is because the politics and stakes of belonging or otherwise for all parties—be they claimants or adjudicators of belonging—are bundled in a constellation of affection, rights, entitlements, and locales of homemaking.

Bracketed belonging as an analytical tool and framework may be apprehended as I have done through three interrelated dimensions—time and shifts, generational convergences and divergences, and the role of institutional actors. These three dimensions overlap with one another and demonstrate how belonging and not-belonging through changing practices of bracketing take place from the moment of Gurkha enlistment toward the varying social and political constellations in which diasporans act or not. Belonging changes with time given that social actors' biographical phases, experiences, and encounters in different contexts shape and reshape their sentiments of belonging or otherwise. Where temporality and shifts in belonging affect the individual, these are further enabled if not constrained by external factors and changes in the law and in immigration policies over time, as I have also demonstrated in this book.

Given the various contexts in which the Gurkhas and the British presence continued in such countries as Hong Kong and Singapore, and including the presence of retired Gurkhas who now work as security contractors in other parts of the world hired by PMSCs, might these constitute a case of "unfinished decolonization" (Hack 2019)? In tandem, Coburn (2018, 335) points out that the United States is continuing British colonial practices, using Nepali security contractors to exert its influence globally in a manner that is politically and economically incapable of doing by relying solely on US soldiers.[3] If that is the case as is being interpreted here, the lasting legacies of the British Empire, even if unintended, continue to exact its influence. Bracketed belonging and its extent, limit, degree, and variegated forms continue to be negotiated by Gurkha families in the countries that I have addressed. Moreover, even if Gurkha security work—both during the period of the British Empire and its conquests, as well as in the postindependence era of its former colonies—continues to be both mobile, transnational, and fluid in the wider global security industry that continues to interface the Global North with the Global South (Chisholm and Stachowitsch 2017), the paradox is that the Gurkhas and their families cannot entirely or sufficiently feel suitably entrenched or belong to any particular location per se. Therein lies the contradictory nexus of security work mobility and how belonging constantly needs to be negotiated between state and nonstate actors.

What would be the long-term impact of colonial institutions in the case of the Gurkhas and their families? The complex social contract between military migrants and nation-states in a global militarized world is contingent on a use-and-repatriate policy, though the degree and extent of belonging and legitimacy differ from country to country, and across different time periods. Where use is concerned, bracketed belonging, transnational ties, and the need for neutrality determine how these Gurkha soldiers or police are sustained in each of the countries where they make their living. In terms of repatriation, nation-states would need to ensure the doling out of pensions and compensations in the post-service period, including immigration policies that determine if citizenship is to be awarded or not. There are also ramifications arising from such policies, which influence where their children may stay or not.

Belonging and Its Limits

There are limits and timelines to how belonging is perceived, experienced, or shifts. Social actors are either subject to the constraints imposed structurally or socially that determine the extent of whether they may belong; or they themselves place and bracket limits based on their experience, location, and aspiration. Such cognizance is reflected through conscious acts of bracketing belonging, the core idiom that this book has engaged with. Consequently, these acts elucidate the malleability and transformative aspects of how diasporans find their grounding across the different countries where Gurkha families are located. In the wake of empire, not only has the Gurkha diaspora taken different shapes and forms, but military security and theaters of war have inadvertently, through the construction of martial races, expanded police and security networks beyond the nation as a category.

There are therefore three ways to think about diaspora and belonging. The first pertains to a sustenance of home/hostlands, enacted by the British government prior to the 2000s when Gurkhas were to be recruited and retired in Nepal. In this thread, the home/hostland axial stands up to a certain point in the timeline of immigration policies and their concomitant changes. The second relates to the shifting brackets of what constitutes home/host when claims to rights, and changes in legal and immigratory structures propel a rethinking of where home is, and who the foreigners are who then turn into good and deserving migrants in establishing home outside of Nepal. The third has to do with the transnational expansion of security forces and networks, where the Gurkhas continue to deliver sustained security services for other nations. This also means a different approach toward understanding the contours of the Gurkha diaspora in the postempire or postcolonial era. The Gurkhas, in their second-career policing and security positions, disrupt the first thread of home/host dynamics given their flexible mobilities and police/security contract work across the globe. Policing space is also widened in the global security industry due to the Gurkhas' reputation in the military context, thereby adding a newer perspective on police militarization. Their jungle warfare expertise, bravery, and loyalty pave the way for later entry into the global security industry covering different aspects of policing, security, and peacekeeping. In addition to pivotal aspects of affective and aspirational practices or plans to belong as illustrated by my discussion of my interlocutors' varying biographies and experiences, the politics of belonging and what would be at stake, may also be interpreted as a form of "postcolonial claims-making" (Laubenthal and Schumacher 2020, 1133). In the current-day context, remnants of empire remain visibly present.

As migrants and security contractors, Gurkhas and families continue to negotiate the varied permutations of bracketed belonging as a perennial undertaking. This continual endeavor intersects both state and nonstate actors in multifarious ways as I have analyzed herein. I regard belonging as a relational and intersubjective process that enmeshes and interfaces different cultural schemas or repertoires all at once. Paying attention to processes and acts of bracketing further brings out the relational logic of how social actors draw up and determine their varied senses of belonging or not to particular social groups and to nation-states. Even if sentiments of belonging or otherwise may stem from affective and emotive experiences of place, memories, and social relations, these feelings either of individuals or social groups are also broadly determined by institutional, legal, and policy frameworks. They include the state, the military, and police bodies interfacing or interacting in relation to the different scales of institutional encounters, control, and management. Nation-states and their paramilitary institutional structures are accompanied by different rules and regulations of bracketing armed services, immigration policies, rights to citizenship, education, and pension. The key institutional actors in my book include the British, Singapore, Nepali, and Hong Kong PRC governments. I have discussed at length the varying structures and bracketed approaches through which the extent, degree, and temporality of belonging for Gurkhas and their families across these respective countries pan out over time and under shifting colonial/postcolonial contexts. Gurkha families continue to reside within the context of a postimperial limbo where together, these different individual and institutional actors form constellations that may build, reject, or alter conditions and sentiments of belonging and not-belonging.

Notes

INTRODUCTION

1. One example of such PMSCs is the Gurkha Security Guards. This company provided ex-Gurkhas as security forces in Sierra Leone in order to both deliver training for the Republic of Sierra Leone Armed Forces and to offer protection for Sierra Rutile, a mining company that oversees US-Australian mining activities (Zack-Williams 2012).

2. Kathmandu and Pokhara—these are the two main areas in Nepal that comprise sizeable Gurkha settlements (Chisholm 2016). In the United Kingdom, I carried out fieldwork in Eastleigh, Farmsborough, London, and Winchester.

3. These terms are commonly used to refer to the children of Gurkhas, with the former term referring to nephews, and the latter referring to nieces (Kiruppalini 2016).

1. CONSTRUCTING A GURKHA DIASPORA

1. One problem might be that of recruits who were outlaws and fugitive criminals who managed to "pass themselves off as genuine Gurkhas" in entering British service. Without the Government of Nepal's cooperation, their identity could not be ascertained (Banskota 1994).

2. The Himachal Punjab Gorkha Association is one of the oldest associations in Dharamshala. Established in 1916, the main aim of this organization is to provide financial assistance to Gurkha widows and orphans, as well as to preserve Gurkha language and culture, and to create employment opportunities for Gurkha pensioners through seeking government assistance (Purthi 2011).

3. Interestingly, Farwell (1984, 81) points out that most British officers were prejudiced against "line boys"—the sons and grandsons of soldiers who were born "in the family lines of a Gurkha battalion in India or Malaya" and who therefore had attended school and picked up foreign or non-Nepalese ways. The British officers felt that these young men did not possess the hardy virtues as compared to those from the hills, and they had also grown too clever for their own good (see also Bolt 1967).

4. Ruchika Uniyal, "Why Kathmandu Wants a Relook at Gorkha Pact," *Times of India*, 2 August 2020, https://timesofindia.indiatimes.com/india/why-kathmandu-wants-a-relook-at-gorkha-pact/articleshow/77310714.cms.

5. Ranjit Rae, "View: Nepal Must Think Before Testing Gurkha Traditions," *Economic Times,* 12 August 2020, https://economictimes.indiatimes.com/news/defence/view-nepal-must-think-before-testing-gurkha-traditions/articleshow/77475715.cms.

6. The recruitment takes place in Nepal, which is administered by HQ British Gurkhas who act on behalf of the Singapore government. The enlistment age spans between sixteen and twenty-one years of age, where Gurkhas may serve up to no more than forty-five years of age, or to opt for early retirement with a reduced pension—see letter by Hugh Davies on "The Gurkhas in Singapore," dated 19 June 1979—File DEFE 24/1818, "Loan Service and Trg Teams: Review of Singapore Gurkha Contingents," National Archives, Kew, UK.

7. For other works on the Gurkhas written in Nepali, see Thapa and Mainali 2002; Jhalak 2012; Rai 2015; Sangroula 2019; Surendra 2062 V.S; and Rai 2070 V.S. "V.S."

following the year of publication in this list refers to the Nepali calendar. This calendar is approximately fifty-six years and eight months ahead of the English/Gregorian calendar.

8. "Gurkhas Are the Public's Great Friends," *Sunday Standard*, 22 April 1951.

9. "Taj Goes to School," *Straits Times*, 31 March 1950.

10. "Prison Gurkha Unit to Join Police Force," *Straits Times*, 30 March 1981.

11. "These 37 Wives Don't Go Out," *Straits Times*, 31 March 1950.

12. "Bartley School's Gurkhas," *Singapore Monitor*, 19 April 1985. In 1993, it was reported that Gurkha children formed more than half of the four hundred students at Elling Primary School. These Nepalese children "joined the school without knowing a word of English." However, their "fighting spirit helps them learn English within two months," according to the Principal—indicating here, perceptions of the Gurkha community's resilience and hardiness that are usually associated with Gurkha soldiers. "Primary 1 Pupils Helping their Nepalese Classmates in English," *Straits Times*, 17 May 1993.

13. File DEFE 24/1818 "Loan Service and Trg Teams: Review of Singapore Gurkha Contingents," National Archives, Kew, UK.

14. "Gurkha Recruitment," https://www.army.mod.uk/who-we-are/corps-regiments-and-units/brigade-of-gurkhas/gurkha-recruitment/.

15. "Gurkhas for Defence of Brunei," *Straits Times*, 25 June 1964.

16. "Deployments: Brunei," https://www.army.mod.uk/deployments/brunei/.

17. "Hive Information Centres: Location Overview Brunei," https://www.army.mod.uk/media/1578/lo-brunei-june-16.pdf.

18. Many retired Gurkha servicemen had acquired land in Manipur and had gone into dairy farming. Specifically, the area of Kanglatombi Kangpokpi became the main locale in which Gurkha retirees toiled as dairy farmers. Other retired Gurkha settlements that practiced dairy farming are found in Mizoram, Meghalaya, and Arunachal Pradesh (Nath 2006).

19. The Gurkhas were relocated from their training depot in Sungai Petani, in the Kedah state of Malaya to Hong Kong (O'Neill and Evans 2018). They were at that time combating communist insurgence threats posed during the Malayan Emergency (1948–60) (Kiruppalini 2016).

20. Smith (1973, 161) writes: "The cold winters in the New Territories reminded Gurkhas of their native land and undoubtedly had beneficial effects on the health of their wives and children in the unit family lines."

21. Gurung (2020, 139) further elaborates that at the end of the two-year tour of this battalion, the Gurkhas returned to Malaya, while their families had to stay behind in Hong Kong. This was because the tented camps back in Malaya were not yet ready to house them altogether. It was only after six months' time that these families could join their Gurkha kin. Over this period of time, this group of sixty-five families were housed in a Kowloon hutted camp, previously a "Japanese prisoner-of-war cage." This scenario was probably one of the earliest instances of Gurkha families being located in Hong Kong in forming part of the broader Gurkha diaspora.

22. Minami (2007) notes that a number of Nepali associations began to spring up in Hong Kong in the 1990s. They include the British Gorkha Ex-Servicemen's Association which was founded in 1994, the Hong Kong Adivasi Sangha (Hong Kong Indigenous People's Association), the Far East Overseas Nepalese Association, the Hong Kong Nepalese Federation, the Hong Kong Gurkhas Forum, the Hong Kong Nepalese Women's Association, as well as the Association of the Gurkhas' Sons and Daughters Hong Kong, among others.

23. IOR L/MIL/7/7054, No. 427, British Library, London.

24. IOR L/MIL/7/7054, No. 427.

25. IOR L/MIL/7/7054, No. 427.

26. IOR L/MIL/7/7054, No. 427.

27. IOR L/MIL/7/7054, No. 427.

28. IOR L/MIL/7/7054, No. 428, British Library, London.

29. IOR L/MIL/7/7054, No. 430, British Library, London.

30. IOR L/MIL/7/7054, No. 430.

31. According to Forbes (1964) who had served with the Gurkhas in the British and Indian Army. Forbes writes about his tour in Singapore in 1963 after the Malayan Emergency and singles out his visit to Alexandra Grammar School. This former elementary school was refitted into a Grammar School for children of army personnel of the British and Indian Armies, as well as the Singapore GC. The author notes that Gurkha boys were admitted to the school, where they stayed in a nearby boarding hostel. These students "were studying in a language that was not their mother tongue." Given the medium of instruction, this led Forbes to ponder: "By bringing them up in a British school, are we turning them into something that is alien from their own homeland? Will those who do not join the army get completely out of touch with Nepal, and turn their backs on their native country, or will they take their knowledge and *savoir-faire* back there to benefit their own people as best they can?" (1964, 153). A similar school, Bourne School was set up in 1954 in Kuala Lumpur to provide education for children of the British armed forces in Malaysia, including the Gurkhas (Bennett 1958).

32. This would relate to what Useugi has pointed out with regard to state "instigation of immigrants' transnationalism" (2007, 403).

2. THE WARRIOR GURKHA

1. "Gurkhas—The Mighty Atoms!" *Straits Times*, 18 October 1953.

2. Legend has it that the term *Gurkha* is taken from Guru Gorakhnath, an eight-century Hindu warrior-saint. There was a teenager by the name Bappa Rawal who was on a hunting expedition with friends in Rajasthan. The group chanced on the warrior saint who was then in deep meditation. Bappa Rawal chose to stay behind to care for the saint. When Guru Gorkhnath awoke, he was impressed with the devotion of Bappa Rawal. He then gave Bappa Rawal the kukri, and told Bappa that "he and his people would henceforth be called Gurkhas, the disciplines of Guru Gorkhnath, and their bravery would become world famous" (Purthi 2011, 92–93).

3. Historian David Omissi calls the recruitment differentiation of the various clans in Nepal as an "atomizing ethnographic enterprise" which essentially produces not individuals but "specimens" (Omissi 1994, 31).

4. Taken from "British Gurkhas Nepal: Pre-arrival Pack Booklet I," June 2009, 16–17.

5. Cross (2009) suggests that the genesis of this motto may be traced to a letter written by Kaji Amar Singh Thapa to the king of Nepal, dated 2 March 1915. He wrote, "If we are victorious we can easily adjust our differences, if we are defeated, death is preferable to a reconciliation of humiliating terms" (2009, 23).

6. This motto is said to be quoted by "many old soldiers to their young sons as they set out to enlist in the British army" (Smith 1973, 175). Interestingly, when Des Chene cited this motto to a group of Gurung *lahures*, not only had they not heard of it, but that they responded in this way: "Perhaps it is better to be clever than dead" (1991, 234).

7. See Lee Hsien Loong, Facebook, 10 April 2019, https://m.facebook.com/leehsien loong/photos/a.344710778924968/2383177671744925/?type=3&source=48&__tn__= EHH-R.

8. Lee Hsien Loong, Facebook, 10 April 2019.

9. "The Gurkha Contingent, an Elite Security Force, has been Stationed in S'pore before S'pore was Born," *Mothership*, 12 June 2018. In particular, one media report utilized

the Gurkhas' sense of dependability in association with organ donation. It was reported that their renowned traits of "loyalty and dependability" became evident when they had "voluntarily pledged their kidneys to the National Kidney Foundation." These 630 Gurkhas were at first concerned over their colleague who had renal failure and who had to be placed on kidney dialysis for close to two years ("630 Gurkhas Pledge their Kidneys," *Straits Times*, 25 June 1988).

10. "Gurkhas in New York," *Today*, 1 October 2004; "Maintaining a Proud Tradition," *The New Paper*, 22 January 1996; "Gurkhas Are Here to Stay," *Straits Times*, 14 March 1987; "In a Globalised World, Focus on Our Similarities," *Today*, 25 September 2014; "Gurkha Wife Gets a Star," *Straits Times*, 5 August 2014; "Gurkha Contingent Did Well to Contain Riot," *Today*, 16 December 2013; "Gutsy Gurkhas Will Let Their Legs Do the Talking Again," *Straits Times*, 15 April 1993; "Exhibition on Sentosa Salutes the Hardy Gurkhas," *Straits Times*, 1 February 1987; "The Small Men with Great Courage," *Straits Times*, 2 April 1978; "Tradition of Gurkhas Fading Away," *New Nation*, 28 April 1976.

11. See also, Stirr (2017) on how Nepali songs, or *dohori*, both celebrate military masculinity as well as lament familial separation of Gurkhas from their loved ones, including the inevitability of death for some.

12. " 'Scuffles' in Gurkha Camp Over Pay Issues," *Today*, 21 June 2008.

13. "Gurkha Stole ATM Card," *Straits Times*, 1 June 1985; "Six-Death Army Driver Is Fined $150," *Straits Times*, 18 February 1967; "Civilian Gurkha on Hurt Charge," *Straits Times*, 26 October 1950; "Gurkha Cop Jailed Nine Months over Clarke Quay Brawl," *Straits Times*, 24 May 2012; "Kidnappers' Motive Was Revenge: Police," *Today*, 7 April 2009; "Home Guards Surprise Gurkha Deserter and Siamese Girlfriend," *Straits Times*, 27 October 1958; "Two-Hour Manhunt for ex-Gurkha Officer," *Straits Times*, 26 June 2012; "Gurkha on Arms Charge," *Straits Times*, 2 November 1949; "Mutiny Ringleader is Jailed for 10 Years," *Straits Times*, 27 June 1963; "Jail for 5 Gurkha officers involved in unlicensed cross-border money transfers," *Today*, 5 September 2024; "Gurkha to Hang," *Singapore Standard*, 11 August 1950; "Insane, He Murdered an Officer," *Straits Times*, 13 August 1952; "I'm Not Mad But I've Shot Him," *Straits Times*, 25 January 1956.

14. Gurkha Security Services, Farnborough, UK, https://gurkhasecurityservices.co.uk/contact-us/.

15. See Gurkha Security Services, Management Team, Farnborough, UK, https://gurkhasecurityservices.co.uk/about-us/management-team/.

16. See Gurkha Security Services, Management Team, Farnborough, UK.

17. See Gurkha Security Services, Management Team, Farnborough, UK.

18. Gurkha Security Services, Management Team, Farnborough, UK.

19. See "History of the Gurkhas," https://gurkhasecurityservices.co.uk/history-of-gurkhas/.

20. "History of the Gurkhas."

21. See "Gurkha Security Services: Testimonials," https://gurkhasecurityservices.co.uk/testimonials/.

22. "Gurkha Security Services: Testimonials."

23. See "Standard-Gurkhas (G3s) Security Services Ltd," https://www.gurkhasgroup.com/security.

24. See personnel profiles, Gurkhas Group, https://www.gurkhasgroup.com/our-people.

25. See "Q&A: Ex-Gurkhas in Hong Kong," https://www.gurkhasgroup.com/q-a-ex-gurkhas.

26. "Q&A: Ex-Gurkhas in Hong Kong."

27. See "Who Are The Gurkhas? 10 Quick Facts," https://www.gurkhasgroup.com/who-are-the-gurkhas.

28. "Who Are The Gurkhas?"

29. "Who Are The Gurkhas?"

30. Gurkha International Security Services, https://gurkha-asia.com/special-security-operatives/.

31. Gurkha International Security Services, https://gurkha-asia.com/.

32. Gurkha International Security Services, https://gurkha-asia.com/bodyguards-and-vvip-escorting-team-guard-force/.

33. For another example of a Malaysian security company that builds on the Gurkha reputation, see Sri Waja Security Services, https://www.sriwajasecurity.com/gurkha-guards.html.

34. Chico Force, https://www.chicoforcesecurity.com/?page_id=356.

35. Chico Force, https://www.chicoforcesecurity.com/?page_id=1842.

36. Chico Force, https://www.chicoforcesecurity.com/?page_id=1842.

37. Chico Force, https://www.chicoforcesecurity.com/?page_id=1842.

38. See for example, "G4S Macau—Gurkha Service," https://www.g4s.com/en-mo/what-we-do/services/gurkha-service; though now defunct, see Open Corporates, https://opencorporates.com/companies/nz/4596939; see Gurkha Security, https://www.gurkha-security.com; see, for example, http://www.gurkhasecurity.org.np/site/index.php; and Gurkha Max, https://www.gurkhamax.com/programs/gurkha-security-guard-training/; IDG Security, which operates in Afghanistan, Myanmar, and Somalia, traces its heritage to the "culture, expertise and values of the Brigade of Gurkhas of the British Army." See https://idg-security.com/about-us/.

39. Farwell (1984) briefly discusses the unknown extent of homosexuality in Gurkha regiments. Through the autobiography of John Morris (1960), who was a junior officer with the Brigade of Gurkhas (2/3rd), Farwell mentions how Morris had chosen Umar Sing, a "handsome teenaged boy in his company" to be his orderly. This Gurkha orderly had apparently slipped into Morris's bed after consuming liquor. Morris eventually "succumbed" to Sing's "loosened inhibitions" (Farwell 1984, 130). Limbu (2015), a Gurkha sergeant who had taken operation tours in Afghanistan learned about the tea boys who were a source of sexual satisfaction for Afghan men in lieu of the high costs of getting married. Limbu then notes that in his village, boys who were good friends would at times "walk around with their arms over each other's shoulders," though "sex between men was completely unheard of" (2015, 123).

40. Hutt (2012) ventures an explanation as to why Nepali writers appear to adopt a censorious approach when it comes to crafting narratives about the Gurkhas. He suggests that as the Nepali language and its literature have over the years translated important components of an integrated national culture, Nepali writers are in this context and climate, "inherently nationalistic" (2012, 24). For those writers whom he has discussed, he is of the view that they have combined their "instinctive nationalism with an avowedly Marxist approach," which run counter to national ideology (2012, 24).

41. A Gurkha child studying in Singapore was reported to have been helped by his local classmates to learn the English language. Rabin Pun said: "It was difficult for me to learn English, but not as difficult as chasing cows and climbing mountains in Nepal." "Primary 1 Pupils Helping Their Nepalese Classmates in English," Straits Times, 17 May 1993.

42. "Gurkha Contingent Donates Kidneys," Straits Times, 23 June 1988.

43. In Kuala Lumpur, Malaysia, some Gurkhas donated blood as part of an emergency appeal from the Kuala Lumpur Blood Bank ("SOS for Blood and Bank Is 13 Pints Richer," Straits Times, 8 December 1959).

44. "Gurkha Wife Helps to Mellow Warrior Image," Straits Times, 5 May 1973.

45. "Gurkha Wife a Heroine in Her Community," Straits Times, 4 March 1973.

46. Caplan (1995b) identifies at least four different forms of Gurkha literature. They range from regimental histories, memoirs, autobiographies, and diaries to coffee-table picture books, and books that relate the Gurkha story for general readership.

47. See Caplan (1991, 591) for detailed examples of how Gurkhas have essentially been portrayed as similar to the image of a British public schoolboy; not unlike Woodyatt (1922) who describes the Gurkhas as cheerful public school boys. Compare these with Gould who suggests that the Gurkhas are a "cheaper version of Europeans" and for which the former were equal to the latter in terms of "courage and fidelity" (1999, 110).

48. It has been argued that where Nepali poetry prior to the twentieth century either celebrated war as an "embankment of the state" or championed the Gurkhas as a "valorous race," poets at the turn of the next century have become disillusioned with such "discursive constructs." Instead, these Nepali poets seemed to have come to the realization that Buddha's message of universal peace wielded more significance than war and its destructive nature (Paudyal and Baral 2021, 12).

3. THE MIGRANT GURKHA

1. There are two recruitment centers in Nepal—at Dharan in the east (established in 1953; Subba 2007), and at Pakhlihawa in the west. Parker (1999) notes that these centers are "magnificent oases of British military life" given the barracks, excellent sports facilities, and training grounds that were located in the "midst of the spectacular landscape" accompanied by their own communications and transport, not to mention a "first-class hospital fully staffed by British medical teams and made available for community use" in the case of Dharan. Recruitment was "met as always by thousands of willing and eager young men" (1999, 183).

2. See for example, Ku et al. (2010) who talk about the lives of South Asians living and working in Hong Kong, including the Gurkhas.

3. The application for British citizenship includes tests such as for English language ability, as well as the "Life in the UK" test—evaluations that reflect how "national identity values enter the application process" (Prabhat 2018, 14). Such values are requisite for foreign born migrants-turned-citizens, as they also "affirm or swear their allegiance to the Queen and pledge their loyalty to the UK" as part of a citizenship ceremony (Andreouli and Dashtipour 2014, 100).

4. Nepal has undergone periods of democratic politics and armed conflict since the 1990s. The country has seen its fair share of constitutional changes occurring in 1990, 2007, and 2015, two major popular movements taking place in 1990 and 2006 that championed for democracy, including the Maoist People's War (a civil war that broke out between the Maoist Communist Party and the government of Nepal) which spanned a decade from 1996 to 2006. By November 2013, Nepal saw the election of a new Constituent Assembly, with a coalition formed between the Nepali Congress and the Nepal Communist Party. In the 2017 national elections, these two parties campaigned together and took majority votes and formally merged after the elections (Hutt 2020).

5. Rob Andreouli, "The Race to be a Gurkha," *The Telegraph* 8 March 2014, https://www.telegraph.co.uk/news/uknews/defence/10677559/The-race-to-be-a-Gurkha.html.

6. The possibility of Gurkha women joining the army was already raised in the 1950s. Two Gurkha women (Bimala Dewan, eighteen, and Radha Rawat, twenty-two) were selected to attend a three-year training course in England in order to qualify as State Registered Nurses. If they had completed the training successfully, they would have been the first Gurkha women officers to join the British Army ("They Want to be the First Gurkha Nurses in History of Nepal," *Straits Times*, 1 March 1957).

7. Haley Dixon, "Gurkhas to Recruit Women for First Time," *The Telegraph* 15 July 2018, https://www.telegraph.co.uk/news/2018/07/15/gurkhas-recruit-women-first-time/.

8. Dixon, "Gurkhas to Recruit Women."

9. "Nepalese Women Set to Join Gurkha Regiment of British Army," *Economic Times*, 16 July 2018, https://economictimes.indiatimes.com/news/defence/nepalese-women-set-to-join-gurkha-regiment-of-british-army/articleshow/65010875.cms?from=mdr.

10. Some concerns include the possibility of having to reduce combat training standards for male Gurkhas so as to avoid potential legal suits of sexual discrimination when females join. Additionally, if female enlistees were to be restricted to noninfantry units, which was in line with the army's policy on all women recruits (now revised), and still to serve alongside their male counterparts, that would also lead to a legal problem as it is illegal to both recruit and train women and men differently to do the same job. See Matthew Hickley, "Hiring Gurkha Girls Will Weaken British Army, Warns Top Brass," *Daily Mail,* 24 October 2008, https://www.dailymail.co.uk/news/article-1080104/Hiring-Gurkha-girls-weaken-British-army-warns-brass.html.

11. This parallels Enloe's discussion whereby the domain of military service was thought to be a male preserve, and where it was assumed to ought to be "run by men and for men according to masculine ideas and relying solely on *man* power" (1983, 7; emphasis in original).

12. Sunita Gurung, GAESO Kathmandu District Committee, https://www.efe.com/efe/english/life/british-army-s-elite-gurkha-regiment-to-welcome-women-recruits-in-2020/50000263-3696843.

13. In 2007, hundreds of Nepalese women, many of whom were Maoist rebels, had already begun training in hopes of joining Gurkha service through this pilot entry scheme when the British Army begun considering changes in their recruitment policies. See Dan McDougall, "Women Set to Join the Gurkhas," *The Guardian* 24 July 2007, https://www.theguardian.com/world/2007/jun/24/gender.uk.

14. Asmita Manandhar, "Who Wants to Be a Gurkha? Women," *Kathmandu Post*, 18 Feb 2019, https://kathmandupost.ekantipur.com/news/2019-02-18/who-wants-to-be-a-gurkha-women.html.

15. Manandhar, "Who Wants to Be a Gurkha?"

16. Manandhar, "Who Wants to Be a Gurkha?"

17. "India Opens Vacancies for Nepali Women in Military Police," *Times of India*, 5 July 2021, https://timesofindia.indiatimes.com/india/india-opens-vacancies-for-nepali-women-in-military-police/articleshow/83534371.cms.

18. Pratichya Dulal, "British Army's Plan to Recruit Nepali Women Draws Mixed Reaction," *SBS Nepal*, 20 March 2019, https://www.sbs.com.au/yourlanguage/nepali/en/article/2019/03/20/british-armys-plan-recruit-nepali-women-draws-mixed-reaction.

19. Manandhar, "Who Wants to Be a Gurkha?"

20. Dulal, "British Army's Plan to Recruit Nepali Women."

21. "Girl Gurkhas," *Nepali Times*, 23 July 2019, https://www.nepalitimes.com/banner/girl-gurkhas/.

22. Hannah King, "Talks Continuing Over Allowing Women To Join Gurkhas," *Forces.net*, 8 March 2021, https://www.forces.net/news/talks-continuing-over-recruitment-women-gurkhas.

23. "Phase 3 (Final Selection) Gurkhas," https://www.army.mod.uk/who-we-are/corps-regiments-and-units/brigade-of-gurkhas/gurkha-recruitment/.

24. "How to Apply to Become a Gurkha," https://www.gurkhabde.com/becoming-a-gurkha/.

25. Audrey Gillan, "The Great Gurkha Race," *The Guardian*, 6 December 2005, https://www.theguardian.com/uk/2005/dec/06/military.audreygillan. The total number

of candidates who applied for Gurkha recruitment in 2005 was 15,106. Out of these, 572 qualified for the central selection round in competing for the 307 available positions.

26. Rob Blackhurst, "The Race to Be a Gurkha," *The Telegraph*, 8 March 2014, https://www.telegraph.co.uk/news/uknews/defence/10677559/The-race-to-be-a-Gurkha.html.

27. "Phase 3 (Final Selection) Gurkhas," https://www.army.mod.uk/who-we-are/corps-regiments-and-units/brigade-of-gurkhas/gurkha-recruitment/phase-3-final-selection/.

28. "Phase 3 (Final Selection) Gurkhas," https://www.army.mod.uk/who-we-are/corps-regiments-and-units/brigade-of-gurkhas/gurkha-recruitment/recruit-registration/.

29. Audrey Gillan, "The Great Gurkha Race."

30. Blackhurst, "The Race to be a Gurkha."

31. Blackhurst, "The Race to be a Gurkha."

32. Gillan, "The Great Gurkha Race."

33. For example, the Gurkha Brothers Training Academy is located in Lalitpur and is described as the "leading pre-British Army and Singapore Police Training Centre in Nepal." See "Gurkha Brothers Training Academy," https://www.facebook.com/gurkhabrothersacademy/about/?ref=page_internal.

34. Comparatively, in a 1948 press report, a Gurkha soldier has been described as such as he learns English in Malaysia: "With his sten gun on the desk beside him, a Gurkha Corporal toils in the Basic English Class at the Gurkha School of Education at the FARELF Training Centre in Johore." "Basic English for Gurkhas," *Straits Times*, 20 November 1948.

35. On the converse, it has also been reported in Hong Kong news media that some Gurkhas who were stationed there—be they single or married—found romantic companionship in Filipino domestic workers. See "How Hong Kong's Gurkha Soldiers Found Love—and a Chance to Choose—with Filipino Domestic Helpers," *South China Morning Post*, 9 May 2022.

36. In general, young brides of Gurkhas who were away from Nepal usually spent substantial amounts of time in their natal homes. Among the Limbus, aside from a number of constraints, a young woman in her natal residence is free to associate with other young men at the *dhan nac*, or "rice dances," that are held frequently. If she were to choose to enter into a relationship with a man there, she was actually able to do so, so long as *jarikal* (compensation) was paid either by herself or her new beau (Caplan 1995b).

37. Some retired Gurkhas had also played fairly influential roles in Nepal politics (Coburn 2018). For example, a good number of these retirees who were associated with the Nepali Congress pushed for more political rights in agitating against the monarchy (Karki and Seddon 2003).

38. I have found through my archival research, a number of job advertisements in Malaysia and Singapore (between the 1950s and 1970s) for watchman, security guards, or drivers that request for ex-Gurkhas. Examples include "Wanted: An Able Bodied Gurkha or Pathan Watchman for an Estate in Kedah," *Straits Times*, 9 September 1964; "Required Young, Energetic, Khaskura-speaking Gurkha Watchman Preferably Gurung or Magar for Oil Palm Factory . . . ," *Straits Times*, 30 September 1964; "Wanted: Reliable Handyman Driver . . . Ex-service Gurkhas Acceptable," *Straits Times*, 28 January 1967. In Hong Kong, ex-Gurkhas have been recruited in security services in the private sector: "Banks Hire Gurkhas to Beef up Security," *South China Morning Post*, 24 October 1993; "Former Gurkha Soldiers in Demand to Keep Hong Kong Secure," *South China Morning Post*, 7 July 2004; as well as the airport site, "Call to Use Gurkhas at Airport Site," *South China Morning Post*, 23 October 1994.

39. Chisholm (2016, 145) points out in her research on ex-Gurkhas working as security contractors in Kabul that they are known as TCNs (third country nationals)—men who work in security who come from the Global South.

40. Such a course used to be called a "rehabilitation programme": "Rehabilitation Programme for 8,000 Gurkhas," *Eastern Sun*, 7 February 1968.

41. See Singapore Gurkha Polyclinic, https://singpoly.com.np/.

42. Singapore Gurkha Polyclinic.

43. This is a pseudonym that I use for purposes of anonymity.

44. Where post-1997 Gurkha retirees were granted UK residency in September 2004, a landmark policy reform in April 2009 saw the British Parliament vote to grant Gurkha veterans residency so long as they have fulfilled a minimum of four years of service (Pariyar 2020).

45. Through my archival research of media reports, I found an article about a Nepalese boy, Megh Bahadurgurang, who donated SGD$5 from Singapore to Nepal via the Malaysian Red Cross Society. This was for the earthquake of 1966 that occurred in Nepal. The report writes that donations such as these would be "one way in which Malaysians could repay the friendship and bravery of the Gurkha soldiers during the Emergency." "More Donations for Nepal Homeless," *Straits Times*, 3 September 1966.

46. When an earthquake hit Nepal in 1988, the Singapore government dispatched ten Gurkha police officers together with thirteen officers from the Civil Defence to Kathmandu for relief support. The dispatch included supplies comprising ground sheets, blankets, and *dahl*. "Singapore Sends Supplies to Quake-hit Nepal," *New Paper*, 3 September 1988.

47. "Nepalese in Singapore In Touch with Families," *Straits Times*, 27 April 2015.

48. "Nepalese in Singapore In Touch with Families." Furthermore, three women who were daughters of retired Singapore Gurkhas—Anita Rai, Himalee Pun, and Shashikala Pun—heard about the Singapore Armed Forces' plan to set up a clinic in Gorkana and volunteered to help as translators for the medical team. "Daughters of Gurkhas Lend a Hand," *TODAY*, 25 May 2015.

49. "Red Cross, Mercy Relief Appeal for Urgent Donations," *Straits Times*, 27 April 2015. Gurkha outfits in Brunei, namely, The Gurkha Palace Restaurant and Gurkha Jewellery, both offered themselves as collection points for donations of medical supplies and daily necessities to be sent to Nepal. "JUST IN: Gurkha Palace Restaurant Collecting Donations to Help Nepal Earthquake Victims," http://www.bt.com.bn/bookmarks-breaking/2015/04/26/just-gurkha-palace-restaurant-collecting-donations-help-nepal.

50. See "School with Close Ties to Nepal Raises $20k," https://www.mfa.gov.sg/Overseas-Mission/Geneva/Mission-Updates/2015/05/press_201505080.

51. "Nepal Earthquake: British Army Send 100 More Gurkhas to Help with Relief Effort," http://www.mirror.co.uk/news/world-news/nepal-earthquake-british-army-send-5669463.

52. See "Nepal Earthquake Appeal- Fundraiser," http://www.gofundme.com/BGNCW.

53. "Comment: It's Britain's Turn To Fight For The Gurkhas," 28 April 2015, http://forces.tv/38337240.

54. Interestingly, Pariyar (2016) argues as to how certain Nepali customs such as house warming rituals, death rites, or Dashain cannot be carried properly in the ways that they can be done back in Nepal. Therefore, some Gurkha immigrant communities overseas are not able to forge closer connections with their deities and consequently experience "isolation from their spiritual realms" (2016, 276).

55. Another factor that ex-Gurkhas take into consideration in terms of citizenship application is that Nepal does not allow dual citizenship (Sharma 2021).

56. See "County Council Support for Gurkha 200 Year Celebrations," http://news.warwickshire.gov.uk/blog/2015/03/26/county-council-support-for-gurkha-200-celebrations/; see also Robin Cottle, "200 Years of Gurkhas Marked with Arctic Expedition, Everest Climb and Launch of Gurkha 200," *Daily Star*, 10 April 2015, https://www.dailystar.co.uk/

news/latest-news/200-years-gurkhas-arctic-expedition-17334379; see Man Aman Singh Chhina, "The Gorkha Rifles of the Indian Army to Turn 200," *Indian Express*, 21 April 2015, http://indianexpress.com/article/india/india-others/the-gorkha-rifles-of-the-indian-army-to-turn-200/ and https://sandbag.asia/?event=the-sandbag-gurkha-200-dinner.

4. GURKHA WIVES AND CHILDREN

1. "These 37 Wives Don't Go Out," *Straits Times* 31 March 1950.

2. "Gurkhas Were So Very Shy . . . ," *Straits Times* 13 April 1950.

3. Special quarters have been allocated by the army where Gurkha wives "can look after their husbands and children." "Gurkhas' Wives in Colony Camp," *Straits Times* 29 March 1948.

4. It is also interesting to see how on the one hand, Gurkhas have been depicted as brave and steadfast in their warfare skills and loyalty. On the other hand, their wives have been portrayed to be the exact opposite for the most parts, in being typified as shy and withdrawn per se.

5. The return to Hong Kong was not always an easy transition. For example, when some of the Gurkha children had returned to take up residency, the application process for identity cards took months, which is further exacerbated by the exit of the British Army in 1997 after the handover. For those who are Hindus, names for newborns are only given after eleven days of their birth, which thereby explains why their names are missing from their birth certificates. Moreover, discrepancies in terms of dates and translations have also slowed down the process of vetting done by the Immigration Department staff. Previously, before the 1997 handover, they could verify claims by contacting the British Army in Hong Kong. Since the handover, however, such checks will need to go through the British Gurkha Records Office in Nepal. These changes have thus created delays in which the usual waiting time of six weeks has now stretched to over seven months for applicants. "Army Departure Brings Long Wait for ID Cards," *South China Morning Post*, 1 February 1998.

6. There is an ongoing oral history project about Gurkha veterans and wives put together as a heritage endeavor to record the life stories of retired Gurkhas living in Colchester, Essex. Out of the twenty stories posted on the website (https://gurkhastories.com), three feature the experiences of Gurkha wives Bhui Maya Rana, Rup Maya Pun, and Tham Maya Pun.

7. For example, we learn of very brief biographies of some Gurkha women in Farwell's (1984) study. Khemkala had served the 1st/6th Gurkhas as a midwife for twenty-six years before she died in 1967, while Sobha Kumari Chhetri contributed thirty-four years as the midwife of the 10th Gurkhas between 1938 and 1972. Sobha's son was serving in the Gurkha Transport Regiment as a major, while her son-in-law was a Gurkha captain.

8. Aadesh's father-in-law served in the British Army and was based in Hong Kong. His wife was born there, and he has the right to abode in Hong Kong as her dependant.

9. Not unlike Bilhana's experience of living with her in-laws in the absence of her husband, Prisha and Parijat were from the same village and got married through their parents' arrangement. When Prisha was left with her in-laws while Parijat was overseas on Gurkha service, the three of them got along fairly well given that theirs was an arranged marriage. If it were a "love marriage," said Parijat, then his/the parents might not have liked it and thus Prisha would have had "a very hard time with the in-laws . . . [for it would have been] like living in hell."

10. I am also aware that there have been Gurkha widows who have chosen to apply for the right to settlement in the United Kingdom as well. This is based on my perusal of court cases pertaining to Gurkha veterans' and Gurkha adult children's appeals to the

UK government with regard to pension and rights to settlement in the United Kingdom respectively for which I discuss in chapter 5. Widows' applications are facilitated by the UK Immigration Directorate Instructions (IDI). Annex K of Chapter 15 of the IDI contains a discretionary policy that allows widows to be granted settlement in the UK (see *Saru v Entry Clearance Officer* [2021] HU/18159/2019, at [7]). Examples of Gurkha widows who have applied through the IDI for settlement may be seen in the following cases: *Shahi v Secretary of State for the Home Department* [2021] HU/06331/2019, at [13]; *Gurung v Secretary of State for the Home Department* [2021] HU/18592/2019(V), at [3]; and *Rai v Entry Clearance Officer* [2021] HU/02600/2020, at [1].

11. Press release of speech by Mr Mohamad Maidin Packer Mohd, Parliamentary Secretary (Education) at Macpherson Primary School Speech Day, 19 November 1999. Document number mmpm19991119a, National Archives of Singapore.

12. There was a Gurkha school in Singapore in the 1950s, located at Ulu Pandan. The school was paid for and managed by the army with Gurkha and Sikh teachers ("Services Children at School," *Straits Times*, 1 December 1950). Another Singapore school that "children of Gurkha policemen" attend is Bartley Primary School, which saw a total of 121 of these children who schooled there. They formed a third of its entire student population as reported in 1985 ("Bartley School's Gurkhas," *Singapore Monitor*, 19 April 1985).

13. "Singapore's Little Nepal." *The New Paper*, 7 August 2000.

14. "Singapore's Little Nepal."

15. "Singapore's Little Nepal."

16. "Singapore's Little Nepal."

17. "Singapore's Little Nepal."

18. See rules of Gurkha Brigade, https://www.army.mod.uk/who-we-are/corps-regiments-and-units/brigade-of-gurkhas/gurkha-recruitment/recruit-registration/.

19. Based on the latest Gurkha recruitment criteria for 2022 outlined by the Ministry of Defence, UK, the minimum height stands at 158cm (see https://www.army.mod.uk/who-we-are/corps-regiments-and-units/brigade-of-gurkhas/gurkha-recruitment/recruit-registration/).

20. It was reported in the *South China Morning Post* that ex-Gurkhas working as bodyguards can earn HK$30,000 (approximately US$3,822) per month. For employers who hire them as individual security officers, their salary can be as high as HK$60,000 (approximately US$7,644) per month. As for security officers who are experienced and occupy managerial or commander positions, they can get HK$100,000 (approximately US$12,740) in addition to housing and car allowances. "Cost of a Bodyguard in Hong Kong Rises with Increasing Demand," *South China Morning Post*, 7 May 2015.

21. See also "Nepalese Community Struggles for Acceptance in the City They Call Home," *South China Morning Post*, 6 April 2014.

22. In 2014, some members of the Nepali community in Hong Kong, including children of Gurkhas, have importuned for a memorial in order to "preserve the Gurkha's story in Hong Kong." Others also suggested building a Gurkha museum. Descendants of Gurkhas have argued that "they had no say in where they were brought up. A museum in the city, therefore, would enable them to remember their roots and culture, give the younger generation a sense of their identity in the city, and share their heritage with fellow Hongkongers as a way to better integrate into local society." "The Nepalese Community in Hong Kong Looks to Preserve Gurkha Legacy," *South China Morning Post*, 28 March 2014.

23. "Nepalese Community Struggles for Acceptance."

24. "'Small Fry' Gets 17 Years in Jail," *South China Morning Post*, 18 December 1996.

25. "Daughters of Gurkhas Lend a Hand," *TODAY* 25 May 2015.

26. "Daughters of Gurkhas Lend a Hand."

27. "Daughters of Gurkhas Lend a Hand."

5. AT THE EDGE OF BELONGING?

1. See *Ghising v Secretary of State for the Home Department* [2012] UKUT 00160 (IAC).

2. From 2004 onward, the British Government began to revise its stance toward Gurkha veterans. It was only in 2009 that Mr. L. Ghising became eligible to apply for entry. He did so, and was granted indefinite leave to enter the United Kingdom on 4 August 2009. His wife was granted indefinite leave to enter the United Kingdom on 16 September 2009. They arrived in the United Kingdom on 25 September 2009.

3. From *Ghising v Secretary of State for the Home Department* [2012] UKUT 00160.

4. From Ruth Cadbury (shadow minister for International Trade) at the UK Parliament debate on Gurkha Pensions. 704 Parl. Deb. H.C. "Gurkha Pensions." (22 November 2021). Col. 8 WH.

5. From Carol Monaghan (shadow SNP spokesperson for Education and for Armed Forces and Veterans) at the UK Parliament debate on Gurkha Pensions. 704 Parl. Deb. H.C. "Gurkha Pensions." (22 November 2021) Col. 10 WH.

6. See for example, Jennifer Ngo, "Nepalis Strangers in Their Own City: Language Barrier and Bias Limit Opportunities Despite Official Rhetoric About Equality, Observers Say," *South China Morning Post*, 6 May 2012. There have also been many immigration cases in Hong Kong whereby spousal visas for Gurkha families to settle in the Hong Kong as dependents have been denied. See among others, "Judge Throws Out Dependency Bid Visa Job Stance Illogical, Absurd: Lawyer," *South China Morning Post*, 16 June 1999; "Strict Entry Criteria Backed." *South China Morning Post*, 26 October 1999; "Wife Challenges Government's Right to Refuse Husband a Visa," *South China Morning Post*, 11 January 2000; *Durga Maya Gurung v Director of Immigration* in the High Court of the HKSAR Court of Appeal, Civil Appeal no 1077 of 2001 (On Appeal from HCAL No. 1487 of 2000) on 19 Apr 2002) as well as refusing children of Gurkhas the permanent resident status under the Basic Law (see "Gurkha Children Fight to Stay," *South China Morning Post*, 4 October 1998).

7. Issues that Singapore Police Gurkhas face include pay and pension inequities, lack of sufficient welfare support for widows, lack of adequate medical support when they retire in Nepal, and the denial of Singapore citizenship for Singapore-born Gurkha children, among others. See Om Gurung, "Plight of the Singapore Gurkhas," *Kathmandu Post*, 28 December 2021.

8. *Ghising and others v Secretary of State for the Home Department and Entry Clearance Officer* [2013] UKUT 00567 (IAC), at [21].

9. *Ghising and others v Secretary of State*.

10. I focus on the United Kingdom given that the contexts in Singapore and Hong Kong are different as these are not the main bases from which the British Army nor the Gurkhas operate. Besides, the Singapore repatriation policy remains in place as I have earlier indicated, while those in Hong Kong do possess the right to abode since the 1980s. In the Hong Kong context as I have discussed, the larger issues have to do with securing good education and employment especially for Gurkha children.

11. See for example, *Gurung and others v Ministry of Defence* [2002] EWHC 2463.

12. Geeta Sangroula calls these Gurkhas "rights-holders" in the context of how their deservedness of equal pay and pension as a form of "human rights-based claim" (Sangroula 2019, 36) continues to be elided by the United Kingdom. She discusses such elision by raising cardinal human rights principles of nondiscrimination and equality as provisions of different judicial and administrative bodies. They comprise, among others, the European Convention of Human Rights; the UN Universal Declaration of Human Rights; the International Covenant on Economic, Social, and Cultural Rights; and the International Labor Organization (of which the United Kingdom is a member).

13. There are a number of Gurkha organizations listed in Laksamba et al. 2013 that have attended assiduously to raising various inequalities that Gurkhas have experienced. Established from 1990, some examples of these organizations include the Gurkha Army Ex-Servicemen's Organization (GAESO), the Nepal Ex-Servicemen Organization (NESO), the British Gurkha Welfare Society (BGWS), and the British Council of Gurkhas (BCG), among others (see Laksamba et al. 2013, 92–97). These organizations, formed by retired Gurkhas, have brought many legal and political issues to Parliament and the Supreme Court of Nepal for a start. Since 2001, they have shifted their approach to the United Kingdom and have filed a number of complaints to the UK Parliament, the International Labor Organization, as well as the UK's high courts.

14. See among many examples, *Purja and ORS v Ministry of Defence* [2003] EWHC 445, at [3] and [33]; and *Gurung and others v Secretary of State for Defence* [2008] EWHC 1496, at [4] and [37].

15. See *Purja and ORS v Ministry of Defence* [2003] EWHC 445, at [53].

16. The Gurkha Justice Campaign, which took place from 2008, was led by Joanna Lumley, a British actress and daughter of an army major who had served alongside the Gurkhas. The campaign, which "forced the issue of citizenship and military service into the public domain" (Ware 2009, 59), fought for parity for Gurkhas who had served in the British Army pertaining to their TACOS (Carroll 2012; Ware 2009, 2013).

17. See *British Gurkha Welfare Society and others v Ministry of Defence* [2010] EWHC 3, at [7].

18. See *British Gurkha Welfare Society and others v Ministry of Defence* [2010] EWHC 3, at [9].

19. Gould (1999) points out that where Indian Gorkhas had the right to settle in India, the British Gurkhas did not have such an option to settle in the United Kingdom prior to changes in immigration rules.

20. Based on the British Army's service structure, upon recruitment Gurkha soldiers were first placed on a four-year contract. Upon the completion of this first contract, they then had to sign further contracts of three, three, and two years, which then totaled twelve years of service. After these twelve years of service, they then had to sign a further three years' re-engagement contract in order to continue their military employment. Together, these contracts from the beginning, add up to the fifteen years of service that Gurkhas deliver (Laksamba et al. 2013).

21. Under the GPS framework, Gurkhas are divided into two core groups—pensioners and nonpensioners. Those belonging to the latter comprise three groups: those who had retired before 1948, a substantial number of those who were made redundant before 1975, and a few hundred Gurkhas who had retired after 1975 (Laksamba et al. 2013).

22. See *British Gurkha Welfare Society and others v Ministry of Defence* [2010] EWHC 3, at [13].

23. See *British Gurkha Welfare Society and others v Ministry of Defence* [2010] EWHC 3, at [12].

24. See *British Gurkha Welfare Society and others v Ministry of Defence* [2010] EWHC 3, at [14].

25. See *British Gurkha Welfare Society and others v Ministry of Defence* [2010] EWHC 3, at [15].

26. See *British Gurkha Welfare Society and others v Ministry of Defence* [2010] EWCA Civ 1098, at [4].

27. See *British Gurkha Welfare Society and others v Ministry of Defence* [2010] EWHC 3, at [7].

28. *British Gurkha Welfare Society and others v Ministry of Defence* [2010] EWHC 3, at [7].

29. From "Gurkhas Discharged Before 1 July 1997 and Their family Members. Version 1.0," Published for Home Office staff, United Kingdom, 28 December 2017, 6.

30. "Gurkhas Discharged Before 1 July 1997 and Their family Members," 6

31. "Gurkhas Discharged Before 1 July 1997 and Their family Members," 6.

32. From "Gurkhas Discharged Before 1 July 1997 and Their Family Members. Version 1.0," Published for Home Office staff, UK, 28 December 2017, 11.

33. *British Gurkha Welfare Society and others v The United Kingdom* [2016] ECHR 44818/11.

34. See *Limbu and others v Secretary of State for the Home Department, Entry Clearance Officer and Entry Officer* [2008] EWHC 2261.

35. See *Limbu and others v Secretary of State for the Home Department, Entry Clearance Officer and Entry Officer* [2008] EWHC 2261, at [20/iv].

36. *Purja and ORS v Ministry of Defence* [2003] EWHC 445, at [4].

37. *Purja and ORS v Ministry of Defence* [2003] EWHC 445, at [3].

38. *Purja and ORS v Ministry of Defence* [2003] EWHC 445, at [3].

39. *Purja and ORS v Ministry of Defence* [2003] EWHC 445, at [3].

40. *Purja and ORS v Ministry of Defence* [2003] EWHC 445, at [33].

41. It should be pointed out that long leave as an entitlement for the Gurkhas has been framed as an example of "undoubted benefits" enjoyed by them, which are "not available to British soldiers"—see *Purja and ORS v Ministry of Defence* [2003] EWHC Civ 1345, at [46].

42. *Purja and ORS v Ministry of Defence* [2003] EWHC 445, at [47].

43. *Purja and ORS v Ministry of Defence* [2003] EWHC 445, at [48].

44. *Purja and ORS v Ministry of Defence* [2003] EWHC 445, at [98].

45. *Purja and ORS v Ministry of Defence* [2003] EWHC 445, at [99].

46. *Purja and ORS v Ministry of Defence* [2003] EWHC 445, at [99].

47. [2008] EWHC 2261, at [25].

48. [2008] EWHC 2261, at [25], my emphasis.

49. *Limbu and others v Secretary of State for the Home Department, Entry Clearance Officer, and Entry Officer* [2008] EWHC 2261, at [27].

50. *British Gurkha Welfare Society and others v Ministry of Defence* [2010] EWHC 3, at [33].

51. *British Gurkha Welfare Society and others v Ministry of Defence* [2010] EWHC 3, at [42].

52. *British Gurkha Welfare Society and others v Ministry of Defence* [2010] EWHC 3, at [42].

53. *Limbu and others v Secretary of State for the Home Department, Entry Clearance Officer, and Entry Officer* [2008] EWHC 2261, at [2].

54. *Limbu and others v Secretary of State for the Home Department, Entry Clearance Officer, and Entry Officer* [2008] EWHC 2261, at [3].

55. *Limbu and others v Secretary of State for the Home Department, Entry Clearance Officer, and Entry Officer* [2008] EWHC 2261, at [3].

56. *Limbu and others v Secretary of State for the Home Department, Entry Clearance Officer, and Entry Officer* [2008] EWHC 2261, at [4].

57. *Limbu and others v Secretary of State for the Home Department, Entry Clearance Officer, and Entry Officer* [2008] EWHC 2261, at [4].

58. *Limbu and others v Secretary of State for the Home Department, Entry Clearance Officer, and Entry Officer* [2008] EWHC 2261, at [7].

59. *Limbu and others v Secretary of State for the Home Department, Entry Clearance Officer, and Entry Officer* [2008] EWHC 2261, at [59].

60. *Limbu and others v Secretary of State for the Home Department, Entry Clearance Officer, and Entry Officer* [2008] EWHC 2261, at [60].

61. *Limbu and others v Secretary of State for the Home Department, Entry Clearance Officer, and Entry Officer* [2008] EWHC 2261, at [60].

62. *Limbu and others v Secretary of State for the Home Department, Entry Clearance Officer, and Entry Officer* [2008] EWHC 2261, at [62].

63. *Limbu and others v Secretary of State for the Home Department, Entry Clearance Officer, and Entry Officer* [2008] EWHC 2261, at [62].

64. *Limbu and others v Secretary of State for the Home Department, Entry Clearance Officer, and Entry Officer* [2008] EWHC 2261, at [62].

65. *Limbu and others v Secretary of State for the Home Department, Entry Clearance Officer, and Entry Officer* [2008] EWHC 2261, at [70].

66. *Limbu and others v Secretary of State for the Home Department, Entry Clearance Officer, and Entry Officer* [2008] EWHC 2261, at [71].

67. *Limbu and others v Secretary of State for the Home Department, Entry Clearance Officer, and Entry Officer* [2008] EWHC 2261, at [68vi].

68. *Limbu and others v Secretary of State for the Home Department, Entry Clearance Officer, and Entry Officer* [2008] EWHC 2261, at [72].

69. *Limbu and others v Secretary of State for the Home Department, Entry Clearance Officer, and Entry Officer* [2008] EWHC 2261, at [66].

70. From Audrey Gillan and James Meikle, "Gurkhas Win Right to Settle in the UK," *The Guardian*, 21 May 2009, https://www.theguardian.com/world/2009/may/21/gurkha-uk-settle-rights-lumley.

71. See among many examples, Gillan and Meikle, "Gurkhas Win Right to Settle in the UK"; "Gurkha Military Veterans on Hunger Strike in London over Pensions Row with UK," https://www.scmp.com/news/world/europe/article/3145412/gurkha-military-veterans-hunger-strike-london-over-pensions-row; and "Gurkha Justice Campaign," https://kathmandupost.com/columns/2022/04/14/gurkha-justice-campaign.

72. *Gurung and others v The Secretary of State for Defence* [2008] EWHC 1496, at [37] and [43].

73. *Gurung and others v The Secretary of State for Defence* [2008] EWHC 1496, at [1].

74. *Gurung and others v The Secretary of State for Defence* [2008] EWHC 1496, at [1].

75. *Gurung and others v The Secretary of State for Defence* [2008] EWHC 1496, at [37].

76. *Gurung and others v The Secretary of State for Defence* [2008] EWHC 1496, at [37].

77. *Gurung and others v The Secretary of State for Defence* [2008] EWHC 1496, at [43].

78. *Gurung and others v The Secretary of State for Defence* [2008] EWHC 1496, at [40].

79. *Gurung and others v The Secretary of State for Defence* [2008] EWHC 1496, at [43].

80. *Gurung and others v The Secretary of State for Defence* [2008] EWHC 1496, at [33].

81. *Limbu and others v Secretary of State for the Home Department, Entry Clearance Officer, and Entry Officer* [2008] EWHC 2261, at [68v].

82. *Limbu and others v Secretary of State for the Home Department, Entry Clearance Officer, and Entry Officer* [2008] EWHC 2261, at [63] and [64]. It is interesting that the trope of morality, either of debt or obligation, continues in succeeding court cases. It has been said that "despite the changes made in the Gurkhas' TACOS since 1997 *to reflect not only legal but moral obligations*, the Gurkhas believe that the Government has not yet gone far enough" (*British Gurkha Welfare Society and others v Ministry of Defence* [2010] EWHC 3, at [47], my emphasis). Entwining the legal and the moral therefore becomes a part of how newer ways to bracket belonging need to consider not only the legality of rights or debts owed, but that of a moral "obligation" where Gurkhas' claims are concerned.

83. See *Purja and Others v Ministry of Defence* [2003] EWCA Civ 1345, at [60].

84. *Limbu and others v Secretary of State for the Home Department, Entry Clearance Officer, and Entry Officer* [2008] EWHC 2261, at [57].

85. *British Gurkha Welfare Society and others v Ministry of Defence* [2010] EWHC 3, at [15].

86. *British Gurkha Welfare Society and others v Ministry of Defence* [2010] EWHC 3, at [24].

87. There were around 3,400 Gurkhas in active service, and 2,200 who had retired on or after 1 July 1997 (case 9 item 24/10).

88. *British Gurkha Welfare Society and others v Ministry of Defence* [2010] EWHC 3, at [8].

89. *Limbu and others v Secretary of State for the Home Department, Entry Clearance Officer, and Entry Officer* [2008] EWHC 2261, at [12], emphasis in original.

90. *Limbu and others v Secretary of State for the Home Department, Entry Clearance Officer, and Entry Officer* [2008] EWHC 2261, at [12], emphasis in original.

91. *Limbu and others v Secretary of State for the Home Department, Entry Clearance Officer, and Entry Officer* [2008] EWHC 2261, at [28].

92. *Entry Clearance Officer v Pun and others* [2011] UKUT 00377 (IAC), at [2]. Case 14 item 2.

93. Note that settlement arrangements listed here are not applicable to Gurkha families alone. They are equally applicable to any of the dependents of all commonwealth and foreign nationals who seek settlement in the United Kingdom upon their father's discharge from HM Forces (*UG and others v Entry Clearance Officer* [2012] EWCA Civ 58, at [1]).

94. *Entry Clearance Officer v Pun and others* [2011] UKUT 00377 (IAC), at [4].

95. *TT v Secretary of State for the Home Department* [2013] EWCA Civ 1068, at [6].

96. *Entry Clearance Officer v Pun and others* [2011] UKUT 00377 (IAC), at [10].

97. *Gurung and others v The Secretary of State for the Home Department and others* [2013], EWCA Civ 8, at [26], emphasis in original.

98. UKUT 480 (IAC); UKUT 00117 (IAC); *Entry Clearance Officer v UR and others* [2010] UKUT 480 (IAC), at [14].

99. *Entry Clearance Officer v KG* [2011] UKUT 00117 (IAC), at [8].

100. *Entry Clearance Officer v UR and others* [2010] UKUT 480 (IAC), at [14].

101. *Entry Clearance Officer v UR and others* [2010] UKUT 480 (IAC), at [14].

102. UKUT 480 (IAC).

103. *Entry Clearance Officer v UR and others* [2010] UKUT 480 (IAC), at [18].

104. See *Ghising v The Secretary of State for the Home Department* [2012] UKUT 00160 (IAC), at [8].

105. *Entry Clearance Officer v UR and others* [2010] UKUT 480 (IAC), at [19].

106. UKUT 00117 (IAC).

107. *Entry Clearance Officer v KG* [2011] UKUT 00117 (IAC), at [8].

108. *Entry Clearance Officer v Pun and others* [2011] UKUT 00377 (IAC), at [13].

109. *Entry Clearance Officer v KG* [2011] UKUT 00117 (IAC), at [13].

110. *Entry Clearance Officer v KG* [2011] UKUT 00117 (IAC), at [14]. In a separate case in which an adult dependent child (Ruma Rai) of her mother and sponsor (who was the widow of a former Gurkha soldier) had appealed against an ECO's refusal for her entry clearance to the United Kingdom, bank statements from the Standard Chartered Bank served as documentary evidence of Miss Rai's financial dependency on her mother. The former was able to withdraw monies from the latter's bank account in Nepal using an ATM card and hence the bank statements were "clearly demonstrative of the fact that the Sponsor/mother provided the Appellant/daughter with financial support" (see *Rai v Entry Clearance Officer* [2021] HU/02600/2020, at [6]).

111. *Entry Clearance Officer v KG* [2011] UKUT 00117 (IAC), at [15]. Article 8 has routinely been invoked in various other cases brought forward by the adult children of Gurkhas. See Case 14 in note 92 here for examples.

112. For a full record of Article 8 and its items, see https://www.echr.coe.int/documents/guide_art_8_eng.pdf; *Entry Clearance Officer v KG* [2011] UKUT 00117 (IAC), at [10].

113. *Entry Clearance Officer v KG* [2011] UKUT 00117 (IAC), at [15].

114. See *UG and others v Entry Clearance Officer* [2012] EWCA Civ 58 for various examples on the complexities of legal diction as well as educational and residential arrangements that would influence the exercise of discretion.

115. See also *Rai v Entry Clearance Officer* [2017] EWCA Civ 320 at [13] and [20], and *Gurung v The Secretary of State for the Home Department* [2021] HU/24446/2018, at [22] for debates on the problematics of evidencing family life vis-à-vis affection, emotional and financial dependency, among others.

116. *Huang v The Secretary of State for the Home Department* [2007] 2 AC 167, at [18].

117. I draw instances from the cases of Miss KG and Roshan Ghising to illustrate this balance. In the case of Miss KG, it was pointed out that further verification of her physical and mental unfitness may be traced to her having reached the age of thirty-eight but who still remained single. This apparently "suggests that a malady has prevented her from doing what would be expected of her in her culture" (*Entry Clearance Officer v KG* [2011] UKUT 00117 (IAC), at [13]). As for the case of Roshan Ghising, his father pointed out the mutual dependency between Roshan and his parents pertaining to "financial, practical and emotional support and guidance." Roshan was their only child who was still living at home, where his father specified that "it is the custom among Nepalese people for the youngest son to remain living with his parents, even after marriage, to care for them when they become elderly" (*Ghising v The Secretary of State for the Home Department* [2012] UKUT 00160 (IAC), at [22]). This custom was presented as evidence that was "undisputed" (*Ghising v The Secretary of State for the Home Department* [2012] UKUT 00160 (IAC), at [99]).

118. *Ghising v The Secretary of State for the Home Department* [2012] UKUT 00160 (IAC), at [17] and [26].

119. Petition supporting Gurkha hunger strikers, https://petition.parliament.uk/petitions/594155.

120. Petition supporting Gurkha hunger strikers.

121. From BBC, "Gurkha Back at Downing Street Hunger Strike after Being Taken Ill," *BBC*, 18 August 2021, https://www.bbc.com/news/uk-england-hampshire-58254634).

122. From Tom Batchelor, "Gurkha on Hunger Strike Outside Downing Street Rushed to Hospital with Heart Issues," *The Independent,* 18 April 2021, https://www.independent.co.uk/news/uk/home-news/gurkha-hunger-strike-heart-attack-b1904659.html.

123. Batchelor, "Gurkha on Hunger Strike Outside Downing Street."

124. For the full report, see "Report of the Technical Committee on Gurkha Veterans," 2018, http://2ndgoorkhas.com/wp-content/uploads/2018/03/20180314-Final_Report_Gurkha_Technical_Committee_1a1.pdf.

125. From page 3 of "Report of the Technical Committee on Gurkha Veterans," 2018. This committee comprised representatives from the UK Embassy of Nepal, the Army Secretariat of the MOD, as well as representation from Gurkha Satyagraha and the GAESO.

126. Page 3 of "Report of the Technical Committee on Gurkha Veterans," 2018.

127. Page 3 of "Report of the Technical Committee on Gurkha Veterans," 2018.

128. In March 2019, however, the UK government had announced support packages for 22,000 Gurkhas and their families. A £15-million increase in the GPS would translate into accompanying increases in veterans' pensions by no more than 34 percent extra.

Alongside pension increases, the MOD had also announced a new £25-million investment that was to go to medical support for Gurkha veterans over the next decade. See Ministry of Defense, "Enhanced Package of Support for Gurkha Veterans." 7 March 2019, https://www.gov.uk/government/news/enhanced-package-of-support-for-gurkha-veterans.

129. These points include, among others, equal pensions and benefits for Singapore Gurkha widows relative to their British counterpart, and to grant work permits and residential visas for Singapore Gurkha families.

130. See "A Memorandum to Gurkha Welfare All-Party Parliamentary Group to be presented by Gurkha Army Ex-Servicemen's Organization," https://gurkhainquiry.files.wordpress.com/2014/03/gurkha-army-ex-servicemens-gaeso.pdf.

131. "A Memorandum to Gurkha Welfare All-Party Parliamentary Group, page 4.

132. "A Memorandum to Gurkha Welfare All-Party Parliamentary Group, page 5.

133. "A Memorandum to Gurkha Welfare All-Party Parliamentary Group, page 5.

134. 704 Parl. Deb. H.C. "Gurkha Pensions" (22 November 2021), Col. 19WH. https://hansard.parliament.uk/commons/2021-11-22/debates/FE019D2B-2CD9-40D8-BE50-9A4189E5CB4A/GurkhaPensions.

135. 704 Parl. Deb. H.C. "Gurkha Pensions" (22 November 2021), Col. 18WH. (David Linden).

136. 704 Parl. Deb. H.C. "Gurkha Pensions" (22 November 2021), Col. 17WH.

137. 704 Parl. Deb. H.C. "Gurkha Pensions" (22 November 2021), Col. 13WH.

138. 704 Parl. Deb. H.C. "Gurkha Pensions" (22 November 2021), Col. 7WH.

139. 704 Parl. Deb. H.C. "Gurkha Pensions" (22 November 2021), Col. 7WH.

140. 704 Parl. Deb. H.C. "Gurkha Pensions" (22 November 2021), Col. 10WH.

141. 704 Parl. Deb. H.C. "Gurkha Pensions" (22 November 2021), Col. 12WH.

142. 704 Parl. Deb. H.C. "Gurkha Pensions" (22 November 2021), Col. 12WH.

143. 704 Parl. Deb. H.C. "Gurkha Pensions" (22 November 2021), Col. 13WH.

144. 704 Parl. Deb. H.C. "Gurkha Pensions" (22 November 2021), Col. 14WH.

145. 704 Parl. Deb. H.C. "Gurkha Pensions" (22 November 2021), Col. 22WH.

146. 704 Parl. Deb. H.C. "Gurkha Pensions" (22 November 2021), Col. 22WH.

147. 704 Parl. Deb. H.C. "Gurkha Pensions" (22 November 2021), Col. 22WH.

148. 704 Parl. Deb. H.C. "Gurkha Pensions" (22 November 2021), Col. 1WH.

149. 704 Parl. Deb. H.C. "Gurkha Pensions" (22 November 2021), Col. 1WH.

150. 704 Parl. Deb. H.C. "Gurkha Pensions" (22 November 2021), Col. 2WH.

151. 704 Parl. Deb. H.C. "Gurkha Pensions" (22 November 2021), Col. 2WH.

152. 704 Parl. Deb. H.C. "Gurkha Pensions" (22 November 2021), Col. 4. WH.

153. 704 Parl. Deb. H.C. "Gurkha Pensions" (22 November 2021), Col. 11 WH.

154. 704 Parl. Deb. H.C. "Gurkha Pensions" (22 November 2021), Col. 5 WH.

155. 704 Parl. Deb. H.C. "Gurkha Pensions" (22 November 2021), Col. 5 WH.

156. 704 Parl. Deb. H.C. "Gurkha Pensions" (22 November 2021), Col. 11 WH.

157. 704 Parl. Deb. H.C. "Gurkha Pensions" (22 November 2021), Col. 14 WH.

158. 704 Parl. Deb. H.C. "Gurkha Pensions" (22 November 2021), Col. 15 WH.

159. 704 Parl. Deb. H.C. "Gurkha Pensions" (22 November 2021), Col. 16 WH.

160. 704 Parl. Deb. H.C. "Gurkha Pensions" (22 November 2021), Col. 16 WH

161. 704 Parl. Deb. H.C. "Gurkha Pensions" (22 November 2021), Col. 24 WH.

162. 704 Parl. Deb. H.C. "Gurkha Pensions" (22 November 2021), Col. 16WH.

163. Gurkha Brigade Association, https://www.gurkhabde.com/gurkha-pension-scheme-2022-award/.

CONCLUSION

1. Special guests invited to the premiere included the Nepali ambassador to the United Kingdom Gyan Chandra Aryal, the former inspector general of the Armed Police Force, as well as British Gurkha Army officers and official representatives of different Nepalese organizations and diplomatic missions to the United Kingdom. See "Historic International Premiere of 'Gurkha Warrior' in London," *Ratopati,* 11 September 2023, https://english.ratopati.com/story/30463/premiere-of-%27gurkha-warrior%27-.

2. "PM Sunak's Best Wishes to 'Gurkha Warrior' Movie,'" *NepalNews,* 23 August 2023, https://nepalnews.com/s/entertainment-and-lifestyle/pm-sunak-s-best-wishes-to-gurkha-warrior-movie.

3. The United States has been hiring private security contractors in Iraq and Afghanistan over the past twenty years (Coburn 2018).

References

Abdullah, Noorman. 2010. "Comfort Food, Memory, and 'Home': Senses in Transnational Contexts." In *Everyday Life in Asia: Social Perspectives on the Senses*, edited by Deborah Kalekin-Fishman and Kelvin E.Y. Low, 157–76. Surrey: Ashgate.

Adhikari, Jagannath. 2007. "Urbanization and Change in Pokhara, Nepal." In *Nepalis Inside and Outside Nepal*, edited by Hiroshi Ishii, David N. Gellner, and Katsuo Nawa, 17–57. New Delhi: Manohar.

Adhikari, Jagannath, and David Seddon. 2002. *Pokhara: Biography of a Town*. Kathmandu: Mandala Book Point.

Adzmi, Azian Muhamad, and Norliza Saiful Bahry. 2020. "'Silaturrahim,' Malaysia Diaspora and Social Media." *Jurnal Komunikasi* 36 (1): 263–77.

Al-Hilo, Mujtaba, and Mohamad Marandi. 2020. "The Wandering Jew Phenomenon: A Post-Diaspora Success." *Al-Ustath Journal for Human and Social Sciences* 59 (2): 11–22. doi.org/10.36473/ujhss.v59i2.1111.

Alinejad, Donya, et al. 2019. "Diaspora and Mapping Methodologies: Tracing Transnational Digital Connections with 'Mattering Maps.'" *Global Networks* 19 (1): 21–43. doi.org/10.1111/glob.12197.

Allen, Nick. 1976. "Approaches to Illnesses in the Nepalese Hills." In *Social Anthropology and Medicine*, edited by J. B. Loudon, 500–552. London: Academic Press.

Allwood, Audrey. 2020. *Belonging in Brixton: An Ethnography of Migrant West Indian Elders in Brixton, London*. Cham: Springer International.

Amelina, Anna, and Thomas Faist. 2012. "De-naturalising the National in Research Methodologies: Key Concepts of Transnational Studies in Migration." *Ethnic and Racial Studies* 35 (10): 1707–24. doi.org/10.1080/01419870.2012.659273.

Amelina, Anna, et al. 2013. "Methodological Predicaments of Cross-Border Studies." In *Beyond Methodological Nationalism: Research Methodologies for Cross-Border Studies*, edited by Anna Amelina et al., 1–19. New York; London: Routledge.

Anderson, Bridget. 2013. *Us and Them? The Dangerous Politics of Immigration Control*. Oxford: Oxford University Press.

Andreouli, Eleni, and Parisa Dashtipour. 2014. "British Citizenship and the 'Other': An Analysis of the Earned Citizenship Discourse." *Journal of Community & Applied Social Psychology* 24 (2): 100–110. doi.org/10.1002/casp.2154.

Ang, Ien. 2007. "Beyond 'Asian Diasporas.'" In *Asian Diasporas: New Formations, New Conceptions*, edited by Rhacel Salazar Parreñas and Lok C.D. Siu, 285–90. Stanford, CA: Stanford University Press.

Anjali, Anju. 2013. "Soldiers, War and My Question." In *Gurkha War Poems*, edited by Mijas Tembe, Apjase Kanchha, and Kangmang Naresh Rai, 7–8. Bloomington, IN: Authorhouse.

Antonsich, Marco. 2010. "Searching for Belonging—An Analytical Framework." *Geography Compass* 4 (6): 644–59. doi.org/10.1111/j.1749-8198.2009.00317.x.

Aryal, Deepak. 2008. "Discourses of Biratā (Bravery) and Shānti (Peace) in School Level Nepalese Textbooks." *Bodhi: An Interdisciplinary Journal* 2 (1): 89–116.

Bammi, Lt. Gen. Y. M. 2009. *Gorkhas of the Indian Army*. New Delhi: Life Span Publishers.

Banskota, Purushottam. 1994. *The Gurkha Connection: A History of Gurkha Recruitment in the British Indian Army*. Jaipur: Nirala.

Barkawi, Tarak. 2017. *Soldiers of Empire: Indian and British Armies in World War II*. Cambridge: Cambridge University Press.

Beckles-Raymond, Gabriella. 2020. "African-Caribbean Women, (Post)? Diaspora, and the Meaning of Home." *African and Black Diaspora: An International Journal* 13 (2): 202–14. doi.org/10.1080/17528631.2020.1750168.

Bellamy, Chris. 2011. *The Gurkhas: Special Force*. London: John Murray.

Bennett, W. J. 1958. "In a British Army Secondary School." *Geography* 43 (2): 114–17.

Berg, Mette Louise. 2011. *Diasporic Generations: Memory, Politics, and Nation among Cubans in Spain*. Oxford: Berghahn.

Berg, Mette Louise. 2014. "Generations." In *Migration: A COMPAS Anthology*, edited by Bridget Anderson and Michael Keith. COMPAS, Oxford.

Bhandari, Kalyan. 2017. "Travelling at Special Times: The Nepali Diaspora's Yearning for Belongingness." In *Tourism and Memories of Home: Migrants: Displaced People, Exiles and Diasporic Communities,* edited by Sabine Marschall, 113–31. Bristol: Channel View.

Bhandari, Nagendra B. 2021. "Representations of the Gurkha (Lahures) in Modernist Narratives." *Unity Journal* 2: 153–62. doi.org/10.3126/unityj.v2i0.38822.

Bharadwaj, Atul. 2003. 'Privatization of Security: The Mercenary-Market Mix.' *Defence Studies* 3 (2): 64–82. doi.org/10.1080/14702430308405063.

Bishop, Edward. 1976. *Better to Die: The Story of the Gurkhas*. London: New English Library.

Blachnicka-Ciacek, Dominika, et al. 2021. "Do I Deserve to Belong? Migrants' Perspectives on the Debate of Deservingness and Belonging." *Journal of Ethnic and Migration Studies* 47 (17): 3805–21. doi.org/10.1080/13691 83X.2021.1932444.

Bolt, David. 1967. *Gurkhas*. New York: Delacorte Press.

Bose, Pablo S. 2021. "Diaspora, Development, and the Reshaping of Homelands in an Evolving World." In *Routledge Handbook of Asian Diaspora and Development*, edited by Ajaya K. Sahoo, 95–106. London: Routledge.

Brocket, Tom. 2020. "From 'In-betweenness' to 'Positioned Belongings': Second-Generation Palestinian-Americans Negotiate the Tensions of Assimilation and Transnationalism." *Ethnic and Racial Studies* 43 (16): 135–54. doi.org/10.1080/0 1419870.2018.1544651.

Brown, Judith. 2006. *Global South Asians: Introducing the Modern Diaspora*. Cambridge: Cambridge University Press.

Brubaker, Rogers. 2005. "The 'Diaspora' Diaspora." *Ethnic and Racial Studies* 28 (1): 1–19. doi.org/10.1080/0141987042000289997.

Brubaker, Rogers. 2010. "Migration, Membership, and the Modern Nation-State: Internal and External Dimensions of the Politics of Belonging." *Journal of Interdisciplinary History* 41 (1): 61–78. doi.org/10.1162/jinh.2010.41.1.61.

Bullock, Christopher. 2009. *Britain's Gurkhas*. London: Third Millennium.

Bunnell, Tim, Jamie Gillen, and Elaine L.E. Ho. 2018. "The Prospect of Elsewhere: Engaging the Future through Aspirations in Asia." *Annals of the American Association of Geographers* 108 (1): 35–51. doi.org/10.1080/24694452.2017. 1336424.

Callahan, Raymond. 2007. "The Great Sepoy Mutiny." In *A Military History of India and South Asia: From the East India Company to the Nuclear Era*, edited by

Daniel P. Marston and Chandar S. Sundaram, 16–33. Bloomington: Indiana University Press.

Caplan, Lionel. 1991. "'Bravest of the Brave': Representations of 'The Gurkha' in British Military Writings." *Modern Asian Studies* 25 (3): 571–97. doi. org/10.1017/S0026749X00013937.

Caplan, Lionel. 1995a. "Martial Gurkhas: The Persistence of a British Military Discourse on "Race." In *The Concept of Race in South Asia*, edited by Peter Robb, 260–81. Oxford: Oxford University Press.

Caplan, Lionel. 1995b. *Warrior Gentleman: "Gurkhas" in the Western Imagination.* Oxford: Berghahn Books.

Carroll, Peter. 2012. *Gurkha: The True Story of a Campaign for Justice.* London: Blackwell.

Cassarino, Jean-Pierre. 2004. "Theorising Return Migration: The Conceptual Approach to Return Migrants Revisited." *International Journal on Multicultural Societies* 6 (2): 253–79. ssrn.com/abstract=1730637.

Castles, Stephen. 2007. "Twenty-first-century Migration as a Challenge to Sociology." *Journal of Ethnic and Migration Studies* 33 (3): 351–71. doi.org/10.1080/13691830701234491.

Chakrabarti, Shantanu. 2008. "Growth and Implications of Private Military Corporations." *Journal of Defence Studies* 2 (1): 109–21.

Chakraborty, Anup Shekhar. 2018. "'Moving Out' and the Social Imaginaries at Play: Construing the Trends in Migrations in Darjeeling Hills and Plains (2005–2015)." *Refugee Watch: A South Asian Journal on Forced Migration—Migrants, Communities and Political Ecology.* 51/52: 30–61.

Chakraborty, Anup Shekhar. 2020. "Shared Heritages, Belonging, Rootedness, and the Notion of Bhoomiputra: Gleaning the Literary Engagements of the Gorkha in South Asia." *Quest: The Journal of UGC-HRDC Nainital* 14 (2–3): 107–29.

Chetri, Nilamber. 2016. "Interrogating Gorkha as Martial Race: Category based on Discrete Identities." *Journal of Studies in History & Culture* 2 (2): 94–125.

Chisholm, Amanda. 2014. "Marketing the Gurkha Security Package: Colonial Histories and Neoliberal Economies of Private Security." *Security Dialogue* 45 (4): 349–72. doi.org/10.1177/0967010614535832.

Chisholm, Amanda. 2016. "Ethnography in Conflict Zones: The Perils of Researching Private Security Contractors." In *The Routledge Companion to Military Research Methods,* edited by Alison J. Williams et al., 138–52. London: Routledge. doi.org/10.4324/9781315613253.

Chisholm, Amanda. 2022. *The Gendered and Colonial Lives of Gurkhas in Private Security: From Military to Market.* Edinburgh: Edinburgh University Press. doi.org/10.3366/edinburgh/9781399501156.001.0001.

Chisholm, Amanda, and Hanna Ketola. 2020. "The Cruel Optimism of Militarism: Feminist Curiosity, Affect, and Global Security." *International Political Sociology* 14 (3): 270–85. doi.org/10.1093/ips/olaa005.

Chisholm, Amanda, and Saskia Stachowitsch. 2017. "Military Markets, Masculinities and the Global Political Economy of the Everyday: Understanding Military Outsourcing as Gendered and Racialised." In *The Palgrave International Handbook of Gender and the Military*, edited by Rachel Woodward and Claire Duncanson, 371–86. London: Palgrave. doi.org/10.1057/978-1-137-51677-0_23.

Chiu, Stephen W. K., and Kaxton Y. K. Siu. 2022. "Hong Kong as a Migration Haven? Ethnic Minorities in the Global City." In *Hong Kong Society: High-Definition Stories beyond the Spectacle of East-Meets-West,* edited by Stephen W. K. Chiu and Kaxton Y. K. Siu, 71–107. Singapore: Springer Verlag. doi.org/10.1007/978-981-16-5707-8.

Chong, Zi Liang. 2014. *The Invisible Force: Singapore Gurkhas*. Singapore: Ethos Books.

Christensen, Maya M. 2017. "Shadow Soldering: Shifting Constellations and Permeable Boundaries in "Private" Security Contracting." *Conflict and Society* 3 (1): 24–41.

Christou, Anastasia. 2009. "Emulating the Homeland—Engendering the Nation: Agency, Belonging, Identity and Gender in Second-Generation Greek-American Return-Migrant Life Stories." In *Return Migration of the Next Generations: 21st Century Transnational Mobility* edited by Dennis Conway and Robert B. Potter, 101–16. Surrey: Ashgate. doi.org/10.4324/9781315244242.

Chudal, Alaka Atreya. 2020a. "Storytelling in Prison: Oral Performance of a Gurkha Prisoner of World War I." *European Bulletin of Himalayan Research* 54: 5–35. doi.org/10.4000/ebhr.286.

Chudal, Alaka Atreya. 2020b. "What Can A Song Do to You? A Life Story of a Gurkha Prisoner in World War I." *South Asia: Journal of South Asian Studies* 43 (3): 392–406. doi.org/10.1080/00856401.2020.1752974.

Coburn, Noah. 2018. *Under Contract: The Invisible Workers of America's Global War*. Stanford, CA: Stanford University Press.

Cohen, Robin. 2008. *Global Diasporas: An Introduction*. 2nd ed. London: Routledge.

Cohen, Robin. 2009. "Solid, Ductile and Liquid: Changing Notions of Homeland and Home in Diaspora Studies." In *Transnationalism: Diasporas and the Advent of a New (Dis)order* edited by Eliezer Ben-Rafael and Yitzhak Sternberg , 117–33. Leiden: Brill. doi.org/10.1163/ej.9789004174702.i-788.34.

Cohen, Robin. 2022. "Citizenship: From Three to Seven Principles of Belonging." *Social Identities: Journal for the Study of Race, Nation, and Culture* 28 (1): 139–46. doi.org/10.1080/13504630.2021.1987874.

Constable, Nicole. 2014. *Born Out of Place: Migrant Mothers and the Politics of International Labor*. Hong Kong: Hong Kong University Press. www.jstor.org/stable/10.1525/j.ctt5vjzj1.

Conway, Dennis, and Robert B. Potter. 2009. "Return of the Next Generations: Transnational Migration and Development in the 21st Century." In *Return Migration of the Next Generations: 21st Century Transnational Mobility* edited by Dennis Conway and Robert B. Potter, 1–18. Surrey: Ashgate. doi.org/10.4324/9781315244242.

Crew, Bob. 2004. *Gurkha Warriors*. London: Metro Publishing.

Croissant, Aurel, and Philip Lorenz. 2018. *Comparative Politics of Southeast Asia*. Cham: Springer. doi.org/10.1007/978-3-319-68182-5.

Cross, J. P. 2009. *The Call of Nepal*. Ann Arbor: Nimble Books.

Cross, J. P., and Buddhiman Gurung. 2007. *Gurkhas at War: Eyewitness Accounts from World War II to Iraq*. London: Greenhill Books.

Darnell, Chris. 2012. *So You Want To Be a Gurkha: A Personal Story*. London: Endeavour Press.

Davis, Victor A. B. 2000. "Sierra Leone: Ironic Tragedy." *Journal of African Economies* 9 (3): 349–69. doi.org/10.1093/jae/9.3.349.

Denman, Terence. 1996. "'Ethnic Soldiers Pure and Simple?' The Irish in the Late Victorian British Army." *War in History* 3 (3): 253–73. https://doi.org/10.1177/096834459600300301.

Des Chene, Mary K. 1991. "Relics of Empire: A Cultural History of the Gurkhas, 1815–1987." PhD diss., Stanford University.

Des Chene, Mary K. 1992. "Traversing Social Space: Gurung Journeys." *Himalaya, the Journal of the Association for Nepal and Himalayan Studies* 12 (1/2): 1–10.

Des Chene, Mary K. 1998. "Fate, Domestic Authority, and Women's Wills." In *Selves in Time and Place: Identities, Experience, and History in Nepal*, edited by Debra

Skinner, Alfred Pach III, and Dorothy Holland, 19–50. Lanham: Rowman and Littlefield.

Des Chene, Mary K. 1999. "Military Ethnology in British India." *South Asia Research* 19 (2): 121–35. doi.org/10.1177/026272809901900202.

De Vienne, Marie-Sybille, and Jeremy Jammes. 2020. "China's Maritime Nexus in Southeast Asia: Economic and Geostrategic Challenges of the Belt and Road Initiative in Brunei." *Asian Survey* 60 (5): 905–27. doi.org/10.1525/as.2020.60.5.905.

Dhakal, Rajendra P. 2016. "The Indian Gorkhas: Changing Orientation of a Diasporic Society." In *Nepali Diaspora in a Globalized Era,* edited by Tanka Bahadur Subba and Awadhesh Coomar Sinha, 93–107. Oxon: Routledge. doi.org/10.4324/9781315685069.

Dixit, Priya. 2017. "Reflections on Encounters with Gurkhas in Nepal." *Critical Studies on Security* 5 (2): 194–97. doi.org/10.1080/21624887.2017.1320878.

Dutt, Srikant. 1981. "Brunei: The Forgotten State of Southeast Asia." *China Report* 17: 33–41. doi.org/10.1177/000944558101700605.

Enloe, Cynthia H. 1980. *Ethnic Soldiers: State Security in Divided Societies.* Athens: University of Georgia Press.

Enloe, Cynthia H. 1983. *Does Khaki Become You? The Militarization of Women's Lives.* London: Pluto Press.

Enloe, Cynthia H. 2014. "The Recruiter and the Sceptic: A Critical Feminist Approach to Military Studies." *Critical Military Studies* 1 (1): 3–10. doi.org/10.1080/23337486.2014.961746.

Erni, John Nguyet, and Lisa Yuk-Ming Leung. 2014. *Understanding South Asian Minorities in Hong Kong.* Hong Kong: Hong Kong University Press. www.jstor.org/stable/j.ctt14jxs35.

Ervine, Jonathan. 2008. "Citizenship and Belonging in Suburban France: The Music of Zebda." *ACME* 7 (2): 199–213. doi.org/10.14288/acme.v7i2.803.

Espiritu, Yen Le, and Thom Tran. 2002. "Viet Nam, nuoc toi (Vietnam, My Country): Vietnamese Americans and Transnationalism." In *The Changing Face of Home: The Transnational Lives of the Second Generation,* edited by Peggy Levitt and Mary C. Waters, 367–98. New York: Russel Sage Foundation.

Faist, Thomas, and Devrimsel D. Nergiz. 2013. "Concluding Remarks: Reconsidering Contexts and Units of Analysis." In *Beyond Methodological Nationalism: Research Methodologies for Cross-Border Studies,* edited by Anna Amelina et al., 239–44. New York: Routledge. doi.org/10.4324/9780203121597.

Farwell, Byron. 1984. *The Gurkhas.* London: Allen Lane.

Forbes, Duncan. 1964. *Johnny Gurkha: A Fascinating Account of the Gurkha People.* London: Robert Hale.

Fortier, Anne-Marie. 1999. "Re-membering Places and the Performance of Belonging(s)." *Theory, Culture & Society* 16 (2): 41–64. doi.org/10.1177/02632769922050548.

Francis, David J. 1999. "Mercenary Intervention in Sierra Leone: Providing National Security or International Exploitation?" *Third World Quarterly* 20 (2): 319–38. doi.org/10.1080/01436599913785.

Freyer, Ana Vila. 2019. "Multiple Belongings and Composite Identities of Young People from the South of Guanajuato, Mexico." *Migration Letters* 16 (2): 255–64.

Gautam, Neha. 2013. *Neither Here Nor There: Children of the Gurkha Contingent in Singapore and Nepal.* Unpublished Academic Exercise, Department of Sociology, National University of Singapore.

Gellner, David N. 2015. "Associational Profusion and Multiple Belonging: Diaspora Nepalis in the UK." In *Diasporas Reimagined: Spaces, Practices and Belonging,* edited by Nando Sigona, Alan J. Gamlen, Giulia Liberatore, and Hélène Neveu Kringelbach, 78–82. Oxford: Oxford Diasporas Programme.

Gellner, David N. 2018. "Introduction: The Nepali/Gorkhali Diaspora Since the Nineteenth Century." In *Global Nepalis: Religion, Culture, and Community in a New and Old Diaspora,* edited by David N. Gellner and Sondra L. Hausner, 1–24. New Delhi: Oxford University Press.

Glenn, Evelyn Nakano. 1983. "Split-household, Small Producer, and Dual Wage Earner: An Analysis of Chinese-American Family Strategies." *Journal of Marriage and the Family* 45 (1): 35–46. doi.org/10.2307/351293.

Glick Schiller, Nina. 2010. "A Global Perspective on Transnational Migration: Theorising Migration without Methodological Nationalism." In *Diaspora and Transnationalism: Concepts, Theories and Methods,* edited by Rainer Bauböck and Thomas Faist, 109–29. Amsterdam: Amsterdam University Press.

Golay, Bidhan. 2009. "Rethinking Gorkha Identity: Outside the Imperium of Discourse, Hegemony, and History." In *Indian Nepalis: Issues and Perspectives,* edited by Tanka Bahadur Subba et al., 73–94. New Delhi: Concept Publishing.

Gould, Tony. 1999. *Imperial Warriors: Britain and the Gurkhas.* London: Granta Books.

Graf, Samuel. 2017. "Diaspora Tourism and the Negotiation of Belonging: Journeys of Young Second-Generation Eritreans to Eritrea." *Ethnic and Racial Studies* 40 (15): 2710–27. doi.org/10.1080/01419870.2016.1262542.

Guibernau, Montserrat. 2013. *Belonging: Solidarity and Division in Modern Societies.* Cambridge: Polity Press.

Gurung, Dil Bahadur. 2017. "The Conditionally Brave People." *Center for Academic Research and Services* 2: 103–24.

Gurung, Muna. 2018. "Aama, 1978." In *Go Home!,* edited by Rowan Hisayo Buchanan, 63–71. New York: Feminist Press.

Gurung, Shibaji. 2011. "British Gurkha Recruitment and Higher Education of Gurung Young Men." *Dhaulagiri Journal of Sociology and Anthropology* 5: 143–70.

Gurung, Tejimala. 2009. "Gorkhas as Colliers: Labour Recruitment and Racial Discourses in the Coal Mines of Assam." In *Indian Nepalis: Issues and Perspectives,* edited by Tanka Bahadur Subba et al., 259–73. New Delhi: Concept Publishing.

Gurung, Tejimala. 2016. "Gurkha Displacement from Burma in 1942: A Historical Narrative." In *Nepali Diaspora in a Globalized Era,* edited by Tanka Bahadur Subba and Awadhesh Coomar Sinha, 203–20. Oxon: Routledge.

Gurung, Tim I. 2020. *The Gurkhas: A True Story.* Singapore: Penguin Books.

Haaland, Gunnar, and Poonam Gurung. 2007. "Globalization of Interaction Systems and the Culture in Ethnicity: Popular Songs and Production of Nepali Ethnoscapes in Southeast Asia." *International Journal of Diversity in Organisations, Communities and Nations* 7 (3): 77–84. doi:10.18848/1447-9532/CGP/v07i03/39380.

Hack, Karl. 2019. "Unfinished Decolonization and Globalization." *Journal of Imperial and Commonwealth History* 47 (5): 818–50. doi.org/10.1080/03086534.2019.1677337.

Hackl, Andreas. 2022. "Good Immigrants, Permitted Outsiders: Conditional Inclusion and Citizenship in Comparison." *Ethnic and Racial Studies* 45 (6): 989–1010. doi.org/10.1080/01419870.2021.2011938.

Haikkola, Lotta. 2011. "Making Connections: Second-Generation Children and the Transnational Field of Relations." *Journal of Ethnic and Migration Studies* 37 (8): 1201–17. doi.org/10.1080/1369183X.2011.590925.

Hamilton, Francis. 1819. *An Account of the Kingdom of Nepal and of the Territories Annexed to this Dominion by the House of Gorkha*. Edinburgh: Constable.

Hamzah, Abu Bakar. 1989. "Brunei Darrusalam: Continuity and Tradition." *Southeast Asian Affairs*: 91–104. www.jstor.org/stable/27911971.

Han, Enze. 2019. "Bifurcated Homeland and Diaspora Politics in China and Taiwan Towards the Overseas Chinese in Southeast Asia." *Journal of Ethnic and Migration Studies* 45 (4): 577–94. doi.org/10.1080/1369183X.2017.1409172.

Hausner, Sondra. 2014. "Belonging and Solitude among Nepali Nurses in Great Britain." In *Facing Globalization in the Himalayas: Belonging and the Politics of the Self*, edited by Gerard Toffin and Joanna-Pfaff Czarnecka, 185–208. Delhi: SAGE.

Hausner, Sondra. 2018. "Afterword: Rethinking Diaspora Consciousness." In *Global Nepalis: Religion, Culture, and Community in a New and Old Diaspora*, edited by David N. Gellner and Sondra L. Hausner. 508–11. New Delhi: Oxford University Press.

Hedetoft, Ulf. 2004. "Discourses and Images of Belonging: Migrants Between New Racism, Liberal Nationalism and Globalization." In *The Politics of Multiple Belonging: Ethnicity and nationalism in Europe and East Asia*, edited by Flemming Christiansen and Ulf Hedetoft, 23–44. Aldershot: Ashgate.

Ho, Elaine Lynn-Ee. 2019. *Citizens in Motion: Emigration, Immigration, and Re-migration Across China's Borders*. Stanford, CA: Stanford University Press.

Hodgson, B. H. 1833. "Origin and Classification of the Military Tribes of Nepal." *Journal of the Asiatic Society* 17: 217–24.

Hölzle, Eva Rozalia, and Joanna Pfaff-Czarnecka, eds. 2023. *The Price of Belonging: Perspectives from Asia*. Leiden: Brill. brill.com/display/title/64241?contents=toc-50344.

Hutt, Michael. 2012. *Eloquent Hills: Essays on Nepali Literature*. Kathmandu: Martin Chautari.

Hutt, Michael. 2020. "The Changing Face of Nepal." *Current History* 119: 141–15. www.jstor.org/stable/48614528.

Imy, Kate. 2019. *Faithful Fighters: Identity and Power in the British Indian Army*. Stanford, CA: Stanford University Press.

Iriye, Akira. 2013. *Global and Transnational History: The Past, Present, and Future*. Basingstoke: Palgrave Macmillan. doi.org/10.1057/9781137299833.

Izuyama, Marie. 1999. "British Imperial Strategy and the Gurkha Negotiations." *Journal of the Japanese Association for South Asian Studies* 11: 51–70. doi.org/10.11384/jjasas1989.1999.51.

Jackman, Gil. 2009. *Cruise: The Real World of Cruising Today*. Indiana: IUniverse.

Jacobsen, Knut A., and Pratap P. Kumar. 2018. "Introduction." In *South Asians in the Diaspora: Histories and Religious Traditions*, edited by Knut A. Jacobsen and Pratap P. Kumar, ix–2. Leiden: Brill. doi.org/10.1163/9789047401407_001.

Jarvie, Ian C. 1977. "Epistle to the Anthropologists." *American Anthropologist* 77 (2): 253–66.

Jenkins, Fiona. 2014. "Pledging Allegiance: The Strangers Inside Democracy and Citizenship." In *Allegiance and Identity in a Globalised World* edited by Fiona Jenkins, Mark Nolan, and Kim Rubenstein, 169–91. Cambridge: Cambridge University Press.

Jones, Paul, and Michal Krzyzanowski. 2011. "Identity, Belonging and Migration: Beyond Constructing 'Others.'" In *Identity, Belonging and Migration*, edited by Gerard Delanty, Ruth Wodak, and Paul Jones, 38–53. Liverpool: Liverpool University Press. doi.org/10.5949/UPO9781846314537.003.

Jones-Correa, Michael. 2002. "The Study of Transnationalism among the Children of Immigrants: Where We Are and Where We Should be Headed." In *The Changing Face of Home: The Transnational Lives of the Second Generation,* edited by Peggy Levitt and Mary C. Waters, 221–41. New York: Russel Sage Foundation.

Jung, Pravesh G. 2016. "Mythical Entrapment of the Self and the Notion of Nepali Diaspora." In *Nepali Diaspora in a Globalized Era,* edited by Tanka Bahadur Subba and Awadhesh Coomar Sinha, 76–92. Oxon: Routledge. doi. org/10.4324/9781315685069.

Kabeer, Naila 2005. ed. *Inclusive Citizenship: Meanings and Expressions.* London: Zed Books.

Kananen, Marko. 2020. "Citizens of Ambivalence: How Educated Young Somali Americans Perceive their Transnational Being and Belonging?" *Journal of International Migration and Integration* 21 (1): 171–84. doi.org/10.1007/s12134-019-00709-5.

Karki, Arjun, and David Seddon. 2003. "The People's War in Historical Context." In *The People's War in Nepal: Left Perspectives,* edited by Arjun Karki and David Seddon, 3–39. New Delhi: Adroit Publishers.

Karki, Hari Bivor. 2009. *Johnnie Gurkha's Is With Me: An Amazing Story and Experience of Life.* Ilfracombe: Arthur H. Stockwell.

Kendall, Gavin, Ian Woodward, and Zlatko Skrbis. 2009. *The Sociology of Cosmopolitanism: Globalisation, Identity, Culture and Government.* Basingstoke: Palgrave Macmillan.

Kershaw, Roger. 2003. "Partners in Realism: Britain and Brunei Amid Recent Turbulence." *Asian Affairs* 34 (1): 46–53. doi.org/10.1080/0306837032000054270.

Kershaw, Roger. 2018. "Royal Writ and British Residency in the Sultanate of Brunei: A Fluid Partnership." *Asian Affairs* 49 (1): 82–102. doi.org/10.1080/03068374. 2018.1419015.

Khagram, Sanjeev, and Peggy Levitt. 2007. *The Transnational Studies Reader: Intersections and Innovations.* New York: Routledge.

Khan, Rimi. 2021. "Pragmatic Belonging: Migrant Young People Making Claims on the Nation." *Journal of Intercultural Studies* 42 (2): 127–42. doi.org/10.1080/07256868.2021.1884054.

Khanal, Prakash. 2013. "Diaspora Volunteering and Development in Nepal." In *Diaspora Engagement and Development in South Asia,* edited by Tan Tai Yong and Md Mizanur Rahman, 162–75. Basingstoke: Palgrave Macmillan. doi. org/10.1057/9781137334459_9.

Kheresh, Devendra. 2013. "War." In *Gurkha War Poems,* edited by Mijas Tembe, Apjase Kanchha, and Kangmang Naresh Rai, 25. Bloomington, IN: Authorhouse.

Kirk-Greene, Anthony H. M. 1980. "'Damnosa Hereditas': Ethnic Ranking and the Martial Races Imperative in Africa." *Ethnic and Racial Studies* 3 (4): 393–414. doi.org/10.1080/01419870.1980.9993313.

Kiruppalini, Hema. 2011. "Silenced Guards: The Foreigner Positionality of Singapore Gurkhas." In *Home in Motion: The Shifting Grammars of Self and Stranger,* edited by Pedro F. Marcelino, 153–59. Leiden: Brill. doi.org/10.1163/9781848880788_017.

Kiruppalini, Hema. 2013. "From Sentries to Skilled Migrants: The Transitory Residence of the Nepali Community in Singapore." In *The Political Economy of South Asian Diaspora: Patterns of Socio-Economic Influence,* edited by Gopinath Pillai, 59–80. Basingstoke: Palgrave Macmillan. doi. org/10.1057/9781137285973_4.

Kiruppalini, Hema. 2016. "Riots, 'Residence,' and Repatriation: The Singapore Gurkhas." In *Nepali Diaspora in a Globalised Era*, edited by Tanka Bahadur Subba and Awadhesh Coomar Sinha, 259–73. Oxon: Routledge.

Kissau, Kathrin, and Uwe Hunger. 2010. "The Internet as a Means of Studying Transnationalism and Diaspora." In *Diaspora and Transnationalism: Concepts, Theories and Methods*, edited by Rainer Bauböck and Thomas Faist, 245–65. Amsterdam: Amsterdam University Press.

Kivisto, Peter, and Thomas Faist. 2007. *Citizenship: Discourse, Theory, and Transnational Prospects*. Malden: Blackwell.

Kochhar-George, Ché Singh. 2010. "Nepalese Gurkhas and their Battle for Equal Rights." *Race & Class* 52 (2): 43–61. doi.org/10.1177/0306396810379073.

Koshy, Susan. 2008. "Introduction." In *Transnational South Asians: The Making of a Neo-Diaspora*, edited by Susan Koshy and R. Radhakrishnan, 1–41. New Delhi: Oxford University Press.

Kraska, Peter B. 2021. "Police Militarisation 101." In *Critical Issues in Policing*, edited by Roger G. Dunham, Geoffrey P. Alpert, and Kyle D. McLean, 445–58. Long Grove IL: Waveland Press.

Ku, Hok Bun, et al. 2010. *(Re)Understanding Multiracial Hong Kong: Eight Stories of South Asians in Hong Kong*. Hong Kong: Centre for Social Policy Studies, Research Report Series Number 16, Department of Applied Social Sciences, The Hong Kong Polytechnic University.

Ku, Hok-bun, Kam-wah Chan, and Karamajit Kaur Sandhu. 2005. *A Research Report on the Education of South Asian Ethnic Minority Groups in Hong Kong*. Hong Kong: Centre for Social Policy Studies, Department of Applied Social Sciences, the Hong Kong Polytechnic University.

Kumar, Bal. 2004. "Migration, Poverty and Development in Nepal." *Asian and Pacific Migration Journal* 13 (2): 205–32. doi.org/10.1177/011719680401300204.

Laguerre, Michael S. 2009. "The Transglobal Network Nation: Diaspora, Homeland, and Hostland." In *Transnationalism: Diasporas and the Advent of a New (Dis)order*, edited by Eliezer Ben-Rafael and Yitzhak Sternberg, 193–210. Leiden: Brill. doi.org/10.1163/ej.9789004174702.i-788.67.

Laksamba, Chandra K. 2012. "Battlefields to Civvy Street: Gurkhas' Struggles in Britain." In *Nepalis in the United Kingdom: An Overview*, edited by Krishna P. Adhikari, 102–22. Kathmandu: Lusha Press/Centre for Nepal Studies United Kingdom.

Laksamba, Chandra K., et al. 2013. *British Gurkha Pension Policies and Ex-Gurkha Campaigns: A Review*. Reading: Centre for Nepal Studies United Kingdom.

Lamont, Michelle, and Virag Molnar. 2002. "The Study of Boundaries in the Social Sciences." *Annual Review of Sociology* 28: 167–95. doi.org/10.1146/annurev. soc.28.110601.141107.

Lan, Pei-Chia. 2020. *Raising Global Families: Parenting, Immigration, and Class in Taiwan and the US*. Stanford, CA: Stanford University Press.

Laubenthal, Barbara, and Schumacher, Daniel. 2020. "Colonial Memories and Transnational Mobilizations: Asia's Colonial Veterans and their Struggle for British Citizenship, c. 1980–2015." *Memory Studies* 13 (6): 1129–43. doi. org/10.1177/1750698018784113.

Law, Kam-Yee, and Lee Kim-Ming. 2013. "Socio-political Embeddings of South Asian Ethnic Minorities' Economic Situations in Hong Kong." *Journal of Contemporary China* 22 (84): 984–1005. doi.org/10.1080/10670564.2013. 795312.

Leander, Anna, ed. 2013. *Commercializing Security in Europe: Political Consequences for Peace Operations*. New York: Routledge.

Leathart, Scott. 1998. *With the Gurkhas: India, Burma, Singapore, Malaya, Indonesia, 1940–1959*. Edinburgh: Pentland Press.

Lee, Kuan Yew. 1998. *The Singapore Story: Memoirs of Lee Kuan Yew*. Singapore: Times Editions.

Lee, Kuan Yew. 2000. *From Third World to First: The Singapore Story, 1965–2000*. New York: Harper Collins.

Lems, Annika. 2020. "Phenomenology of Exclusion: Capturing the Everyday Thresholds of Belonging." *Social Inclusion* 8 (4): 116–25. doi.org/10.17645/si.v8i4.3282.

Leonard, R. G. 1965. *Nepal and the Gurkhas*. London: HMSO.

Leung, Lisa Yuk-Ming. 2021. *Ethnic Minorities, Media and Participation in Hong Kong: Creative and Tactical Belonging*. Oxon and New York: Routledge. https://doi.org/10.4324/9781003006480.

Levitt, Peggy, and Mary C. Waters. 2002. "Introduction." In *The Changing Face of Home: The Transnational Lives of the Second Generation,* edited by Peggy Levitt and Mary C. Waters, 1–30. New York: Russel Sage Foundation. jstor.org/stable/10.7758/9781610443531.5.

Ley, David, and Audrey Kobayashi. 2009. "Back to Hong Kong: Return Migration or Transnational Sojourn?" In *Return Migration of the Next Generations: 21st Century Transnational Mobility,* edited by Dennis Conway and Robert B. Potter, 119–38. Surrey: Ashgate. doi.org/10.1111/j.1471-0374.2005.00110.x.

Lim, Joo Jock. 1976. "Brunei: Prospects for a 'Protectorate.'" *Southeast Asian Affairs* 149–64. jstor.org/stable/27908276.

Lim, Peter H. L., ed. 2009. *Chronicle of Singapore 1959–2009: Fifty Years of Headline News*. Singapore: EDitios Didier Millet.

Limbu, Kailash. 2015. *Gurkha—Better to Die than Live a Coward: My Life with the Gurkhas*. London: Little Brown.

Limbu, Kailash. 2021. *Gurkha Brotherhood: A Story of Childhood and War*. London: Michael O'Mara Books.

Ling, Choon Chi. 1999. *The Gurkhas: A Community in Honor*. Unpublished Academic Exercise, Department of Sociology, National University of Singapore.

Long, Norman, and Ann Long. 1992. eds. *Battlefields of Knowledge: The Interlocking of Theory and Practice in Social Research and Development*. London: Routledge.

Low, Choo Chin. 2020. "De-commercialization of the Labor Migration Industry in Malaysia." *Southeast Asian Studies* 9 (1): 27–65. doi.org/10.20495/seas.9.1_27.

Low, Kelvin E.Y. 2014. *Remembering the Samsui Women: Migration and Social Memory in Singapore and China*. Vancouver: UBC Press.

Low, Kelvin E.Y. 2015. "Migrant Warriors and Transnational Lives: Constructing a Gurkha Diaspora." *Ethnic and Racial Studies* (online first). doi.org/10.1080/01419870.2015.1080377.

Mabo, Lila Seling. 2022. *Memoirs of a Gurkha Wife During Lockdown*. Bloomington, IN: Authorhouse.

MacDonell, Ranald, and Marcus Macauley. 1940. *A History of the 4th Prince of Wales' Own Gurkha Rifles, 1857–1937*. Vols. 1 and 2. Edinburgh: W. Blackwood.

Macleish, Kenneth. 2012. "Armor and Anesthesia: Exposure, Feeling, and the Soldier's Body." *Medical Anthropology Quarterly* 26 (1): 49–68. doi.org/10.1111/j.1548-1387.2011.01196.x.

Mahmood, Tahir, and Amjad A. Khan. 2017. "Collaboration, Political Control and the British Strategic Imperatives in Colonial Punjab." *Pakistan Vision* 18 (2): 15–31.

Malinowski, Bronislaw. 1922. *Argonauts of the Western Pacific: An Account of Native Enterprise and Adventure in the Archipelagoes of Melanesian New Guinea.* London: Routledge.

Mani, Ratna. 2020. "The Gurkha Recruitment: Remittances and Development." *International Journal of Recent Advances in Multidisciplinary Research* 7 (9): 6256–62. 10.22161/ijels.55.27.

Marenin, Otwin. 2005. "Building a Global Police Studies Community." *Police Quarterly* 8 (1): 99–136. doi.org/10.1177/1098611104267329.

Maunaguru, Sidharthan. 2019. *Marrying for a Future: Transnational Sri Lankan Tamil Marriages in the Shadow of War.* Seattle: University of Washington Press.

Maxwell, Kenneth. 1999. "Macao: The Shadow Land." *World Policy Journal* 16 (4): 73–95. www.jstor.org/stable/40209665.

Mee, Kathlee, and Sarah Wright. 2009. "Geographies of Belonging." *Environment and Planning A* 41(4): 772–79. doi.org/10.1068/a41364.

Menon, K. U. 1988. "A Six-Power Defence Arrangement in Southeast Asia?" *Contemporary Southeast Asia* 10 (3): 306–27. www.jstor.org/stable/25798017.

Minami, Makito. 2007. "From *Tika* to *Kata*? Ethnic Movements Among the Magars in an Age of Globalization." In *Nepalis Inside and Outside Nepal*, edited by Hiroshi Ishii, David N. Gellner, and Katsuo Nawa, 443–66. New Delhi: Manohar.

Morrice, Linda. 2017. "British Citizenship, Gender and Migration: The Containment of Cultural Differences and the Stratification of Belonging." *British Journal of Sociology of Education* 38 (5): 597–609. doi.org/10.1080/01425692.2015.1131606.

Morris, John. 1960. *Hired to Kill: Some Chapters of Autobiography.* London: Hart-Davis.

Muller, Tanja R., and Milena Belloni. 2020. "Transnational Lived Citizenship: The Case of the Eritrean Diaspora." *Africa Spectrum* 56 (1): 3–18. doi.org/10.1177/00020397211005472.

Murphy, Dervla. 1967. *Waiting Land: A Spell in Nepal.* London: John Murry.

Mustassari, Sanna, Anna Maki-Petaja-Leinonen, and Anne Griffiths. 2017. "Identities and Intersections: Critical Perspectives on the Person of the Law." In *Subjectivity, Citizenship and Belonging in Law,* edited by Anne Griffiths, Sanna Mustassari, and Anna Maki-Petaja-Leinonen, 3–26. London: Routledge.

Nath, Lopita. 2006. "Migration, Insecurity and Identity: The Nepali Dairymen in India's Northeast." *Asian Ethnicity* 7 (2): 129–48. doi.org/10.1080/14631360600734384.

Navaro-Yashin, Yael. 2007. "Make-Believe Papers, Legal Forms and the Counterfeit: Affective Interactions between Documents and People in Britain and Cyprus." *Anthropological Theory* 7 (1): 79–98. doi.org/10.1177/1463499607074294.

Nedelcu, Mihaela. 2012. "Migrants' New Transnational Habitus: Rethinking Migration through a Cosmopolitan Lens in the Digital Age." *Journal of Ethnic and Migration Studies* 38 (9): 1339–56. doi.org/10.1080/1369183X.2012.698203.

Nedumaran, N. 2017. *The Forgotten Sentinels: The Sepoys of Malaya, Singapore and Southeast Asia.* Chennai: Pixar Graphics.

Ngai, Mae M. 2004. *Impossible Subjects: Illegal Aliens and the Making of Modern America.* Princeton: Princeton University Press. jstor.org/stable/j.ctt5hhr9r.

Nieswand, Boris. 2011. *Theorising Transnational Migration: The Status Paradox of Migration.* New York: Routledge.

Northey, W. Brook 1938. *The Land of the Gurkhas or The Himalayan Kingdom of Nepal.* Cambridge: Hefer and Sons.

Northey, W. Brook, and C. J. Morris. 1987. *The Gurkhas: Their Manners, Customs and Country.* New Delhi: Cosmo Publications.

Omissi, David. 1994. *The Sepoy and the Raj: The Indian Army, 1860–1940*. London: Palgrave Macmillan.

O'Neill, Mark, and Annemarie Evans. 2018. *How South Asians Helped to Make Hong Kong*. Hong Kong: Joint Publishing.

Ong, Aihwa. 1996. "Cultural Citizenship as Subject-Making: Immigrants Negotiate Racial and Cultural Boundaries in the United States." *Current Anthropology* 37 (5): 737–62. doi.org/10.1086/204560.

Onta, Pratyoush. 1996. "Creating a Brave Nepali Nation in British India: The Rhetoric of *Jati* Improvement, Rediscovery of Bhanubhakta, and the Writing of *Bir* History." *Studies in Nepali History and Society* 1 (1): 37–76.

Orjuela, Camilla, and Dhananjayan Sriskandarajah. 2008. "The Sri Lankan Tamil Diaspora: Warmongers or Peace-Builders?" In *Transnational South Asians: The Making of a Neo-Diaspora*, edited by Susan Koshy and R. Radhakrishnan, 325–44. Delhi: Oxford University Press.

Osborne, Myles. 2014. *Ethnicity and Empire in Kenya: Loyalty and Martial Race Among the Kamba, c. 1800 to the Present*. Cambridge: Cambridge University Press. https://doi.org/10.1017/CBO9781107447714.

Parajuly, Prajwal. 2013. *The Gurkha's Daughter*. London: Quercus.

Pariyar, Mitra. 2016. "Dreams of Sacrifice: Changing Ritual Practices Among Ex-Gurkha Immigrants in the UK." In *Nepali Diaspora in a Globalized Era*, edited by Tanka Bahadur Subba and Awadhesh Coomar Sinha, 274–90. Oxon: Routledge.

Pariyar, Mitra. 2018. "Caste Discrimination Overseas: Nepali Dalits in England." In *Global Nepalis: Religion, Culture, and Community in a New and Old Diaspora*, edited by David N. Gellner and Sondra L. Hausner, 404–34. New Delhi: Oxford University Press.

Pariyar, Mitra. 2019. "Travelling Castes: Nepalese Immigrants in Australia." *South Asian Diaspora* 11 (1): 89–103. doi.org/10.1080/19438192.2018.1523091.

Pariyar, Mitra. 2020. "Caste, Military, Migration: Nepali Gurkha Communities in Britain." *Ethnicities* 20 (3): 608–27. doi.org/10.1177/1468796819890138.

Pariyar, Mitra, Bal Gopal Shrestha, and David N. Gellner. 2014. "Rights and a Sense of Belonging: Two Contrasting Nepali Diaspora Communities." In *Facing Globalization in the Himalayas: Belonging and the Politics of the Self*, edited by G. Toffin and J. Pfaff-Czarnecka, 134–58. Delhi: SAGE.

Parker, John. 1999. *The Gurkhas: The Inside Story of the World's Most Feared Soldiers*. Kent: Headline Book.

Parreñas, Rhacel Salazar, and Lok C.D. Siu. 2007. "Introduction: Asian Diasporas—New Conceptions, New Frameworks." In *Asian Diasporas: New Formations, New Conceptions*, edited by Rhacel Salazar Parreñas and Lok C. D. Siu, 1–27. Stanford, CA: Stanford University Press.

Paudyal, Mahesh, and Raj Kumar Baral. 2021. "The Politics of Gorkha Martial Valour: A Critical Introduction to Modern Nepali War Poetry." *Cogent Arts & Humanities* 8 (1): 1–16. doi.org/10.1080/23311983.2021.1923896.

Pawley, Laurence. 2008. "Cultural Citizenship." *Sociology Compass* 2 (2): 594–608. doi.org/10.1111/j.1751-9020.2008.00094.x.

Peers, Douglas M. 2007. "The Martial Races and the Indian Army in the Victorian Era." In *A Military History of India and South Asia*, edited by Daniel P. Marston and Chandar S. Sundaram, 34–52. Connecticut: Praeger Security International.

Pemble, John. 1971. *The Invasion of Nepal: John Company at War*. Oxford: Clarendon.

Perumal, Elan. 2018. "Foreign Workers: Nepal Slams the Door, Unhappy with Company Monopoly." *Star Online*. July 28. www.thestar.com.my/news/

nation/2018/07/28/no-more-nepaleseworkers-for-msia-embassy-discrepancies-in-recruitment-process-pushed-our-govt-to-st/#UVuMwuJkkHWK0EW9.99.

Pettigrew, Judith 2000. "'Gurkhas' in the Town: Migration, Language, and Healing." *European Bulletin of Himalayan Research* 19: 7–39.

Pfaff-Czarnecka, Joanna. 2013. "Multiple Belonging and the Challenges to Biographic Navigation." MMG Working Paper 13–05, Max Planck Institute for the Study of Religious and Ethnic Diversity, Göttingen.

Pfaff-Czarnecka, Joanna. 2020. "From 'Identity' to 'Belonging' in Social Research: Plurality, Social Boundaries, and the Politics of the Self." *European Scientific Journal* 16 (39): 113–32.

Pfaff-Czarnecka, Joanna. 2022. *Belonging in Motion: Contested Social Boundaries in South Asia*. Kathmandu: Himal Books.

Pickering, Michael. 2001. *Stereotyping: The Politics of Representation*. Basingstoke: Palgrave.

Piya, Avash. 2020. "Just Like a *Lahure*: Appropriating Identities and Virtues of the Gurkhas." *Studies in Nepali History and Society* 25 (2): 327–52.

Prabhat, Devyani. 2018. *Britishness, Belonging and Citizenship*. Bristol: Policy Press.

Pries, Ludger. 2001. "The Disruption of Social Geographical Space: Mexican-US Migration and the Emergence of Transnational Social Spaces." *International Sociology*, 16 (1): 55–70. doi.org/10.1177/0268580901016001005.

Purthi, R. K. 2007. *Nepalese Gorkhas*. New Delhi: Sumit Enterprises.

Purthi, R. K. 2011. *The Gurkhas: A Study of Manners, Customs and Country*. New Delhi: Sumit Enterprises.

Qureshi, Kaveri, and Benjamin Zeitlyn. 2013. "British Muslims, British Soldiers: Cultural Citizenship in the New Imperialism." *Ethnicities* 13 (1): 110–26. doi.org/10.1177/1468796812449705.

Ragsdale, T. A. 1989. *Once a Hermit Kingdom: Ethnicity, Education and National Integration in Nepal*. Delhi: Manohar.

Rai, Bandana. 2009. *Gorkhas: The Warrior Race*. Delhi: Kalpaz Publications.

Rai, Daya Krishna. 2013. "The Buddhas Inside War." In *Gurkha War Poems*, edited by Mijas Tembe, Apjase Kanchha, and Kangmang Naresh Rai, 67–68. Bloomington, IN: Authorhouse.

Rai, Ganesh. 2020. *Gurkha Guns: The Authentic Voice of a British Gurkha Soldier Who Fought in the Falklands War 1982*. Kent: Conrad Press.

Rai, Naresh Kangmang. 2015. *Khukuriko Dhaarmaa* [in Nepali]. Kathmandu: Brother Books.

Rai, Puran. 2070 V.S. *British Gorkha Sainik Sahityako Itihas* [in Nepali]. Kathmandu: Shami Sama Prakashan Griha.

Rai, Rajesh. 2014. *Indians in Singapore, 1819–1945: Diaspora in the Colonial Port City*. New Delhi: Oxford University Press. https://doi.org/10.1093/acprof:oso/9780198099291.001.0001.

Ralph, David, and Lynn. A. Staeheli. 2011. "Home and Migration: Mobilities, Belongings and Identities." *Geography Compass* 5 (7): 517–30. doi.org/10.1111/j.1749-8198.2011.00434.x.

Rand, Gavin. 2006. "'Martial Races' and 'Imperial Subjects': Violence and Governance in Colonial India, 1857–1914." *European Review of History: Revue européenne d'histoire* 13 (1): 1–20. https://doi.org/10.1080/13507480600586726.

Rashid, Maria. 2020. *Dying to Serve: Militarism, Affect, and Politics of Sacrifice in the Pakistan Army*. Stanford, CA: Stanford University Press.

Rathaur, Kamal Raj Singh. 2000. *The Gurkhas: A History of the Recruitment in the British Indian Army*. New Delhi: Nirala.

Rathaur, Kamal Raj Singh. 2001. "British Gurkha Recruitment: A Historical Perspective." *Voice of History* 16 (2): 19–24.

Ratzmann, Nora. 2021. "Deserving of Social Support? Street-level Bureaucrats' Decisions on EU Migrants' Benefit Claims in Germany." *Social Policy & Society* 20 (3): 509–20. doi.org/10.1017/S1474746421000026.

Ray, Subhasish. 2013. "The Nonmartial Origins of the "Martial Races": Ethnicity and Military Service in Ex-British Colonies." *Armed Forces and Society* 39 (3): 560–75. doi.org/10.1177/0095327X12449427.

Röttger-Rössler, Birgitt. 2018. "Multiple Belongings. On the Affective Dimensions of Migration." *Zeitschrift für Ethnologie* 143: 237–62. jstor.org/stable/26899773.

Rottmann, Susan B., Ivan Josipovic, and Ursula Reeger. 2020. "Beyond Legal Status: Exploring Dimensions of Belonging among Forced Migrants in Istanbul and Vienna." *Social Inclusion* 8 (1): 241–51. https://doi.org/10.17645/si.v8i1.2392.

Roy, Kaushik. 2001. "The Construction of Regiments in the Indian Army: 1859–1913." *War in History* 8 (2): 127–48. doi.org/10.1177/096834450100800201.

Roy, Kaushik. 2013. "Race and Recruitment in the Indian Army: 1880–1918." *Modern Asian Studies* 47 (4): 1310–47. doi.org/10.1017/S0026749X12000431.

Safran, William. 2009. "The Diaspora and the Homeland: Reciprocities, Transformations, and Role Reversals." In *Transnationalism: Diasporas and the Advent of a New (Dis)order*, edited by Eliezer Ben-Rafael and Yitzhak Sternberg, 75–99. Leiden: Brill.

Sahoo, Ajaya K. 2021. "Introduction: Asian Diaspora and Development." In *Routledge Handbook of Asian Diaspora and Development*, edited by Ajaya K. Sahoo, 1–14. Oxon: Routledge.

Samsi, Aznita, Norehan Abdullah, and Lim Hock Eam. 2020. "Foreign Labour and Job Creation in Malaysian Manufacturing Sector." *Journal of Critical Reviews* 7 (8): 1526–30.

Sangroula, Geeta P. 2019. "Gurkha's Quest for Justice: Possible Remedies for Gurkhas Under International Human Rights System." *Kathmandu School of Law Review* 7 (2): 14–36.

Sangroula, Yubaraj. 2019. *Gorkha Brigade (1814–2014): Nepali Yuwaamathi 200 Barshako Shoshan* [in Nepali]. Bhaktapur: Lex and Juris Publications.

Schein, Richard H. 2009. "Belonging Through Land/scape." *Environment and Planning A* 41 (4): 811–26. doi.org/10.1068/a41125.

Schrooten, Mieke. 2012. "Moving Ethnography Online: Researching Brazilian Migrants' Online Togetherness." *Ethnic and Racial Studies* 35 (10): 1794–809. doi.org/10.1080/01419870.2012.659271.

Seddon, David. 2022. *Lahure Women: Two Centuries of Struggle, Service and Silent Fortitude*. New Delhi: Adroit Publishers.

Seddon, David, et al. 2002. "Foreign Labour Migration and the Remittance Economy of Nepal." *Critical Asian Studies* 34 (1): 19–40. doi.org/10.1080/146727102760166581.

Seeberg, Jens. 2016. "Competing Perspectives on the Gurkhas and Identity Politics in Nepal." In *Nepali Diaspora in a Globalised Era*, edited by Tanka Bahadur Subba and Awadhesh Coomar Sinha, 55–75. Oxon: Routledge.

Seo, Seonyoung. 2019. "Temporalities of Class in Nepalese Labour Migration to South Korea." *Current Sociology* 67 (2): 186–205. doi.org/10.1177/0011392118792925.

Shams, Tahseen. 2020. *Here, There, and Elsewhere: The Making of Immigrant Identities in a Globalized World*. Stanford, CA: Stanford University Press.

Sharma, Jeevan, and Ian Harper. 2017. "Britain-Nepal Relations through the Prism of Aid." *European Bulletin of Himalayan Research* 50: 145–61.

Sharma, Pratima. 2021. "Diaspora Diplomacy: Emerging Priority of Nepal's Foreign Policy." *Journal of Political Science* 21: 86–99.

Sharma, Samir. 2022. "'The North Remembers!' Virtual Publics and Limits of Digital Interventions in the Darjeeling Hills." *Studies in Nepali History and Society* 27 (2): 356–84.

Sharma, Sanjay, et al. 2022. "Relationship in Progress: Absent Gurkhas and Their Proud but Disconnected Children." *Asian Studies: Journal of Critical Perspectives* 58 (2): 71–99.

Sharma, Sanjay. 2017. "Mere 'Mercenaries' to Equal Citizens: Political and Social Negotiations by Gurkhas in the UK." MA diss., Central European University.

Shivakoti, Richa. 2019. "When Disaster Hits Home: Diaspora Engagement After Disasters." *Migration and Development* 8 (3): 338–54. doi.org/10.1080/21632324. 2019.1565383.

Shrestha, Tina. 2018. "Aspirational Infrastructure: Everyday Brokerage and the Foreign-Employment Recruitment Agencies in Nepal." *Pacific Affairs* 91 (4): 673–93. doi.org/10.5509/2018914673.

Simonsen, Kristina B. 2016. "How the Host Nation's Boundary Drawing Affects Immigrants' Belonging." *Journal of Ethnic and Migration Studies* 42 (7): 1153–76. doi.org/10.1080/1369183X.2016.1138854.

Singh, Bhupinder, and Bawa Singh. 2020. "Punjab under the British Rule: Historicising the Local Transformations." *Indian Historical Review* 46 (2): 207–26. doi. org/10.1177/0376983619889520.

Singh, Harischandra Lal. 1980. *Principal Records of Nepal.* Kathmandu: Satish Singh.

Singh, Khushwant. 1962. *Ranjit Singh: Maharaja of the Punjab.* London: George Allen and Unwin.

Sinha, Vineeta. 2019. "Modern Hindu Diaspora(s)." In *The Oxford History of Hinduism: Modern Hinduism*, edited by Torkel Brekke, 179–202. Oxford: Oxford University Press. doi.org/10.1093/oso/9780198790839.003.0011.

Sinha, Vineeta. 2022. "Interrogating a 'Diasporic' Lens: Narrating Singapore's Indian Communities." In *New Perspectives on The Indian Diaspora*, edited by Ruben Gowricharn, 78–103. New York: Routledge. doi.org/10.4324/9781003191063.

Siu, Lok C. D. 2005. *Memories of a Future Home: Diasporic Citizenship of Chinese in Panama.* Stanford, CA: Stanford University Press.

Sivis, Selin. 2022. "Who is (Un)deserving? Differential Healthcare Access and the Interplay Between Social and Symbolic Boundary-drawing Towards Syrian Refugees in Turkey." *Journal of Ethnic and Migration Studies* (online first). doi. org/10.1080/1369183X.2022.2058470.

Smith, Eric David. 1973. *Britain's Brigade of Gurkhas.* London: Leo Cooper.

Stanik, Paulina. 2019. "No More Uncertain: The Future of the Gurkhas in the British Army." *ANGLICA: An International Journal of English Studies* 28 (1): 89–102.

Stirr, Anna M. 2017. *Singing across Divides: Music and Intimate Politics in Nepal.* New York: Oxford University Press.

Streets, Heather. 2004. *Martial Races: The Military, Race, and Masculinity in British Imperial Culture, 1857–1914.* Manchester: Manchester University Press. https:// doi.org/10.7765/9781847793942.

Struck, Bernhard, Kate Ferris, and Jacques Revel. 2011. "Introduction: Space and Scale in Transnational History." *International History Review* 33 (4): 573–84. doi.org/1 0.1080/07075332.2011.620735.

Subba, Khusiyali. 2007. "Drug Users of Dharan: Aspects of Marginalization." In *Nepalis Inside and Outside Nepal*, edited by Hiroshi Ishii, David N. Gellner, and Katsuo Nawa, 283–306. New Delhi: Manohar Publishers.

Suen, Lorna K. P., and Tika Rana. 2020. "Knowledge Level and Hand Hygiene Practice of Nepalese Immigrants and Their Host Country Population: A Comparative Study." *International Journal of Environmental Research and Public Health* 17 (11): 1–17. 10.3390/ijerph17114019.

Sun, Biyang, and Eric Fong. 2021. "Immigrant Entrepreneurship in Hong Kong." In *Immigrant Entrepreneurship in Cities: Global Perspectives*, edited by Cathay Yang Liu, 67–96. Cham: Springer.

Surendra, K. C. 2062 V.S. *Gorkhabharti: Katha-Vyatha ra Aandolan* [in Nepali]. Taplejung: Sabita Prakashan.

Tam, Siumi Maria. 2010. "Dealing with Double Marginalization: Three Generations of Nepalese Women in Hong Kong." *Asian Journal of Women's Studies* 16 (2): 32–59. doi.org/10.1080/12259276.2010.11666087.

Tang, Lik Hang Adalard. 2009. "Constructing 'Second Nepal': The Nepalese Gurkha Community in Kam Tin, Hong Kong." MA diss., The Hong Kong University of Science and Technology.

Tang, Wai-Man. 2017. "Migration, Marginalization and Metropolitaneity: Negotiation of Masculinities of Nepali drug users in Hong Kong." *Gender, Place & Culture* 24 (2): 213–24. doi.org/10.1080/0966369X.2016.1277187.

Teerling, Janine. 2011. "The Development of New 'Third-Cultural Spaces of Belonging': British-born Cypriot 'Return' Migrants in Cyprus." *Journal of Ethnic and Migration Studies* 37 (7): 1079–99. doi.org/10.1080/1369183X.2011.572484.

Tembe, Mijash. 2013. "Me, The Point Man." In *Gurkha War Poems*, edited by Mijas Tembe, Apjase Kanchha, and Kangmang Naresh Rai, 9. Bloomington, IN: Authorhouse.

Teo, Sin Yih. 2011. "The Moon Back Home is Brighter? Return Migration and the Cultural Politics of Belonging." *Journal of Ethnic and Migration Studies* 37 (5): 805–20. doi.org/10.1080/1369183X.2011.559720.

Thapa, Bal Bahadur. 2021. "Global Capitalism and the Lahures: A Study of Modernity in *Anagarik*, a film directed by Rambabu Gurung." *SCHOLARS: Journal of Arts & Humanities* 3 (2): 45–58.

Thapa, Basanta, and Mohan Mainali. 2002. *Lahurekaa Katha* [in Nepali]. Kathmandu: Himal Kitab.

Thapa, Tapasya. 2009. "Being and Belonging: A Study of the Indian Nepalis." In *Indian Nepalis: Issues and Perspectives*, edited by Tanka Bahadur Subba et al., 95–105. New Delhi: Concept Publishing.

Thomas, Nisha, Matt B. Smith, and Nina Laurie. 2020. "Diaspora Volunteering: A Tool for Development or a Channel for Diasporic (Re)engagement with Countries of Origin—A Case Study from Nepal." In *South Asia Migration Report 2020: Exploitation, Entrepreneurship and Engagement*, edited by Irudaya S. Rajan, 207–29. New York: Routledge. doi.org/10.4324/9780429321450.

Thule, Elon. 2011. *Samjhanaamaa Kimberley Cross* [in Nepali]. Kathmandu: Sabda Satabdi Nepal

Thurley, Djuna. 2021a. *The Campaign for Gurkha Pensions*. Commons Library Research Briefing, House of Commons Library, UK, 8 September.

Thurley, Djuna. 2021b. *The Campaign for Gurkha Pensions*. Commons Library Research Briefing, House of Commons Library, UK, 17 November.

Timalsina, Ramji. 2019. "Transnational Perspective in the Theorization of Nepali Diaspora and its Literature." *Migration and Diasporas: An Interdisciplinary Journal* 2 (2): 7–35.

Tinker, Hugh. 1967. *The Union of Burma: A Study of the First Years of Independence*. Oxford: Oxford University Press.

Tonsing, Kareen NingLianChing. 2010. "A Study of Acculturation and Adaptation of South Asians in Hong Kong." *The International Journal of Interdisciplinary Social Sciences* 5 (2): 189–99.

Tran, Van C., Jennifer Lee, and Tiffany J. Huang. 2019. "Revisiting the Asian Second-Generation Advantage." *Ethnic and Racial Studies* 42 (13): 2248–69. doi.org/10.1080/01419870.2019.1579920.

Tuker, Francis. 1950. *While Memory Serves*. London: Cassell.

Uesugi, Taeko. 2007. "Re-examining Transnationalism from Below and Transnationalism from Above: British Gurkhas' Life Strategies and the Brigade of Gurkhas' Employment Policies." In *Nepalis Inside and Outside Nepal*, edited by Hiroshi Ishii, David N. Gellner, and Katsuo Nawa, 383–410. New Delhi: Manohar Publishers.

Uesugi, Taeko. 2015. "Two Aspects of Hinduism Associated with Military Labour Migration: Hinduism in the British Army's Brigade of Gurkhas before the Abolition of the Nepalese Monarchy." *Journal of Contemporary Indian Studies* 5: 15–29.

Uesugi, Taeko. 2019a. "Domesticating Civil-Military Entanglements: Multiplicity and Transnationality of Retired British Gurkhas' Citizenship Negotiation." In *Civil–Military Entanglements: Anthropological Perspectives*, edited by Birgitte Refslund Sørensen and Eyal Ben-Ari, 121–42. New York: Berghahn Books. https://doi.org/10.2307/j.ctv1850gf5.

Uesugi, Taeko. 2019b. "The Transnational Civil Society of Nepali Emigrants and the Nepali Government: Corporatism beyond National Borders." *Japanese Review of Cultural Anthropology* 20 (1): 247–96.

Uprety, Sanjeev. 2011. *Masculinity and Mimicry: Ranas and Gurkhas*. Kathmandu: Baha Occasional Papers 5.

Valenzuela-Silva, Pilar, and Monit Cheung. 2016. "Nepalese Living in Hong Kong: Social Exclusion and Higher Education Enhancement." *Hong Kong Journal of Social Work* 50 (1–2): 47–66. doi.org/10.1142/S021924621600005X.

Van Hear, Nicholas. 2015. "Spheres of Diaspora Engagement." In *Diasporas Reimagined: Spaces, Practices and Belonging*, edited by Nando Sigona et al., 32–35. Oxford: Oxford Department of International Development.

Vansittart, Eden. 1906. *Gurkhas: Handbooks for the Indian Army*. Calcutta: Office of the Superintendent, Government Printing.

Vansittart, Eden. 1993. *The Gurkhas*. Delhi: Anmol Publications.

Vertovec, Steven. 2000. *The Hindu Diaspora: Comparative Patterns*. London: Routledge.

Vertovec, Steven. 2009. *Transnationalism*. London: Routledge.

Vines, Alex. 1999. "Gurkhas and the Private Security Business in Africa." In *Peace, Profit, or Plunder? The Privatization of Security in War-Torn African Societies*, edited by Jakkie Cilliers and Peggy Mason, 129–32. Johannesburg: Institute for Security Studies.

Ware, Vron. 2009. "Why Critical Whiteness Studies Needs to Think About Warfare." *Sociologisk Forskning* 46 (3): 57–64. doi.org/10.37062/sf.46.19213.

Ware, Vron. 2010. "Whiteness in the Glare of War: Soldiers, Migrants and Citizenship." *Ethnicities* 10 (3): 313–30. doi.org/10.1177/1468796810372297.

Ware, Vron. 2011. "'Johnny Gurkha Loves a Party': The Colonial Film Archive and the Racial Imaginary of the Worker-Warrior." In *Film and the End of Empire*, edited by Lee Grieveson and Colin MacCabe, 119–31. Basingstoke: Palgrave Macmillan.

Ware, Vron. 2012. *Military Migrants: Fighting for YOUR Country*. Basingstoke: Palgrave Macmillan.

Ware, Vron. 2013. "Can You Have Muslim Soldiers? Diversity as a Martial Value." In *The State of Race*, edited by Nisha Kapoor, Virinder Kalra, and James Rhodes, 121–45. London: Palgrave. doi.org/10.1057/9781137313089_7.

Ware, Vron. 2015. "The Sinews of Empire in the World of Modern Warfare." In *Diasporas Reimagined: Spaces, Practices and Belonging*, edited by Nando Sigona et al., 14–18. Oxford: Oxford Department of International Development.

Weiss, Anja, and Arnd-Michael Nohl. 2013. "Overcoming Methodological Nationalism in Migration Research: Cases and Contexts in Multi-Level Comparisons." In *Beyond Methodological Nationalism: Research Methodologies for Cross-Border Studies*, edited by Anna Amelina et al. 65–87. New York; London: Routledge.

Werbner, Pnina, and Mark Johnson, eds. 2011. *Diasporic Journeys, Ritual, and Normativity among Asian Migrant Women*. London: Routledge.

Wilding, Raelene. 2007. "Transnational Ethnographies and Anthropological Imaginings of Migrancy." *Journal of Ethnic and Migration Studies* 33 (2): 331–48. doi.org/10.1080/13691830601154310.

Wimmer, Andreas, and Nina Glick Schiller. 2002. "Methodological Nationalism and Beyond: Nation-state Building, Migration, and the Social Sciences." *Global Networks* 2 (4): 301–34. doi.org/10.1111/1471-0374.00043.

Witteborn, Saskia. 2019. "Digital Diaspora: Social Alliances Beyond the Ethnonational Bond." In *The Handbook of Diasporas, Media, and Culture*, edited by Jessica Retis and Roza Tsagarousianou, 179–92. New Jersey: John Wily and Sons.

Wolf, Diane L. 2002. "There's No Place Like 'Home': Emotional Transnationalism and the Struggles of Second-Generation Filipinos." In *The Changing Face of Home: The Transnational Lives of the Second Generation*, edited by Peggy Levitt and Mary C. Waters. 255–94. New York: Russel Sage Foundation.

Wood, Robert E. 2002. "Caribbean of the East? Global Interconnections and the Southeast Asian Cruise Industry." *Asian Journal of Social Science* 30 (2): 420–40. jstor.org/stable/23654713.

Woodyatt, Nigel. 1922. *Under Ten Viceroys: Reminiscences of a Gurkha*. Sherborne: Herbert Jenkins.

Yamanaka, Keiko. 2000. "Nepalese Labour Migration to Japan: From Global Warriors to Global Workers." *Ethnic and Racial Studies* 23 (1): 62–93. doi.org/10.1080/014198700329132.

Yamanaka, Keiko. 2005. "Changing Family Structures of Nepalese Transmigrants in Japan: Split-households and Dual-wage Earners." *Global Networks* 5 (4): 337–58. doi.org/10.1111/j.1471-0374.2005.00123.x.

Yuen, Mary Mee-Yin. 2020. *Solidarity and Reciprocity with Migrants in Asia: Catholic and Confucian Ethics in Dialogue*. Cham: Springer.

Yung, King-Fung Phoenix. 2002. "We Have No Choice! Social Exclusion and Citizenship of the Nepalese Community In Hong Kong." MA diss., Chinese University of Hong Kong.

Yuval-Davis, Nira. 2006. "Belonging and the Politics of Belonging." *Patterns of Prejudice* 40 (3): 197–214. https://doi.org/10.1080/00313220600769331.

Zack-Williams, Tunde. 2012. "Multilateral Intervention in Sierra Leone's Civil War: Some Structural Explanations." In *When the State Fails: Studies on Intervention in the Sierra Leone Civil War*, edited by Tunde Zack-Williams, 13–30. London: Pluto Press.

Zainal, Zakaria. 2012. *Our Gurkhas: Singapore Through Their Eyes*. Singapore: Epigram Books.

Index